Greening Business

Greening Business

Research, Theory, and Practice

Ian Worthington

OXFORD

UNIVERSITY PRESS

Great Clarendon Street, Oxford, OX2 6DP,
United Kingdom

Oxford University Press is a department of the University of Oxford.
It furthers the University's objective of excellence in research, scholarship,
and education by publishing worldwide. Oxford is a registered trade mark of
Oxford University Press in the UK and in certain other countries

First Edition published in 2013

Impression: 1

British Library Cataloguing in Publication Data

Data available

Library of Congress Cataloging in Publication Data

Data available

ISBN 978–0–19–953521–7 (hbk)
      978–0–19–953522–4 (pbk)

Printed in Great Britain by
CPI Group (UK) Ltd, Croydon, CR0 4YY

For Lindsey, Tom, and Georgina with all my love

■ PREFACE

The origins of this book lie in a conversation I had with a colleague in the Leicester Business School at the start of the new millennium. As a long-standing lecturer in business and management, I had become increasingly concerned that the idea of the 'business environment' on most degree courses in UK universities appeared to ignore for the most part the relationship between firms and the natural environment, focusing instead mainly on the economic, political, socio-demographic, and technological contexts of business. When challenged by my colleague to 'do something about it', I set about devising a new elective module entitled 'Greening Business' which was offered to final year undergraduates for the first time in September 2001. To my amazement and delight, the module proved almost an instant success and, within a few years, was attracting over 150 final year students of various nationalities. This book is an attempt to repay the debt to those hundreds of students who have shared my enthusiasm for the subject and my conviction that the environmental performance of business organizations is a key management issue and will become increasingly so in the twenty-first century.

In designing the book, I have tried to focus on what, for me, are the key aspects of the debate on the greening of business, including questions of 'why', 'how', and 'when' firms invest in environmental initiatives. My aim has also been to draw attention to the wide range of international research in the field, including the growing number of contributions by colleagues in southern and eastern Europe, Asia, South America, and elsewhere. This is a very exciting development and one which points to the global nature of environmental issues in both business and government as we move inexorably towards a carbon-constrained future.

As any author knows, the choice of material is as much about what to leave out as it is about what to include; this book is no exception. I hope I have been able to capture most, if not all, aspects of the debate about the greening of business that has occurred over the last thirty to forty years and to emphasize the contested nature of this debate among researchers, practitioners, and policy-makers concerned with the issue of corporate environmentalism. First and foremost, my concern has been to be as objective as possible in presenting the findings of the research, theory, and practice in this domain. I am happy to leave polemical discussions to others far better qualified (and more willing) than I am to adopt a particular stance on business behaviour and decisions.

In carrying out the research for this book and putting all the material together, I have received help and encouragement from numerous sources. I am indebted to the staff of

De Montfort University library (for help with source material), Nicola Smorowinski and Karen Wallace-Jones (for expertly deciphering and quickly typing up my hand-written script), Dr Harvi Boyal-Seth (for invaluable research on aspects of green marketing), Charles-David Mpengula and Rehaana Mohammed (for providing information on some recent developments in the field), and my colleagues in the Leicester Business School (for their constant support and encouragement). I would also like to say a special thank you to the staff (past and present) at Oxford University Press, particularly David Musson, Emma Lambert, and Matthew Derbyshire, who have helped and supported me throughout the project. My biggest debt, however, is to my wife Lindsey and our wonderful children, Tom and Georgina; not only have they all supported me throughout the time I have been researching and writing this book, they have also helped me in numerous practical ways: typing additional material, proof-reading, sorting out diagrams and tables, correcting grammar and punctuation, collating references, and generally giving me space and time to complete the project. It is to them that I dedicate this book, with my love and with immense pride in all their personal achievements and in their many contributions to the public good.

Ian Worthington

Leicester Business School
De Montfort University
January 2012

■ CONTENTS

◾ LIST OF FIGURES

■ LIST OF TABLES

▥ LIST OF BOXES

Section One
Mapping the Territory

1 Organizations and the natural environment: the two faces of business

The environment has been described as a bundle of resources to be used by organizations. The emphasis is on understanding both how environments influence organizations and how organizations can procure, exploit, or compete for environmental resources. The reverse relationship—how organizations have an impact on their environment—has received little attention.

(Shrivastava, 1995*a*)

It is business that produces goods and services that meet so many of our needs, wants and desires, and it is this process of production that is responsible for much of the environmental degradation that has occurred and continues to take place.

(Welford and Starkey, 1996)

Global environmental problems such as climate change that require urgent solutions have increased societal awareness about the impact of business operations on the natural environment.

(Aragón-Correa et al., 2008)

Introduction

In July 2009, the UK government set out an ambitious road map aimed at indicating how the country would meet its legally binding target of a 34 per cent cut in greenhouse gas emissions by 2020 and for setting the United Kingdom on track for a planned 80 per cent reduction by 2050. In reporting on the government's proposals, the *Financial Times* (16 July 2009: 1) noted that large industrial users had claimed that the expected rise in energy costs—a consequence of the plan—could make UK manufacturers uncompetitive in the global economy in the coming decade. Leaving aside the merits (or otherwise) of the government's or industry's positions, the former's decision to set out how it aims to move the United Kingdom towards a low-carbon economy underlines how central an issue the environment has become in the twenty-first century and how environmental problems pervade all areas of daily life, including the world of business and government. Put simply, business activity not only affects the natural environment but, in turn, is affected by it and by government attempts to address environmental problems such as climate change, ozone depletion, resource degradation, pollution, and loss of biodiversity. Business responses to pressures from government and other stakeholders to improve on its environmental performance—including questions of why, how, and when—are the primary focus of this book.

What is business?

As a universal and enduring human activity, business is relatively simple to describe. Dictionary definitions normally portray it as being concerned with buying and selling, with trade and with the pursuit of profits via the satisfaction of consumer needs and wants. To the economist, it is seen as a collective term to describe that part of society which is concerned with the production, consumption, and exchange of goods and services under different types of economic systems, most notably, market-based or mixed economies. The organizations (or firms) which inhabit this domain vary in size, structure, legal identity, and purpose, but the majority depend for their continued existence on securing profits, the excess of revenue from the sale of an organization's outputs over the costs incurred during their production. In such a domain, the market is the focus of business activity and the pursuit of profits a fundamental, though not necessary single, organizational goal or *raison d'être*.

In focusing on the generic processes that define the essence of business activity, systems theorists argue that business is basically concerned with the transformation of inputs into outputs for consumption purposes. Inputs include labour, materials, energy, finance, and technology, what economists usually refer to as the factors of production. The transformation or throughput phase refers to all the activities, systems, processes, and procedures involved in the conversion of these inputs into the organization's output or outputs. The outputs include both tangible and intangible products such as goods, services, information, and ideas that are consumed by individuals and/or other organizations, including other businesses for whom they may represent inputs into their own transformation process. All of this transformation process takes place in what systems thinkers call the environment, the context in which business organizations (or firms) exist, operate, and pursue their objectives.

What is the business environment?

For students of business and management, the term 'the business environment' has traditionally been used to describe the wide range of factors and influences which are external to the organization, which can impact upon its operations and decisions and over which the firm generally has little, if any, direct control (see e.g. Worthington and Britton, 2009). This organization or business environment is often portrayed as comprising two distinct types of influences: those that are broad, general, and contextual (i.e. macroenvironmental variables) and those that are more immediate, operational, and task-focused (i.e. microenvironmental variables). In the strategy and management literature, the former are frequently referred to as the PESTLE factors—an acronym denoting the broad Political, Economic, Social, Technological, Legal, and Ethical influences on business (Johnson et al., 2005). The latter comprise the more day-to-day influences that impact on organizations, most notably those emanating from the firm's stakeholders including its customers, suppliers, creditors, and competitors (Worthington and Britton, 2009).

This perspective of the business environment is represented in Figure 1.1.

Viewed from a systems point of view, businesses are seen as complex, open systems interacting with the many external forces that constitute their environment and which are said to present firms with both threats and opportunities and to act as enabling or constraining influences on business activity. Studies of business, management, strategy, and organizations all recognize the importance of a firm's external environment which finds expression in familiar concepts and theories such as SWOT and PESTLE analysis, Porter's 5 Forces, and strategic positioning. What is missing from much of the early literature in these fields is the notion that an organization's external context also includes the natural environment. Shrivastava (1995a), for example, has argued that scholars of organizational studies have tended to use a denatured, narrow, and parochial conception of the organizational environment that has prevented and devalued the incorporation of the natural environment into organizational theorizing. Winn and Kirchgeorg (2005) have also observed that the concept of the natural environment is largely missing from early management education and that until relatively recently it has been seen as irrelevant to business practice and operations (see Box 1.1).

While consideration of the impact of the natural environment on business activity is implicit in the idea that firms need to deploy resources such as raw materials and energy,

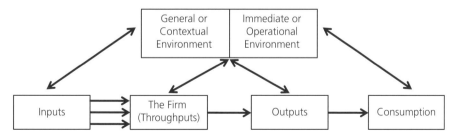

Figure 1.1 The business environment: the traditional view

Source: Adapted from Worthington and Britton (2009).

BOX 1.1 THE CHANGING FACE OF THE BUSINESS/NATURAL ENVIRONMENT RELATIONSHIP

Winn and Kirchgeorg (2005) suggest that the concept of the environment in management studies has evolved over time. In early analyses, the idea of the environment referred to the PESTLE factors and little, if any, attention was paid to the natural environment in relation to business practice. As awareness grew about the impact of human activity on the natural world (see Chapter 2), attention then began to shift towards an analysis of the business/natural environmental interface, exemplified by the emergence of studies of corporate environmental management and the idea of sustainable development. This focus on the consequences of business activity on the natural environment is often referred to as the 'inside-out' view: from the firm to the environment.

The authors argue that we are in the midst of a third phase in our view of the business/natural environment relationship in which natural disasters are becoming 'a recurrent fact of managerial life', creating 'increasingly massive ecological discontinuities' in a new era that will be characterized by 'extreme upheaval, distraction, and chaotic change' (ibid.: 233). They suggest that organizations will need to adopt new perspectives, develop appropriate firm-level capabilities, and fashion innovative long-term strategies if they are to survive. In short, they will need to consider the impact of changes in the natural environment on the organization and its performance: the 'outside-in' view.

this does not invalidate the observation that the notion of the business environment has tended to be narrowly drawn in much of the early management literature. That said, the last decade or so has seen increasing recognition of the impact of the natural environment on business decisions and operations, not least with regard to the potential consequences for the business community of environmental problems such as climate change and resource depletion (see Green Snapshot: Damage to the Economy). It is not an exaggeration to suggest that environmental issues of this kind are increasingly becoming a key business concern at local, national, international, and global levels, and there is clear evidence to indicate that large corporations in particular see the management of their environmental performance as having long-term implications for the way business is conducted and for the development of relationships with the organization's stakeholders (Buchholz, 1998).

GREEN SNAPSHOT: DAMAGE TO THE ECONOMY

In a report published in 2006, the environmental pressure group Friends of the Earth (FOE) suggested that failure to take sufficient steps to address the problem of climate change could cost the global economy US$20 trillion a year by the end of the twenty-first century. Drawing on research from over 100 economic and scientific papers, the group argued that allowing global warming to go unchecked could lead to a temperature rise of 4 degrees centigrade by 2100, resulting in economic damage worth in the region of 8 per cent of global GDP. Published in advance of the UK government's own review of the economics of climate change by Sir Nicholas Stern, the FOE report underlines how the economy and the natural environment are inextricably linked and that failure to tackle global environmental problems will inevitably have consequences for the business communities in all countries.

Indicative of this change in perception has been the gradual incorporation of the natural environment into management theory and practice (see below) and the emergence of a growing number of articles devoted to the business/natural environment interface in mainstream management journals, one of which, the *Academy of Management*, established an 'Organization and Natural Environment' interest group in 1995 (see e.g. Purser et al., 1995). This book aims to capture this important development by examining the theory and practice of corporate greening as portrayed in both the literature and in business responses in the real world.

Business and the natural environment: 'goods' and 'bads'

Business and economic activity generally, undoubtedly give rise to significant benefits at an individual, corporate, and societal level. By employing people to produce goods and services, firms provide individuals with incomes which they can use to purchase products to satisfy their material needs and wants, both now and in the future. The income earned by businesses from selling their outputs provides revenue which can be used for a variety of purposes, including investment, innovation, and rewarding the firm's owners. Much of this economic activity helps to drive economic growth and to provide governments with revenue via taxation which can be invested in public services such as healthcare and education. This 'good' face of business tends to be the one that is stressed in both academic and practitioner circles when attempts are being made to explain the purpose of and rationale for business activity.

As the quotations at the start of this chapter clearly highlight, these 'good' aspects of business come at a price. To use a rather inelegant economic concept, business activity generates 'bads' as well as 'goods', including environmental problems such as the

---

GREEN SNAPSHOT: DAMAGE TO THE ENVIRONMENT

A study for the United Nations, conducted by the London-based consultancy group Trucost (2010), estimated that the cost of pollution and the damage to the natural environment caused by the world's largest companies was worth over US$2 trillion in 2008. Of this, more than half was attributable to the emission of greenhouse gases that have been linked to climate change. The study found that the overall damage equated to around 6–7 per cent of the companies' combined turnover and on average was equivalent to one-third of their profits. By far the most damaging sector was the utilities industries, followed by basic materials (e.g. mining, forestry) and consumer goods (e.g. cars, food, and drink). The total figure for environmental damage was larger than the national economies of all but seven countries in the world in 2008.

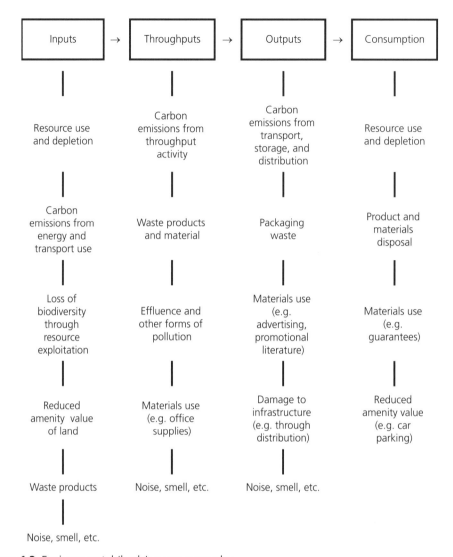

Figure 1.2 Environmental 'bads': some examples

running down of valuable resources and damage to the natural environment which we and other species inhabit and in which firms are located (see Green Snapshot: Damage to the Environment). According to Hawken (1996), business contributes to environmental damage in three main ways—by what it takes, by what it makes, and by what it wastes. This bad face of business activity occurs at all stages of the transformation process (Shrivastava, 1996) and involves environmental problems that occur across all spatial levels from the local to the global (see Figure 1.2).

Another way to capture this symbiotic relationship between business and the natural environment is to recognize that the latter provides three important 'economic'

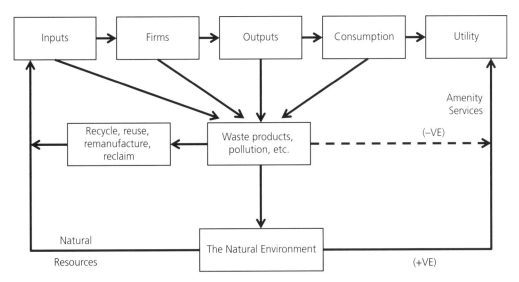

Figure 1.3 Linking the firm and the natural environment

Source: Adapted from Worthington (2005).

Notes: 1. In keeping with economists' definitions, 'utility' is used here to mean satisfaction derived from consumption (e.g. of goods and services and of amenity services such as landscape).
2. The diagram excludes the traditional 'environmental' influences depicted in Figure 1.1.

functions for those involved in business activity (Pearce and Turner, 1990; Worthington, 2005): it is a supplier of resources for business organizations (e.g. raw materials); it is an assimilator of waste products generated by economic activity (e.g. pollution); it is a direct source of amenity value or aesthetic enjoyment for individuals and organizations (e.g. a beautiful landscape). Figure 1.3 illustrates these three economic functions provided by the natural environment and shows how the environmental impact of business can be mitigated to some degree by business practices such as recycling, reuse, and remanufacture, although these activities in turn inevitably involve additional environmental consequences, such as the use of energy and the creation of wastes that are not captured in the diagram.

While a substantial amount of effort has been devoted in the past to exploring the negative impacts (or 'bads') that firms have on the natural environment (i.e. often referred to as an 'inside-out' view), there is a growing acceptance that the natural environment's impact on the businesses is no less important (i.e. the 'outside-in' perspective) for the future well-being and functioning of economic activity and for organizational competitiveness (Porter and Reinhardt, 2007). The Stern Report (2006), for example, estimated that failure to take action to tackle climate change could result in an up to 20 per cent decline in the size of the global economy and a plethora of other recent authoritative reports by national and international bodies paint a picture of how

---

GREEN SNAPSHOT: SOURCES OF GREENHOUSE GAS EMISSIONS

Scientific evidence suggests that climate change and a discernible increase in the level of greenhouse gases (GHGs) in the atmosphere are closely related, with the latter invariably being linked to human economic activity. Drawing on data produced by the World Resources Institute, the Stern Report (2006) identified the main sources of emissions as power generation (24 per cent), land use (18 per cent), industry (14 per cent), transport (14 per cent), and agriculture (14 per cent). A study by the UN Intergovernmental Panel on Climate Change (2007) reached similar conclusions, identifying the main sources of GHGs as energy supply (25.9 per cent), industry (19.4 per cent), forestry (17.4 per cent), agriculture (13.5 per cent), and transport (13.1 per cent).

According to a UN report published in 2008, an industry-based analysis of global CO_2 emissions suggested that major contributors were electricity (24 per cent) and manufacturing (11 per cent), whilst shipping (4.5 per cent) and aviation (2 per cent) had a much smaller, though nevertheless significant, impact.

---

the environmental problems, caused in part by business activity, can impact adversely on the business community (see Green Snapshot: Sources of Greenhouse Gas Emissions). In short, the business/natural environment relationship flows in both directions and is complex, interactive, and dynamic, varying both between places and over time (see e.g. Roberts, 1995). A core concern of this relationship is how the natural environment has become a central issue for a growing number of businesses and how some firms are seeking to manage this relationship in a strategic way. Why, when, and how business organizations do this is a central concern of this book.

Positioning the book

The business/natural environment interface can be, and has been, examined from multiple perspectives, ranging from philosophy, anthropology, and sociology, to economics, law, ethics, and management science. As Bansal and Howard (1997) point out, the perspective(s) taken in analysing this relationship will define the context, the framework for analysis, and the underlying assumptions adopted by researchers. In this book, the primary focus is on the natural environment as a key business/management issue at corporate, business, and functional levels and in particular on the circumstances in which some firms seek to manage their environmental responses in a strategic way, in an effort to gain or maintain a competitive advantage in the market place.

Using the firm as the main unit of analysis, and drawing from a wide range of international literature on the subject, the book focuses on research, theory, and practice related to the greening of business, including the central question of why and how firms deal with environmental issues from a strategic point of view by incorporating the natural environment into their decision-making processes. The aim of the analysis is not to prescribe what firms ought to do nor to adopt a polemical approach to the business/natural environment relationship. Rather the intention is to examine, analyse, and describe firm-level responses to the environmental agenda, by drawing on the insights offered by both academic researchers and practitioners in this domain.

As environmental issues in business cut across functional, corporate, and national boundaries (Bansal and Howard, 1997), the concepts, theories, and models referred to in this text are drawn from a variety of disciplines and sub-disciplines; equally, examples of, and references made to the greening of business at both a practical and theoretical level are designed to provide an international perspective that exemplifies the cross-national nature of many of today's environmental concerns in business. It is interesting to note that whilst much of the early literature in the field of corporate greening focuses on US and European experience, recent years have seen a significant growth in the number of journal articles examining environmental practices in the emerging economies, with China a particularly rich source of information on corporate environmental behaviour.

The organization of the book

To investigate research, theory, and practice on the greening of business, the book is divided into five sections. Following the introductory comments in Section One, the second section (comprising Chapters 2 and 3) places the debate on the business/natural environment relationship within the broader context of public and political concerns over the adverse impacts of business activity. Chapter 2 begins with a discussion of the factors which have led to a growth in environmental awareness among the public and politicians and examines the roots of the demands for corporate action, together with subsequent policy, institutional and conceptual developments. Central to the emerging debate has been the notion of a potential trade-off between economic growth and environmental protection, an issue highlighted in the chapter, together with a discussion of some of the initial business responses to the growing demands for corporate environmental action.

This contextual analysis is continued in Chapter 3 which focuses on how and why governments have responded to the negative environmental externalities linked to business activity. Following a discussion of the idea of externalities as a result of market failure, the chapter examines in detail three main approaches/policy instruments used by national governments to encourage firms to improve on their environmental performance: regulation, market-based instruments, and voluntary agreements. Attention is focused on how each approach is meant to work, the case for and against and on business attitudes to the instrument concerned. The chapter concludes with an analysis of the evolution of the different governmental approaches, most notably the shift away from regulation and towards more market-based instruments, including the use of environmental taxation and tradeable emissions permits.

In Section Three (comprising Chapters 4–7), the focus moves to the firm level and to an examination of the theoretical and empirical contributions to the debate over the greening of business. Chapter 4 addresses the central issue of 'why firms go green', what drives them towards a higher level of environmental performance, and what might be the underlying motivations which could explain their green behaviour. Having examined the concept of a 'green' business, the chapter critically investigates the main organizational drivers and motivations and discusses important moderating and mediating influences on corporate environmental responses. Emphasis is given to Bansal and Roth's model (2000) of corporate ecological responsiveness and to the growing number of studies which have identified the key barriers to environmental change at an organizational level.

While Chapter 4 seeks to address why greening occurs, Chapter 5 looks at how academic researchers and management consultants have used various conceptually and empirically-based systems of classification to categorize firm-level green responses. Following an examination of both stage model and matrix model approaches to the 'how' and 'why' of organizational change, the chapter undertakes a detailed analysis of two specific models and their particular dimensions. It comments on the usefulness of classification schemes to our understanding of environmental practices in business and concludes with a discussion of what have been termed second-generation models of corporate greening.

Underlying much of the debate concerning why and how firms become greener is the question of whether improvements in environmental performance can benefit an organization. A detailed and critical analysis of the business case for corporate greening is the subject matter of Chapter 6. As the discussion illustrates, the idea that greening the firm 'pays'—the so called 'win-win hypothesis'—has been hotly contested and there is conflicting empirical evidence on the claimed link between environmental performance and business performance. The chapter examines the burgeoning literature in this field and asks if the question 'when does it pay' might be more relevant than asking 'if it pays' and whether our idea of the 'business case' may be too narrowly drawn. In investigating the issue of a possible competitive advantage from environmentalism, the analysis draws upon concepts and theories from the strategic management field, most notably Porter's notion of positioning and the resource-based view of the firm.

To conclude Section Three, Chapter 7 looks specifically at the issue of small firm engagement in the environmental agenda, given that small and medium-sized enterprises constitute the overwhelming majority of businesses (>90 per cent) worldwide. Drawing on the relatively limited but growing literature in this field, the chapter investigates small firm attitudes to environmental protection and how far, and in what ways, an organization's perceptions might be reflected in its subsequent behaviour. Echoing the previous idea that it is important to ask why firms might become more environmentally responsible, the chapter analyses both the drivers of and motivations underlying small firm ecological behaviour, including perceptions of the competitive benefits of environmentalism. In undertaking this analysis, it draws attention to the claim that structural influences might be important in explaining variations in small firm environmental responses in different policy jurisdictions.

Against this background of theoretical and empirical analysis of corporate greening, the fourth section investigates what greening business might mean in practice: how might it manifest itself within an organization? Chapter 8 introduces the idea of green strategies and the different strategic postures a firm can take in managing its relationship with the natural environment. The chapter discusses the notion of strategy levels, strategy choice, and strategy implementation and the distinction between reactive and proactive environmental strategies. It also examines a number of alternative strategy responses at firm level and the idea of establishing strategic environmental alliances as an approach to corporate greening.

A key part of the greening process is the idea of managing one's environmental performance in a systematic way; this is the subject matter of Chapter 9 which examines the emergence of environmental management systems (EMSs) with particular emphasis on ISO14001 and the European Eco-Management and Audit Scheme (EMAS). The chapter discusses the idea of an EMS, the EMS cycle, and claimed advantages and disadvantages of EMS implementation, along with a comparison of ISO14001 and EMAS. In keeping with the approach adopted in the previous section, the chapter ends with an analysis of the empirical evidence of researchers in the field, including findings on the reasons for EMS adoption by business organizations and the possible links between adoption and firm-level performance.

To complete the analysis in Section Four, Chapter 10 focuses on greening at a functional level within a business by examining green purchasing and supply chain management, green marketing, and (briefly) the idea of green accounting. Drawing on an extensive literature in this field, the chapter covers a variety of topics including definitions, scope, drivers, barriers, benefits, and ideas such as greening the marketing mix and the notion of the green consumer. It asks how the functional aspects of a business can be reconfigured to demonstrate a firm's commitment to environmental protection and underlines how corporate responses at the functional level can be related to previous observations in areas such as corporate image, stakeholder engagement, risk management, and competitive advantage.

In order to take stock of the progress made towards the greening of business, the concluding section and chapter of the book (Section Five, Chapter 11) investigates the idea of the ecologically sustainable business organization: what is meant by the concept of a 'sustainable business'; what are the indicators of ecological sustainability at firm level; and how can a firm make progress on the sustainability front? In addition to examining possible obstacles on the road towards corporate sustainability, the chapter examines the distinction between 'bolt-on' and 'embedded' sustainability, relating the latter to the 'win-win' school of thought discussed at various points in the text (especially Chapter 6). It ends with a reminder that business responses to calls for more sustainable forms of development need to be seen in context, that we should not forget that firms are first and foremost economic institutions for which environmentalism is only one consideration and the one for which the foreseeable future is likely to be judged predominantly from an economic and commercial point of view by the majority of the business community.

Key issues and themes

As the previous section illustrates, an investigation of the greening of business raises a number of important questions regarding the firm/natural environment relationship. These include the following:

- What are the key pressures being exerted upon firms which might cause them to incorporate environmentalism into their strategic thinking and day-to-day operations?
- What are the underlying motivations which cause some businesses to adopt a greener approach?
- How can firm-level environmental responses be conceptualized?
- To what extent is a firm's environmental performance a potential and/or actual source of competitive advantage?
- How can an organization demonstrate its commitment to environmental protection through its decisions and actions at a functional, business, and corporate level?
- Can a business be truly sustainable in an ecological sense?

In addressing these and other issues, the book looks beyond organizational practice to the theoretical debates that underpin corporate responses and provides a contemporary analysis of corporate environmental management practices, supported by a wealth of empirical evidence and research by international scholars. In the absence of a widely accepted definition of the notion of 'greening', the term is used primarily—though not exclusively—to refer to deliberate attempts by businesses to improve on their environmental performance. A fuller discussion of the concept can be found at the start of Chapter 4.

Supporting material

To supplement the discussion and analysis in each chapter, the book makes use of a range of supporting material. In addition to the usual figures and tables, each chapter contains:

- Boxes—illustrating key concepts, contemporary debates, research findings, and so on;
- Green Snapshots—focusing on recent examples of environmental responses undertaken by business organizations or on environmental impacts or issues;
- A case study—found at the end of each chapter from Chapter 2 onwards. Consistent with Yin's definition (1994), the case studies cover a range of contemporary phenomena, including organizational responses, policy initiatives, and research findings.

An extensive bibliography can be found at the end of the book.

A note on terminology

In keeping with established practice in the literature on organizations and the natural environment, a number of terms have been used interchangeably including ecological and environmental, for example when referring to the responsiveness of businesses to the environmental agenda. The idea of the greening of a firm and the concept of corporate environmentalism have also been used synonymously, while accepting that in reality not all businesses are legally speaking corporate entities. Where an idea, term, or concept has received special attention by academic researchers (e.g. green marketing), this is reflected in the discussions in either the text or the supporting material of the relevant chapter.

Section Two

Greening Business in Context

2 The emergence of corporate environmentalism

Economic growth that does no environmental damage is an unattainable goal. The best governments can hope for is green growth.

(Cairncross, 1995)

Concern about the impact of human activity on the earth's systems and resources has generated a rich debate about the balance between economic development and environmental protection.

(Roome, 1997)

Everything we do has an environmental impact, and economic decisions pervade all we do.

(Pearce and Barbier, 2000)

Introduction

Business responses to the environmental agenda do not take place within a vacuum. As Chapter 1 indicates, firms exist and operate within a multifaceted, dynamic, and spatially diverse external context which helps to shape both their operations and decisions, including those related to the environmental management of the organization. At a broad socio-political level, this external context or business environment includes public and governmental awareness of and responses to environmental challenges posed in part by business activity.

While concern over the impact of this aspect of human activity on the natural environment was only one feature of the late twentieth century *zeitgeist*, there can be little doubt that the increasing willingness of some parts of the business community to demonstrate higher levels of environmental performance in recent decades has been driven at least in part by public and political demands for corporate action (Shrivastava, 1996). The roots of these demands and subsequent policy, institutional and conceptual, developments are the subject matter of this chapter. More detailed analysis of specific policy instruments and the drivers of corporate ecological responsiveness can be found in Chapters 3 and 4, respectively.

The growth of environmental awareness

Environmental problems such as global warming, loss of biodiversity, and pollution are the result of both natural causes (e.g. volcanic activity) and human behaviour. As far as the latter is concerned, the literature suggests that the various forms of environmental degradation confronting the world can—at a general level (see Chapter 3)—be linked to developments that have occurred over time, including the pursuit of economic growth, population increases, industrialization, poverty, and technological change (Buchholz, 1998; Pearce and Barbier, 2000). Given the seemingly inexorable growth in the global population, public expectations of rising levels of affluence, increasing urbanization, and the war on global poverty, the prediction is that without human intervention the natural environment will continue to deteriorate, with potentially catastrophic global human consequences in the future. In the words of the Chairman of the Intergovernmental Panel on Climate Change (IPCC): 'climate change is here, if we don't react, war, pestilence and famine will follow close behind' (quoted in Visser, 2009).

Growing appreciation of, and concern over, the deteriorating state of the global environment cannot be attributed to any single event or historical period. That said, there is a general agreement that a number of factors have proved pivotal in raising levels of awareness and in generally stimulating demands for action at government and corporate levels in the closing decades of the twentieth century. According to researchers (e.g. Roberts, 1995; Buchholz, 1998; Vogel, 2006; Visser, 2009), key influences have been:

- the publication of influential books such as Rachel Carson's *Silent Spring* (1962), Paul Ehrlich's *Population Bomb* (1968), and James Lovelocks's *Gaia* (1979);
- a series of high-profile ecological disasters including the Torrey Canyon (1967), Amoco Cadiz (1978), and Exxon Valdez (1998) oil spills; the dioxin leak at Seveso (1976); the chemical release at the Union Carbide plant in Bhopal (1984); the disaster at the nuclear installation at Chernobyl (1986);
- scientific discoveries and observed natural changes, for example the impact of chlorofluorocarbons (CFCs) on the ozone layer and the problem of greenhouse gas emissions (GHGs);
- a resurgence in interest in socially responsible business principles and practices; and
- media coverage of all of the above.

In helping to place the environment on the public and political agenda, developments such as these also appear to have had other consequences. The emergence of the modern day environmental movement and a change in focus towards environmental protection and more sustainable forms of development (see below) have both been linked to the politicization of environmental issues from the 1960s onwards (Murphy and Bendell,

1997; Buchholz, 1998; Garner, 2000). Similarly, a growth in the amount of environmental legislation, the establishment of special government agencies and departments to oversee environmental matters (e.g. both the UK Department of the Environment and the US Environmental Protection Agency were set up in 1970), and the First World Climate Conference (1979) also date from around this period and formed part of the backdrop against which further initiatives and institutions subsequently developed.

At corporate level too, there were signs that environmentalism was beginning to penetrate, albeit slowly, the boardrooms of some major international companies. In 1972, for example, the Club of Rome—a group of eminent industrialists, economists, and civil servants—commissioned a study by academics at the Massachusetts Institute of Technology, which was subsequently published as *The Limits to Growth* (Meadows et al., 1972). This study investigated the planet's economic, social, and environmental interactions and painted a gloomy picture of the future, given current trends in population growth, industrialization, pollution, food production, and resource depletion (Cairncross, 1995; Visser, 2009). In essence, it predicted that, because of the limited availability of national resources (especially oil), economic growth would not be able to continue indefinitely, a conclusion that led some observers to call for radical or even zero rates of growth in order to avoid a future global economic and environmental catastrophe (Barrow, 1999; Garner, 2000).

Although many believe that hindsight has shown this neo-Malthusian viewpoint to be unduly pessimistic (e.g. see Cairncross, 1995), it did at least draw attention to the relationship between economic growth and its environmental consequences and helped to provide a stimulus to the search for a more palatable alternative to future constraints on growth. This alternative—'sustainable development'—and its link to the growth versus environmental protection debate—are the issues to which we now turn.

Economic growth versus environmental protection

To gain an appreciation of the evolution of the notion of sustainable development, it is helpful to draw upon some basic economic theory and concepts relating to the question of the pursuit of growth, a goal that has remained at the core of the dominant intellectual model of economic and social progress since the end of the Second World War (Jacobs, 1996).

The argument runs essentially along these lines: Economic activity creates jobs, income, consumption, material well-being, and revenue for governments to provide essential public services such as health care and education. In order to maintain employment and its various beneficial consequences, annual growth is necessary and this is dependent on technological advancement and free trade. As the benefits of free trade spread to lesser developed economies, opportunities are created to reduce poverty and to raise global living standards. Moreover, the resources generated from gradually rising levels of free-market economic activity can be used to tackle the social and environmental consequences associated with rising levels of production, consumption, and distribution across the global economy.

As conventionally conceived, growth implies a real increase in a country's output (or income or expenditure) over time and is traditionally measured by annual rises in real net national product, where 'real' means allowing for inflation, 'net' means taking into account depreciation of assets, and 'product' is the output of goods and services produced by the economy over a given time period (e.g. see Worthington and Britton, 2009). While calculating growth in this way rightly allows for the depreciation of a country's capital wealth (e.g. machinery and other assets), it does not normally take account of the running down of what is called its 'natural capital' which is provided by the natural environment and includes scarce, finite resources such as waste assimilation capabilities, the ozone layer, and rich and biodiverse ecosystems. As indicated in Chapter 1, the natural environment, like other assets, provides economic benefits and contributes to economic productivity and well-being both currently and in the future (Pearce and Barbier, 2000). As with other forms of human and physical capital, a country's natural capital can be depleted, as well as built up, over time by pursuing a goal of economic growth. Should such a depletion occur, the true cost of short-term increases in economic growth is likely to be borne both economically and environmentally by future generations, creating what has become known as a 'problem of inter-generational equity'.

From an environmental impact point of view, the precise relationship between growth and environmental degradation is both complex and highly contested (Cairncross, 1995; Daly, 1996; Pearce and Barbier, 2000; York and Venkataraman, 2010). One view is that there is an inevitable trade-off between the two, with environmental problems rising inexorably as growth increases, a relationship captured in Figure 2.1.

An alternative perspective suggests that, as *per capita* levels of income rise over time, problems such as environmental pollution and resource depletion will rise at first but will eventually decline as individuals demand a cleaner environment and countries are

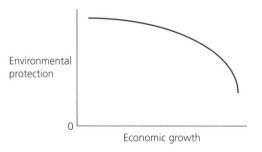

Figure 2.1 Economic growth versus environmental protection

BOX 2.1 THE ENVIRONMENTAL KUZNETS CURVE (EKC)

The following diagram shows a posited EKC for carbon dioxide. The implication of the hypothesis underlying this curve is that there is an inverted U-shaped relationship between a range of indicators of environment pollution (or resource depletion) and the level of *per capita* income, measured by GNP (gross national product). As the curve illustrates, initially CO_2 rises with increases in *per capita* GNP; beyond the turning point ('a' in the diagram) however, increases in income result in environmental improvements (see e.g. Pearce and Barbier, 2000).

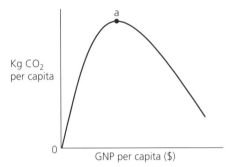

In the context of the debate concerning the impact of economic growth on the natural environment, the EKC implies that growth is not a threat to sustainability and that there are no environmental limits to growth as suggested by the Club of Rome. A study by Gross and Krueger (1995) found no evidence that environmental quality deteriorated steadily with growth in the economy and suggested that proponents of the trade-off view tended to ignore the impact of new technology and structural change on the environment versus economy relationship. In contrast, Stern et al. (1996) claim that the EKC model is based on a number of unrealistic assumptions (e.g. trade has a neutral effect on environmental degradation; there is no feedback from environmental quality to production possibilities) that call into question its usefulness as a theoretical proposition. The authors argue that the economy and the environment are jointly determined and that economic activity inevitably has negative impacts on the environment in some countries. Given the differences between the resource bases upon which economic activity depends, countries which import most of their basic materials may be exporting environmental problems to their trading partners.

driven to devote more of their additional resources to environmental protection—a proposition exemplified by what is called the Environmental Kuznets Curve (EKC) (see Box 2.1).

The central issue raised by these two opposing views is whether it is possible to have both economic growth and a cleaner environment (Cairncross, 1995). It is worth noting that under both positions, growth is seen to have an adverse effect on the natural environment. While the trade-off view suggests this will continue in an upward trend, the EKC relationship posits that, ultimately, economic development will take care of the environment automatically (Pearce and Barbier, 2000). In effect, where environmental protection is concerned, growth is not only a problem but also a possible solution over the longer term.

While there is empirical evidence to suggest that some environmental problems (e.g. sulphur dioxide) have indeed been reduced as *per capita* levels of income have risen (Arrow et al., 1995; Barbier, 1997), it remains far from clear whether economic growth alone offers a solution to all forms of environmental degradation. Current evidence indicates that far from being a panacea, the pursuit of economic growth is helping to put some critical economic resources at risk (e.g. the ozone layer) and to impose a variety of costs on society, including poorer human health, lost productivity, and amenity loss that needs to be recognized (Cairncross, 1995). Put simply, growth carries with it social, economic, and environmental costs, as well as benefits, and these tend to fall disproportionately on certain groups in society (e.g. the poor) and on developing more than developed economies. That being the case, many argue that growth should no longer be the priority for policy makers and that, instead, countries should focus on 'development' and in particular on 'sustainable development' with its emphasis on qualitative rather than quantitative improvements in economic performance (Cairncross, 1995; Pearce and Barbier, 2000).

Sustainable development

The emergence of the concept of sustainable development has been linked to international discussions in the 1970s and 1980s which focused primarily on development, growth, environment, and their human impact at a global level. Murphy and Bendell (1997) have suggested that key building blocks on the road to the establishment of the World Commission on Environment and Development (the WCED or Brundtland Commission)—which popularized the idea of sustainable development—have included the *Limits to Growth* Report (1972), the Stockholm Conference (1972), the Brandt Reports (1980 and 1983), and the World Conservation Strategy (1980), all of which began to identify relationships between social, economic, and environmental concerns that went beyond national boundaries. As Elliott (1999) notes, by the late 1970s, official thinking was beginning to see issues of environment and development, and the concerns of the developed and developing countries, as mutually interdependent rather than separate considerations for policy makers at the national and international levels.

It is generally agreed that the establishment of the Brundtland Commission in 1983 signalled a major attempt to address global environmental and development issues simultaneously. In its well-known report published in 1987, and entitled *Our Common Future* (WCED, 1987), the Commission defined sustainable development as development that 'meets the needs of the present without compromising the ability of the future generations to meet their own needs'. Under this definition, the basic proposition was that, in making choices designed to increase well-being today, countries should ensure that future generations are left no worse off than their current counterparts (Pearce and Barbier, 2000). In environmental terms, this implied *inter alia*, the need to limit environmental degradation, conserve the world's stock of natural capital, preserve essential ecosystem functions, and aim for improvements in the quality of life rather than simply year-on-year increases in *per capita* income (Cairncross, 1995; Jacobs, 1996; Pearce and Barbier, 2000).

The Brundtland Report not only helped to focus attention on a range of issues from equity and social justice to concern for the quality of life (see Box 2.2) but also pointed to the need to accept that there were limitations on the environment's ability to satisfy both the current and future needs and aspirations of the global population, to accept, in Daly's words (1996), that economic activities take place within an ecosystem which is finite, non-growing, and materially closed. From a business point of view, this proposition appeared to run counter to the traditional notion of 'business as usual', with its emphasis on growth and unfettered access to the world's natural resources and environmental services. For political leaders too, the emergence of sustainable development on the international policy agenda represented a considerable challenge, not least in relation to how it could be operationalized at national and international levels.

BOX 2.2 SUSTAINABLE DEVELOPMENT

The Brundtland Commission's oft-quoted definition of sustainable development is only one of many attempts to define this somewhat problematic concept (see e.g. Pearce et al. (1989) *Blueprint for a Green Economy*, Annex: Sustainable Development—A Gallery of Definitions). As Gladwin and Kennelly (1997) have pointed out, the fact that the term tends to be infused with 'multiple objectives and complex interdependencies' has made it 'fuzzy, elusive, and controversial'. This ambiguity in the business/natural environment vocabulary or discourse arguably makes it difficult for researchers and/or other observers of the business scene to assess corporate responses to the sustainability agenda. Can we ever achieve a truly 'sustainable business organization' (see Chapter 11) and if so, what would it look like and how would we recognize it?

In an effort to gain a clearer view of the concept, many writers point to the principal components of the idea that appear to be widely accepted in a majority of the definitions. Welford (1995), for example, argues that sustainable development is made up of three closely connected issues: the need to value the environment as an integral part of the economic process rather than as a 'free good'; the need to deal with the issue of equity; the need to operate on a longer time scale (i.e. the issue of futurity). Gladwin and Kennelly (1997) suggest that it is a process of achieving human development (i.e. widening or enlarging the range of people's choices) in a way which is 'inclusive', 'connected', 'equitable', 'prudent', and 'secure', while Schaltegger et al. (2003) speak of the three pillars of sustainable development: 'eco-efficiency', 'eco-justice', and 'socio-efficiency'. What these interpretations have in common is the idea that morality is no less important than economics and that key concerns should include issues of equity (both inter- and intra-generational), quality of life, and the protection of natural capital. Where the latter is concerned, this implies operating within the carrying capacity of the earth's ecosystems so as to provide for the well-being of future, as well as current, generations.

Policy and institutional developments post-Brundtland

The idea that countries should aim to combine economic development with environmental protection was given further emphasis in the World Development Report published in 1992 by the World Bank (Cairncross, 1995) and was the central theme at the United Nations Conference on Environment and Development (UNCED) held at Rio in the same year. The 'Earth Summit', as it became popularly known, attracted political leaders from across the globe, together with representatives of business, environmentalists, and citizen groups and was tasked by the UN General Assembly with devising strategies aimed at promoting environmental protection and sustainable development across the globe (McCoy and McCully, 1993). As the largest meeting of heads of state in history, the Rio Summit unsurprisingly proved to be a highly politicized occasion at which governments, NGOs, business leaders, and other groups lobbied hard to promote and protect their own interests. Inevitably, its outcomes proved to be something of a compromise and ranged from non-binding statements of broad principles (e.g. the Rio Declaration on Environment and Development; Statement on Forest Principles), through to a non-legally binding blueprint aimed at promoting sustainable development (Agenda 21), to legally binding treaties designed to tackle specific and urgent global environmental problems (e.g. the Convention on Biological Diversity; the Convention on Climate Change) but which did not achieve universal support.

Arguably, one of the Summit's most important contributions was that it helped to focus global attention on the need to address social, economic, and environmental issues at all spatial levels in an integrated manner and to consider the policy and institutional framework necessary to achieve such integration. The result over the next decade was a plethora of initiatives, policy commitments, institutional developments, national plans, and strategies, many of which date from this period and some key examples of which are illustrated below (see Box 2.3).

The Earth Summit also provided a natural stepping stone to discussions aimed at tackling the rapidly rising problem of climate change which had been highlighted in IPCC Reports and which was the focus of the work of the UN Framework Convention that emerged from the Rio process. These discussions culminated in the signing of the Kyoto Protocol in 1997, which came into force in 2005 and which set mandatory targets for greenhouse gas reductions (based on 1990 levels) for the world's leading developed economies that were to be achieved by 2012. Under Kyoto, the global target represented a 5.2 per cent reduction in greenhouse gases against 1990 levels, with some countries (e.g. Iceland) allowed to increase their emissions, while most of the others had to reduce theirs. Within the European Union (EU), the target was an overall 8 per cent reduction, again with variations between EU member states.

BOX 2.3 POLICY AND INSTITUTIONAL DEVELOPMENTS PRE- AND POST-RIO

- 1988—the establishment of the International Panel on Climate Change (IPCC) under the United Nations Environment Programme (UNEP). The IPCC's first report pointed to the problem of global warming and its likely consequences. Subsequent reports were published in 1995, 2001, and 2007 (Visser, 2009).
- 1988 onwards—the drafting of national plans and strategies on sustainable development across OECD and EU countries from Denmark and the Netherlands to South Korea, New Zealand, and Japan (Elliott, 1999; Jänicke and Jörgens, 2000).
- 1992—UN Framework Convention on Climate Change aimed at stabilizing greenhouse gas emissions that are associated with global warming and climate change (Visser, 2009).
- 1992—UN Commission on Sustainable Development set up to review progress after Rio and to encourage international cooperation on sustainable development (Murphy and Bendell, 1997).
- 1992–7—EU 5th Environmental Action Programme which committed EU countries to a policy of sustainable development and discussed how this might be achieved (Enmarch-Williams, 1996; Baker et al., 1997; Clement and Bachtler, 2000; Garner, 2000).
- 1994—'Sustainable Development: the UK Strategy', the UK government's response to the Rio Summit. The UK government had also previously published an Environmental White Paper in 1990 entitled, '*This Common Inheritance*' (Lowe and Ward, 1998) and a growing number of UK local authorities were beginning to draw up sustainable development plans at local level under Local Agenda 21 (Worthington et al., 2003).
- 1997—Earth Summit II which reviewed progress on the implementation of Rio agreements (Murphy and Bendell, 1997).
- 2002—UN World Summit on Sustainable Development (WSSD) in Johannesburg (also known as Rio + 10), which focused on implementing Agenda 21 via a multi-stakeholder approach at national, regional, and international levels.

Although developing economies were not required to set emission reduction targets, and some participants in the discussions subsequently decided not to implement the agreement (e.g. the United States), Kyoto marked a significant first step in tackling greenhouse gas emissions. It also proved a key influence in shaping the environment in which many major international companies would operate in the future, by ushering in the process of carbon trading (see Chapter 3 for fuller details) which helped to institutionalize the idea that global environmental problems could be, and ought to be, tackled in large part via market mechanisms. A generation earlier, the Organisation for Economic Co-operation and Development (OECD) had discussed the desirability of polluters paying for the environmental damage they caused, and the so-called 'polluter pays principle' was also accepted by the EU at this time (Roberts, 1995). By the early 1990s, an international consensus was beginning to emerge that market-based approaches—including the use of economic instruments such as environmental taxes and subsidies and emissions trading—would be an important weapon in tackling major environmental problems such as pollution and climate change. Kyoto proposed a mechanism for achieving this goal that has endured down to the present day (see Box 2.4).

BOX 2.4 KYOTO AND CARBON TRADING

Under the Kyoto Treaty, thirty-seven industrialized countries agreed targets to reduce their carbon emissions in the period 2008–12 by an average of 5 per cent over 1990 levels, with each of the participants given tradable rights associated with their own national budget. To build flexibility into the system, the agreement allowed a country to attempt to achieve its target in a variety of ways beyond simply reducing its emissions through domestic initiatives (e.g. an increased use of renewables). As well as being able to trade rights between themselves (e.g. as within the EU), participating rich countries could also invest in environmental projects in other developed and/or transition economies (known as Joint Implementation) or in emissions-saving projects (e.g. wind turbines, geothermal plants) in developing countries (known as the Clean Development Mechanism (CDM)), using the carbon credits gained to offset against their own emissions target. Alternatively, the credits could be sold on the open market to other polluters. For poorer countries with credits to sell, the flexibility mechanisms had the benefit of providing a welcome source of income; for richer nations, investing in emission reduction measures in poorer countries held out the promise of achieving their national target by cheaper means.

In practice, the carbon offsetting scheme has attracted a certain amount of criticism. Some environmental groups and academics have alleged that the scheme is being abused by some companies (e.g. in the chemical, energy, and water industries) who are claiming credits for schemes that are failing to deliver genuine carbon savings or for projects that are already under way and therefore do not provide for what is called 'additionality'. In May 2008, for example, the US watchdog group, International Rivers, published a study which suggested that nearly three-quarters of all registered CDM projects were complete at the time that their application for credits was approved, thereby calling into question why funding was required to complete the scheme.

Further criticisms include the tendency for CDM projects to be concentrated in a few countries (e.g. China, India, Brazil) at the expense of the least developed nations and the ability of some governments to build up spare credits because of a significant downturn in their economies (e.g. as in Eastern Europe following the collapse of the Soviet bloc) rather than as result of introducing emission-saving measures. The latter is known, in the jargon, as 'hot air'.

Note: 1. For a discussion of corporate responses to Kyoto, including the rent-sharing aspects of the CDM, see Begg et al. (2005), especially chapter 17.

Business responses

The debate by governments over how to address the issue of economic development and environmental protection simultaneously, clearly had implications for the business community and posed an important question regarding how far firms should be prepared to incorporate concern for the environment into their strategic discussions and day-to-day operations. While there were some signs in the post-'*Limits to Growth*' period that business leaders were prepared to engage in both fora and agreements designed to promote greater social and environmental responsibility (e.g. Business in the Community and the International Business Leaders Forum in the United Kingdom were established in 1982 and 1990, respectively; the Responsible Care Programme in the Chemical Industry was launched in 1985; the Montreal Protocol on CFCs was signed in

1987), on the whole it seems fair to say that around the time of the Brundtland Report, many businesses still remained hostile to the idea that environmental protection should act as a constraint on corporate growth.

An important indication that this perspective was beginning to be questioned by some major international business leaders came in 1990 with the establishment of the Business Council for Sustainable Development (BCSD) under the chairmanship of Stephan Schmidheiny, a Swiss industrialist. The BCSD included the chief executive officers of forty-eight of the largest transnational companies in the world (e.g. DuPont, Dow, Shell, Mitsubishi) and was invited to develop a 'business view' for the Earth Summit in Rio in 1992. In its report entitled *Changing Course* (1992), the Council presented the idea that the most effective way to achieve sustainable development was through the market and called for progress towards full-cost pricing and the use of economic instruments—including environmental taxes, charges, and tradable permits—in pursuit of this goal (Schmidheiny, 1992; Holliday et al., 2002).

At the time, a similar stance was taken by the International Chamber of Commerce (ICC) which also produced input for the Earth Summit. The centrepiece of the ICC's strategy was its Business Charter for Sustainable Development, which was designed to be a benchmark statement of the commitment by business organizations to protect the environment and to which firms were voluntarily invited to sign up (Welford, 1997*b*). Subsequent to the publication of the ICC's Charter principles in 1991, the ICC produced a book entitled *From Ideas to Action* (1992) which gave examples of environmental practices and programmes that had been implemented by various companies across different sectors. Like the BCSD, the ICC believed that protecting the natural environment was best achieved through the market rather than regulation and that, given the right conditions, businesses could benefit from integrating environmentalism into their corporate and business strategies (Welford and Gouldson, 1993).

In order to make the notion of sustainable development more appealing and meaningful to businesses, the BCSD held a competition to find a phrase that suggested that there was a clear business case for environmentalism (Holliday et al., 2002). The winning phrase—'eco-efficiency'—subsequently became the watch word of the BCSD's successor organization, the World Business Council for Sustainable Development (WBCSD), created in 1995 following a merger of the BCSD and the World Industry Council of the Environment (WICE) which had been set up by the ICC (Visser, 2009). As defined by the WBCSD (2000), eco-efficiency is achieved 'by the delivery of competitively priced goods and services that satisfy human needs and wants and bring quality of life, whilst progressively reducing ecological impacts and resource intensity throughout the life cycle, to a level at least in line with the Earth's estimated "carrying capacity"'. In short, it was seen as a means of simultaneously delivering environmental and economic performance (De Simone and Popoff, 1997).

How far all this activity in the post-Brundtland period constituted a cultural shift in business attitudes to environmental protection is, of course, open to debate. Frankel

(1998) has argued that *Changing Course* was a defining moment in the history of corporate environmentalism, a challenge to the idea of 'business as usual'. For McCoy and McCully (1993), the report was a 'manifesto for corporate environmentalism', an indication—in Cairncross's words (1995)—that by the early 1990s some businesses were beginning to embrace green philosophy in a big way. Welford (1997*b*), on the other hand, has been highly critical of the idea of eco-efficiency, arguing that it does not tackle the root causes of environmental problems, but instead promotes growth, free trade, and globalization rather than sustainable development. In his opinion, the Rio process was an indication that industry and its representative organizations had 'hijacked' environmentalism, controlling the agenda in political circles in a way that has prevented a more radical debate over the integration of social, economic, and environmental concerns at national and international levels.

While this latter view clearly has some validity, there seems little doubt that the last two decades of the twentieth century were marked by a growing awareness within the international business community that environmental protection was becoming an important business issue and one to which firms would increasingly need to respond under pressure from a variety of stakeholder interests. As indicated above, political, policy, and international initiatives were one important manifestation of such a development. Another was the proliferation in terminology that emanated primarily from the academic community and from its understandable concern to capture the different facets of the economy/ecology debate as a growing number of firms moved from a position of resistant adaptation to external pressures for change towards a more enlightened attitude to environmental management (Fischer and Schot, 1993).

The terminology of sustainability

The debate over how to reconcile economic growth and environmental protection helped not only to raise environmental consciousness among the various stakeholder interests but also to expose a divergence in opinion between those who generally subscribed to a reformist/anthropocentric (or technocratic) view and those who tended towards a more radical/ecocentric approach to sustainable development (Elliott, 1999). Under the former perspective, primacy is given to human beings, and nature is regarded as an expendable resource for furthering the interests of the human species (Gladwin and Kennelly, 1997). Accordingly, economic growth is seen as a desirable goal and environmental protection tends to be regarded as a matter of utilizing resources better and of applying technology to provide for environmental solutions within existing socio-economic and political structures (O'Riordan, 1981; Garner, 2000).

By contrast, ecocentrists are earth-centred, with humans only one of many species with no inherent rights of primacy nor claims on the earth's resources (O'Riordan, 1985). By implication, sustainable development under this view requires the establishment of a new moral and ethical view of nature and commensurate changes in social, economic, and political structures (Baker et al., 1997; Elliott, 1999; Garner, 2000), rather than tinkering with technocratic solutions. As O'Riordan (1981) rightly notes, in practice, the distribution between these two positions is frequently blurred, and individual perspectives and preferences tend to be conditioned by a variety of factors including economic and institutional influences.

This notion of differing viewpoints has been captured well and variously in the environmental literature. Roome (1997) for instance talks of 'deep', 'mid', and 'shallow' green perspectives that can be applied to both individuals and organizations; Porritt (1984) and Dobson (1995) refer to 'light' and 'dark' green approaches, while Naess (1973) uses the terms 'shallow' and 'deep' ecology. Consistent with this idea that there may be a variety of meanings and/or approaches where environmentalism is concerned, Baker et al. (1997) have proposed the notion of a 'ladder of sustainable development' in advanced industrial societies, based on differing ideological beliefs that range from an anthropocentric to an ecocentric (or biocentric) view of nature. At the anthropocentric end of the ladder, the authors talk of 'treadmill' and 'weak sustainable development', characterized by an instrumental approach to the natural environment in which growth is either pursued as desirable in its own right with little or no concern for the environmental consequences ('treadmill') or where growth remains central, but some limited attempts are made to manage environmental problems through market-driven technocratic solutions ('weak sustainable development'). As societies move towards an ecocentric approach, protecting the environment is seen as a precondition to economic development and consequently environmentalism becomes embedded in the policy process in an integrated ('strong sustainable development') or a holistic manner ('ideal' model).

When applied to the management of business organizations, anthropocentrism and ecocentrism imply different management orientations towards protecting the natural environment. Under the former, often called 'traditional management', the exploitation of natural resources is seen as a legitimate, even desirable, activity, and pollution and waste are treated as externalities (see Chapter 3) that result from the free market process (Shrivastava, 1995a). Under the latter, the emphasis is on creating sustainable economic development and improving the quality of life for all organizational stakeholders, by managing the environmental impact of the organization at all stages of the transformation process (see Chapter 1) via initiatives such as ecological designs, resource reduction, and the use of environmentally efficient technologies (Shrivastava, 1995b, 1995c; Buchholz, 1998).

Theoretical support for the view that organizations (and societies) could manage their environmental impact effectively came with the development of ecological modernization (EM) theory in the 1980s (Orsato and Clegg, 2005). Advocates of EM saw it as a way in which capitalism could accommodate the environmental challenge (Gouldson and Murphy, 1996, 1997, 1998; Robbins, 2001), a means by which environmental protection and economic advancement could coexist (Garner, 2000). To achieve this integration at the macro-level, EM theorists called upon nation states to adopt appropriate policy structures and instruments which simultaneously promoted growth and environmental protection (Gouldson and Murphy, 1996), whether this be via the reconfiguration of the regulatory framework or through the increased use of self-regulation and market-based approaches (Mol and Sonnenfeld, 2000; Gunningham and Sinclair, 2002). At the micro-level, the focus has tended to be on the adoption of new technologies and techniques designed to reduce an organization's environmental impact and to promote greater eco-efficiency to the benefit of both the firm and the environment (see Chapter 8 for a fuller discussion).

Unsurprisingly, the idea that growth and environmental protection could be supported on theoretical grounds found favour with a growing number of political leaders in the closing years of the twentieth century and the ideology of EM began to emerge in policy statements and actions at governmental and intergovernmental levels, including the EU's Environmental Action Programmes (Baker et al., 1997; Clement and Bachtler, 2000; Orsato and Clegg, 2005). At corporate level too, the theory had obvious appeal and its underlying philosophy began to be reflected in management practices (e.g. the introduction of environmental management systems) and in debates concerning the advantages of corporate environmentalism, including those put forward by groups such as the BCSD and its successor organization (see above).

While eco-modernist views have undoubtedly had a formative influence on both public policy and current discourses in the environment/economy field—including notions of 'win-win', the 'double divided', or the 'greengold thesis' (see Chapter 6)—not all observers feel it offers a satisfactory and/or desirable approach to the natural environment/economy debate. Some critics have argued that the EM theory is basically defensive and insufficiently radical, a case of 'business as usual' with an added environmental tinge (Welford, 1997b). Others have pointed to its limitations as both a theoretical explanation and a potential policy tool (Roberts and Gouldson, 2000) and to its distinctly anthropocentric view of the value of nature (Baker et al., 1997). Notwithstanding these criticisms, it seems reasonable to suggest that the essentially incrementalist and technocentric approach to addressing environmental problems put forward by prescriptive interpretations of the theory (Gouldson and Roberts, 2000) will continue to have more appeal at both the state and corporate level than more radical proposals. As Baker et al. (1997) have pertinently observed, the philosophy of EM fits well with the overall economic *raison d'être* of a politico-economic structure such as the EU with its emphasis on continual economic growth and an ever-expanding environmental protection policy. Much the same could be said for other market-based economies and for the resonance of EM theory with the goals of profit-seeking private sector organizations within a capitalist economic system (Gunningham and Sinclair, 2002).

From Kyoto to Copenhagen

The 'rich debate'—referred to by Nigel Roome in the opening quotation at the start of this chapter—has continued to the present day. Following the agreements reached at Kyoto, international attention after 1997 became increasingly focused on the key issue of climate change and its perceived and anticipated social, economic, and environmental consequences. In addition to numerous meetings of political leaders under the auspices of the United Nations, the G20 countries, the World Economic Forum, the European Union, and other cross-national groupings, the opening years of the new millennium saw a plethora of official reports (e.g. the Stern Report, 2006; the UN Millennium Ecosystem Assessment Report, 2007)—published at both national and international levels—that re-emphasized the widely accepted links between economic activity and damage to the natural environment. A central theme running through all of this activity was the idea that tackling problems such as climate change was a vital global issue that required action by government, individuals, and businesses alike. Where the latter was concerned, most countries (and large multinationals) tended to favour a dual-track approach, with regulatory and government-designed economic instruments such as emissions trading schemes (see Chapter 3) coexisting alongside voluntary initiatives, many of which were aimed at encouraging business organizations to commit themselves to higher levels of social and environmental responsibility and/or provide information on their environmental impacts that could be of benefit to stakeholder groups such as institutional investors (e.g. the Carbon Disclosure Project, the UN Global Compact, and the Global Reporting Initiative).

To craft a new global treaty to regulate greenhouse gas emissions after the expiry of the Kyoto Protocol in 2012, UN member state governments embarked upon a series of rolling meetings designed to establish a road map for negotiations that were to be concluded in Copenhagen in December 2009. At a conference in Bali in 2007, for example, ministers and officials from participant states eventually finalized an agreement to work towards a new climate change deal to come into effect in January 2013 and to continue negotiations on issues such as financing and technology transfer until a successor treaty was agreed at the Copenhagen summit. As in the run up to the Kyoto meeting more than a decade earlier, the whole process was highly political and subject to substantial lobbying and posturing by individual member states (e.g. the United States), groupings of countries (e.g. the EU; the BRIC countries—Brazil, Russia, India, and China), developed versus developing nations, and vested interests (e.g. industries and large multinationals), all of whom sought to shape the agenda and substance of negotiations before the 2009 meeting.

The years immediately prior to Copenhagen also saw a number of other developments that formed part of the background against which the climate change negotiations were concluded. While some countries continued to resist the setting of targets for greenhouse

---

GREEN SNAPSHOT: THE CARBON DISCLOSURE PROJECT (CDP)

The CDP was launched in 2000 in an effort to encourage corporate responses to climate change, primarily by improving both the quantity and quality of information on the impact of business activity on the global climate. Using an annual, voluntary climate change questionnaire, the CDP collects information and data from thousands of organizations worldwide on their greenhouse gas emissions and on their water management and climate change strategies with the aim of providing public disclosure and transparency and of encouraging participating firms to make performance improvements. The findings can be accessed by a wide variety of interests, including institutional investors, government agencies, policy makers, and academics.

Operating in the world's major economies, and supported by funding from a range of charitable and corporate bodies and national governments, the CDP provides a coordinating mechanism for hundreds of institutional investors with tens of trillions of dollars under their management and for a number of major purchasing organizations, including Dell, PepsiCo, and Wal-Mart. The CDP's website is thought to be the largest repository of corporate greenhouse gas emissions data in the world (see e.g. Visser, 2009) and its reports—accessible via its website—contain detailed information on greenhouse gas emissions and on corporate perceptions of business risks and opportunities associated with climate change from the world's largest business organizations.

---

gas emissions, others such as the United Kingdom voluntarily legislated to set binding cuts on emissions and began to devise strategies to achieve the agreed reductions (e.g. 80 per cent by 2050). In the United States, the election of President Obama raised hopes that the US administration would emulate the stance taken by a significant number of American States, cities, and companies and agree to cuts in emissions as part of a new global deal on climate change. In China too, the world's biggest polluter, there were signs that the government was willing to commit itself to curb its carbon emissions, invest in clean energy and seek to reduce the level of emissions per unit of output over the coming decade.

GREEN SNAPSHOT: CHINA AND CLIMATE CHANGE

While the Kyoto Treaty made no demands on China regarding cuts in carbon emissions, the Chinese government began to signal its willingness to consider ways of reducing its environmental impact in the pre-Copenhagen period. Central to its plan was a commitment to increase its use of wind and solar power in the decade up to 2020 through the direction of hundreds of billions of dollars towards low-carbon investment. It also announced plans to invest large sums in carbon-efficient transport and electricity transmission systems. The hope is that by the end of 2020 around 15 per cent of China's energy production will come from clean sources, making the country a world leader in renewables.

More recently (November 2011), the government has announced its intention of replacing the billions of incandescent light bulbs used annually in China with more energy-efficient models over the next five years, a decision which follows in the wake of similar decisions in Australia, Brazil, the EU, and a number of other countries.

In the event, the Copenhagen summit proved to be a major disappointment for those hoping for a comprehensive global agreement that could be converted into a legally binding treaty. Despite general recognition by participants of the scientific case for limiting future temperature increases to two degrees centigrade, the eventual Copenhagen 'accord'—brokered by the United States, China, Brazil, India, and South Africa—contained no commitment on how this was to be achieved, nor any legally binding emissions targets. Instead, countries were asked individually to make pledges on the extent to which they would reduce emissions by 2020, in effect a bottom-up approach to carbon reduction based on national policies and commitments.

GREEN SNAPSHOT: INVESTING IN CLIMATE CHANGE

Following the failure of the Copenhagen summit in 2009 to deliver an international climate change treaty, more than 450 of the world's major investors—responsible for controlling around $13 trillion of assets—called upon national governments to adopt policies that showed their determination to move towards an economy based on the use of cleaner energy. At a conference held at the United Nations in January 2010, the investors argued that it was essential for governments to adopt rigorous targets for reducing greenhouse gas emissions over the next decade and beyond if they were to be persuaded that investing in a low-carbon economy made commercial sense. What was needed, they suggested, was immediate action by governments at a national and regional level (e.g. in areas such as renewable energy, cleaner vehicles, public transport) in order to attract private sector funding for the transition from fossil fuels to renewable, low-carbon sources of energy.

On the positive side, the summit agreed on an incentive scheme to address the problem of deforestation and to set up a multi-billion dollar fund to support poorer countries to adapt to climate change over the coming years. It also set a target of meeting in Cancun in Mexico in November 2010 in the hope that further progress could be made in finding a follow-on treaty or agreement once Kyoto expired in 2012.

As with the Copenhagen summit, the meeting in Cancun ultimately failed to deliver an international agreement, although it did help to formalize the target emission cuts put forward by some UN member states during and after the Copenhagen process. Agreements were also reached on better monitoring of national plans and the deforestation scheme and on the establishment of a Green Climate Change Fund to help poorer countries, both of which had previously been agreed in outline at Copenhagen. As for a successor to Kyoto, this was deferred to a further summit to be held in Durban in South Africa in late 2011.

After protracted negotiations, the meeting in Durban finally resulted in an agreement between all the participating nations to start work on a new climate change accord which would have legal force and would require both developed and developing countries to cut their carbon emissions. In what some described as 'a deal to agree a deal', 2015 was the date set for countries to reach agreement on the terms of the accord which is scheduled to come into effect in 2020. Initial signs suggest that reaching a binding agreement will be by no means an easy task, with few observers expecting any significant breakthrough by the time of the Earth Summit in 2012 (also known as Rio + 20). Despite continuing pressure on the world's governments from scientific bodies, some large corporate businesses, and investor groups, a combination of global economic problems, persistent crises in the Eurozone, political unrest in the Middle East, and the forthcoming US presidential elections (in 2012) make it almost certain that reaching agreement on a successor to Kyoto will be pushed well down the political agenda in most countries and may yet fail to materialize.

Case Study: The Gulf of Mexico oil spill, 2010

For the average citizen, scientific and scholarly debates about the damage to the environment caused by economic activity can appear somewhat esoteric. Disagreements between scientists/scholars over the causes and effects of problems such as global warming do little to capture the public imagination and often help to generate a considerable amount of distrust and scepticism over the validity of scientific and academic analysis. This is a situation which some individuals and groups (e.g. industry lobbies, some politicians, climate change deniers) are only too willing to exploit in an effort to advance their position, and this invariably causes further confusion in the public's mind.

The reality is different where a major environmental disaster is concerned; the impact tends to be clear for all to see and, whilst the long-term effects may not be immediately apparent or may be underestimated, media coverage of such a disaster helps to raise public awareness of the potential impact of business operations on the natural world when a major incident occurs. Over the years, a plethora of such incidents have proved instrumental in placing the environment firmly on the public and political agenda.

One industry which has had its share of environmental disasters in recent decades has been the oil industry, with the BP oil spill in the Gulf of Mexico in 2010 being a notable and globally well-publicized example. Beginning with an explosion on the company's Deepwater Horizon oil rig in late April of that year, thousands of tonnes of crude oil began to leak into the waters off the US Gulf coast and set in train a frantic effort to stem the flow and to clean up the rapidly growing slick before it caused further ecological and economic damage.

The company's response to the oil spill took a variety of forms. Attempts were made to cap the leaking underwater well using robot-operated submarines; while this was taking place, barrages were deployed to try to prevent the oil from reaching the Gulf coast.

Other techniques included skimming oil off the surface of the water, the use of chemical dispersants, and the burning of surface oil where this was possible. Despite all these efforts, tens of thousands of barrels of oil continued to flow from the well each day and to threaten the coastline of several US states bordering the Gulf of Mexico. It was not long before the spill became larger than the Exxon Valdez disaster that had occurred off the coast of Alaska in 1989.

The impact of the crisis was substantial. Eleven workers lost their lives and others were injured as a result of the explosion. The spill also threatened the livelihoods of those who depended on the sea for employment or who worked in the local tourist industry. It was estimated, for example, that the cost to the fishing industry alone would run into billions of dollars and that this would have a major impact on the local and regional economy over many years.

Ecologically, the disaster threatened to be just as significant. In addition to being an important area for fishing and a major spawning ground for tuna, the Gulf is a highly important habitat for bird species and for dolphins, otters, and turtles. On land it contains a key, but fragile, area of wetland which is home to many species of birds and animals, as well as serving as a buffer against storms and hurricanes. From the outset, it was recognized that the damage to local ecosystems and subsystems was likely to be substantial and could last well into the future.

While much of the threatened ecological damage could be attributed to the impact of the oil itself, there were other environmental consequences, some of which were the result of attempts to address the problem, As well as toxic fumes given off by the oil floating in the water, carbon dioxide was released when some of the oil was set on fire in an attempt to limit the damage, and this also had the effect of causing unpleasant fumes and black smoke which drifted over the area. A further concern was the impact on the marine environment of using chemical dispersants to break up the oil slick in the expectation that this would allow natural processes (e.g. waves) to begin to lessen the damage.

As for BP itself, the crisis proved something of a public relations as well as a commercial disaster. Over the course of several months, the company and its partner organizations (e.g. Haliburton and Transocean) were permanently in the public spotlight and were heavily criticized by US political leaders for their response which was perceived as slow and inadequate given the scale of the leak. As well as facing possible criminal action for negligence and loss of life, the company's activities in the Gulf and elsewhere in America came under serious threat and the corporation saw a dramatic fall in its share price as traders took fright over its future risks and liabilities. In seeking to address the problem, BP was forced to spend billions of dollars, which included the cost of the clean-up and containment; grants to, and claims by, the US government and/or the states affected; legal settlements with affected parties; and ongoing costs of environmental remediation. Unanticipated costs on this scale clearly had important implications for the organization's current shareholders and for potential future investors looking for a safe and profitable haven for their money.

While the BP oil spill in the Gulf of Mexico serves as an important and timely reminder of the potential trade-off between economic activity and environmental protection (see Chapter 3), it also emphasizes the fact that, at the firm level, damaging the environment when engaging in everyday business behaviour can also have significant negative economic and commercial implications for an enterprise. The price paid by the environment as a result of business activity can sometimes rebound on the business community itself, and the cost incurred at corporate level may not simply be in dollars but also in a loss of public image, an erosion of political capital, and a hostile (and potentially crucial) reaction by the markets both in the short and longer term.

3 Government, business, and the natural environment: policy instruments

The market, that mechanism that so marvelously directs human activity to supply human needs, often has no way of putting a proper price on environmental resources. 'Free as the air' is all very well, but it means that factories pay nothing to belch smoke from their stacks. It is easy to put a price on a tree as timber. But that price will take no account of its value as a mechanism for preventing soil erosion, or as a home for rare birds or insects, or as a store of carbon dioxide that might otherwise add to the greenhouse gases in the atmosphere.

(Cairncross, 1993)

It has long been established that free markets will not necessarily deliver efficient outcomes in the absence of appropriate property rights and/or in the presence of externalities.

(Stoeckl, 2004)

While there is some scope for optimism with regard to corporate environmental efforts, it is likely that voluntary initiative falls far short of what is required from an environmental point of view.... Hence there is clear scope for policies aimed at enhancing the introduction of environmentally friendly products.

(Kuhn, 2005)

Introduction

It was suggested in Chapter 1 that environmental problems can be portrayed as one of the inevitable consequences of economic activity—an unwanted output of the productive process and an unwelcome side-effect of people's consumption of the goods and services that satisfy their daily needs and wants. As indicated in Chapter 2, growing recognition of the damage being inflicted on the natural environment by these everyday processes gave rise to a 'rich debate' about how to balance public and political demands for economic growth and development with the need to protect the earth's ecosystems and natural resources upon which current and future well-being depends. A key part of this debate has concerned the role governments can play in promoting more sustainable forms of development and, more specifically, what steps the state can undertake to encourage organizations to improve their environmental performance. In this chapter we focus primarily on the three main approaches adopted by national governments and discuss the evolution of an emerging international consensus on how policy makers at national level and beyond can best encourage businesses to become greener.

Environmental problems: a case of market failure?

In *Blueprint for a Green Economy*, Pearce et al. (1989) argue that the root cause of most environmental problems lies in the failure of the economic system to take account of the valuable services which are provided by the natural environment and which help to promote and sustain economic activity. To understand this claim, it is helpful to briefly consider some of the underlying principles and practices that govern the operation of a modern market-based economy.

As the name suggests, in this type of economy, decisions on production, consumption, and distribution are determined predominantly by a system of markets which facilitate the flow of goods, services, and resources between buyers and sellers in an arrangement underpinned by the existence of private property. In the market for resources such as labour, firms are normally the buyers and individuals the sellers; in the market for goods and services the reverse is often the case. What links buyers and sellers in these markets is a system of prices that determines how economic inputs and outputs are ultimately allocated and which acts as an indicator of the value placed on an asset by those engaged in a transaction. As market conditions change (e.g. a resource becomes more limited in supply), prices tend to adjust and act as a signal to buyers and/or sellers that can elicit a change in their behaviour, with product/resource substitution or investment in new products and/or processes just some of the responses that might occur.

Where environmental protection is concerned, economists have questioned whether relying solely on market forces is sufficient to encourage individuals and organizations to engage in environmentally friendly behaviour. For a start, some environmental assets that provide an economic function (e.g. the air and the sea) are not traded in markets in the traditional sense, hence their value as a resource or as a source of utility cannot be revealed through the usual processes of buying and selling. Being in common ownership rather than someone's private property, these assets are effectively 'free goods' which are available for all to exploit as they see fit and without a market to ration their use. Given a choice between installing expensive equipment to clean up emissions to air from a factory or pumping them into the atmosphere free of charge, a rational firm is likely to choose the latter course of action, assuming there are no controls imposed by government and/or incentives to do otherwise.

In addition to the absence of a market that can prevent overuse of some environmental assets by opportunists, economists point to imperfections in the operation of existing markets for goods and services, most notably the existence of 'externalities' or what Pearce and Barbier (2000) call 'uncompensated third-party effects'. In essence, these occur when the actions of one party have an adverse (or beneficial) impact on another party, as in the case of the pollution of a river by firm 'A' which imposes additional costs on its downstream neighbour firm 'B', which uses water from the river for its production processes. In the absence of incentives, 'A' is likely to take no account of the impact on 'B' when calculating the 'costs' of its activities; in economists' language these additional costs (or, in some cases, benefits) are essentially 'externalized' by 'A' and are experienced by someone who has no direct involvement in a market transaction.

As Figure 3.1 indicates, externalities can be either negative or positive and can occur at different stages of the transformation process (Worthington, 2005). They can also be mixed in the sense that they impact simultaneously on both producers and consumers (e.g. when traffic jams caused by individuals going on holiday increase the distribution costs of firms whose lorries are also stuck in the jam).

For economists, the problem of externalities lies not in the moral question of whether these spill-over effects are right or wrong, but in the fact that they represent a form of 'market failure'; this is the idea that, in terms of efficiency or social desirability, the best result that could have been achieved in the operation of a market was not achieved in

	Production Externality	**Consumption Externality**
+	Firm A trains its workers on computers and some take their skills to firm B	An individual paints her/his house and thereby increases the value of neighbouring properties
−	Firm X pollutes a river which increases the production costs of firm Y	A neighbour plants fast-growing conifers blocking out the light in the next door garden

Figure 3.1 Examples of externalities

Notes: 1. Production externalities exist when the production activities of one firm directly affect the production activities of another firm.
2. Consumption externalities exist when the level of consumption of a good/service has a direct effect on the welfare of another consumer.

Source: Worthington (2005).

BOX 3.1 THE IMPACT OF AN EXTERNAL COST

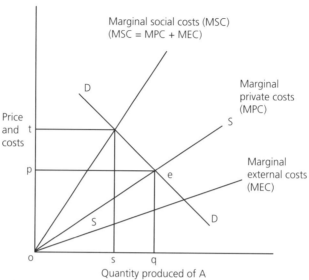

Source: Worthington (2005).

The diagram above illustrates the effects of a negative externality such as pollution. Using simple demand and supply analysis in the market for product A, we can see that the demand curve (DD) and the supply curve (SS), or marginal private costs curve (MPC) intersect at point 'e' giving a market price of 'op' and a market quantity traded of 'oq'. If we assume that producers are imposing external costs on society in the form of pollution (represented by the marginal external costs curve—MEC), then the full social cost of producing product A (MSC) comprises the marginal private costs (MPC) plus the marginal external costs (MEC). If such additional costs are added, the socially optimal level of output becomes 'os' and the optimal price becomes 'ot', that is, pollution would be reduced because fewer goods are traded as the price rises. It is worth noting that pollution is only one example of market failure; others include public goods and asymmetries of information and their effects (i.e. 'moral hazard' and 'adverse selection').

While economists normally portray externalities as spillover effects of behaviour and hence suggest that they can be addressed by allocating property rights (e.g. by state intervention) which will permit the establishment of a market, Callon (1998) asks whether they might prove to be the norm and questions whether they can easily be internalized, since they are often difficult to identify and measure (e.g. what are the causes of global warming, who is responsible, and who is affected and by how much?). This could imply the need for substantial investments aimed at identifying and measuring externalities prior to the establishment of any property rights.

practice (Callon, 1998). As indicated in Box 3.1, externalities (both negative and positive) affect the efficiency of the market as a means of allocating resources because they result in a gap between the social costs (or benefits) of an economic activity and the private costs of that activity that is borne by the participating firm (or individual). Put another way, where markets fail to adequately reflect the environmental costs of economic behaviour, economic activity tends to be orientated towards satisfying private gains rather than social benefits and hence environmental considerations will tend to be downgraded or, in some cases, ignored altogether (Cairncross, 1993; Pearce and Barbier, 2000)—a point clearly demonstrated by the opening quotation to this chapter.

Given market imperfections of this kind and the absence of a market in the case of environmental free goods and services, the general consensus is that government intervention is sometimes necessary to avoid/reduce environmental degradation caused by economic activity. What form(s) this intervention might take, what the consequences might be for firms, and how far it can maximize environmental protection whilst minimizing harm to the economy has been the subject of considerable debate over many decades (see below).

In the next section we examine briefly the main types of policy instrument used by governments to shape the environmental behaviour of firms, prior to undertaking a detailed analysis of the three main approaches most commonly found in national jurisdictions. Each approach has both its advantages and disadvantages and the choice at any point in time will be determined by a variety of factors, including attempts by vested interests to steer the debate on environmental governance towards arenas where they have the greatest influence (Kellow and Zito, 2002).

A typology of policy instruments

In tackling issues of policy concern, governments normally have a range of options they can pursue. The choices they make tend to be determined by questions of relative cost, perceived effectiveness, efficiency, equity, social justice, public acceptability, political feasibility, and so on. In the final analysis, the hope is that the chosen policy and instrument(s) will be at least partially successful in achieving the government's policy goals, in this case addressing the adverse environmental effects associated with business activity. At the risk of oversimplification, this requires the state to decide how far it should be involved in directing the activities of the business community. Should it use, what Bemelmans-Videc et al. (1998) refer to as 'sticks' (e.g. regulations) or should it opt for less constraining approaches such as economic instruments ('carrots') or information provision ('sermons') as a means of shaping corporate behaviour?

Following Pearce and Barbier (2000) and Jordan et al. (2003b), Figure 3.2 presents a simplified typology of alternative environmental policy instruments based on two dimensions: (a) whether a government specifies the goals it wishes firms to achieve and (b) mandates how they should seek to achieve them. Where both the means and the ends are specified by policy makers via the use of government regulation (Cell 1), the chosen policy mode is known as 'command and control', exemplified by the imposition of legally binding emissions targets and the use of a prescribed (or best available) technology (Prakash and Kollman, 2004). Should a government choose not to mandate

---

GREEN SNAPSHOT: A MIXED APPROACH TO ENVIRONMENTAL PROTECTION

The state has a variety of weapons at its disposal when seeking to encourage domestic firms to improve on their environmental performance. These can be applied at either the macro- or micro-level as evidenced by recent decisions taken by the Chinese government. In addition to announcing plans to encourage the development of cleaner energy sources in the run-up to the Copenhagen summit in 2009 (see Chapter 2), Chinese decision-makers stated their intention to set national targets for renewables and to make funding available for low-carbon projects. In October 2010, the government also ordered the closure of over 2,000 factories which were deemed unsafe, highly polluting, or energy inefficient in sectors that included steel, paper, and cement.

   As part of its five-year economic plan from 2011 onwards, the government has indicated its intention of slowing down the rate of economic growth as a means of reducing the environmental impact of the country's economic activity and is planning to take a number of other steps to green the Chinese economy, including making energy efficiency a priority, setting a carbon intensity target, establishing a mandated carbon trading system, and levying taxes on heavy polluters. It has also been fighting a prolonged public relations campaign to persuade UN officials and sympathetic governments to hold western nations responsible for a significant proportion of the country's greenhouse gas emissions by dint of their seemingly inexorable demands for exported Chinese manufactured goods.

	Government/regulator specifies the goal firms have to achieve	Government/regulator does not specify the goal firms have to achieve
Government/regulator specifies how firms should achieve the required goal	Cell 1 Command and control regulation	Cell 2 Technology-focused regulatory standards
Government/regulator does not specify how firms should achieve the required goal	Cell 3 Most negotiated agreements and others (e.g. some MBIs; some forms of regulation)	Cell 4 Market-based instruments (MBIs) and other approaches (e.g. informational devices)

Figure 3.2 A typology of government environmental policy instruments

Source: Adapted from Pearce and Barbier (2000) and Jordan et al. (2003*b*). The latter was based on an earlier version of the typology by Russell and Powell (1996).

what organizations should do nor how they should do it (Cell 4), this is generally known as a 'market-based approach' in that it uses various types of price signal to address instances of market failure (e.g. free environmental goods and negative environmental externalities). Between the two lie options in which the state either specifies what should be achieved but not how to achieve it (Cell 3), or determines the means but not the ends (Cell 2). Most negotiated voluntary agreements between the government and business are indicative of the former, whilst the imposition of technology-based regulatory standards (e.g. the requirement to use the best available technology not entailing excessive cost—BATNEEC) is an example of the latter.

While it is tempting to view these different policy instruments as mutually exclusive, in reality there tends to be a degree of overlap between the categories. Apart from the fact that regulation can be applied to means or ends or both, the use of market-based instruments frequently requires governments to use the law to bring into being and operate the different types of economic incentive/disincentive used in environmental protection (Pearce et al., 1994; Braadbaart, 1998). Moreover, far from being seen as alternative options, policy makers usually view regulatory and other approaches as complementary in that together they can facilitate action at both a general and specific level and can be targeted at firms, industries, sectors, or at the economy as a whole according to the circumstances.

Of the various policy approaches indicated in Figure 3.2, three in particular form the core of governmental attempts at addressing environmental problems at national level and beyond: regulation, market-based instruments, and voluntary approaches. In the next three sections, we discuss each of these in detail, outlining how they work and examining important subgroups within particular categories of governmental response.

Regulatory approaches to environmental protection

ON REGULATION

Regulation as imposed by a governing authority essentially aims to produce outcomes that might otherwise not occur if decisions are left entirely to market forces. In the field of environmental protection, this basically includes the establishment of a system of direct control over organizations and activities which has a legal basis and which is operationalized through a range of structures and procedures, including the use of directives, regulatory bodies, permits, licences, inspection, and enforcement regimes and the application of sanctions in the event of non-compliance (Golub, 1998; Gouldson and Murphy, 1998; Petts, 2000). In the literature, such an approach is frequently referred to as 'command-and-control' regulation and continues to be one of the primary means by which governments seek to pursue their environmental policy objectives, in short, a key driver of firm-level environmental behaviour (see Chapter 4).

Although command and control in its purest form arguably involves governments dictating what firms should do and how they should do it (Russell and Powell, 1996), regulation in practice can vary substantially in style, content, and degree of application and can be aimed at a range of environmental problems from pollution control to resource management. Regulations can be used to outlaw or ban activities or to apply certain quotas and/or standards deemed to be desirable by the regulatory authorities (Gunningham and Sinclair, 2002). They can be used *inter alia* to impose limits on the levels of discharge from specific sources (e.g. a facility or firm); to specify the characteristics required of certain products (e.g. the fuel efficiency of cars); to determine the inputs to be used (e.g. banning toxic materials); to mandate the techniques and/or technology that a firm must apply; and to identify its obligations regarding issues such as recycling, information disclosure, and employee certification (Welford and Gouldson, 1993; Seik, 1996; Kolk, 2000; ACCA, 2002). In some cases, regulatory intervention is aimed at achieving a minimum standard of environmental protection; at other times it may be designed to encourage firms to go beyond compliance, by the adoption of a more flexible regulatory stance backed by incentives for organizations that exceed legal requirements (Gunningham and Sinclair, 2002).

For the governing authorities, the use of environmental laws and regulations requires consideration of a number of key issues including the appropriate level of protection (e.g. a partial or complete ban), whether to apply a standard to a pollutant or to its impact, and whether standards should be applied to all or just some organizations (Cairncross, 1995). Governments must also decide on the extent to which the decision-making process and/or their approach to enforcement is both open and flexible. Andrews (1994), for example, differentiates between open and closed decision-making processes and between rigid/statutory and flexible/negotiated approaches to regulatory enforcement, distinguishing different national responses on the basis of these two dimensions (see Figure 3.3). In a similar vein, a number of writers have argued that different traditions, styles, and institutional settings give rise to contrasting regulatory approaches, with US decision-makers said to prefer a more adversarial and legalistic approach with its emphasis on detail, uniformity, and the use of sanctions, compared to the more collaborative and consensual approach adopted in Europe, where industry involvement, self-regulation, and voluntary approaches are claimed to be more prevalent (Cairncross, 1995; Kolk, 2000; Lofstedt and Vogel, 2001; Gunningham and Sinclair, 2002; Gouldson, 2004).

Generalizations of this kind need to be treated with a degree of caution, however. It is worth remembering that environmental policies and laws emanate from different jurisdictions—from the local to the international—and thus are likely to be influenced by different styles and traditions (Roberts, 1995; Kolk, 2000). Moreover, large differences in approach can occur both *between* countries with the same overlapping regulatory system (e.g. as in the European Union (EU)) and *within* states which have a federal system of government, with authority shared between the centre and sub-national levels of decision-making and with opportunities for each level to take a different stand on how, when, and where to regulate (Kolk, 2000).

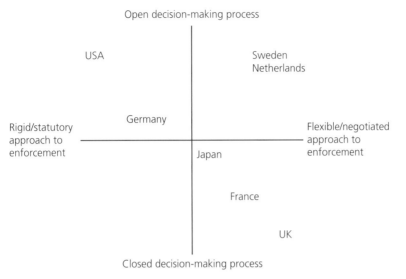

Figure 3.3 Mapping of historical behaviour by key variables

Source: Adapted from Andrews (1994).

To add to the complexity, regulatory approaches also need to take account of a government's broader policy aims. In the EU, for instance, environmental regulation needs to be harmonized with the social and economic goals of the EU, including issues relating to the formation of a single market and to the competitiveness of member states and their firms. Achieving a coordinated and coherent approach requires consideration not only on the content of a regulatory instrument but also its mode of implementation, including the issue of how far each member state is free to choose its own way of achieving the agreed objectives.

THE CASE FOR AND AGAINST REGULATION

Like all environmental policy instruments, regulation has both advantages and disadvantages that relate not only to its operation as a means of shaping behaviour but also to its impact on firms and the economy generally. Key arguments for and against the use of environmental regulations are summarized in Box 3.2.

The essence of the case for regulation centres around issues such as familiarity, certainty, effectiveness, and flexibility. Historically, governments have regularly used legislation and regulation to shape the behaviour of individuals and organizations by identifying what actions are acceptable and what are not. Apart from signalling that the state is responding to the concerns of its citizens regarding environmental protection, the use of a regulatory approach provides for a certain degree of stability and certainty

---

BOX 3.2 THE CASE FOR AND AGAINST ENVIRONMENTAL REGULATION

The case for	The case against
• The market alone is unlikely to protect the environment—legislation and government regulations is necessary	• Regulation imposes additional costs on firms
• Regulation can provide for certainty, stability, familiarity, and dependability	• It often fails to take account of business practices and/or market conditions
• It can be effective in reducing pollution particularly from single media, point-sources	• It can often be inflexible, bureaucratic, and can create a compliance mentality
• Regulation can be flexible and can encourage greater efficiency and innovation	• The burden of regulation can fall unequally on firms
• Properly crafted regulation can provide first-mover advantages by stimulating innovative responses	• It is frequently difficult to enforce, particularly where SMEs are concerned
• Regulation can be used to encourage 'laggard' firms to achieve minimum standards of environmental protection	• It tends to be less suitable for dealing with diffuse sources of environmental impact
	• Uniform responses do not allow firms to tailor their responses to achieve low compliance costs
	• Regulation is vulnerable to political manipulation
	• Regulation can distort management decisions (e.g. new plant locations) and can be used as a trade barrier

Source: Cairncross (1995); Porter and van der Linde (1995*a*, 1995*b*); Gunningham and Grabosky (1998); Kolk (2000); Pearce and Barbier (2000); Majumdar and Marcus (2001); ACCA (2002); Gunningham and Sinclair (2002); Gurtoo and Anthony (2007).

---

within the business community, providing that standards or targets are clear and transparent and there is adequate monitoring and enforcement in place to ensure compliance and to reduce 'free-riding' by unscrupulous operators.

Arguably, environmental regulations tend to be most effective in reducing pollution from large, point-source facilities, particularly where a single medium (e.g. air or water) is involved (Gunningham and Grabosky, 1998; ACCA, 2002). Firms operating such facilities are usually highly visible and are often subject to a series of detailed obligations under the terms of specific permits or licences, thereby giving rise to the expectation that they will be regularly inspected and will be treated fairly and equitably by regulators (Gunningham and Sinclair, 2002).

Despite concerns that the need to devote organizational resources to meet environmental obligations may have a negative impact on businesses (Jaffe et al., 1995), some observers claim that carefully designed and flexible regulations can help to root out inefficiencies in areas such as product design and production and can encourage innovation and value-adding corporate responses (Porter and van der Linde, 1995*a*, 1995*b*). Where regulations allow ample implementation time and set challenging performance goals, it is suggested that they can create significant organizational pressures for change and in doing so can encourage firms to see regulatory imperatives as an opportunity to be exploited rather than as a cost imposed on businesses by the state (Porter and van der Linde, 1995*a*, 1995*b*; Majumdar, 1997; King, 2000; Majumdar and Marcus, 2001; see also the discussion in Chapter 6).

The case against the use of environmental regulation tends to focus on the limitations of regulatory intervention, including its effectiveness in dealing with transitory, mobile, and/or remote firms that can be difficult to track and inspect (Gunningham and Grabosky, 1998; Gunningham and Sinclair, 2002). Doubts have also been expressed regarding the ability of governments to fashion regulations that:

• take account of industry's needs and capabilities;
• encourage innovation rather than a compliance mentality;
• can be easily understood and widely enforced;
• do not stifle entrepreneurship and investment.

In respect of the latter, it has frequently been suggested that national differences in regulations can create an 'unlevel playing field' that could ultimately encourage some firms to move to locations where regulatory demands are less stringent. Empirical investigations of the so-called 'pollution-haven hypothesis' or 'race to the bottom' tend to be contradictory and/or inconclusive, with estimates in the literature ranging from positive and significant to negative and significant across a wide range of studies (see e.g. Dean and Brown, 1995; Levinson, 1996; Dean et al., 2000; Cole and Elliott, 2003; Busse, 2004; Madsen, 2009). For a meta-analysis of environmental regulations and new plant location decisions, see Jeppesen et al. (2002).

BUSINESSES AND REGULATIONS

As the discussion in Chapter 4 will demonstrate, academic studies have shown regulation to be a key factor shaping the environmental actions of firms. This does not imply, however, that businesses approve of the use of regulatory approaches in addressing the problem of environmental protection. If anything, corporate leaders often display an ambivalent attitude to this form of government intervention.

Positive responses to regulation very much mirror the advantages identified in Box 3.3. Firms like the certainty associated with the use of regulation and often see it as preferable to alternative approaches such as the use of environmental taxes and charges (Kolk, 2000; Pearce and Barbier, 2000). Regulation may also act as an incentive for firms to innovate and/or improve their products and processes and could provide new product and/or market opportunities, particularly for organizations willing to go beyond compliance (see Chapter 8).

On the negative side, many firms see regulations as an additional cost to the business that can cause resources to be diverted from other uses (Majumdar and Marcus, 2001). Regulations are also frequently perceived as unfair and inflexible, especially if they differ between firms (e.g. older and newer firms) or countries (e.g. where some countries 'gold plate' their regulations or use regulations as a trade barrier) or if they dictate what technology must be applied to tackling a particular environmental problem (Cairncross, 1995; Pearce and Barbier, 2000; Gunningham and Sinclair, 2002). A common complaint is that some firms can be put at a competitive disadvantage because of disparities in regulatory requirements between countries, with some business leaders claiming they are over-regulated by their governments compared to their overseas rivals. Less frequently mentioned is the fact that powerful businesses, industries, and their representative organizations regularly lobby policy makers in an attempt to forestall or weaken environmental regulations that they deem to be economically and commercially undesirable (Cairncross, 1995; Kolk, 2000; Pearce and Barbier, 2000), interventions which often prove successful.

Market-based (or economic) instruments

ON MARKET-BASED INSTRUMENTS (MBIs)

Whereas regulation basically involves governments in deciding on the best course of action to address environmental problems, market-based or economic instruments essentially leave economic actors free to respond to certain stimuli in ways they themselves see as most beneficial for the organization (OECD, 1994; Braadbaart, 1998). In simple terms, MBIs use various financial (or other) incentives or disincentives to shape firm-level behaviour, using price signals within the market to influence corporate decisions (Cairncross, 1995; Pearce and Barbier, 2000). Sprenger (2000: 3) defines them as 'proxies for market signals in the form of a change to relative prices and/or a financial transfer between polluters and society'. Under this approach, actions taken by firms to reduce their environmental impact are rewarded by the reduction/removal of a financial penalty or by the granting of a financial reward (e.g. a subsidy). Those organizations that persist in engaging in undesirable behaviour face the opposite course of action, being penalized for their decision not to respond to the economic incentive or disincentive put in place by the governing authority (Gunningham and Grabosky, 1998; ACCA, 2002; Sonneborn, 2004).

As Table 3.1 illustrates, the concept of MBIs or economic instruments can cover a wide variety of incentive-based mechanisms, some of which provide positive incentives

Table 3.1 Market-based instruments

Author	Main types of MBI/economic instrument
OECD (1994)	Taxes (including levies and charges), subsidies, tradeable emissions permits, deposit–refund systems
Panayotou (1994)	Property rights; market creation; fiscal instruments and charge systems; financial instruments; liability instruments; performance bonds; deposit–refund systems
Pearce et al. (1994)	Charges, taxes, fees; subsidies; deposit–refund schemes; permits; compensatory incentives; enforcement incentives
Seik (1996)	Charges; subsidies; deposit–refund schemes; market instruments
Braadbaart (1998)	Emission charges; user charges or fees; product charges; marketable permits; deposit–refund schemes; green or Pigovian taxes
Andersen and Sprenger (2000)	Charges/taxes; deposit–refund schemes; market creations; subsidies; liability schemes
Pearce and Barbier (2000)	Charges, taxes, fees; subsidies; deposit–refund or fee rebate systems; tradeable permits; compensatory incentives; enforcement incentives
Sonneborn (2004)	Pollution fees/taxes; subsidies; deposit–refund systems; permit trading systems; performance bonds and liability payments; fuel source information; incentive marketing schemes; licensing and quota systems

and others negative. Some of these instruments involve schemes in which the government allocates property rights and creates a market for certain environmental goods and services; others are based on the modification of existing markets via the use of fiscal instruments such as taxes, charges, and subsidies (Gunningham and Grabosky, 1998; Gunningham and Sinclair, 2002). To Pearce and Barbier (2000), MBIs broadly cover two kinds of policy measure: those that involve an administered price and those that revolve around an administered market. With the former, this means creating a price where none previously existed (e.g. a tax placed on emissions) or modifying an existing price (e.g. placing an additional charge on a polluting product) to reflect environmental impacts. In the case of the latter, the government's approach is to create a market that did not previously exist, as in the case of tradeable pollution permits that can be bought and sold by participating organizations (see below).

To gain a more detailed insight into the use of market-based instruments, including their strengths and weaknesses, the next two subsections focus on two major examples that have grown in prominence in recent decades: environmental taxes and tradeable pollution permits. The former is a prime example of an administered price, with taxes setting a price on pollution that—in theory at least—reflects the cost imposed on society by polluters. The latter, on the other hand, focuses on quantity rather than price, with governments allocating rights to firms to pollute up to certain predetermined levels and allowing organizations to trade these rights if they so wish in the administered market that policy makers have created (Pearce et al., 1994; Cairncross, 1995; Gunningham and Sinclair, 2002).

ENVIRONMENTAL TAXES

Environmental taxes are a form of fiscal instrument used to encourage environmentally responsible behaviour through full (or partial) cost pricing of consumption or production (Gunningham and Grabosky, 1998; Sonneborn, 2004); they can also be used to achieve other government goals, including revenue raising and promoting innovation.

The different purposes for which environmental taxes are levied are reflected in the literature. Echoing the European Environmental Agency's (EEA) Report on Environmental Taxes (1996), Ekins (1999) classifies them into three main types according to their primary objectives:

- Cost-covering charges
- Incentive taxes
- Revenue-raising taxes (or fiscal environmental taxes).

Cost-covering charges are those where the individuals (or organizations) making use of the environment have to contribute to the cost of controlling and monitoring that use, for example via regulation. They include both 'user charges' that are paid for a specific environmental service such as waste disposal and 'earmarked charges', where the revenue earned from the charge is used on related environmental services of general benefit (e.g. water treatment). Incentive taxes are designed to change the behaviour of economic actors towards more environmentally friendly products, practices, and/or processes, whilst revenue-raising taxes are used primarily as revenue-raising devices that contribute broadly to government income and which may or may not subsequently be used for environmental purposes (i.e. 'hypothecated taxes'). In practice, these three main functions of environmental taxes are not always mutually exclusive (EEA, 1996; Ekins, 1999).

The theoretical foundations of environmental taxation have been traced back to the work of the economist Arthur Pigou in the early twentieth century, who identified the existence of market externalities and proposed the use of a tax as a way to bridge the gap between the private and social costs of economic activity—a so-called 'Pigovian tax' (Pearce and Turner, 1990; Cairncross, 1993). As Box 3.3 illustrates, the basic argument is that the application of a tax which incorporates the costs of environmental services and damage into the prices of the products or activities that cause them provides a means of internalizing negative externalities and of applying the polluter (or user) pays principle (EEA, 1996; Ekins, 1999; Pearce and Barbier, 2000; Prakash and Kollman, 2004). In doing so, the hope is that the resultant increase in prices caused by the imposition of a tax might encourage producers (or consumers) to change their behaviour in a way that benefits the natural environment (e.g. finding less polluting production methods, consuming greener products), thereby creating both a positive incentive (i.e. behavioural change) and an environmental effect (i.e. improved environment) through the use of the fiscal instrument.

BOX 3.3 POLLUTION CONTROL THROUGH TAXATION

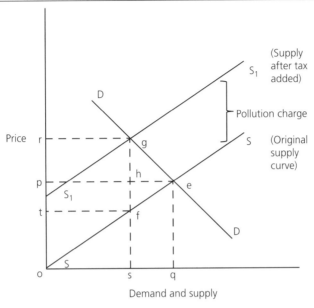

Source: Worthington (2005).

Notes: 1. 'op' is the original paid (before charge).
2. 'or' is the price including the charge (equivalent to 'gf').
3. 'ot' is the price received by producers after the charge.
4. The areas 'ghe' and 'hef' represent the loss in consumer and producer surplus respectively that is not captured by the government when imposing this tax.

Box 3.1 illustrates how the private costs of production underestimate the full social costs where a negative externality (e.g. pollution) is present. If a government imposes a tax on polluters equivalent to the marginal external costs of their activities (represented by the vertical distance 'gf' above), then this would increase market price from 'op' to 'or' and the quantity traded would fall from 'oq' to 'os'. At the new market price—which now includes a pollution tax or charge—total consumer expenditure is 'orgs' compared to 'opeq' before the tax. For the producer, total revenue falls from 'opeq' to 'otfs', a loss of 'tpef' of which 'tphf' is the tax paid (see Note 4 above).

As will be evident, the relative contributions of producers and consumers depend upon the slope of the demand and supply curves (i.e. the price elasticities of supply and demand). In markets which are competitive on the supply side for example, consumers should be asked to shoulder less of the burden of a pollution tax.

In addition to taxes on polluters, governments also use environmental subsidies and tax concessions as alternative forms of fiscal instrument. Rather than taxing pollution to encourage firms to reduce it, the subsidy approach offers financial rewards to firms for reducing their negative environmental impact: that is, it is a mirror image of pollution taxes. Firms which fail to reduce pollution have to forgo the financial payment.

As an approach to environmental protection, subsidies tend to be unpopular with economists. They contravene the polluter pays principle and could encourage new entrants into a market in order to gain the financial reward. In extreme cases, this could have the perverse effect of increasing total pollution. As Pearce and Barbier (2001) note, the definition of market-based instruments often now includes the removal of subsidies and other public policy interventions which distort the private costs of resource use and pollution discharge.

How far in practice a government is able to equate the tax levied to the damage caused is of course a moot point. Bluffstone (2003), for example, distinguishes between three levels of environmental tax in the context of practices in the developing and transition economies. First-best environmental taxes (Pigovian taxes) are those where the government is able to balance the costs and benefits of environmental protection, a process which he suggests would be particularly demanding in information terms if the authorities are to set the appropriate goals and the right level of tax in order to maximize the total net benefits to society. For practical reasons, he argues that less efficient but more feasible environmental taxes tend to be used in the real world, with the level of tax set exogenously according to political processes, including 'rule of thumb' approaches (second-best taxes) or levied on products or inputs rather than being concerned with questions of environmental performance (third-best environmental taxes).

Despite this apparent mismatch between theory and practice, studies indicate the relatively widespread use of environmental taxes by national governments (see Table 3.2), coupled with a general acceptance that using the price mechanism to shape the behaviour of economic actors has certain advantages often not evident in other approaches. In addition to helping to correct the market for negative externalities and embodying the polluter pays principle, environmental taxes are said to provide incentives for behavioural change both now and in the future; allow firms to make their own choices; work with the grain of the market; act as a spur to investment and innovation; be more effective and efficient than regulation in environmental and economic terms; raise

Table 3.2 Examples of environmental tax by country

Country	Examples of environmental tax
Australia	Aircraft noise; oil recycling; petroleum tax
Chile	Petroleum; motor vehicle ownership; domestic waste collection
Czech Republic	Air pollution; electricity use; natural gas; solid fuels
Denmark	Carbon dioxide; sulphur; coal; electricity; water quality
Finland	Waste; water usage; nuclear waste; tyres
Germany	Aviation; aircraft noise; electricity; waste water
Japan	Aviation fuel; sulphur dioxide; petroleum; coal
Netherlands	Petrol; energy; water pollution; aviation noise
New Zealand	Waste disposal; petroleum fuels; road use
Norway	Sulphur; electricity consumption; pesticides
South Africa	Vehicle emissions; electricity; aviation fuel
United Kingdom	Landfill; air passenger duty; climate change levy

Notes: 1. The examples include taxes imposed in the form of levies and user charges.
2. In federal systems of government, some taxes are levied at sub-national level (e.g. in states, provinces, regions).
3. The OECD has an extensive database of environmental policy instruments by countries, including environmental taxes.

revenue for government; and provide opportunities for structural change within the tax system and the economy generally (Cairncross, 1995; EEA, 1996; Gunningham and Grabosky, 1998; Marshall Report, 1998; Ekins, 1999; Pearce and Barbier, 2000; ACCA, 2002; Gunningham and Sinclair, 2002).

As might be anticipated, using taxes to address environmental problems is also seen to have a number of disadvantages. Criticisms include the difficulty of setting taxes at an appropriate level; their potential adverse effect on firm, sector, and national competitiveness; their tendency to be regressive, inflationary, and politically unpopular; uncertainties regarding their effectiveness; difficulties in separating the impact of taxation from other elements of the instrument mix; and the potential for a clash of interest between the environmental protection aspect of taxation and its use as a revenue-raising mechanism (EEA, 1996; Marshall Report, 1998; Ekins, 1999; OECD, 2001; ACCA, 2002; Gunningham and Sinclair, 2002). An additional concern is that imposing taxes and other charges may be perceived as legitimating or condoning environmentally harmful behaviour, given that it appears to imply that the state will allow pollution at a price, a strategy which may be deemed by some as inferior to one which outlaws it altogether (Gunningham and Sinclair, 2002).

GREEN SNAPSHOT: FRANCE AND A CARBON TAX

Putting a preferred policy into effect can often prove extremely difficult as President Nicholas Sarkozy of France discovered with regard to his plans to introduce a carbon tax aimed at encouraging French families and businesses to reduce their use of fossil fuels. Announced with a fanfare in 2009 as part of a fight to 'save the human race' from global warming, the plan would have made France the largest European economy to levy a carbon tax, following the introduction of other successful schemes in the Nordic countries in the 1990s. Since most electricity generation in France comes from nuclear plants which have low emissions, the plan was to exempt electricity from the tax which was to be aimed at the use of gas, oil, and coal. Green campaigners argued that the proposed scheme lacked ambition, allowed too many exemptions for big industrial polluters, and was a wasted opportunity. Business groups (including transport companies and farmers) complained that the scheme was unfair and would affect the country's competitiveness.

Following an adverse judgement in the French constitutional court just before the scheme was scheduled to come into effect at the start of 2010, the French government announced (in March of that year) its intention of delaying the implementation of the plan, pending an agreement with its European partners on a pan-European carbon tax, in order to protect France's competitiveness. A European-wide tax on CO_2 had been mooted in September of the previous year as a way of meeting the EU's emission targets and raising revenue, but progress had been slow because of opposition from a number of member states. By mid-2010, the discussions had effectively stalled because of continued opposition (e.g. from Germany, Poland, the United Kingdom), a worsening economic climate, and lobbying by business interests and consumer groups.

Postscript: A report in *Le Figaro* in September 2011 suggested that the French government might introduce a one-off levy on carbon-intensive firms as a way of reducing its budget deficit, a proposal which will inevitably face fierce opposition from business groups.

TRADEABLE PERMITS

As indicated previously, tradeable or marketable permits are an example of market creation where a government creates tradeable pollution (or resource) rights, issues quotas, allowances, or permits up to the agreed level and then allows the holders of those rights to trade them like any other commodity (Gunningham and Grabosky, 1998; Andersen and Sprenger, 2000). The trading of rights (e.g. relating to greenhouse gas emissions or natural resource exploitation) usually takes place under prescribed rules and may be external (e.g. between different enterprises or countries) or internal (e.g. between different plants within the same firm), within a free or controlled permit market (Pearce and Barbier, 2000).

The notion of creating tradeable rights to address environmental problems such as greenhouse gas emissions was a key outcome of the Kyoto process (see Chapter 2, Box 2.4) and is exemplified by the European Emissions Trading Scheme (ETS) discussed in the case study at the end of this chapter.[1] Gunningham and Grabosky (1998) describe this approach as a hybrid between direct regulations and free market environmentalism in that governments decide on the overall quantity of pollution (or resource exploitation) allowable, while market forces determine the eventual distribution of rights between participating firms or countries. In practice, of course, governments can influence the market in a variety of ways, for example by varying the number of permits issued, charging for permits or allocating them for nothing, preventing permit hoarding, and allowing flexibility of various kinds as under Joint Implementation and the use of the Clean Development Mechanism (Cairncross, 1995; see also Chapter 2). A tradeable permit system also provides a government with a means of lowering the level of pollution over time by gradually reducing the number of permits allocated to participants, thereby effectively increasing their market price.

Like other government approaches to environmental protection, tradeable permits have their benefits and drawbacks. On the positive side, market creation, unlike direct regulation, offers greater flexibility to firms in determining their responses to their individual circumstances without the regulatory authorities needing to know the particulars of each firm's pollution reduction capacities (Gunningham and Grabosky, 1998; Gunningham and Sinclair, 2002). Given that the cost of reducing a particular pollutant is likely to vary between businesses, creating a market for pollution permits provides a mechanism for exploiting differences in the marginal costs of abatement, with firms that are able to keep their pollution below the allocated level benefiting from selling unused permits to businesses that have exceeded their quota. Either way, the system provides incentives for all participants to reduce their emissions so far as they efficiently can and allows them the flexibility to do so in the least-cost manner (Golub, 1998; Gunningham and Sinclair, 2002).

On the negative side, operating a tradeable permit system faces a number of important practical difficulties. These include issues relating to permit allocation; questions of enforcement, particularly when there is a large number of small and mobile sources of

---

GREEN SNAPSHOT: PROFITING FROM POLLUTION

According to a report by the carbon trading think tank Sandbag (2011), some of Europe's largest corporations have been able to acquire billions of euros from the operation of the European ETS. Through a combination of over-allocation of permits by national governments and a downturn in the global economy, it is estimated that leading firms in the steel, chemical, paper, cement, and ceramic sectors have acquired excess pollution credits which can be either sold or hoarded for future use. The report places the steelmaker Arcelor Mittal in first place in the list of beneficiaries with a surplus estimated to be around 1.7 billion euros. Other key net gainers include the cement group Lafarge, Tata Steel, and steelmaker Thyssen Krupp. The report also found that most of the firms identified in its analysis were buying pollution permits on the international market, mainly from Indian and Chinese businesses. As indicated in the case study at the end of this chapter, these permits can be used within the EU's trading scheme, allowing the holders to retain the more valuable European permits for future use or sale when market conditions become more favourable.

---

pollution; problems of measuring discharges easily and economically; and the danger of cheating and uncompetitive market practices (Cairncross, 1995; Gunningham and Grabosky, 1998; Marshall Report, 1998; Gunningham and Sinclair, 2002). At an international level, the use of tradeable permits also raises questions of effectiveness and equity, with richer nations more able to buy offsets in poorer countries to meet their national targets, in effect, exporting the problem of pollution reduction.

BUSINESS AND MARKET-BASED INSTRUMENTS

Taken at face value, MBIs appear to be more business friendly than regulatory approaches to environmental protection. Despite lacking the certainty associated with the latter, market-based instruments offer firms the flexibility to make their own decisions on whether and how to respond; provide them with the opportunity to tailor their responses to their own particular circumstances; and open up the possibility that businesses can achieve both static and dynamic efficiency gains (EEA, 1996; Marshall Report, 1998; Pearce and Barbier, 2000; OECD, 2001; ACCA, 2002; Sonneborn, 2004). Of the two approaches examined above, it has been suggested that industry tends to prefer tradeable permits over taxation since there is less risk that governments can abuse the system for other ends (e.g. revenue raising); the polluter only pays for pollution that is above a pre-agreed level; businesses feel that they have more control over a permit system where the parameters are known in advance (Pearce and Barbier, 2000).

In reality, of course, not all firms are affected equally by the use of MBIs. The impact of environmental taxes, for example, will vary according to factors such as the level of taxation, the nature of the production process, the opportunities for gaining exemptions, and the degree of recycling of taxation undertaken by the government (e.g. shifting taxation from labour to environmental protection). Similarly, how far businesses can pass on some of the tax burden to consumers will also tend to differ between polluters given the variations in the price elasticity of demand for different products. In short, as with other approaches to environmental protection, MBIs can create inequalities between firms and sectors, with some businesses benefiting while some are disadvantaged (Kolk, 2000; OECD, 2001). They can also give rise to different corporate responses ranging from compliance, through lobbying over the design of a permit scheme or for a reduced tax burden (e.g. on the grounds of international competitiveness), to offering to undertake voluntary initiatives either with or without state involvement (Prakash and Kollman, 2004).

Voluntary approaches (VAs)

MAJOR TYPES OF VOLUNTARY INSTRUMENT

Alongside regulation and market-based initiatives, VAs are an important, broad category of environmental policy instrument that has grown in use over recent decades. Paton (2000) describes the various forms of voluntary environmental initiative as public or private efforts to improve the environmental performance of firms beyond existing legal requirements. As a major report on VAs has indicated, this definition encapsulates a wide range of instruments, the three main types of which are public voluntary programmes, negotiated agreements, and unilateral commitments (Borkey et al., 1998).

Public voluntary programmes essentially involve commitments that are devised by an environment agency and in which individual firms are invited to participate. The agency concerned normally sets the targets and individual businesses are asked to sign up to the environmental objectives, sometimes being offered an incentive to do so (e.g. technical or financial assistance; public relations benefits). Kolk (2000) and Pearce and Barbier (2000) use the term voluntary agreement to indicate that the choice to participate in a given initiative is left to companies and the agreed objectives are not enforceable. Well-known examples include the EU's Eco-Management and Audit Scheme (EMAS) and the US programmes known as Greenlight (concerning the use of energy efficient lighting) and 33/50 (covering emissions of toxic chemicals), with the latter attracting considerable academic attention (Arora and Casson, 1995, 1996; Darnall, 2002; Lyon and Maxwell, 2007).

Negotiated agreements (also confusingly sometimes called voluntary initiatives or voluntary agreements) involve commitments that emerge through a process of bargaining between a public authority (e.g. national government) and industry (e.g. an industry sector). Agreements of this type normally contain a target to achieve and a time schedule for industry to achieve it (Borkey et al., 1998). In return, the public authority usually undertakes not to introduce any new piece of legislation, though this remains an option should voluntarism fail to reach the desired objective (Gunningham and Sinclair, 2002). In Europe, negotiated agreements are a particularly popular approach to environmental protection and have been a key element of the National Environmental Policy Plan in the Netherlands, where the term 'covenants' is used (Borkey et al., 1998; Golub, 1998; Paton, 2000; Gunningham and Sinclair, 2002).

The third type, unilateral commitments, denotes environmental programmes set up by firms independently of any involvement of a public authority and which may be aimed at achieving a variety of objectives such as protecting the firm's reputation, impressing its stakeholders, and/or forestalling government regulation. In addition to a wide range of individual initiatives, where a firm decides both the targets and the means of achieving its objectives, some commitments of this kind involve individual businesses signing up to a voluntary code of conduct or charter (e.g. the CERES Principles) or an industry association committing itself to self-regulation. A prime example of the latter is the Chemical Manufacturers' Association (CMA) Responsible Care Progamme, which was established in response to a decline in public confidence in the chemical industry and which is a voluntary code of conduct developed, monitored, and enforced by the CMA (Gunningham and Grabosky, 1998; Prakash, 1999, 2000b; King and Lenox, 2000).

Although unilateral commitments are not strictly a public policy instrument per se, Richard Andrews (1998) has suggested that they are perhaps best seen as lying on a continuum of relationships—between regulation and self-regulation—that is marked by varying degrees of involvement of the public authorities in defining ways of addressing the issue of environmental protection. It is worth reiterating that even unilateral beyond-compliance corporate initiatives of the kind highlighted in the coming chapters still operate under the shadow of government, with regulatory intervention always an option should the authorities deem it necessary or desirable (Prakash, 1999; Pearce and Barbier, 2000; Clemens and Douglas, 2006).

Being one element of a policy mix aimed at encouraging greener responses in the private sector, VAs are thought to have some discernible advantages, particularly over regulation. These include flexibility; greater cost-effectiveness; greater sensitivity to industry needs and market circumstances; and suitability in addressing newly emerging issues for which no policy framework currently exists (Gunningham and Grabosky, 1998; Paton, 2000; Gunningham and Sinclair, 2002; Jordan et al., 2003a; Steelman and Rivera, 2006). On the downside, critics point to problems such as the degree of free-riding; questions concerning their effectiveness in delivering environmental protection; doubts over their economic efficiency compared to regulation; weak standards and enforcement procedures; an absence of explicit sanctions; and ill-defined objectives and performance measures (Arora and Casson, 1996; Borkey et al., 1998; Golub, 1998; Gunningham and Grabosky, 1998; King and Lenox, 2000; Gunningham and Sinclair, 2002; Lyon and Maxwell, 2003; Prakash and Kollman, 2004). As a number of writers have pointed out, VAs to environmental protection are perhaps best seen as complementary rather than as an alternative to environmental regulations and market-based instruments, being unlikely ever to be adequate in themselves (Andrews, R.N.L., 1998; Golub, 1998; King and Lenox, 2000).

BUSINESS AND VOLUNTARY APPROACHES

An established approach to environmental protection in OECD countries and beyond, unsurprisingly VAs generally find favour with the business community. In broad terms, voluntary initiatives and the various forms of self-regulation and co-regulation are perceived as offering greater freedom to firms over how far and in what ways they respond (Prakash and Kollman, 2004). As well as the increased flexibility associated with VAs, voluntarism also provides a means of avoiding further regulation and may help businesses to enhance stakeholder relationships and achieve corporate competitiveness via improved public image and green differentiation (Cairncross, 1995; Andrews, R.N.L., 1998; King and Lenox, 2000; Anton et al., 2004), an issue discussed in more detail in forthcoming chapters.

The assumption that firms will invariably prefer policies that give them more freedom needs to be treated with a degree of healthy skepticism however (Prakash and Kollman, 2004). As organizations with differing resources and competencies, firms are likely to exhibit different preferences over alternative policy approaches, with some businesses preferring the certainty of regulation while others see voluntary approaches or economic instruments as more in keeping with industry and market practices.

While the received wisdom is that some firms and industries may use voluntary action to reduce the likelihood of further regulatory intervention by a determined government, it is equally possible that others might support environmental legislation because it might give them a competitive advantage or because they already take a pro-environmental position for internal and/or external reasons (Prakash and Kollman, 2004). Under the latter view, stronger regulation could be said to be built upon an existing solid foundation of voluntarism that is reflected in different forms of mutual interest in business/government alliances. A less generous interpretation of the evolution of VAs sees them as an outcome of a weak government, a consequence of industry pressures on the regulatory authorities, which renders more stringent regulations politically infeasible (Lyon and Maxwell, 2003).

The evolution of environmental policy instruments

Although regulation has remained the backbone of governmental approaches to environmental protection for at least two generations, the closing decades of the twentieth century undoubtedly witnessed a gradual shift in emphasis at international, intergovernmental, and national levels (e.g. the Brundtland Report; the EU's Fifth Environmental Action Plan, 1993–2000; the Dutch National Environmental Policy Plan, 1988–9; the Marshall Report in the United Kingdom, 1998) towards more flexible and business-focused environmental policy instruments (EEA, 1996; Borkey et al., 1998; Golub, 1998; Gunningham and Grabosky, 1998; Ekins, 1999; Kolk, 2000). These 'second-generation' or 'new environmental policy instruments' (NEPIs) as they are sometimes called, include not only those discussed above but also informational devices such as eco-labels and the use of more flexible regulations designed to encourage beyond compliance behaviour (Gunningham and Sinclair, 2002; Jordan et al., 2003*a*, 2003*b*; Mol, 2003; Tews et al., 2003; Gouldson, 2004). Their increasing deployment and diffusion across national and supranational jurisdictions represent an important reshaping of the regulatory landscape and mark a discernable shift in emphasis from what Stoker (1998) terms 'government' to 'governance', exemplified by the growing use of public/private partnerships in environmental policy making (Gunningham and Sinclair, 2002; Jordan et al., 2003*a*, 2003*b*; Mol, 2003).

In discussing the reasons for the gradual convergence in governance patterns in environmental policy, researchers have pointed to a variety of contingent factors. In addition to a growing awareness of the limitations of a command and control approach, it has been suggested that key influences on governmental decision-makers have included the resurgence of a free-market ideology; the need for greater cost-effectiveness and flexibility; growing stakeholder pressures; the focus on the polluter pays principle; pressures from industry for a reduced regulatory burden; the growth of powerful non-governmental organizations; emerging new environmental problems; and the processes of international policy transfer and diffusion (EEA, 1996; Andrews, R.N.L., 1998; Gunningham and Grabosky, 1998; Ekins, 1999; Gunningham and Sinclair, 2002; Khanna and Anton, 2002*a*; Jordan et al., 2003*a*, 2003*b*; Mol, 2003; Tews et al., 2003). When reduced to its essence, the claim is that developments in the institutional, economic, political, and ideological environment in the 1980s and 1990s have helped to shift the balance in governmental approaches to environmental protection away from the use of direct regulation and towards the greater use of markets and collaborative forms of policy making.

Theoretical analysis of the evolution of environmental policy instruments illustrates the wide variety of lenses through which the gradual reconfiguration of the regulatory state can be viewed. Jordan et al. (2003*a*, 2003*b*), for example, suggest two broad theoretical perspectives: the first—'ideational theories'—emphasizing the importance of policy learning in driving the selection of instruments; the second—'institutional theories'—stressing the importance of national institutional forms and the historical-institutional context in influencing the choice between different policy modes. For Gunningham and Sinclair (2002), five theoretical frameworks help to conceptualize the process of regulatory reconfiguration: reflexive regulation, regulatory pluralism, environmental partnerships, civil regulation and participatory governance, ecological modernization, and the 'greengold thesis'. As the authors suggest, while none of these perspectives works well in relation to all sectors, contexts, or enterprise types, they can help to enrich our understanding of the individual policy instruments and of the process by which they were selected and adopted by environmental policy makers in different national jurisdictions.

On the issue of joint environmental policy making in Europe, Mol's study (2003) of particular policy areas in three comparable European countries (Austria, Denmark, the Netherlands) suggests that neither the theory of political modernization nor deregulation is sufficient to explain the emergence of the phenomenon, with the specific political and institutional context seen as decisive in how public/private environmental partnerships are organized and implemented. Contextual influences also figure predominantly in a study of the international diffusion of NEPIs by Tew et al. (2003), which they ascribe to the inner dynamics of international processes of policy transfer or diffusion (e.g. political, economic, and institutional linkages between nation states) and which they claim make it increasingly difficult for national policy makers to ignore new approaches to environmental protection that have already been put into practice in 'pre-runner' countries.

Case Study: The European Emissions Trading Scheme

As a market-based approach to environmental protection, Emissions Trading Schemes (ETS) comprise the basic elements found in normal markets: there is a commodity to be traded (i.e. greenhouse gases), a demand for that commodity (i.e. from firms emitting those gases), and a structure within which trading can occur (i.e. the scheme). In essence, such schemes are designed to encourage polluters to reduce their emissions below a predetermined level by, for example, investing in new, cleaner technology; in doing so they can earn emissions credits which can be sold on to polluters who exceed their agreed limit because compliance costs are higher than purchasing additional credits in the market. The overall aim is that emissions will be held within a given 'cap' and that this quantitative limit will gradually be reduced over time. Since trading of emissions credits occurs within the total limit, schemes are often referred to as 'cap and trade' schemes.

The establishment of the European ETS in 2005 followed in the wake of a US scheme set up in 1995 aimed at emissions trading in sulphur dioxide and a UK scheme introduced in 2002 which was aimed at the emission of greenhouse gases and which gave UK participants (e.g. BP, Sainsbury, Shell, Barclays, Caterpillar) some experience of emissions trading prior to the introduction of the European ETS. Set up under an EU directive, the first phase of the European scheme in the period 2005–7 was basically used as a 'warm-up' exercise for the second phase which has operated for the five years between 2008 and 2012 and was designed to be congruent with the compliance period of the Kyoto Protocol (see Chapter 2) under which the EU was obliged to reduce its emissions levels by 8 per cent on average compared to the baseline year of 1990. Phase 3 is expected to run for a further five years after 2012.

In keeping with the idea of cap-and-trade, the European ETS requires each member state government to set an emissions cap for all installations covered by the scheme and to have its plans ratified at the EU level. Once a national plan is agreed concerning the allocation of emissions between sectors and firms, allowances are given to the participating organizations which indicate what quantity of greenhouse gases are permitted during the commitment period. Trading of allowances can occur between organizations during this period and it is possible to use emissions reductions from outside the EU to meet an agreed limit (e.g. under Joint Implementation and the Clean Development Mechanism— see Box 2.4). Companies are also now allowed to bank any spare permits (i.e. allowances) they have for use in the third phase after 2012.

Hailed as a major policy innovation and as a cheaper and more effective way of tackling climate change than the use of regulation, the European ETS cannot be said to have been an unqualified success. There is widespread agreement that too many permits were issued in Phase 1 of the scheme and this resulted in the price of carbon in the market becoming almost worthless. While some steps were taken to address this issue in Phase 2, environmental campaigners still believe that there was an over-supply of carbon credits and since these were largely issued freely, and some firms have gained an effective subsidy which they have been able to turn into windfall profits by selling their spare allowances (see Green Snapshot: Profiting from Pollution). It is also claimed that further gains were made by energy companies which were passing on the 'cost' of free permits to consumers, thereby gaining further revenue from the operation of the scheme.

The European ETS has also been criticized on a number of other grounds, including:

- its failure to include some big emitters of greenhouse gases (e.g. airlines are only required to join the scheme after 2012);
- its failure to set a minimum 'floor price' for carbon, thereby acting as a disincentive for firms to invest in carbon reduction measures;
- the practice of allowing offsetting, which can encourage some companies to buy credits from developing companies rather than investing in abatement measures;
- the ability of firms to hoard permits which can be used to offset future emissions without reducing pollution or which may be sold at a profit if the carbon price increases;
- the ability of firms to profit from selling spare permits as the economy slows down;

- the danger that the over-supply of permits will depress carbon prices, thereby discouraging investment in cleaner energy;
- serious doubts over whether the scheme will deliver significant carbon savings as it was designed to do.

There is also evidence that the operation of the multi-billion euro ETS has been subject to manipulation by speculators and has been the target of fraudsters seeking to capitalize on the scheme's less than robust governance arrangements.

■ NOTE

1. Useful sources of information on the European ETS include the EU's Europa website and the websites of government departments that manage the scheme at national level. The scheme has also attracted academic attention (see e.g. Kruger and Pizer, 2004; Engels et al., 2008; Engels, 2009) as well as substantial media coverage.

Section Three
Theoretical and Empirical Perspectives

4 Why firms go 'green': drivers and motivations

Environmental pressures in the coming decade are going to force organisations to become more environmentally responsive. Greening organisations is going to be a high priority item on the agendas of corporate and public sector organisations.

(Shrivastava and Hart, 1994)

...bringing about a better world to live in environmentally appears to depend on the interactions between government, customers, suppliers, owners, managers and employees in companies.

(Lindell and Karagozoglu, 2001)

...the organisational environment itself is not a constant, and firms play a role in constructing it. Firms may take a proactive approach not just toward improving environmental performance but also to influencing the institutional setting in which they operate.

(Etzion, 2007)

Introduction

All organizations face pressures from their external environment, which can affect their operations and decisions, including those related to their mission, core values, and strategies. Where a firm's impact on the natural environment is concerned, these pressures include the social, political, and legal influences discussed in Chapters 2 and 3 and which have formed a major part of the broad external context in which business responses to the environmental agenda have emerged over recent decades (Cairncross, 1991; Shrivastava and Hart, 1994; Lindell and Karagozoglu, 2001). These responses—often referred to as 'corporate environmentalism' or the 'greening of organizations' (see below)—have taken various forms and have been linked to developments in the regulatory, market, and social domains of business (Shrivastava and Hart, 1994; Cairncross, 1995; Henriques and Sadorsky, 1996, 1999; Bansal and Roth, 2000).

In this chapter, we examine two key questions relating to the greening of business:

- What are the key drivers of corporate ecological responsiveness?
- What motivates firms to become more environmentally responsive?

In addressing these questions, the analysis draws on an extensive literature on why firms go green and investigates key variables that can influence firm-level environmental behaviour. The direction of business responses, including how they have been categorized by academic researchers and consultants, is discussed in the next chapter.

The concept of 'greening' business

What is meant by the notion of 'greening' or a 'green' business has been the subject of some debate (Chryssides and Kaler, 1993), much of which has been focused at the organizational level of analysis and at outcome-related aspects of corporate environmental management (Gladwin, 1993; Winn and Angell, 2000). Under this perspective, 'green' or 'greened' firms are generally held to be those that have been involved in a deliberate process of internal change which is aimed at addressing adverse environmental and human impacts brought about by their activities. The resultant changes can relate to a firm's core values, policies, products, systems, processes, and/or technologies (Shrivastava, 1992; Bansal and Roth, 2000). They can impact at all phases of the transformation process (see Chapter 1) and can have implications for an organization's revenues and/or costs; its competitiveness (see Chapter 6); its resources and capabilities (Hart, 1995; Russo and Fouts, 1997); its relationships with key stakeholder groups such as customers, suppliers, and regulators (Sharma and Henriques, 2005); and even for the moral commitment of organizational members (Crane, 2000).

The tendency of scholars to focus predominantly on outcome-related indicators of corporate greening is well represented in the extant literature. Henriques and Sadorsky (1996, 1999), for instance, define 'environmentally responsive firms' as those that formulate an official plan for dealing with environmental issues and suggest that 'environmental commitment' is demonstrated by what a firm has done or is doing to improve its environmental performance. Bansal and Roth (2000) use the term 'corporate ecological responsiveness' to denote a set of corporate initiatives aimed at mitigating an organization's impact on the natural environment, whereas Banerjee et al. (2003) portray 'corporate environmentalism' as the recognition by a firm of the importance of environmental issues and their subsequent integration into the strategic plans of the organization.

As all of these definitions imply, the idea of corporate greening can also denote an internal process by which firms address and manage their environmental impact and which includes notions of awareness, attitude, and orientation ('thinking greenly'), together with an affective element, what Gladwin (1993) has called 'feeling greenly'. Conceived in this way, the focus is not simply on the results of greening but also on the processes by which these results are achieved, including the role of individuals in championing environmental issues within a business (Andersson and Bateman, 2000). Georg and Fussel (2000) have argued that greening can be treated as a case of sense-making in which environmental commitment emerges via a process of social interaction within an organizational context. Their claim that greening is shaped by emotional factors is also echoed by Fineman (1997) who links pro-environmental changes within an organization to the emotional meanings managers attribute to pressures to green the business.

Whether examined at an individual, organizational, or inter-organizational level, a recurring theme in the 'greening as a process' literature is the importance of senior executives and managers in shaping organizational responses (see Chapter 5), including those that go beyond compliance with existing regulations. Drawing from insights offered by institutional theory, the corporate social performance literature, and stakeholder analysis, Prakash (2000a, 2001) argues that 'beyond compliance' environmental responses can be linked to two types of intra-firm process: those that are power-based and those that are leadership-based. Thus, while external pressures create expectations and incentives for managers to adopt a particular environmental stance, it is—according to Prakash—intra-firm politics that influences how managers perceive and interpret these pressures and subsequently act upon them.

This idea that combining different literatures and theoretical approaches can help to shed light on the corporate greening process is also reflected in Winn and Angell's study (2000) of German consumer goods producers. Using concepts and models derived from the corporate social performance, strategy, and environmental management literatures, the authors investigate the internal processes of corporate greening and identify (a) policy commitment to environmental issues and (b) approaches to implementing green activities as two independent dimensions of the corporate greening process. By utilizing these two dimensions, Winn and Angell identify four types of greening which portray different configurations along the two dimensions (see Chapter 5 for a fuller discussion). The implication of their analysis is that alternative paths of greening can exist and that this raises questions about the dynamic relationship between corporate activities and policy commitment and about the role of top management in shaping environmental change at firm level.

The drivers of 'green' behaviour

Academic researchers have long been interested in the factors that predispose firms to adopt different forms of socially responsible behaviour (Burke and Logsdon, 1996; Porter and Kramer, 2002; McWilliams et al., 2006; Worthington et al., 2008). With regard to corporate greening, studies of the phenomenon have focused at different levels of analysis (Hoffman, 1993, 1999; Henriques and Sadorsky, 1999; Bansal and Roth, 2000; Cordano and Frieze, 2000; King and Lenox, 2000; Sharma, 2002; Sharma and Henriques, 2005) and have pointed to a variety of external and internal influences that can affect the environmental practices and attitudes of firms of different sizes (Petts et al., 1999; Tilley, 1999; Patton and Worthington, 2003; Williamson et al., 2006; Zhang et al., 2009), in different industries (Zhuang and Synodinos, 1997; Sharma and Henriques, 2005), and in different geographical locations (Ytterhus and Synnestvedt, 1996; Lindell and Karagozoglu, 2001; Peart, 2001). Since greening the firm is normally seen as a management prerogative, some of these studies have taken a stakeholder approach in investigating the underlying drivers of a green response, arguing that the nature, extent, and managerial perceptions of a firm's stakeholder influences can be an important variable in determining corporate environmental decisions (Williams et al., 1993; Henriques and Sadorsky, 1996, 1999; Angell and Rands, 2002; Sherman et al., 2002; Sharma and Henriques, 2005).

Whilst there is general agreement that a firm's stakeholders are likely to prove an important influence on its behaviour (see below), this is not the only factor seen as influential in driving corporate ecological responsiveness. Having investigated the prior research on organizations and the natural environment, Bansal and Roth (2000) also point to the impact of legislation/regulation, economic opportunities, and ethical influences as key antecedent conditions driving firms to reduce their environmental footprint (see Figure 4.1). In a similar vein, Post and Altman (1994) speak of three distinct forms of environmentalism—compliance-based, market-driven, and value-driven—which emerged in the closing decades of the twentieth century, while Hoffman (2001*a*) suggests that industrial environmentalism, regulatory environmentalism, environmentalism as social responsibility, and strategic environmentalism were emblematic of the period between 1960 and 1993.

In essence, all these writers agree that a combination of regulatory, market, ethical, and stakeholder pressures can explain why firms respond to the environmental agenda and that their responses to these factors provide an insight into managerial motivations for going green. In the following subsections, we examine each of these drivers in more detail and offer a critical analysis of their role in shaping corporate environmental

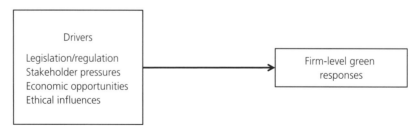

Figure 4.1 The drivers of green behaviour

behaviour. An investigation of possible motivations underlying the greening of organizations is contained in a subsequent section of this chapter.

LEGISLATION/REGULATION

Chapter 3 has highlighted how governments can use legislation and regulation to shape the environmental behaviour of firms. The importance of the law in influencing organizational decisions has been widely recognized in the corporate greening literature and is frequently held to be the single most significant external factor in inducing businesses to undertake green initiatives (Welford and Gouldson, 1993; Post, 1994; Henriques and Sadorsky, 1996; Andrews, R.N.L., 1998; Bansal and Roth, 2000; Lindell and Karagozoglu, 2001; Darnall, 2002; Etzion, 2007).

From a firm's point of view, pro-environmental responses to pressures of this kind are not difficult to rationalize. Failure to comply with regulatory requirements can result in an organization incurring fines, penalties, and legal costs and may threaten the position of a firm's directors and/or its reputation as a commercial enterprise (Henriques and Sadorsky, 1996; Bansal and Roth, 2000; Etzion, 2007). Compliance can also help to leverage advantage with legislators and with other key stakeholders (see below) and can help to reduce current and future risks and liabilities, including the dangers of a loss of competitiveness as regulations become increasingly demanding and/or corporate customers use environmental performance as a criterion for contract compliance (Henriques and Sadorsky, 1996; Wubben, 1999).

In practice, of course, the response of firms to regulatory pressures can vary substantially and may even be idiosyncratic within an individual industry (Etzion, 2007). Industry-leading firms may see legislation and regulation as an important entry barrier and may encourage regulators to introduce stricter rules and stronger monitoring and enforcement mechanisms in order to put laggards at a competitive disadvantage. The latter, in turn, may use lobbying and other strategies to pre-empt tougher regulations and/or promote industry self-regulation and voluntary approaches in the hope of reducing governmental pressures for change (Lyon and Maxwell, 1999; Gunningham and Sinclair, 2002).

The extent to which legislation/regulation acts as a driver of corporate ecological responsiveness can also be affected by a variety of other factors including different regulatory styles, organizational culture, organizational flexibility, the role of industry associations, other stakeholder pressures, and the perceptions of organizational decision-makers regarding the impact of regulation on a firm's competitiveness. Businesses that react to regulatory imperatives with innovative responses (Porter and van der Linde, 1995a, 1995b; Etzion, 2007) are more likely to focus on the opportunities afforded by a proactive environmental stance. Those that see regulation as a threat to their relative competitiveness may attempt to preserve the status quo by creating a buffer between themselves and the outside world, although ultimately this may give rise to a process of incremental changes that subsequently engenders higher levels of environmental protection (King, 2000).

It is worth re-emphasizing that, while governments are ultimately responsible for environmental laws and regulations, these are frequently shaped by different stakeholder interests, including businesses, business representative organizations, environmental NGOs and the media. Moreover, while such legal interventions are frequently focused at specific industries and environmental problems, they also serve to raise awareness of environmental issues and concerns among different stakeholder interests and the public generally (Sharma, 2002). As Chapter 2 has demonstrated, this awareness constitutes an important influence in the broader external context of business and serves to highlight the interrelationship between the regulatory, market, and social domains within which organizations exist and operate.

STAKEHOLDER PRESSURES

Alongside the regulatory demands imposed by governments, firms also face pressure to become greener from other constituencies. Customers, competitors, suppliers, creditors, investors, shareholders, employees, community groups, environmental lobbies, and the media can all be instrumental in inducing corporate ecological responsiveness, although the precise extent of their influence is frequently unclear or may be limited in practice according to the resource dependency between the firm and a particular stakeholder

---

GREEN SNAPSHOT: TESCO'S FIRST ZERO CARBON STORE

As consumers have become increasingly aware of environmental issues, many organizations have felt compelled to demonstrate their green credentials by announcing a range of high-profile environmental initiatives and programmes. Leading UK grocery retailers, including Marks and Spencer, Tesco, Asda, and Waitrose, provide a good example of this trend, with initiatives in areas such as reduced or recyclable packaging, local sourcing, greener products, and reduced energy use just some of the schemes introduced in recent years. Marks and Spencer, for example, announced its 'Plan A' in early 2007 which committed the company to spending around £200 million on reducing its environmental impact over the next five years. Tesco, the leading supermarket in the United Kingdom, quickly followed suit, with a twenty-point plan which included a proposal to add 'carbon footprint' labels to many of its food products and to make green choices available to consumers at affordable prices. Tesco also underlined its commitment to become a carbon-neutral company by 2050 by building its first zero carbon store in 2010, using timber-frame technology, increased use of natural light, energy saving refrigerators, and a combined heat and power plant using renewable biofuels. Tesco chief executive Sir Terry Leahy claimed that, whilst the store cost more to build than a conventional store, the fact that it used considerably less energy—in an era of high oil prices—meant that this in itself provided a solid business case for the decision to seek to reduce its carbon impact.

BOX 4.1 STAKEHOLDER INFLUENCES

Stakeholder group	Possible responses/strategies inducing corporate ecological responsiveness
Customers (including other organizations)	Purchase/not purchase; boycott; litigation; supply chain pressure from purchasing organization
Competitors	Environmental innovations; lobbying for stricter or weaker regulation; environmental leadership
Suppliers	Supply/withhold supply; supply chain pressure; contract compliance
Investors/shareholders	Invest/withhold or withdraw investment; shareholder activism
Financiers and insurers	Provide credit or insurance/withhold credit or insurance
Employees (including managers)	Seek employment/leave employment; voice discontent; whistle blowing; lobby managers
Environmental NGOs	Endorse/criticize a firm and/or its products; lobby for change; positive or adverse publicity; seek or reject an environmental partnership
Local community	Request regulatory hearings; support or challenge the organization; protest; provide or withhold a licence to operate
Media	Positive or adverse publicity; mobilize public opinion; lobby the firm and/or regulators and other stakeholders

---

group (Lawrence and Morell, 1995; Henriques and Sadorsky, 1996, 1999; Berry and Rondinelli, 1998; Bansal and Roth, 2000; Green et al., 2000; Hoffman and Ventresca, 2002; Marshall et al., 2005; Sharma and Henriques, 2005).

The opportunity for the different stakeholder groups to exercise some degree of influence over the environmental behaviour of a firm (or firms generally) is normally related to their ability to impact an organization's bottom line (either directly or indirectly) via their responses. As Box 4.1 illustrates, these responses can be both positive and negative in approach and reflect the different relationships between, and priorities of, the various stakeholder interests and the firm (Sharma and Henriques, 2005).

While the stakeholder management literature generally argues that an organization's primary stakeholders (e.g. customers, suppliers) are likely to exercise more influence over its strategies and decisions by dint of their importance, power, legitimacy, and leverage (Freeman, 1984; Angell and Rands, 2002), the reality tends to be more complex and ambiguous (Etzion, 2007). Each firm—even within the same industry—has a unique relationship with its stakeholders; the way managers interpret and respond to the various stakeholder pressures therefore can vary between organizations as well as over time, thereby giving rise to a range of different organizational responses (Lindell and Karagozoglu, 2001). Thus, whilst logic might suggest that all firms will seek to reduce negative reactions and build stakeholder support by becoming more ecologically responsive (Lawrence and Morell,

1995; Henriques and Sadorsky, 1996, 1999), this will not necessarily always be the case. As with regulatory pressures, firm-level responses to stakeholder demands and expectations will be conditioned by a variety of factors, including managerial perceptions of the relative costs and benefits of corporate action or inaction (Angell and Rands, 2002). To paraphrase Gladwin (1993), it is not inevitable that 'thinking and/or feeling greenly' will result in a firm 'behaving greenly' as tends to be implied by rational choice models of corporate behaviour.

ECONOMIC OPPORTUNITIES

Organizations may seek to improve on their environmental performance as a means of providing an economic and commercial benefit to the enterprise. The emergence of the notions of 'eco-modernization' and 'eco-efficiency' in the later years of the twentieth century promoted the idea that pro-environmental responses could benefit the firm as well as the environment by generating opportunities on both the demand and supply side of business. By seeking ways to reduce their environmental impact, organizations might simultaneously be able to lower the costs of production, for example by reducing waste and/or the price or quantity of inputs (Porter and van der Linde, 1995*a*, 1995*b*; Bansal and Roth, 2000), and create revenue-raising opportunities by developing green products and processes and by enhancing the organization's resources and capabilities, including its corporate reputation (Dechant and Altman, 1994; Hart, 1995; Russo and Fouts, 1997; Christmann, 2000). A detailed and critical examination of the business case for corporate ecological responsiveness is provided in Chapter 6.

ETHICAL INFLUENCES

Alongside the various external drivers of corporate social and environmental responsibility, researchers have also pointed to the importance of ethical influences in shaping firm-level responses (Drumwright, 1994; Waddock et al., 2002; Worthington et al., 2008). This line of argument suggests that some organizations may be motivated to improve on their environmental performance because they believe it is the 'right thing to do' and is in keeping with the norms and values of the organization (Bansal and Roth, 2000; Takala and Pallab, 2000; Wulfson, 2001). Normative explanations such as this do not of course imply that ethically driven responses invariably override other considerations, including the need to be competitive and commercially successful. As numerous writers have pointed out, socially and environmentally responsible behaviour can be rationalized on various grounds, ranging from altruism, through compulsion to strategic intent (Jones, 1999; Van Marrewijk, 2003; Husted and De Jesus Salazar, 2006). It can be difficult for scholars to distinguish between those actions which are motivated by genuinely ethical considerations and those which are undertaken deliberately and primarily for organizational and/or personal gain (Worthington et al., 2008).

Liedtka's assertion (1991) that it is individuals rather than organizations which make decisions points to the fact that ethically driven green responses can often be linked to the role played by individual environmental 'champions' and/or members of the senior management team operating within a given organizational context (Lawrence and Morell, 1995; Andersson and Bateman, 2000; Egri and Herman, 2000; Prakash, 2000a, 2001; Starik and Marcus, 2000; Aragón-Correa et al., 2004). Where the culture and values of an organization are conducive to an ecologically responsible approach, envir- onmental leaders will be better placed to drive through the changes necessary if a firm is to achieve higher levels of environmental commitment (Andersson and Bateman, 2000; Egri and Herman, 2000; Ramus and Steger, 2000; Starik and Marcus, 2000; Angell and Rands, 2002). Research suggests that the opportunities to achieve such changes will also be conditioned by a variety of other factors, including the levels of discretion given to environmental champions; their relative power, influence, and subjective norms; and the role they play in establishing the organization and the direction it takes (Flannery and May, 2000; Prakash, 2000a, 2001; Schaper, 2002; Marshall et al., 2005).

GREEN SNAPSHOT: KOKOYU AND SOCIAL RESPONSIBILITY

Research by Dubey (2008) into the strategic dimension of green marketing by Japanese companies indicates that Kokoyu, a major manufacturer of stationery and office furniture, has been progressively developing greener products out of a sense of moral obligation and social responsibility towards its customers. The company established an environmental action charter in 1993 and began to develop and market its eco-products as part of its main product lines two years later. Consistent with Bansal and Roth's observation (2000) that firms often pursue green strategies for multiple motives, Dubey notes that Kokoyu recognized from the outset that its aim to be a socially responsible business also provided it with an opportunity to exploit a market that was increasingly being shaped by pro-environmental public policies and legislation on issues of recycling and waste management.

Drivers of a green response: mediating and moderating variables

The drivers of a green response discussed above tend to overlap and/or interrelate in quite complex ways. Stakeholder groups, for example, may not only pressurize firms to become greener, they may also induce governments to increase their regulatory oversight of business, and this in turn may encourage further demands on firms from interests such as investors, shareholders, customers, and the media. Whether examined theoretically or empirically, what academic analysis indicates is that pro-environmental behaviour by firms can be linked to a variety of interacting external and internal factors operating in the regulatory, market, and social domains of business. It also indicates that the influence of these factors on an organization's responses will be conditioned by a range of moderating and mediating variables which may help to shed light on the timing, direction, and content of corporate ecological decisions.

In broad terms, a moderating variable is one that influences the strength of a relationship between two other variables, for example, between any one of the drivers of green behaviour illustrated in Figure 4.1 and the extent to which an organization ultimately responds to these drivers. Mediating variables, in contrast, are essentially those that help to explain the relationship between two other variables, in this case between the driver and the firm's response (Baron and Kenny, 1986). As the examples in Box 4.2 indicate, researchers have suggested a wide range of variables that can impact on why, when, and how business decisions-makers respond to external pressures aimed at greening the firm. These influences can be both external and internal to the organization; operate at firm, industry, or macro-environmental level; may be intangible or tangible;

BOX 4.2 EXAMPLES OF MEDIATING AND MODERATING VARIABLES IN THE LITERATURE

Author(s)	Variable(s)	Main argument(s)
Henriques and Sadorsky (1996)	• Level of stakeholder pressure • Financial position of firm • Size of firm • Extent of industry regulation • Firm's attitude to environmental issues	The likelihood that a firm will draw up an environmental plan will depend on factors such as the degree of stakeholder pressure, the availability of financial resources, the importance given to environmental issues, the cost of coordination, and the degree of regulation within its industry.
Cramer (1998)	• Coincidence of increased eco-efficiency and market opportunities • Internal structure and culture of the organizations • Nature and extent of external pressures	How far firms will go to improve on their environmental performance will depend on a combination of internal and external factors, including the role of influential individuals within the organization.
James et al. (1999), Faulkner et al. (2005)	• Leadership • Technology • Human resource and capital capability • Organizational adaptability • Opportunity cost assessment	Leadership role (including style, commitment, concern, objectives) is a key mediating factor shaping the decision-making process. Practical considerations such as technology, resources and flexibility will act as important moderators limiting a firm's potential responses.

(continued)

BOX 4.2 (CONTINUED)

Bowen (2000*a*, 2000*b*)	• Visibility—organizational and issue	The visibility of an organization and of environmental issues can affect both the timing and the content of the response.
Angell and Rands (2002)	• Organizational context	A firm's organizational context, including its size, industry, and level of organizational commitment creates a filter through which external pressures are experienced, recognized, and considered.
Bowen (2000*a*, 2002)	• Organizational slack (actual and potential)	Organizational slack can fulfil a range of functions in relation to corporate greening including facilitating innovative green behaviour.
Darnall (2002), Hilliard (2004)	• Organizational capabilities	Differences in the internal capabilities of a firm can influence its capacity to respond to external and internal pressures.
Banerjee et al. (2003)	• Top management commitment • Industry type	Top management acts as a mediator of the drivers of corporate response, while industry type (e.g. high and moderate impact sectors) acts as a moderator.
Etzion (2007)	• Strategic attributes (e.g. workforce perceptions) • Contingent attributes (e.g. size, slack) • Industry (e.g. 'dirty' vs. 'clean' industries) • The broader environment (e.g. stakeholders)	Factors operating at firm, industry, and the macro-environmental level can influence corporate performance.

and include managerial perceptions, attitudes, and predispositions regarding corporate environmentalism at any given point in time.

The picture that emerges from the research on organizations and the natural environment is one of considerable complexity which belies the implied stimulus response model suggested by Figure 4.1. To understand what encourages firms to go green, it is necessary to go beyond a basic analysis of the key drivers of corporate ecological responsiveness and consider how factors such as the size of the firm, the industry in which it operates, the resource context of the organization, and the attitudes and beliefs of the firm's senior management might shape firm-level responses to external pressures. Figure 4.2 seeks to capture this complexity, albeit still in a simplified form.

Presented in this way organizational responses to ecological issues can clearly vary substantially (see Chapter 5), even for firms of the same size and in the same industry, and this can be related to the unique internal and external contexts faced by each firm.

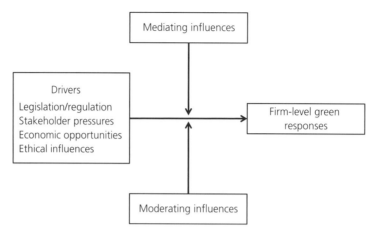

Figure 4.2 Factors driving a green response

Thus, while some organizations might embrace the demands of external stakeholders for improvements in their environmental performance, others in apparently similar circumstances may not even comply with existing regulations (Bansal and Roth, 2000). Apart from such differences in firm-level green responses, the evidence indicates that organizations may also exhibit variations in the motivations underlying their behaviour (Bansal and Roth, 2000; Winn and Angell, 2000). To investigate why firms go green requires consideration not only of the different drivers of corporate greening but also of the alternative motives that may underpin specific organizational responses to the various stakeholder pressures being experienced by a firm.

Motivations for corporate greening

Discussions about why firms go green frequently conflate the drivers of and motivations for corporate ecological responsiveness (see e.g. Cairncross, 1995; Ghobadian et al., 1995; Henriques and Sadorsky, 1996; Morrow and Rondinelli, 2002). While the two are clearly interrelated, investigating a firm's motives for engaging in green behaviour takes us beyond a simple consideration of the internal and external pressures experienced by an organization to an examination of the underlying rationale of a pro-environmental response (see also Chapter 6). As Bansal and Roth (2000) have noted, understanding why green behaviour occurs can help to expose the mechanisms that can foster ecologically sustainable organizations and can allow researchers, corporate decision-makers, and governments to assess the relative efficacy of the various approaches to corporate greening that were discussed in Chapter 3.

A survey of the literature of corporate greening indicates that firms are motivated to go green for three broad reasons: it provides benefits or creates opportunities for the organization; it reduces threats or risks to the enterprise; it accords with the firm's ethical stance. In practice, an organization's actions could reflect multiple motivations and any one of its motivations can be expressed in several ways (Bansal and Roth, 2000).

Benefit- or opportunity-focused explanations of corporate greening link a firm's actions to various strategic advantages thought to emanate from a green response. In attempting to reduce its environmental impact, an organization may be seeking to meet stakeholder or societal expectations; gain legitimacy in the eyes of external and internal interests; achieve market-related benefits such as product differentiation, exploiting green market niches, cost saving, or eco-efficiencies; improve working conditions for employees; and enhance the organization's image and/or corporate reputation (Dechant and Altman, 1994; Cairncross, 1995; Fineman, 1997; Prakash, 1999, 2001; Driscoll and Crombie, 2001; Florida and Davison, 2001; Fryxell and Szeto, 2002; Khanna and Anton, 2002*b*; Morrow and Rondinelli, 2002; Hahn and Scheermesser, 2006; Lynes and Dredge, 2006; Lynes and Andrachuk, 2008). In examining motivations of this kind, researchers have investigated organizations in different national settings and/or in different industries and have frequently focused on individual green initiatives being pursued at the firm level (see e.g. Ghobadian et al., 1995; Fryxell and Szeto, 2002; Morrow and Rondinelli, 2002; Hahn and Scheermesser, 2006; Lynes and Dredge, 2006). It has to be said that it is not always clear from some of this analysis whether corporate perceptions of organizational benefits or opportunities were *ex ante* explanations for a firm's actions or *ex post* rationales aimed at persuading key stakeholders that there was a sound business case for investing in proactive green behaviour (see Chapter 6).

GREEN SNAPSHOT: GREEN PRODUCT DEVELOPMENT AT BRASKEM

As environmental regulations become tighter and customers begin to seek greener alternatives, opportunities open up for firms to profit from proactive green responses. The Brazilian industrial company Brasken provides a good example of how firms can benefit from responding to external demands for more environmentally friendly products. In 2007, the company announced that it had begun production of what it described as the world's first internationally certified renewable polyethylene packaging, based on sugarcane ethanol. Compared to bio-degradable plastic packaging which emits methane as it decays in landfills, green renewable bioplastics are said to have a much smaller environmental footprint as a result of their ability to reduce carbon emissions and lower waste management costs and cut the demand for petroleum. As a leader in what is expected to be a huge global market for renewable packing, Braskem has the potential to gain a competitive advantage through its investment in green product development, which has put it at the forefront of a rapidly growing industry.

Risk- or threat-focused explanations claim that for some organizations the decision to engage in green behaviour is a way of protecting themselves from adverse stakeholder reactions and/or the consequences that accrue from a negative or limited response to the drivers of corporate ecological change. Reduced current and future liabilities and risks—including fines, adverse publicity from non-compliance, fiscal consequences, potential loss of business, the danger of legislative sanctions—have all been suggested as key influences shaping firm-level behaviour (Dechant and Altman, 1994; Ghobadian et al., 1995; Fineman, 1997; Lindell and Karagozoglu, 2001; Khanna and Anton, 2002). While this perspective suggests a predominantly defensive rationale, it is not always easy to separate risk-based motives from the more opportunity-related explanations and/or outcomes of a firm's pro-environmental behaviour. Put simply, some firms that exhibit environmental commitments may not only reduce risks, but may also simultaneously create opportunities to gain from their environmental stance. Which is the dominant motivation, if any, shaping firm-level green behaviour is not always easy to discern.

While the two previous explanations for why firms go green suggest that corporate decision-makers are motivated primarily by economic and commercial considerations, the third broad explanation stresses the ethical and normative context of organizational responses, namely, the belief that firms have a moral obligation to protect the natural environment (Bansal and Roth, 2000; Egri and Herman, 2000; Takala and Pallab, 2000; Hahn and Scheermesser, 2006). Ethical explanations of corporate ecological responsiveness reflect the concern that an organization has for its obligations to the wider society, its elevation of notions of the social good over that of self-interest. That said, as with other manifestations of corporate social responsibility, a firm's ethical stance vis-à-vis the natural environment may also help it to gain a strategic advantage over its rivals, particularly if its actions are seen as an important aspect of doing business by key stakeholders such as customers, investors, and financiers (Post and Altman, 1994; Hoffman, 2001b; McWilliams and Siegel, 2001; Porter and Kramer, 2002).

A model of corporate ecological responsiveness

Key insights into what drives and motivates firms to engage in pro-environmental activity came with the publication of Bansal and Roth's study of UK and Japanese industries in 2000. Using prior research on the drivers of corporate greening to develop a preliminary model of corporate ecological responsiveness, the authors undertook a multi-stage investigation of the factors underpinning firm-level responses and of the contextual influences shaping organizational decisions. Their findings—depicted in the form of an advanced model—portray the relationships between the motivations and their contexts and provide examples of corporate initiatives that reflect the different explanations for green behaviour suggested by their research findings.

Bansal and Roth's empirical investigations identify three dominant motivations which they labelled 'competiveness', 'legitimation', and 'ecological responsibility'. 'Competiveness' is defined as the potential to improve long-term profitability by undertaking green initiatives which could give rise to competitive advantage borne out of demand and/or supply side developments such as cost savings, reputational gains, and new business opportunities. 'Legitimation' refers to the desire of the organization to improve the appropriateness of its actions in relation to an established set of regulations, norms, values, or beliefs, as in the case of regulatory compliance, undertaking environmental audits or engaging in impression management. 'Ecological (or environmental) responsibility' denotes a firm's concern for its social obligations and values, as exemplified by donations to environmental causes as well as the use of life cycle analysis and/or recycling.

Heeding Starik and Rands's call (1995) for a multi-level analysis of corporate ecological behaviour, Bansal and Roth examine the different contexts in which a firm's motivations emerged and identify three key contextual dimensions that appear to be influential in explaining why firms go green. These three dimensions are termed 'issue salience' (the ecological context), 'field cohesion' (the organizational field context), and 'individual concern' (the individual context) and refer to the extent to which an ecological issue has meaning for an organization's constituents (issue salience), the intensity and density of formal and informal network ties between organizational constituents (field cohesion), and the degree to which organizational members value the environment and have discretion to act on their values (individual concern).

By linking together the two aspects of their research, Bansal and Roth have produced a model which suggests how a firm's motivations might be influenced by contextual considerations. A simplified version of the anticipated relationships between context and motivation is depicted in Table 4.1. For instance, where ecological issues were seen as of primary concern (e.g. high profile environmental accidents or crises), the authors

Table 4.1 Motivations and their contexts

Contexts	Motivations		
	Competiveness	Legitimation	Ecological responsibility
Issue salience	Positive	Positive	N/A
Field cohesion	Negative	Positive	Negative
Individual concern	N/A	Positive	Positive

Note: Adapted from Bansal and Roth (2000).

argue that this was likely to have a positive association with both the motivations of competiveness and legitimation, given the likely reaction of key stakeholders to the firm's impact on the natural environment. In situations where environmental issues are of low salience, the authors posit that there is likely to be less of an impact of this contextual factor on a firm's competitiveness and legitimacy, with organizational constituents less likely to impose pressures on the firm or to provide it with opportunities to achieve a competitive advantage.

In exploring links between the drivers and motivations of corporate ecological respon-siveness and between the different motivations and contexts of organizational responses, Bansal and Roth's analysis is a timely reminder that corporate decisions do not take place within a vacuum. Understanding why firms go green requires consideration of a range of complex and interacting antecedent conditions and influences operating at different levels and subject to change over time. The environment in which firms operate and make their decisions is not a constant; it shapes, and is shaped by, what organizations do, including their responses to the green agenda (Etzion, 2007). Applying only a single paradigm (e.g. economic theory) to the study of corporate greening paints an incomplete picture of the reality of organizational life and fails to take account of the multi-faceted and multi-layered nature of corporate experience and behaviour (Starik and Rands, 1995; Bansal and Roth, 2000).

Barriers to environmental change

Whereas much of the literature of corporate greening focuses on the drivers, motiv-ations, and contexts of corporate ecological responsiveness, some writers have rightly drawn attention to the existence of barriers to corporate environmentalism. To complete the analysis of why firms go green, it is appropriate to conclude this chapter with a brief examination of the view that many businesses face countervailing pressures when deciding if, when, and how to react to expectations of higher levels of environmental performance. These barriers (or resistant forces) have been used to explain why some firms have been reluctant, unwilling, or unable to engage in pro-environmental activities, notwithstanding external demands for change (see e.g. Tilley, 1999).

As will be evident from the examples given in Box 4.3, the 'barriers to environmental change' literature also identifies a wide range of internal and external factors that can help to explain differences in how firms react to the drivers of corporate environmental-ism. Apart from the obvious issues of a firm's resources and capabilities, the research suggests that actual or potential obstacles to corporate greening include individual biases, organizational and industry factors, and institutional arrangements. Small firms in particular are often portrayed in the literature as ill-equipped to go much beyond

BOX 4.3 BARRIERS TO ENVIRONMENTAL CHANGE

Author(s)	Focus of research	Key barriers	Examples
Post and Altman (1994)	Managing environmental change processes	Industry and organizational barriers	Capital costs; regulatory constraints; information; financial knowledge; attitudes of personnel; top management deficiencies; past practice
Tilley (1999)	Small firms—attitudes and behaviour	Organizational and institutional barriers	Poor eco-literacy; low environmental awareness; economic barriers; inadequate institutional infrastructure
Harris and Crane (2002)	The greening of organizational culture	Individual and organizational barriers	Individual resistance to change; lack of internal coordination; organizational politics
Hoffman et al. (2002)	New forms of cooperation on environmental practice	Cognitive and institutional barriers	Management attitudes; individual biases and perceptions; changing institutional roles; organizational inertia within the regulatory agencies
Steger et al. (2003)	Greening Chinese business	Organizational and institutional barriers	Inadequate management; lack of technical expertise; poor education and training; weak enforcement arrangements
Hoffman and Bazerman (2005)	Changing practice on sustainability	Organizational and psychological barriers	Cognitive biases; individual perceptions; self-interest; over-reliance on regulatory standards; capital budgets; segmented organizational responsibilities
Kasim (2007)	Malaysian hotel sector	Industry and institutional barriers	Industry policy and economics; lack of adequate infrastructure; lack of conviction of environmental management by key institutions
Okereke (2007)	Carbon management in the FTSE 100	Organizational barriers	Lack of strong policy framework; uncertainties over government action and the marketplace
Walker et al. (2008)	Environmental supply chain management practices	Internal and external barriers—organizational, industry, and institutional	Costs; lack of legitimacy; poor supplier commitment; regulatory barriers

compliance, and some will undoubtedly be non-compliant or at best 'vulnerably compliant' (Petts et al., 1999), either through choice or ignorance, particularly if the drivers of environmental change are relatively weak, as tends to be the case for many smaller organizations (see Chapter 7 for an extended discussion).

In focusing on the idea that change within an organization is often met with resistance, the barriers-to-change approach points to the need to examine in detail the particular context of a firm's green responses and to consider the relative strength of the drivers of and barriers to corporate environmentalism. Thus, while many organizations face substantial pressures for a 'greener' approach which are likely to prove irresistible (Shrivastava and Hart, 1994; Roberts, 1995), others, for a variety of reasons including uncertainty, may be less well-placed or slow to adopt green management processes and practices. Given variations in the internal and external circumstances facing each individual business, we should not be surprised to find differences in both the nature and strength of corporate ecological responses. These differences, how they are categorized by researchers and their indicative dimensions, form the subject matter of the next chapter.

Case Study: Uniqlo

The Fast Retailing Group is a Japanese clothing organization whose core business is Uniqlo, a casual wear brand known for its coloured sweaters, polo shirts, and jackets. Other brands that are part of the global business include g.u., theory, and princesse tam. tam. Currently, the group has over 1000 stores, around 80 per cent of which are based in Japan and some of which are operated on a franchise basis. The company also has a presence in other parts of Asia and in the United States, the United Kingdom, France, and Russia.

Under its founder and CEO, Tadashi Yanai, Uniqlo's guiding principle is that the most critical question an organization can ask itself is whether its existence and operations are good for society. Yanai believes that what people wear can change their lives and this gives clothing retailers and producers considerable power; this power, he contends, also comes with responsibility and this ethical stance lies at the heart of the organization's activities. Exemplifying Yanai's commitment to corporate social responsibility (CSR) is the company's 'All Product Recycling Initiative' which started in Japan and Korea and which was introduced into its stores in the United Kingdom, the United States, and France from the start of September 2011.

Building on a fleece recycling programme which began in 2001, the new scheme essentially involves collecting used clothing items from customers who no longer want them and passing them on to refugees and internally displaced persons around the world, thereby maximizing the value obtained from an item. Any reusable clothing handed in is first separated into categories, cleaned, and then delivered to those in greatest need, as identified through the offices of the UN High Commissioner for Refugees. It is estimated that, in the period from 2006 (when the scheme began) to July 2011, over 11 million items had been collected and delivered to recipients, largely across the developing world. Clothes which are deemed unfit for further wear are either converted into industrial fibre or are used as a fuel to generate electricity.

Uniqlo sees its All Product Recycling Initiative as part of its attempt to demonstrate its commitment to CSR and to meet the needs of its key stakeholders (i.e. customers, employees, shareholders and investors, business partners, and the local community), all of whom, it believes, share an interest in its approach to corporate governance, business ethics, and the environment. Where environmental protection is concerned, the scheme is seen as an important element in its overall aim of reducing its environmental impact at every stage of the product life cycle, from cradle to grave. Other initiatives in this area include schemes to reduce packaging waste and improve energy and resource efficiency, as well as a commitment to incorporate environmental considerations into all its products.

In September 2010, Uniqlo also launched a social enterprise, in a joint venture with Grameen Bank, aimed at addressing issues such as poverty, sanitation, and education in Bangladesh through the production and sale of clothing, using locally sourced labour and raw materials.

5 Models of corporate greening

Developing and using classification systems are familiar conceptual processes. Ordering concepts, objects or entities into groups or classes on the basis of their similarities enables us to increase our understanding of observed complexity and to communicate our observations more easily'

(Hass, 1996)

Firms' responses to (these) different types of pressure, and to the potential market benefits of an environmental strategy, have varied greatly. Some have just been reactive, others proactive.

(Kolk, 2000)

The history of scholarship focusing on the management of organisations in the natural environment is relatively brief, compared to that in other environments-oriented academic fields, and it has often followed both the organizational practice in, and practitioner writing on, environmental management.

(Starik and Marcus, 2000)

Introduction

Reference has already been made to the growth of interest shown in corporate environmentalism over recent decades and to the burgeoning academic and practitioner literature that has accompanied this important development. Subsequent reviews of published work on organizations and the natural environment (ONE) have pointed to the rich diversity of topics, issues, theories, models, and empirical analysis which have exercised writers in the field (Gladwin, 1993; Sharma and Aragón-Correa, 2005; Etzion, 2007; Srivastava, 2007) and which have increasingly appeared in mainstream management journals as well as those specifically devoted to environmental aspects of business (see e.g. the *Academy of Management Review*, 1995, Special Issue on 'Ecologically Sustainable Organizations'). Within this eclectic mix, some researchers have sought to enhance our understanding of firm-level green behaviour by investigating the characteristics and evolution of organizational responses to the environmental agenda. The result has been the emergence of a variety of models and typologies of corporate greening which help to shed light on what Van de Ven and Poole (1995) call the 'how' and 'why' of the organizational change process and which are the central focus of this chapter.

Classification systems in environmental management

The development of classification schemes is a well-established practice in the field of business and management (see e.g. Miles and Snow, 1978; Porter, 1985) and one that has spawned a plethora of concepts which are sometimes used somewhat indiscriminately by writers in these fields. Doty and Glick (1994) argue that terms such as 'typology', 'taxonomy', and 'classification scheme' are frequently used interchangeably and that this semantic confusion can help to obscure important differences between these various conceptual tools. They suggest that classification schemes and taxonomies are systems of classification that categorize phenomena (e.g. environmental strategies) into mutually exclusive and exhaustive sets with a series of discrete decision rules, whereas a typology refers to conceptually derived interrelated sets of ideal types, each of which represents a unique combination of attributes thought to determine the relevant outcome(s). For Bailey (1994), the essential difference between a taxonomy and typology is that the former is the outcome of empirical investigation whilst the latter is conceptually based, often derived from researcher intuition or experience and not necessarily subjected to empirical investigations at a later date.

The use of classification systems—including taxonomies and typologies—has been particularly prevalent in the literature of environmental management, with over fifty models appearing since the late 1980s (Kolk and Mauser, 2002). At the risk of oversimplification, most of the models proposed generally fall into two main types based on their underlying structure: stage or continuum models and categorical or matrix models (Hass, 1996). Stage models are linear classification schemes that designate a series of 'stages' (or phases) by which firms become progressively greener, as exemplified by their attitudes, actions, postures, and strategies vis-à-vis environmental issues (Hass, 1996; Schaefer and Harvey, 1998). Matrix models, on the other hand, categorize and rate firm-responses along different dimensions of environmental management (e.g. environmental risk versus market opportunity; high versus low), with the resultant matrix of responses representing 'ideal types' of behaviour or performance that do not necessarily imply progression in environmental protection. Both these approaches are discussed in more detail below, prior to examination of particular examples from the corporate greening literature.

STAGE MODELS

Stage models of corporate environmental behaviour conceptualize the greening of business as a developmental process in which firms move towards higher levels of environmental performance over time. At their simplest, these models posit three basic phases of environmental response, ranging from little or no consideration given to environmental issues, through basic compliance with environmental regulations (and possibly societal expectations), to beyond compliance behaviour by the more environmentally responsive organizations (see Figure 5.1). As Hass (1996) has suggested, this approach appears to be based on either explicit progression or on evolutionary assumptions and a sequential logic and frequently carries with it the implication that firms *should* aspire to move along this continuum in order to reduce their impact on the natural environment.

An examination of a sample of published models of this kind reveals considerable diversity along several dimensions (Hass, 1996; Schaefer and Harvey, 1998; Kolk and Mauser, 2002). Key differences include:

- the overall focus of the model;
- the number of designated stages;
- the terminology used to describe firm-level responses; and
- the number of, and defining criteria for, the different stages identified (see Box 5.1).

Moreover, while some models of this kind are purely conceptual, others are supported with empirical evidence drawn from a variety of industries, sectors, and geographical contexts, including cross-national comparisons of corporate environmental attitudes and behaviours. A fuller investigation of the various models and their similarities and differences can be found in Kolk and Mauser's article on the evolution of environmental management, published in the *Business Strategy and the Environment* journal in 2002.

As Box 5.1 illustrates, the three basic phases of environmental response shown in Figure 5.1 are frequently extended to five stages or more and are generally portrayed as progressive levels of environmental management or strategic response. Implicit in most, if not all, models of this kind is the idea that firms have a choice of environmental strategy or position and that movement through the various stages tends to occur as businesses become increasingly engaged in the environmental agenda (Schaefer and Harvey, 1998). It is also assumed that rating of firms on the specified dimensions is possible within a continuum, thereby effectively reducing the multi-dimensional character of the environmental management strategy construct to a primarily one-dimensional stage-like progression (Hass, 1996).

Figure 5.1 A simple stage model of environmental management

BOX 5.1 SELECTED STAGE MODELS OF ENVIRONMENTAL MANAGEMENT/STRATEGY

Author(s)	Model title	Number of stages	Names of stages or positions
Petulla (1987)	Approaches of Environmental Management (EM)	3	Crisis-orientated; cost-orientated; enlightened EM
Hunt and Auster (1990)	Developmental Stages of Corporate Environmental Management Programs	5	Beginner; fire fighter; concerned citizen; pragmatist; proactivist
Winsemius and Guntram (1992)	Development Stages in Environmental Policy Planning	4	Reactive; sectoral; topical; comprehensive
Roome (1992)	Strategic Options Model	5	Non-compliance; compliance; compliance plus; commercial and environmental excellence; leading edge
Azzone and Bertele (1994)	Environmental Contexts	5	Stable; reactive; anticipatory; proactive; creative
Arthur D. Little (1996)	Stages of EM Evolution	4	Reactive; responsive; proactive; competitive
Berry and Rondinelli (1998)	Stages of Corporate EM	3	Non-compliance; compliance; beyond compliance

GREEN SNAPSHOT: BEYOND PETROLEUM?

Stage models of corporate greening portray companies as moving progressively along a continuum as they respond positively to increasing pressures to improve on their environmental performance. It is not unknown for a firm to signal its claimed, increasing environmental proactivity through evocative advertising, and the use of green symbols/logos or even a clever change of slogan, as exemplified by BP's use of a stylized green sun symbol and its adoption of the notion of 'Beyond Petroleum'.

Unanticipated events (e.g. the Gulf of Mexico oil spill; see Chapter 2) and changes of policy and leadership can, however, raise important questions about a firm's green credentials and its direction of travel. In addition to the public relations disaster resulting from the Deepwater Horizon incident, critics of BP have accused it of retreating—at least in part—from its commitment to expand beyond fossil fuels. In 2009, the company closed its alternative-energy headquarters in London, accepted the resignation of its most senior executive in this division of the business, and imposed further, large cuts in the alternative energy budget. It also announced its intention of closing or selling off its interests in a number of renewable businesses in India, Spain, and the United States. Coupled with its plans to move into the highly controversial exploitation of oil from Canada's tar sands, critics could be forgiven for thinking that BP might be moving 'back to petroleum' rather than beyond it.

MATRIX MODELS

Whereas stage models present firm-level responses to environmental management or strategy as a kind of continuum along which organizations can (and do) move, matrix or categorical models characterize a firm's position according to predetermined dimensions without assuming any growing responsiveness on its part. A basic and common structure is shown in Figure 5.2 and can be used to illustrate the link between an organization's environmental management concerns and its observed generic environmental strategies. The placing of a firm's responses in this 2×2 matrix is determined by both the dimensions that define the axes and by the rating of each business (e.g. high versus low; strong versus weak) on each of these chosen dimensions. The resultant matrix identifies four positions a firm faces (or may be placed in) with respect to its environmental management policies or strategic responses/posture. Firms occupying the same cell in such a matrix may, of course, adopt different strategies in response to their interpretation of their operating domain (Hass, 1996; Kolk and Mauser, 2002).

Some examples of models of this kind are shown in Box 5.2. As with stage models, categorical approaches show some diversity. Steger (1993), for example, presents a 2×2 matrix based on the dimensions of 'corporate environmental risk' and 'market opportunities through environmental protection', with both scales rated as small to large. Rondinelli and Vastag (1996) and Vastag et al. (1996) also use the notion of risk, but this appears on both dimensions of their four-cell model (i.e. 'endogenous risk' and 'exogenous risk'),

Dimension 1 (e.g. perceived environmental risk)

		Rating scale (e.g. low/weak/small)	Rating scale (e.g. high/strong/large)
Dimension 2 (e.g. perceived market opportunity)	Rating scale (e.g. low/weak/small)	1	2
	Rating scale (e.g. high/strong/large	3	4

Figure 5.2 A simple matrix model of environmental management

Notes: Cell 1 = low risk/low opportunity.
       Cell 2 = high risk/low opportunity.
       Cell 3 = high opportunity/low risk.
       Cell 4 = high risk/high opportunity.

BOX 5.2 SELECTED MATRIX MODELS OF ENVIRONMENTAL MANAGEMENT/STRATEGY

Author(s)	Model title	Number of cells	Names of stages or positions
Steger (1993)	Generic Environmental Strategies	4	Indifferent; defensive; offensive; innovative
Rondinelli and Vastag (1996)	Classification of Environmental Policies	4	Reactive; proactive; crisis preventive; strategic
Brockhoff et al. (1999)	Environmental Business Strategy	4	Defender; escapist; dormant; activist
Winn and Angell (2000)	Corporate Greening	4	Deliberate reactive greening; unrealized greening; emergent active greening; deliberate proactive greening
Levy and Kolk (2002)	Responses to Climate Change	4	Resistant; avoidant; compliant; proactive

---

while Roome's focus (1992) is on 'public perception' and 'scientific significance of environmental impact' when producing his threat response assessment of corporate vulnerability, prior to outlining a five-phase stage model of strategic options. As these examples illustrate, categorical approaches to classifying firm-level behaviour tend to assume that firms can be rated along the chosen dimensions and that the dimensions that define the axes are able to differentiate between different businesses (Hass, 1996).

Two models of corporate greening

To gain a clearer view of how classification schemes have been developed in the field of environmental management, it is helpful to examine two specific models of corporate greening in more detail: Hunt and Auster's five-stage Environmental Development Continuum (1990) and Steger's Generic Environmental Strategies Model (1993). These well-known models can be seen as exemplars of the two major approaches to the classification discussed above.

HUNT AND AUSTER'S MODEL

Hunt and Auster's investigations into corporate environmental management practices grew out of the recognition that managing a firm's environmental impact was rapidly becoming a major business issue. Faced with a combination of increased regulatory demands, growing consumer pressures, and higher levels of risk and uncertainty, the authors argued that US corporations should see environmental management as a critical component for sustaining a competitive advantage. In their opinion, firms not only needed a change in perspective but also to accept that, in order to sustain long-term profitability, they might need to invest sufficient resources in preventative environmental management programmes to protect their competitive position.

On the basis of an analysis of environmental management programmes at various companies in a range of industries, Hunt and Auster suggested five distinct phases of programme development, ranging from essentially no protection against environmental risk at the lower end of the development continuum to a programme of proactive environmental management at the other end of the scale. Whereas the former approach reflected the view that environmental management was unnecessary and/or too costly to afford, firms at the proactivist end of the continuum saw managing environmental risks as a business priority requiring an open-ended commitment of corporate resources. At the time of their analysis, the authors suggested that few US corporations appeared to have reached the highest stage of programme development as portrayed in their five-phase model.

For Hunt and Auster, each stage in their model represents a generic characterization, with the specific requirements for any organization dependent on company size, type of business, complexity of the corporate structure, and the range of potential environmental

---

GREEN SNAPSHOT: A MIXED PICTURE FOR UK FIRMS

One way in which a firm can demonstrate its green credentials is to set targets to reduce its environmental impact. Where greenhouse gas emissions targets are concerned, UK firms appear to have something of a mixed record. A report from the Carbon Disclosure Project (CDP) (see Chapter 2) in early 2010 suggested that big polluters in the energy, materials, and utilities sectors were lagging significantly behind other large businesses when setting annual targets for emissions reductions, despite being responsible for almost 90 per cent of the emissions produced by FTSE 100 firms. The report also pointed out that almost a third of all companies that had set targets did so on the basis of carbon intensity rather than on absolute reductions in greenhouse gas emissions, a decision which allowed them to increase their overall emissions while appearing to have become greener.

A subsequent study by the Carbon Trust (June 2011) found that nearly half of the country's top companies had not set targets on greenhouse gas emissions, significantly down on the 77 per cent who claimed to have set them according to the CDP analysis referred to above. The Carbon Trust study indicated that most carbon reduction targets set by FTSE companies tend to be short-term and some firms that had previously set targets had not renewed them when they expired. One company highlighted for its positive commitment was Kingfisher, the UK parent company of the do-it-yourself retailer B&Q. The firm's CEO claimed that setting measurable targets and objectives had helped it to improve on its performance and this had made an important contribution towards meeting its environmental goals. Since part of the CEO's bonus is linked to the firm's environmental performance, this was no doubt a welcome outcome.

problems and risks a business faces. Given the variations in these dimensions, they argue that a perceived 'proactivist' stance in one industry (e.g. banking) may only be marginally adequate in another (e.g. petrochemicals), a position that serves to re-emphasize the need to avoid broad and acontextual generalizations where corporate environmental management is concerned. Nor is it possible in their opinion to categorize any entire industry (e.g. chemicals) at one particular stage of development, given that the environmental management needs of some firms in the industry (e.g. small, one product) will invariably differ from those of others where the size, scale, complexity, and diversity of the organization present considerable risk-management challenges for the organization's decision-makers.

Under Hunt and Auster's model, a firm's environmental management programme was categorized using three basic criteria. These were the degree to which a programme reduces environmental risk, the commitment of the organization, and the programme design. In the case of the latter two criteria, these were broken down into a number of sub-component parts such as the mindset of managers, resource commitment by the organization, top management involvement and support, and the degree of integration and reporting structures in operation within the organization. Firms that performed relatively poorly with respect to the various criteria (e.g. by exhibiting little or no protection against environmental risks, limited commitment; negligible or no real indication of addressing environmental problems within the organization) were designated as either 'Beginners' or 'Fire Fighters' and were placed in the early stages of the development continuum. As an organization's performance improved in relation to the defining criteria, movement would occur along the continuum, indicating a higher level of protection against environmental risk and an increasingly active commitment to environmental management within the enterprise.

Hunt and Auster called the highest level of performance 'proactivist', a posture which offered the firm maximum protection from current and future environmental risks. Seven universal components of a proactivist stance which they regarded as the key requirements in protecting the organization were:

- top level support and commitment;
- corporate policies that integrate environmental issues;
- effective interfaces between corporate and business unit staff;
- a high degree of employee awareness and training;
- a strong auditing programme;
- a strong legal base; and
- established ownership of environmental problems.

For Hunt and Auster, proactivism required a change in attitudes as well as behaviour and an acceptance that a comprehensive environmental management programme needed to give consideration to structures, culture, policies, programmes, people, and relationships

---

GREEN SNAPSHOT: L.L. BEAN AND THE ENVIRONMENT

Founded in 1912, the US-based mail-order, online, and rental company L.L. Bean claims a long history of involvement in environmental stewardship both through its products and its operations. Its current environmental policies and initiatives include using paper from certifiable sustainable sources; working with the Environmental Protection Agency to develop a long-term greenhouse gas emissions reduction programme; energy conservation measures; designing and building more eco-efficient buildings; converting its truck fleet to biodiesel; reducing packaging use; establishing a corporate recycling programme; and working with suppliers and other organizations to minimize harmful substances in its products and to develop more sustainable alternatives. The company also has an ongoing Environmental Charitable Giving programme and encourages its employees to adopt environmentally friendly commuting options such as carpooling and biking.

---

throughout the organization, from top to bottom. Taken as a whole, their analysis points to environmental responses as essentially a top-down process, dependent on the leadership shown by senior executives at corporate level and on their willingness to commit time, money, and effort in addressing the firm's impact on the natural environment both now and in the future.

While some stage models offer little, if any, insight into how organizations might be able to move to a higher level of environmental performance, Hunt and Auster's study discussed the key processes firms needed to engage in, in order to implement a more proactive environmental management programme. As well as assessing the full range of environmental risks, they suggested that firms needed to sell the rationale for good practices throughout the organization; implement changes designed to facilitate programme visibility, accessibility, and effectiveness; recruit suitably qualified personnel; manage and utilize the flow of information; and re-evaluate and reform as necessary existing policies and programmes.

STEGER'S GENERIC ENVIRONMENTAL STRATEGIES MODEL

Like Hunt and Auster, Steger began his analysis of corporate responses to environmentalism with the observation that changes in the business environment were helping to make firms more aware of the possible benefits of beyond compliance behaviour. Given the technological developments, supply chain pressures, and changing consumer reactions, he argued that firms had an opportunity to be more proactive and to exploit the potential competitive advantages of engaging in sound environmental practices. Whether beyond compliance behaviour represented an attempt by firms to use environmentalism as a stimulus to innovation and market development was, for Steger, a key

Market opportunities for environmental protection

		Small	Large
Corporate environmental risk	Small	Indifferent	Offensive
	Large	Defensive	Innovative

Figure 5.3 Steger's generic environmental strategies model

Source: Adapted from Steger (1993). From *Environmental Strategies for Industry* edited by Kurt Fischer and Johan Schot. Copyright © 1993 Island Press. Reproduced by permission of Island Press, Washington, DC.

question. In addressing this issue, the author proposed a model of four possible generic strategies that businesses could pursue, prior to reporting on a piece of empirical research into pro-environmental management practices amongst German manufacturing and service companies which was carried out in the early 1990s.

Steger's oft-quoted model of alternative strategic responses is shown in Figure 5.3. As the model indicates, the choice of strategy a firm could implement was thought to be determined by two major factors: the company's potential to gain market opportunities via environmental protection; and the degree of environmental risk inherent in its day-to-day activities. By examining firms along these two dimensions, Steger identified four generic strategies: 'indifferent', 'defensive', 'offensive', and 'innovative'. Since the first of these implied that environmental protection was of no strategic importance, Steger's analysis focused on the other three and examined how they might work in practice.

For businesses where the environmental risks may be large, but the opportunities small, the model proposed that corporate decision-makers were likely to adopt a defensive strategy, with the focus on complying with environmental legislation. In risk-based industries of this type (e.g. electricity generation using fossil fuels), Steger argued that regulatory demands and the need to install expensive end-of-pipe technologies made firms in the industry vulnerable to changes in market conditions, such as buyers seeking cheaper substitutes or competitors introducing new technologies. While environmental compliance was clearly necessary, his contention was that a defensive response was not sufficient because of new environmental market pressures and innovative opportunities, and he called on firms to switch to an offensive or innovative strategy as a means of gaining from environmentalism and of securing their competitive position in the changing market place.

The underlying conditions that support an offensive approach are where environmental risks are relatively insignificant, but where firms could gain substantial market opportunities through corporate greening. Steger suggested that such a situation could occur where firms were able to provide additional benefits to the consumer by either modifying existing products or developing more environmentally sound goods or services. In adopting such an approach, he stressed the need for a firm to be an early mover and to communicate its product's environmental advantages to its customers through its marketing activities. It also needed to ensure that environmental action took place across its entire product range in order to prevent consumers from switching to alternatives under the same brand.

Where both risks and opportunities are deemed large, Steger regarded an innovative approach as desirable, albeit that this tended to be the most challenging strategy for corporate executives to pursue. To exploit the market potential inherent in this situation required, in his opinion, a major change in the production process or a complete new product design capable of achieving long-term success for the innovating organization. In addition to discussing the potential benefits of this strategic approach (e.g. early mover advantages, product differentiation, reduced future regulatory costs), Steger also underlined the risks involved, including high R&D costs, demand uncertainty, and doubts over product quality. Balancing these risks and opportunities, he accepted, provided a considerable challenge for most businesses, especially in situations where the environmental advantage of a new product or process was far from clear.

In reporting on the empirical findings of his study of German companies, Steger noted that, while environmental concerns were increasingly becoming a market issue, most businesses were still not implementing an offensive or innovative strategy, but instead were tending to focus on avoiding risk rather than grasping new market opportunities via environmentalism. Moreover, while many organizations recognized that environmental protection was a question of social and ecological responsibility, few appeared to be approaching the issue in a comprehensive and integrated manner. For most firms questioned, a primary motive for engaging in pro-environmental behaviour seemed to be regulatory compliance, with attention largely focused on production and technical considerations. Recognition of the value-adding potential of corporate environmental protection (e.g. cost reductions or revenue gains) appeared to be largely absent among the respondent organizations.

Although Steger's concern was clearly that firms should adopt more offensive or innovative approaches in response to the new environmental market pressures, he offered only limited insight into how a firm could move away from a defensive mode of behaviour. His analysis appears to imply that to achieve the desired change required a top-down approach in which board members took steps to ensure that environmental protection was integrated into the firm's corporate and business strategies and reflected in the goal structure of the organization. How this was to be achieved is not entirely clear, although he hinted at the need for systematic planning, cross-functional coordination, and awareness-raising and training of corporate employees, especially those involved in a firm's marketing and R&D functions. While Steger accepted that much remained to be done in these areas, he argued that a majority of German corporations were moving towards the goal of a comprehensive environmental strategy in which environmental protection and business performance were seen as complementary. For him, the process of learning and change had begun; what was needed was time for firms to rise to the new challenge and opportunities inherent in greening the organization.

An assessment

The development of classification systems of the types discussed above is not without its merits. By categorizing different forms of corporate environmental response, writers in the field have helped to enhance our understanding of environmental management practices and have drawn attention to the wide range of reactions of corporate decision-makers to the growing tide of environmentalism (Kolk and Mauser, 2002). Bailey (1994) argues that good classification schemes help to reduce complexity, highlight similarities and differences between observed phenomena, and can form an important bridge between concept, theory, and empirical research. Moreover, by providing a parsimonious framework for understanding corporate behaviour and/or outcomes, such systems have tended to capture the imagination of scholars, managers, and students alike (Doty and Glick, 1994), thus proving a useful stimulus to further investigations in this as in other problem domains.

Being an essentially heuristic device, both stage and categorical models have been subjected to considerable criticism. Cramer (1998), for example, argues that some of the assumptions inherent in certain models (e.g. the progressional nature of firm responses; the separation of environmental strategy from business strategy; the existence of a single environmental stance) are not necessarily true to reality and she points to the need to recognize that corporate responses will be shaped by a variety of internal and external factors, including the structure and culture of the organization and market conditions. Others have argued that models often tend to be highly prescriptive (Schaefer and Harvey, 1998); are too simplistic to deal with organizational complexities (Kolk and Mauser, 2002); may be inadequately specified (Schaefer and Harvey, 1998); are frequently lacking in any discussion of how an organization can move between different levels of environmental performance (Hass, 1996); and are generally difficult to operationalize (Hass, 1996; Schaefer and Harvey, 1998; Kolk and Mauser, 2002).

With regard to the last of these issues, it is interesting to note that empirical testing of certain models has provided contradictory findings. A study of Canadian firms by Henriques and Sadorsky (1999) was largely supportive of the models of Hunt and Auster (1990) and Roome (1992), whereas both Hass's (1996) and Schaefer and Harvey's (1998) investigations question their utility in interpreting firm-level green responses. In Hass's study of Norwegian firms in two industries, she found the Hunt and Auster model inadequate as a research framework both in an operational and contextual sense, and a similar conclusion was reached by Schaefer and Harvey when testing the two models in a UK context. As the latter authors have pointed out, continuum models basically imply linear and one-dimensional progression on all fronts, when in reality environmental responses are generally more complex and multi-faceted. Added to this, many models tend to use relatively vague criteria which are not consistently defined across the various stages and which do not necessarily reflect the differences that tend to exist between industries, firms, and even sites (Schaefer and Harvey, 1998). Applying these criteria to actual behaviour therefore becomes highly problematic as Kolk and Mauser (2002) have rightly observed.

Second-generation models

It has been suggested that the flaws inherent in conceptualizing corporate environmental behaviour as a series of stages on a continuum helped to encourage the development of a number of 'second-generation models' in the late 1990s (Kolk and Mauser, 2002). To conclude this chapter, two of these models—those of Ghobadian and colleagues (1998) and Winn and Angell (2000)—are briefly considered below.

The basic premise underlying Ghobadian et al.'s adapted, non-linear progression model is that, in order to plot and describe a company's strategic environmental policy, it is necessary to take account of a set of key external and internal influences and constraints (e.g. mediating and moderating influences), examples of which were discussed in Chapter 4. Using evidence from a survey of seventy-eight top UK corporations, the authors argued, that when these factors were considered, substantial doubt is cast upon the evolutionary assumptions inherent in stage models of corporate greening. In particular, they questioned whether corporate decisions (*a*) demonstrate a linear progression towards excellence over time, (*b*) develop in a sequential and incremental manner, and (*c*) indicate a move towards globalized standards of performance. The idea of a continuum with inevitable forward momentum was, in their opinion, not entirely reasonable because of a failure to recognize that there were strategic options that could lie outside the basic model depicted in Figure 5.1.

Utilizing Roome's basic sequential model (1992) as a base on which to build their own extended linear approach, Ghobadian et al. identified three alternative corporate responses to those suggested by the traditional model. These were:

- restrained commitment—where a firm had no incentive to advance towards excellence;
- speculative commitment—where a firm adopted a fast-track approach to excellence in order to take a short-cut to advancing its corporate goals;

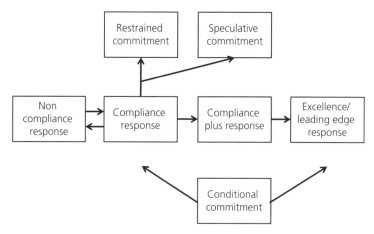

Figure 5.4 Ghobadian et al.'s extended linear approach

Note: Adapted from Ghobadian et al. (1998).

- conditional commitment—where a firm adopted a pragmatic approach to environmental policy at any given time and in any given place (e.g. by pursuing different policies for the different geographical locations of its sites).

Figure 5.4 shows how these responses relate to Roome's basic stage model.

In essence, the basic argument was that firms have a much wider range of strategic policy options than those suggested by previous researchers who had not always taken into account the wide range of factors shaping policy choices. In highlighting apparent weaknesses in the linear approach, the authors drew attention to the possibility of non-sequential corporate responses and to alternative policy choices by a firm operating in different business contexts. As Kolk and Mauser (2002) have observed, however, this recognition of increased complexity in modelling corporate environmental behaviour comes at a price, since it renders the revised model more difficult to apply than those that seek to simplify complex reality.

The focus of Winn and Angell's research was on the internal aspects of the corporate greening process. On the basis of a study of German firms in the consumer goods industry, the authors identified two independent dimensions of environmental management—a firm's policy commitment and its approach to policy implementation—that were similar to influences identified in Hass's earlier work (1996) on modelling environmental behaviour. Using these two dimensions, they proposed a four-cell matrix model (or typology) that drew on previous concepts in the strategic management, corporate social performance (CSP), and corporate environmental management literatures. A basic version of their conceptual model is depicted in Figure 5.5.

Winn and Angell's typology identified four ideal types of corporate response. 'Deliberate reactive' greening (Cell 1) they described as an unsystematic, reactive, and reluctant

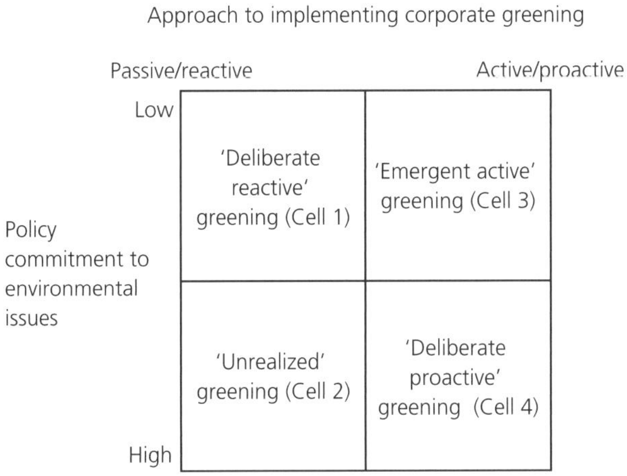

Approach to implementing corporate greening

	Passive/reactive	Active/proactive
Low	'Deliberate reactive' greening (Cell 1)	'Emergent active' greening (Cell 3)
High	'Unrealized' greening (Cell 2)	'Deliberate proactive' greening (Cell 4)

Policy commitment to environmental issues

Figure 5.5 Winn and Angell's factor-based model of corporate greening

Source: Adapted from Winn and Angell (2000).

response by a firm's top management to issues of environmental responsibility. A firm of this type they described as an environmental follower rather than leader which did not incorporate environmental considerations into its decision-making processes. In contrast, businesses that demonstrated 'emergent active' green responses (Cell 3) took a proactive approach to environmental protection and managed this through their products and their supply chain. In such a firm, prevention had become part of the organization's capability set and it engaged in planning and external monitoring in order to anticipate future changes in its operating environment. That said, the firm's lack of commitment to environmental issues generally meant that the management's response to environmental protection remained very limited and hence was not systematically considered across all major functional areas.

The apparent contradiction in this form of green response can also be seen in what Winn and Angell called 'unrealized' greening (Cell 2). Here, top management appeared highly committed to the environment, but the firm took an essentially passive/reactive approach to implementing corporate greening via its products, processes, systems, or supply chain relationships. As in the case of the deliberate reactive approach, firms exhibiting this stance were environmental followers and remained basically unprepared for new developments because of a lack of formal planning and monitoring of the internal and external environments.

The fourth cell in the factor-based model of corporate responses—'deliberate proactive' greening—depicted a firm that was an environmental innovator, with both its commitment and approach to implementation at the high end of the scale. Organizations in this category had a top management highly committed to environmental protection and this was reflected in all aspects of the firm's activities at corporate, business, and functional levels. Inputs, throughputs, outputs, and suppliers were all managed with the environment in mind and the organization possessed a general capability for prevention through its planning, monitoring, and review systems and processes.

While Winn and Angell's profiles of four ideal types of corporate greening are able to accommodate conflicting theoretical perspectives put forward in the various strategic, CSP, and environmental management literatures, the authors accepted that they were less clear on the issue of the underlying dynamics of greening and the possible patterns or paths of greening processes. Thus, to shed light on these issues, four follow-up case studies were employed which subsequently provided more detailed insights into issues such as the drivers of and barriers to corporate greening and how a firm's stance on environmental protection was reflected in its activities, structures, and processes. A key finding to emerge from this additional research was that the initial four profiles suggested by the factor-based model may mask alternative configurations (or subcategories) within types, particularly where there is inconsistency along the two dimensions (see above). As Winn and Angell point out, these alternative configurations (e.g. lack of implementation under 'unrealized greening' could be explained by insufficient time or organizational limitations or lack of intent) have critical implications for our understanding of business responses to the environmental agenda and underline the variety, complexity, and dynamics of internal greening processes often not captured in extant models of corporate environmental management.

Case Study: Modelling business responses to climate change

Most models of corporate greening of the types discussed above tend to use classification schemes to categorize business responses to environmental issues generally. As this case study illustrates, however, models can also be used to discuss the different ways in which firms can or may approach specific environmental concerns that impact upon the business and which require some form of strategic response, even if that response is to do nothing. Two such schemes are discussed here: Kolk and Pinkse's model of strategic options (2005) for climate change and Levy and Kolk's typology of responses (2002) to climate change by multinational companies (MNCs) in the oil industry.

KOLK AND PINKSE'S STRATEGIC OPTIONS MODEL

Kolk and Pinkse's analysis comprised two main components: a model of the strategic options available to firms; and an examination of the actual patterns of market-orientated actions being undertaken by businesses, based on data provided by 136 large organizations that were part of the Global 500. We discuss each of these in turn.

The construction of the authors' six-cell strategic options matrix model (or typology) was based on the observation that firms have certain choices in responding to climate change policies and that these choices can involve different degrees of interaction with other organizations. With regard to the available choices, the authors identified two broad forms of market strategy that firms could pursue under a flexible regulatory regime: 'innovation' and 'compensation'. The former involves the development of new environmental technologies or services aimed at reducing emissions, an approach that helps to improve the company's assets and organizational competencies. The latter denotes some form of transfer of emissions or emission-generating activities, a process that leaves a firm's own competencies and technological assets essentially unaltered. Under either approach, an organization could act entirely on its own, or alternatively interact with external actors, including other companies in its supply chain or industry, competitors, companies in different sectors, NGOs, and regulatory agencies.

Kolk and Pinkse captured these two aspects of strategic response in the form of a typology, depicted in Figure 5.6. The horizontal axis indicates the two main forms of strategic response, namely innovation and compensation; the vertical axis identifies the degree to which a company chooses to interact with other organizations in pursuing its objectives. Where a firm acts alone, this represents an internal organizational response. Should the organization choose to cooperate or collaborate with other organizations, its interaction may be either within its own supply chain (a vertical interaction) or with organizations outside its supply chain (a horizontal interaction), as exemplified by the

| | | Strategic approach | |
		Innovation	Compensation
Type of interaction	Internal (within the firm)	Process improvement (Cell 1)	Internal transfer of emissions reductions (Cell 2)
	Vertical (within the supply chain)	Product development (Cell 3)	Supply-chain measures (Cell 4)
	Horizontal (beyond the supply chain)	New product and/or market combinations (Cell 5)	Acquisition of emissions credits (Cell 6)

Figure 5.6 Strategic options for climate change

Source: Figure 1 in Ans Kolk and Jonatan Pinkse, 'Business Responses to Climate Change: Identifying Emergent Strategies', in *California Management Review* vol. 47, no. 3 (Spring 2005), pp. 6–20. © 2005 by the Regents of the University of California. Reprinted by permission of the University of California Press.

practice of forming partnerships with competitors and/or NGOs to develop low-emissions technologies.

As Figure 5.6 illustrates, within each strategic response, organizations have choices about how to address the issue of climate change. Under an innovative approach, a firm could seek improvements in the production process (Cell 1), or develop existing and/or new emission-reducing products (Cell 3), or explore new product/market combinations (Cell 5) via a strategic alliance or some other form of inter-firm cooperation. In the case of compensation, it might engage in the transfer of emissions within the company (Cell 2); or develop external relationships within or beyond the supply chain (Cell 4 and Cell 6) aimed at achieving its objectives through, for example, purchasing emission credits from other organizations or partnering in offset projects as under the Kyoto Protocol (see Chapter 2). As the latter approach illustrates, innovative and compensatory responses are frequently interrelated in that an innovating firm may be the source of surplus emission credits purchased by an organization that has chosen to adopt a compensatory approach to the problem of climate change.

As the authors have pointed out, companies that take action with regard to climate change do not necessarily adopt all the measures indicated by the typology, but it is probable that they may use different combinations of approach as part of their overall environmental strategy. In order to explore actual corporate responses, Kolk and Pinkse subsequently developed a measurement instrument based on their typology which they applied to information that was provided under the Carbon Disclosure Project (see Chapter 2). With the aid of cluster analysis, their investigations revealed six different strategy configurations for climate change. Table 5.1 gives a brief description of the emergent patterns of corporate response identified in the empirical analysis.

Table 5.1 Patterns of corporate response

Type of response	% of companies involved	Basic orientation/posture
Cautious planners	31	Preparing for action, but with little activity with regard to the different policy options
Emergent planners	36	Primarily involved in target setting but at an early stage with regard to implementing the necessary organizational changes
Internal explorers	14	Focus on internal targets and improvements in the production process (e.g. energy efficiency measures)
Vertical explorers	10	Focus on developing measures upstream and/or downstream in the supply chain
Horizontal explorers	5	Primarily focused on exploring opportunities in markets beyond their current operations, including via inter-firm cooperation
Emissions traders	4	Main approach is engaging in emission markets and offset projects

On the basis of the figures in Table 5.1, two-thirds of businesses fell into the first two categories, suggesting that for many firms the implementation of strategies aimed at addressing climate change was still at a preliminary stage. For the one-third of organizations that were more proactive in their responses, a majority tended to focus on the opportunities available either within the organization or in the firm's supply chain, whilst just under 10 per cent were involved in emission trading or exploring the benefits of market diversification and collaboration. As Kolk and Pinkse observed, managers have various strategic options when addressing the market aspects of responding to climate change, and current strategies suggested different combinations of the various market possibilities. In their opinion, different managerial perceptions of the risks and/ or opportunities related to climate change could lead companies to choose different approaches, some of which may not necessarily be path dependent.

LEVY AND KOLK'S TYPOLOGY OF OIL MNC RESPONSES TO CLIMATE CHANGE

Levy and Kolk's analysis took as its starting point the fact that companies in the same industry often exhibited different strategic responses in addressing the issue of climate change. The authors argued that these responses—which were a blend of market and non-market strategies—developed within an environment where there were both divergent and convergent pressures facing organizational decision-makers. Within the oil industry, Levy and Kolk identified the home country environment and each individual firm's history and experiences as major divergent institutional pressures shaping corporate responses, with the participation of oil MNCs in the global industry and in the climate change issue itself seen as the main convergent influences impacting on company decisions. The balance between these two sets of forces, they believed, was liable to shift over time as the level of certainty surrounding the issue tended to increase.

Using data gathered from four major oil multinationals based in both the United States and Europe, Levy and Kolk examined the question of why businesses with similar internal competencies and external market conditions might pursue different strategies. As part of their analysis, they adopted a two-dimensional typology (or matrix) originally put forward by Gladwin and Walter (1980) to classify each company's environmental strategy (see Figure 5.7). On one axis, responses were designated either 'uncooperative' or 'cooperative' depending on the degree of support for mandatory emission controls and investment in renewable energy technologies. On the other axis, companies were deemed either 'assertive' or 'unassertive' according to the level of support or opposition to regulatory efforts. The resultant four-cell matrix provided a means of identifying four strategic postures which were named 'resistant', 'avoidant', 'compliant', and 'proactive'.

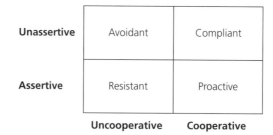

	Uncooperative	Cooperative
Unassertive	Avoidant	Compliant
Assertive	Resistant	Proactive

Figure 5.7 Strategic responses to climate change

Source: Figure 1 in Ans Kolk and Jonatan Pinkse, 'Business Responses to Climate Change: Identifying Emergent Strategies', in *California Management Review* vol. 47, no. 3 (Spring 2005), pp. 6–20. © 2005 by the Regents of the University of California. Reprinted by permission of the University of California Press.

The four case study firms were then placed within the matrix and the authors indicated their perceived direction of movement between cells as the balance of convergent and divergent pressures changed over time.

Overall, Levy and Kolk's investigations suggested that the discernable differences in corporate responses to climate change within the oil industry could not be adequately explained by the conventional drivers of strategy. By focusing on the institutional context within which corporate decisions are formulated and implemented, the authors highlighted how a firm's strategic options are shaped by multiple competing pressures including regulatory expectations, norms governing business/government relations, and perceptions concerning future technologies. These various influences were associated with the institutional context of the MNC's home county and with the specific history of each company, pointing to the importance of local context in influencing initial corporate reactions. With the shifting balance of divergent and convergent pressures over time, Levy and Kolk argued that home country and firm-level context become less important as convergent pressures at a global and issue level tend to predominate. Given the frequent interactions within this changing institutional context, oil MNCs have tended to develop similar outlooks on markets and technologies. Only time will tell whether this trend will continue.

6 Examining the business case for corporate greening

To believe that environment regulations improve corporate competitiveness, it is necessary to believe that the average company routinely misses profitable opportunities to develop environmental products or install anti-pollution devices.

(Cairncross, 1995)

Managers need to go beyond the question 'Does it pay to be green?' and ask instead 'Under what circumstances do particular kinds of environmental investments deliver benefits to shareholders?'

(Reinhardt, 1999a)

Companies that manage and mitigate their exposure to climate-change risks while seeking new opportunities for profit will generate a competitive advantage over rivals in a carbon-constrained future.

(Lash and Wellington, 2007)

Introduction

Writing about the 'market for virtue', David Vogel (2006: 16) argues that 'it is impossible to exaggerate the significance of the contemporary claim that there is a business case for corporate responsibility, business ethics, corporate citizenship, environmental stewardship, pollution control, sustainable development and the like.' As Vogel points out, the reasons why firms engage in socially and environmentally responsible forms of behaviour can be many and various and are not always related to improving the bottom line. That said, his contention is that, while profitability may not be the only reason why businesses will or should behave virtuously, it has become the most influential consideration for managers and one which is evidenced by the large and growing literature on whether corporate social responsibility 'pays' (see e.g. Worthington, 2009).

Where environmental protection is concerned, business case arguments have increasingly come to the fore since the emergence of ecological modernization theory in the closing decades of the twentieth century. This theory challenged the long-established belief that economic advancement and environmental protection tended to be inimical and helped to support the as-yet minority view amongst business leaders that corporate environmentalism could be economically and commercially beneficial. Under what became known as the 'win-win', 'double dividend', or 'greengold hypothesis', it was argued that by engaging in voluntary environmental initiatives businesses could improve their profitability and competitiveness—a 'win' for the firm and a 'win' for the environment. Subsequent development of this pro-greening argument saw the marshalling of theoretical and empirical support for the 'win-win' case and for the claim that some firms were clearly motivated to invest in green initiatives because it offered an opportunity to improve their long-term profitability and competitive advantage (Bansal and Roth, 2000).

As might be anticipated, the win-win position has not gone unchallenged, nor has there been any shortage of attempts by researchers to investigate whether corporate greening actually 'pays', either in the short or longer term. In this chapter, we examine this debate in detail and highlight the findings of numerous empirical studies of the claimed relationship between environmental and business performance. The analysis shows that, despite a large and still growing literature on the business case for corporate greening, there is still no consensus of opinion on whether greening ultimately pays. Considerable progress has been made, however, on identifying some of the key variables that can affect whether beyond-compliance environmental responses can benefit the firm and in providing a theoretical explanation of the claimed link between proactive environmental strategies and competitive advantage at the firm level.

GREEN SNAPSHOT: WAL-MART

For many larger organizations, including Wal-Mart, the claimed link between environmental performance and business performance is no longer in dispute. In October 2005, the company announced its belief that sustainability was the route to becoming an even better company and identified three areas where it could become a more sustainable enterprise and simultaneously gain economic and commercial benefits: action on climate change, waste reduction, and sustainable products. Wal-Mart's objectives include ultimately becoming entirely supplied by renewable energy, creating zero waste, and selling products that help to conserve resources and protect the environment.

Central to its belief that sustainability makes good business sense is the conviction that economic value can be created by driving innovation along its extended value chain, from the raw materials that eventually go into its products to the disposal of those products at the end of their lifecycle. Porter and Kramer (2011) report that by taking action in its value chain (e.g. by reducing its packaging and rerouting its delivery vehicles), the company has been able to lower its carbon emissions and made savings of $200 million in costs in 2009, despite shipping more products overall. In its 2010 Global Sustainability Report, the company accepts, however, that it still faces considerable challenges with regard to further reductions of packaging and eliminating PVC.

Does it pay to be green? The early debate

In a celebrated article in the *New York Times Magazine* in 1970, Milton Friedman argued that firms that engaged in beyond-compliance social and environmental initiatives were acting against the interests of their shareholders. Friedman's view was not only that a firm's directors were ill-equipped to make decisions on issues of social and environmental responsibility, but that as agents for the firm's owners (the principals) they also had a fiduciary responsibility to the shareholders, not to some broader conception of the social good (Worthington, 2009). The social responsibility of a business, suggested Friedman, was to increase its profits so long as it complied with the law and operated in an ethical manner; accordingly, spending the owners' money on pollution control expenditures beyond what was required by law was tantamount to practising pure and unadulterated socialism.

As Hoffman (2001*a*) subsequently observed, Friedman's apparent antagonism to proactive environmental management resonated with business sentiment of the time. In keeping with what is generally known as the traditional or neo-classical view of economics, environmental protection was seen by business leaders at best as a necessary evil and at worst as a temporary inconvenience. Put at its simplest, the claim was that, if firms were obliged to invest in environmental improvements in order to reduce their environmental impact, this would increase their costs, reduce their profits and result in a loss of competitiveness (Jaffe et al., 1995; Lanoie and Tanguay, 2000). In short, a win for the environment meant that the firm would lose out; greening, in other words, conflicted with the achievement of other key business objectives.

The 'win-lose' position is exemplified by Walley and Whitehead's article in the 1994 May/June edition of the *Harvard Business Review* which suggested that responding to environmental problems has always been a no-win proposition for managers. The authors argued that with environmental costs skyrocketing at most companies and with little chance of economic payback in sight, the idea that it can pay firms to be green appeared highly unrealistic. Instead of focusing on win-win solutions, they advised firms to concentrate on what they called 'the trade-off zone', where any environmental benefit that might be derived from undertaking environmental initiatives was weighed judiciously against the value destruction such investment might occasion.

Walley and Whitehead were not alone in voicing scepticism of the position being adopted by eco-modernists. Cairncross (1995), for example, claimed that most of the 'low hanging fruit' had probably already been picked, ensuring that any further expenditures on environmental improvements would result in rising business costs. Maxwell (1996) argued that greening the firm would create losers as well as winners and that what might prove a competitive advantage for some would be a competitive disadvantage for others. Echoing Walley and Whitehead, Palmer et al. (1995) suggested that the increasing complexities of environmental issues and the scale of environmental expenditures meant that opportunities to gain from corporate environmentalism tended to be rare.

In cautioning against an optimistic view of corporate greening, the sceptics were responding to a new perspective of environmental management which was attracting support amongst politicians, practitioners, and academics alike (Russo and Fouts, 1997). Foremost amongst these was Harvard Professor Michael Porter who argued that the conventional wisdom that environmental regulations drove up business costs was based on a static view of the business environment (Porter, 1991; Porter and van der Linde, 1995a, 1995b; Esty and Porter, 1998). The essence of the Porter hypothesis, as it became known, was that given the dynamic nature of the environment in which businesses operated, properly designed environmental standards and regulations could drive corporate decision-makers to seek innovative solutions to environmental problems, thereby enhancing resource productivity and generating what he called 'innovation offsets'. Far from being a threat to the firm, Porter argued that regulation could encourage businesses to uncover and implement more efficient and cost-saving opportunities (Ng, 2005), a net positive force driving the private sector and the economy as a whole towards greater competitiveness in international markets (Jaffe et al., 1995; Russo and Fouts, 1997; Karagozoglu and Lindell, 2000).

This idea that greening the firm could prove both profitable and a source of competitive advantage had support in various quarters. Dechant and Altman (1994) claimed that the practice of environmental management was becoming an essential part of doing business rather than a side issue, an observation supported by Shrivastava (1992) and by Welford and Gouldson (1993) amongst others. Bonifant et al. (1995) suggested that firms could gain a competitive advantage by undertaking environmental investments that helped to reduce business costs and create market opportunities. Gallarotti (1995) reached a similar conclusion, arguing that the emergence of the green movement and stricter environmental regulations meant that firms would be able to profit from environmentally sound strategies that could help reduce organizational costs, achieve better market penetration, reduce corporate risk, improve stakeholder relationships, and provide rent-seeking opportunities via manipulation of the supply chain.

GREEN SNAPSHOT: BLOOM ENERGY

California-based technology company Bloom Energy is confident that it has developed an ideal win-win product, one that allows its customers to save money and at the same time reduce their carbon footprint. Based on a sand-like powder, rather than precious metals or corrosive materials, the firm's Energy Servers have been described as a mini power station containing fuel cells that can run on anything from natural gas to renewables, creating electricity in a far more efficient and less polluting way than existing technologies. It is claimed that a stack of fuel cells no larger than a shoe box could produce enough electricity to power an average home, while a freezer-sized unit could meet the energy needs of 200 homes or a small office building.

Bloom's claim that its device can help its customers to lower their energy costs, reduce their carbon footprints, enhance their energy security, and promote their commitment to a greener future simultaneously appears to have some credibility in corporate circles. Current users of its technology include Coca Cola, eBay, Federal Express, Google, Safeway, and Wal-Mart.

In recognition of these two opposing positions, the *Harvard Business Review* commissioned the views of twelve experts on whether greening the firm pays; these were published in the 1994 July/August edition of the journal. While some supported either Walley and Whitehead's or Porter's views on the question of environmental management, others adopted a midway position or argued that the views of the two camps were often misunderstood or misconstrued. In a rejoinder, Walley and Whitehead claimed that they were not calling for firms to give up on environmental action, but that the challenge was to decide on how fast and how far to go; each decision should be judged on its merits, not on seductive claims that environmental responses inevitably give rise to improved business performance.

The assertion that corporate responses to environmental management could vary according to circumstances was subsequently picked up by Rugman and Verbeke (1998*a*) who produced a useful organizing framework (see Box 6.1) for the literature on corporate strategy and environmental regulations and positioned the views of the main protagonists and the twelve experts within the resultant matrix. An important insight to emerge from Rugman and Verbeke's analysis was that, at the firm level, environmental regulations could evoke a range of managerial responses and could have a wide variety of impacts on a firm's economic performance. This implied that a simple linear relationship between environmental performance and a positive or negative economic outcome did not fully reflect reality, but needed to include an investigation of the circumstances under which (i.e. when) greening might or might not pay (Reinhardt, 1999*a*, 1999*b*). Fuller consideration of this issue can be found below, following an examination of a representative

---

BOX 6.1 AN ORGANIZING FRAMEWORK OF CORPORATE STRATEGIES AND ENVIRONMENTAL REGULATIONS

		Impact of regulations on industrial versus environmental performance	
		Conflicting	Complementary
Time horizon of managerial response	Static	Conventional economic view	'Win-win' view
	Dynamic	Walley and Whitehead view	Porter hypothesis

Source: Adapted from Rugman and Verbeke (1998*a*).

Notes: 1. Industrial performance at firm level includes profitability and growth.
2. Environmental performance includes ecological impact, resource usage, and emission levels.
3. The time horizon axis relates to managerial perceptions of the longer term (dynamic) or more immediate (static) impact of environmental regulations.

cross-section of empirical investigations of the relationship between a firm's environmental management practices and its subsequent business performance.

Testing the 'win-win' hypothesis: the empirical evidence

Much of the early debate on the business case for corporate greening was conducted at a theoretical and conceptual level and was often supported by anecdotal evidence of organizations that had or had not benefited from investing in environmental improvements (Cordeiro and Sarkis, 1997; Sharma and Aragón-Correa, 2005). One often-quoted example of gains from environmental action was 3M's Pollution Prevention Pays (3Ps) programme which at the time was hailed as a practical demonstration of the win-win position (Hart and Ahuja, 1996) and a confirmation of Porter's view that pollution represented a form of inefficiency that revealed flaws in product design, the choice of production inputs, and/ or the manufacturing process (Porter and van der Linde, 1995*a*, 1995*b*; Nehrt, 1996). Understandably, proponents of the win-lose persuasion focused their attention on firms with contrasting experiences, including Texaco, whose total investments in environmental compliance and emission reduction in the late 1990s were said to be three times the book value of the company and twice the size of its current asset base (Hart and Ahuja, 1996).

The first serious and consistent attempts to investigate whether corporate greening represented a competitive asset or liability began to emerge around the mid-1990s with the publication of a stream of empirical research on the link between environmental strategy/management and various measures of business performance (Sharma and Aragón-Correa, 2005). In addition to testing statistically the validity of the win-win hypothesis, some authors also developed models or conceptual frameworks to illustrate the hypothesized links that were thought to lie at the heart of the business case for investing in environmental improvements. A selection of these models/frameworks is illustrated below in Box 6.2.

The examples contained in Box 6.2 indicate that the general consensus among researchers was that some form of linear relationship existed between a firm's environmental strategies and/or management practices and its subsequent business performance, with the former impacting on the latter either positively or negatively according to circumstances. As Hart and Ahuja (1996) and King and Lenox (2001) have insightfully pointed out, however, it is not entirely clear whether environmental initiatives at firm level result in an improved financial situation or whether financially successful firms are the ones that can afford to spend money on environmental improvements in keeping with what became known as 'slack-resources' theory (see Chapter 4).

BOX 6.2 SELECTED MODELS/FRAMEWORKS OF THE ENVIRONMENTAL MANAGEMENT/STRATEGY AND BUSINESS PERFORMANCE RELATIONSHIP

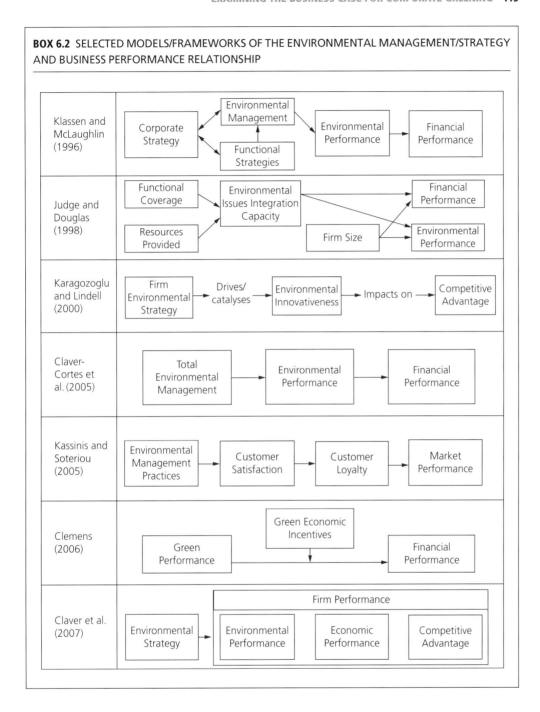

The models/frameworks illustrated above also indicate that researchers varied in their views as to the key building blocks and relationships thought to explain how

environmental performance could affect business outcomes. In Klassen and McLaughlin's model (1996), the firm's environmental management practices were linked to its corporate and functional strategies and together were seen to determine its environmental performance, which in turn affected its financial performance by two main pathways, namely cost saving or market opportunities. In contrast, Judge and Douglas (1998) adopted a resource-based perspective which emphasized functional coverage and the resources provided by firms as key antecedents of the development of a capability that could integrate environmental issues into the strategic planning process. This capability was deemed to be the source of a firm's environmental and financial performance, with these two performance measures separated in the authors' model rather than interrelated.

Given such differences in theoretical approach, it is perhaps not surprising to discover that the empirical findings of the various studies that have been published between the mid-1990s and the present day provide mixed evidence on the question of whether corporate greening pays. Table 6.1 indicates that results range from the positive through neutral to the negative, although research that indicates a positive relationship between environmental performance and firm performance tends to predominate. This disparity in research findings can also be found in studies that have examined the link between firm performance and both quality management and corporate social responsibility practices in private sector business organizations (see e.g. Claver-Cortés et al., 2005; Salzmann et al., 2005).

Table 6.1 also illustrates that considerable variation exists in both the designs and implementation aspects of the different research projects, including:

• study focus—with some studies examining the link between environmental regulation and competitiveness while most tend to explore how environmental strategy and/or environmental management practices impact on financial performance;
• research design and methodology—with examples of cross-sectional, longitudinal, and case study approaches as well as different data collection and analysis techniques employed, including the use of surveys, archival searches, interviews, event studies, regression analysis, etc.;
• geographical coverage—with both single-country (especially the United States) and cross-national studies evident and a clear focus on the developed economies;
• firms, industries, and sectors studied—with varieties in firm size, industry or industries studied, and sectorial focus. Large firm research in heavily polluting industries figures prominently;
• environmental performance variables—with a diverse range of measures employed, including third-party environmental ratings, toxic release data, and environmental investments. As Claver-Cortés et al. (2005) point out, some studies use environmental management variables, while others focus on environmental performance;

Table 6.1 The environment–business performance link: some key texts

Authors	Study focus	Research approach and methodology	Geographical coverage	Firms/industries/ sectors	Environmental performance variables employed	Business performance variables employed	Summary of study main findings
Hamilton (1995)	Media and stock market reactions to TRI data	Event study; data from TRI and stock market	United States	436 publicly-traded companies	TRI emissions and TRI publications	Stock price	No relationship for amount of emissions; negative relationship for TRI publications
Hart and Ahuja (1996)	Emission reduction and firm performance	Longitudinal study using published data bases; multiple regression analysis	United States	127 firms	Emissions reductions based on TRI	ROA; ROE; ROS	Pollution prevention has a positive influence on financial performance within one to two years
Klassen and McLaughlin (1996)	Impact of environmental management on firm performance	Event study using archival data of performance	United States	US firms with environmental awards and crises. Several industries involved	Environmental awards	Stock market returns	Environmental awards led to significant positive changes in market valuation; crises had a negative impact
Cordeiro and Sarkis (1997)	Environmental proactivism and firm performance	Analysis of published accounting data and industry analyst's forecasts. Cross-sectional design	United States	523 firms submitting TRI data	TRI releases—data on emissions and waste releases	Industry analyst earnings-per-share growth forecasts	A significant negative relationship between environmental performance and earnings-per-share growth forecasts
Russo and Fouts (1997)	Corporate environmental performance and profitability	Two-year study using published data	United States	243 firms from several sectors	Environmental ratings based on compliance, expenditures and waste reduction	ROA	Environmental performance had a positive and significant effect on ROA; moderated by industry growth

(continued)

Table 6.1 Continued

Authors	Study focus	Research approach and methodology	Geographical coverage	Firms/industries/ sectors	Environmental performance variables employed	Business performance variables employed	Summary of study main findings
Hitchens et al. (1998)	Company competitiveness and environmental regulation	Matched-pair approach using published data and interviews	Germany, Italy, Northern Ireland, Republic of Ireland	67 food processing firms across European countries	Comparative costs of environmental compliance and practices	Value-added per employee; productivity; export share; employment growth	No clear relationship between company competitiveness and the size of regulation costs
Klassen and Whybark (1999)	Environmental technology and manufacturing performance	Cross-sectional study using focus group, interviews, and surveys	United States	69 firms in the furniture industry	Environmental technology portfolio and TRI released data	Manufacturing performance—objective and perceptual measures	Environmental technology has a positive and significant effect on manufacturing and environmental performance
Wubben (1999)	Environmental legislation and competitiveness	Case study approach using a survey and interview methodology	European Union	EU chemical industry	European laws relevant to the industry	Short-term profitability and long-term innovativeness	Legislation has created a rat-race among larger players at a longer term cost to smaller companies
Dowell et al. (2000)	Impact of global environmental standards on market value	Three-year study using published data on environmental standards and market value	US-based multinational enterprises	Manufacturing and mining firms in S&P 500	3rd party environmental standards	Stock market value (Tobin's Q)	Firms adopting a single stringent standard have a higher market value
Gilley et al. (2000)	Environmental initiatives and anticipated economic performance	Event study based over thirteen-year period using published data	United States	Firms in manufacturing and service industries with environmental announcements	Announced environmental initiatives/events in the study period	Stock returns	No apparent overall effect on stock returns of announced initiatives

Karagozoglu and Lindell (2000)	Progressive environmental policies and their financial and competitive impact	Cross-sectional study using a survey of company CEO's	United States	Hi-tech and traditional manufacturing industry firms	Self-rated environmental performance	Self-rated financial performance	A proactive environmental strategy leads to environmental innovation and environmental competitive advantage
Halme and Niskanen (2001)	Environmental protection measures and shareholder value	Longitudinal analysis of industry data using an event study methodology	Finland	Forestry industry firms	Environmental investments announced by the press	Share price—stock return window	Environmental investments have a negative instantaneous effect on share price but no adverse and permanent impact on firm value
King and Lenox (2001)	Environmental performance and financial valuation	Longitudinal study using TRI data and corporate data via Compustat	United States	652 manufacturing firms	Total emissions and other emission measures	Financial performance measured by Tobin's Q	Negative association between relatively high toxic emissions and the firm's Tobin's Q. Evidence of an association between lower pollution and high financial valuation
Sarkis and Cordeiro (2001)	Environmental practices and firm performance	Cross-sectional study using published TRI and financial data	United States	482 firms in multiple industries	TRI data variables on emissions, waste discharges, recycling, etc.	ROS	Both pollution prevention and end-of-pipe efficiencies are negatively associated to ROS, with the relationship larger and more significant for pollution prevention

(continued)

Table 6.1 Continued

Authors	Study focus	Research approach and methodology	Geographical coverage	Firms/industries/sectors	Environmental performance variables employed	Business performance variables employed	Summary of study main findings
Wagner and Schaltegger (2003)	Corporate environmental strategy, economic and environmental performance	Cross-sectional survey using the European Business Environment Barometer	Various European Countries	European manufacturing industry	Self-assessed multiple performance measures including resource reductions, emission reductions, reduced risk	Environmental profit indices based on environmental competitiveness survey	Firms with shareholder value-oriented strategies have a more positive relationship between economic and environmental performance
Darnall and Ytterhus (2005)	Environmental and financial performance	Cross-sectional study using survey data collected for an OECD project	Canada, France, Germany, Hungary, Japan, Norway, and US	Manufacturing firms	Reduction in environmental impact measures	Profitability	No significant difference in the profitability between dirty and clean sectors and between early and later mover sectors
Kassinis and Soteriou (2005)	Environmental management practices and firm performance	Cross-sectional approach using a survey and pilot interviews	Austria, France, Germany, Greece, Italy, Portugal, Spain, UK, and others	Hotel industry across the EU—at the high-end of the market	Environmental management practices including recycling, energy and water saving	Growth in profit, revenues, and sales	The relationship between environmental performance and market performance is indirect, it is mediated by customer satisfaction and loyalty
Wagner (2005)	Environmental strategies, economic and environmental performance	Cross-sectional analysis using a purposive survey methodology	Germany, Italy, Holland, UK	European manufacturing industry—pulp and paper	Various emissions and input measures	Profitability ratios—ROS, ROCE, ROE	Pollution prevention appears to have a more positive impact than end-of-pipe approaches but no significant relationships

Study	Topic	Method	Country	Sample	Green performance measure	Financial performance measure	Findings
Clemens (2006)	Small firm green performance, financial performance, and green economic initiatives	Cross-sectional study using a survey instrument	United States	Small US scrap yards in the steel industry	Relative green performance self-rated by respondents, including environmental responsiveness and consciousness	Relative profitability—self-rated items included growth in earnings and revenue market share, ROA, profitability	A positive relationship exists between green practices and financial performance and this strengthens when green incentives are fewer
Claver et al. (2007)	Environmental management and firm performance	Case study methodology using surveys, interviews, and archival data	Spain	Farming cooperative—fruit, vegetables, oil, spices	Environmental protection measures based on a prevention logic	Relative profitability and valued added, including ROA	Environmental management has a positive effect on firm performance
Aragón-Correa et al. (2008)	Environmental strategy and performance in small firms	Cross-sectional study using interviews and a survey instrument	Spain	108 automotive repair small businesses	Innovative preventive and eco-efficient practices self-assessed by respondents	Perceptual measures of financial performance	Firms with the most proactive environmental practices exhibited a significantly positive financial performance
Clarkson et al. (2010)	Consequences of proactive environmental strategies	Longitudinal analysis using published data from the TRI and other sources	United States	Pulp paper, chemical, oil and gas, and metals and mining, 242 firms	Toxic releases	ROA and operating cash flows, ratio of total debts to total assets	Significant improvements (or declines) in environmental improvements in the prior periods can lead to improvements (or declines) in financial performance in subsequent periods

- business performance variables—again, considerable variety is evident in the research, including measures of financial performance which is the most popular variable employed by researchers.

As several observers have indicated, conceptual and methodological differences such as these may go a long way towards explaining why research findings point to different verdicts on the validity of the win-win hypothesis (Klassen and McLaughlin, 1996; Russo and Fouts, 1997; Schaltegger and Synnestvedt, 2002; Claver et al., 2007).

A closer examination of the studies highlighted in Table 6.1 equally reveals that some researchers have identified factors that appear to affect the strength of the relationship between environmental performance and business outcomes. Russo and Fouts (1997), for instance, suggest that the positive effect of environmental proactivity on economic performance increases with industry growth, while Wagner and Schaltegger (2004) point to the impact of different environmental strategies on a firm's economic performance. To develop the analysis further, we now turn to an examination of some of the key variables that are thought to moderate the relationship between business and environmental performance. In short, we ask, under what circumstances does greening the firm pay/not pay?

When does greening pay?

All investments by firms represent something of a risk; some will be successful and will bring net advantages to the organization, and others will fail or will generate costs that far outweigh the benefits gained. In purely economic and commercial terms, investments in environmental improvements are no different from other types of corporate expenditure (Willard, 2002). If such investments are seen as a business rather than social responsibility issue, the key question is when does corporate greening pay (Reinhardt, 1998; King and Lenox, 2001; Orsato, 2006). Reinhardt's observation (1998) that there is no one-size-fits-all environmental policy points to a simple answer to this question: it depends upon the circumstances.

Academic investigations of possible contingent influences identify a number of internal and external variables that appear to affect the relationship between a firm's environmental strategy/management practices and its subsequent business performance. Externally, an organization's ability to create value through environmental action and capture it from other economic actors has been linked to the existence of favourable (or unfavourable) conditions in its various operating domains (Reinhardt, 1998, 1999*a*, 1999*b*; Hart and Milstein, 1999; Karagozoglu and Lindell, 2000; Wagner and Wehrmeyer, 2002; Ambec and Lanoie, 2008). For example, Karagozoglu and Lindell's study (2000) of the key variables at the core of the win-win model suggests that supportive/

less supportive regulations act as a moderator of the relationship between environmental innovativeness and environmental competitive advantage, although they do not appear to trigger innovation as suggested by Porter and van der Linde (1995*a*, 1995*b*). Stoeckl (2004) maintains that the firms most likely to gain from proactive responses will be those operating in highly competitive markets, where product differentiation is possible on environmental grounds and where consumers are more willing to pay higher prices for greener products.

Regarding internal influences, the research generally focuses on the characteristics of the firm and the quality of its management. In one of the earlier studies, Hart and Ahuja (1996) found that emission reduction strategies enhanced financial performance more for higher polluters than for businesses with lower emission levels, with a time lag before pollution prevention measures appeared to drop to the bottom line. Timing, together with the intensity of environmental investments, also featured in Nehrt's cross-national research (1996) of the chemical-bleached paper pulp industry, with earlier investors in pollution-reducing processing equipment having higher profit growth than later investors, irrespective of national differences in environmental regulations.

With respect to managerial aspects, several studies have suggested that the ability to leverage financial and/or competitive advantage from green investments will tend to be contingent on factors such as managerial integration capacities, executive creativity, risk management capabilities, commitment to proactive environmental strategies, and the choice of environmental technologies (Shrivastava, 1995*b*; Judge and Douglas, 1998; Wagner and Wehrmeyer, 2002; Ng, 2005; Lash and Wellington, 2007). One important contribution to this debate has been Christmann's investigations (2000) of the role of complementary assets as moderators of the relationship between a firm's environmental actions and its competitiveness. Drawing on survey data from eighty-eight US chemical companies, Christmann has argued that firms need to possess certain resources if they are to capture the benefits associated with a particular environmental strategy, technology, or innovation. Insofar as not all firms necessarily possess these assets, this could explain why some are unable to gain a cost advantage from environmental proactivity, while others are able to do so via best practice environmental management (see below).

In keeping with Christmann's resource-based perspective, a more recent study of environmental strategy and performance in Spanish small firms (Aragón-Correa et al., 2008) suggests that even small and medium-sized enterprises (SMEs) can adopt proactive environmental practices and that these practices can lead to superior financial performance via specific capabilities that are based on the unique strategic characteristics of smaller enterprises. As with larger businesses, differences between smaller firms regarding the acquisition and deployment of valuable organizational capabilities could help explain why win-win opportunities are more apparent in some SMEs than in others, with firm size a relevant rather than a deterministic factor (Aragón-Correa et al., 2008).

Extending the business case construct

While the notion of the business case for corporate greening tends to be associated primarily with measurable economic and financial advantages accruing to business organizations (see Table 6.1), the concept can be used in its broadest sense to mean any important benefit that firms can gain from investing in environmental initiatives. Defined in this way, it is clear from observations made in this and previous chapters that firms that undertake environmental improvements may gain organizational benefits in at least four key areas. These interrelated strands to the business case—improved organizational performance, building stakeholder relationships, contributing to strategic objectives, and responding to a changing external environment—are depicted in Figure 6.1.

With regard to improved organizational performance, the focus has largely been on greening as a means of achieving financial and risk-bearing economies (Dechant and Altman, 1994; Bonifant et al., 1995; Gallarotti, 1995). As indicated in Chapter 4, research suggests that the ability to leverage economic opportunity and/or to reduce threats and risks to the organizations are two of the key motivations that explain why firms engage in beyond-compliance environmental behaviour. On the upside, it has been argued that greening may give rise to a variety of corporate advantages including:

• improvements in product quality, process efficiency, and resource productivity (Gallarotti, 1995; Porter and van der Linde, 1995a, 1995b);
• cost savings via access to cheaper capital, reductions in resource usage, energy consumption, and waste production and disposal (Dechant and Altman, 1994; Bonifant et al., 1995; Hart and Ahuja, 1996; Lanoie and Tanguay, 2000; Esty and Winston, 2006);

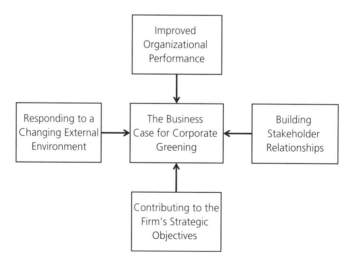

Figure 6.1 The business case for corporate greening

Source: Worthington (2009). Reproduced by kind permission of Springer Science+Business Media.

- increased revenue from exploiting new green market niches (Gallarotti, 1995; Ambec and Lanoie, 2008);
- enhanced brand image and corporate reputation (Guimaraes and Liska, 1995; De Simone and Popoff, 1997).

On the downside, the focus has been on the management of potential threats/risks such as costly litigation and fines associated with environmental accidents, potential loss of reputation, being behind the regulatory curve, and adverse customer reactions to a firm's environmental performance (Russo and Fouts, 1997; Lankoski, 2006; Lash and Wellington, 2007).

As will be evident from the above discussion, many of the claimed improvements in organizational performance have been linked, at least in part, to the firm's capacity to enhance its stakeholder relationships via its environmental actions. Reference has already been made to the fact that stakeholder pressures are regarded as one of the key drivers of corporate ecological responsiveness (see Chapter 4), although the precise influence of the various stakeholder groups at firm level will tend to vary according to circumstances (Henriques and Sadorsky, 1999; Aragón-Correa and Rubio-López, 2007). By undertaking environmental investments, it is claimed that firms can gain legitimacy in the eyes of key stakeholders, including customers, regulators, creditors, suppliers, employees, NGOs, and the wider community (Dechant and Altman, 1994; Gallarotti, 1995; De Simone and Popoff, 1997; Coulson and Monks, 1999; Miles and Covin, 2000; Florida and Davison, 2001; Claver et al., 2007; Ambec and Lanoie, 2008), thereby helping to induce positive stakeholder responses (e.g. brand loyalty; increased employee morale) and to reduce the threat of adverse stakeholder reactions brought about by a poor environmental performance (e.g. customer boycotts; threat of further regulation; hostile media comment).

In responding positively to calls for higher levels of environmental protection, a firm may also be able to achieve what is called—in the strategic management literature—a better 'fit' between the organization's internal environment (i.e. its resources, capabilities, structures, etc.) and its changing external context. Given the rising public and political expectations that businesses should demonstrate as well as their social and environmental responsibility, organizations will face increased pressures to examine their internal practices, processes, and procedures, including how these impact on the natural environment. Failure to do so could give rise to a significant reputational risk in the court of public opinion, resulting in a negative effect on brand and shareholder value and on a firm's competitiveness in domestic and international markets (Lash and Wellington, 2007).

Demonstrating one's green credentials is not simply a matter of risk reduction, but can also be used strategically to capture value for the organization. Firms that see environmentalism strategically undertake environmental expenditures in the hope of gaining a competitive edge over their rivals while simultaneously leveraging the performance and stakeholder benefits discussed above. In Esty and Winston's memorable assertion

---

GREEN SNAPSHOT: BENEFITTING FROM ACTION ON CLIMATE CHANGE

While UK companies have something of a mixed record where greenhouse emissions reduction targets are concerned (see Green Snapshot in Chapter 5), the 2011 Carbon Disclosure Project (CDP) Annual Report indicates that a majority (68 per cent) of the world's largest corporations now claim that action on climate change lies at the heart of their business strategies. Companies ranked in the top ten by the CDP, on the basis of the amount of information they disclosed and their performance in reducing carbon emissions, included Philips, BMW, Honda, Tesco, Bank of America, Bayer, and Sony. Apple and Amazon were evidently among the companies that chose not to disclose information.

 The report—which was drawn up by consultants PriceWaterhouseCoopers—also highlights a correlation between high carbon performance and improved stock market performance, with a majority of initiatives on emissions reduction apparently achieving a payback within three years or less. According to the CEO of the CDP, there was clear evidence that managing and reducing carbon emissions make good business sense, particularly in an era of rising energy prices and concerns over the security of energy supplies. Companies yet to respond to the changing environment, he suggested, would have to work hard to remain competitive in an increasingly resource-constrained, low-carbon economy.

(2006), smart companies are those that use environmental strategy to innovate, create value, and build competitive advantage. Theoretical explanations as to how environmentalism and competitive advantage are linked are considered in the concluding section below.

Competitive advantage via environmentalism: theoretical perspectives

While undertaking environmental initiatives may give rise to the kinds of organizational benefits discussed above, it does not follow that investing in corporate environmentalism will invariably help to give a firm a competitive advantage in the market place. Reinhardt's assertion (1999a) that we need to ask when greening pays, needs to be supplemented by a further question: how can environmentally related investments become a source of competitive advantage at firm level (see e.g. Welford and Gouldson, 1993; Denton, 1994; Bonifant et al., 1995; Holliday et al., 2002; Laszlo, 2008).

 As a business concept, competitive advantage has been widely discussed in the strategic management literature and is most readily associated with the work of Michael Porter (1980, 1985). At its simplest, the term denotes the ability of a firm to perform better than its rivals; to create more economic value than its competitors; and to do things better and more quickly than the other firms in its industry, thereby providing the organization with a competitive edge (Cockburn et al., 2000; Lash and Wellington, 2007; Barney and Hesterley, 2009). In relation to corporate environmentalism, Welford and Gouldson (1993), for example, have argued that the constituent elements of competitive advantage include reduced costs, improved stakeholder relationships, improved product quality, and reduced risk exposure. Insofar as these advantages could presumably be available to all firms that invest in environmental management, the question still remains as to how greening can be used strategically to set a firm apart from its competitors. In short, how are superior performance and greening linked?

Broadly speaking, at a theoretical level, there are two main schools of thought regarding the sources of competitive advantage via environmentalism: 'positioning' and the 'resource-based view of the firm' (Orsato, 2006). With regard to the former, Porter (1980, 1985) has basically argued that firms can gain a competitive advantage by acquiring a dominant position in their industry either through delivering the same benefits as competitors but at a lower cost (i.e. a cost advantage); or delivering benefits to consumers that exceed those of competing products or services (i.e. a differentiation advantage). Either of these positional advantages can be achieved in a broad market segment or in a particular market niche, what Porter has called a 'focus' strategy.

As far as a cost advantage is concerned, proponents of the win-win hypothesis see environmentalism as a means to reducing operational expenditures and of managing current and future environmental and regulatory risks that have associated costs (Bonifant et al., 1995; De Simone and Popoff, 1997; Esty and Winston, 2006; Lash and Wellington, 2007). Porter and van der Linde (1995a, 1995b) have suggested, however, that sustained competitive advantage rests not on such static efficiency gains, nor on optimizing within fixed constraints, but on a firm's capacity for innovation and improvement within a constantly changing business environment. By responding innovatively to environmental regulations, the authors argue, firms will achieve increases in resource productivity and this will help to lower a product's costs or improve its value to consumers, thereby building long-term competitiveness.

In addition to helping to reduce a firm's costs, investing in environmental improvements may also allow an organization to create products or employ processes that provide greater environmental benefits or smaller environmental costs than those of its rivals; differentiating its offering in this way may enable it to command higher prices, to capture a larger share of the market, or to achieve both (Reinhardt, 1998, 1999a; Esty and Winston, 2006). Orsato (2006) notes that environmental differentiation strategies can take the form of beyond-compliance leadership or of eco-branding, with the former focusing on investing to gain a positive reputation with key stakeholders, while the latter seeking competitiveness via exploiting an environmental market niche. As has been pointed out, however, an organization's capacity to gain a differentiation advantage is contingent on a number of factors, including the responsiveness of consumers to the claimed environmental benefits, their willingness to pay premium prices to gain such benefits, and the ability of the firm to defend its innovation against imitation by competitors (Reinhardt, 1998; Orsato, 2006; Ambec and Lanoie, 2008).

Whereas the positioning school regards competitive advantage as emanating from an organization's response to its changing external environment, the resource-based view focuses on differences in the internal aspects of rival organizations. Critics of Porter (e.g. Hilliard, 2004) have argued that his analysis was deficient in this respect. Under resource-based theory—or what Marcus (2005) prefers to call a 'view' (RBV)—a firm's superior performance and its capacity to achieve above-average economic rent is seen as an outcome of its ability to successfully acquire, generate, and deploy valuable and heterogeneously distributed resources and capabilities (see e.g. Prahalad and Hamel, 1990; Barney, 1991; Oliver, 1997; Cockburn et al., 2000). Resources are essentially the factors owned and controlled by the business and can be both tangible (e.g. financial assets, technology and buildings) and intangible (e.g. patents, reputation, brand equity, information). Capabilities are the various skills and aptitudes the organization possesses (e.g. the ability to absorb information and knowledge, to innovate and learn) that allow it to use its resources effectively in pursuit of its goals and that, when aggregated, give rise to particular organizational proficiencies or competencies. Where a firm possesses resources, capabilities, and competencies that have value, are rare, are difficult to imitate, and have few substitutes, it is argued that this can give rise to a sustainable competitive advantage for the organization (Barney, 1991).

In an early application of RBV theory to the study of the firm and its relationship with the natural environment, Hart (1995) argued that businesses will become increasingly constrained by and dependent upon ecosystems and that their strategies and competitive advantage will be rooted in capabilities that facilitate environmentally sustainable economic activity, what he called a natural-resource-based view of the firm (see Box 6.3). One important insight to emerge from Hart's analysis was that a firm could pursue different, though interconnected, environmental strategies and that these were associated with particular driving forces, key resources, and sources of competitive advantage.

Like Hart, Russo and Fouts (1997) have suggested that the resource-based view offers researchers a useful tool for examining the relationship between a firm's environmental and economic performance in that organizations are trying to develop their resources against a background of public scrutiny and expectations relating to environmental protection. Reflecting Hart's observation that firms can pursue different policy responses, Russo and Fouts assert that firms that engage in beyond-compliance environmental strategies will differ in their resource base from those that are merely seeking to comply with regulatory requirements. The claim is that environmental proactivism tends to involve resource and capability enhancement and results in increased complexity in resource deployment which makes it difficult for rivals to imitate. In testing their hypothesis that higher levels of corporate environmental performance are associated

BOX 6.3 HART'S NATURAL-RESOURCE-BASED VIEW OF THE FIRM

Hart begins his analysis with the observation that management theory has tended to ignore the impact of the natural environment when examining the context in which firms operate and compete. Given the growing impact of environmental problems, his contention is that existing theory is likely to prove deficient when identifying emerging sources of competitive advantage in the future.

Drawing on resource-based views of the firm put forward by researchers in the field of strategic management, Hart points to the link between a firm's resources and capabilities and its subsequent performance in the market place. In simple terms, the theory suggests that resources help to develop capabilities which in turn can yield competitive advantage; the latter may be manifest as a cost or differentiation advantage, or as an early mover advantage (pre-emption), or in the form of a more secured future position. This is depicted in the generic diagram below.

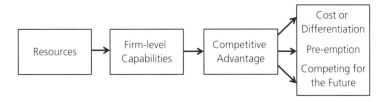

Central to Hart's argument is the claim that future challenges and constraints posed by the natural environment will impact significantly on a firm's resources and capability development and hence on its ability to compete. Competitive advantage, he argues, will increasingly be rooted 'in a set of emerging capabilities such as waste minimization, green product design and technology cooperation in the developing world' (p. 991). This being the case, firms will need to develop their strategies accordingly to ensure that they develop capabilities that give rise to competitive advantage via environmentally sustainable economic activity.

Hart puts forward a conceptual framework incorporating three such interconnected strategies: pollution prevention, product stewardship, and sustainable development. He identifies the environmental driving forces behind each, the associated key resources, and the basis of the firm's competitive advantage under each strategy. Pollution prevention, for example, is driven by the need to minimize emissions, effluents, and waste products under pressure from external stakeholders. By pursuing such a strategy, Hart argues that firms will develop a capability of continuous improvement and this can give rise to a cost advantage over rival businesses. Under product stewardship and sustainable development, Hart argues that the source of the firm's competitive advantage will be its ability to pre-empt its competitors (for example, by gaining exclusive access to limited resources) or to secure its future position (for example, by investing in market development), respectively.

In the final part of his article, Hart discusses the theoretical implications of his natural-resource-based view of the firm and the interconnections between the three strategies, including the notion of path dependence. The culmination of his discussion is the development of a number of propositions which he hopes will be used to guide future empirical investigations. As Hart notes in his final remark, much work still needs to be done when examining the relationships between the three environmental strategies and indicators of financial and market performance. In his opinion, the natural-resource-based view of the firm opens up a number of potentially productive avenues for research in this regard.

with enhanced profitability, Russo and Fouts found that proactivism translates into competitive advantage and that the apparent benefits of greening seem to strengthen with industry growth (see above).

Following Hart's pioneering analysis, a number of empirical studies have emerged which have enhanced our understanding of both the antecedents and outcomes of environmental capability generation (Sharma and Aragón-Correa, 2005). Fuller details of these studies can be found in Table 6.1. In summary, the research suggests that firms that have a competitive advantage tend to be those that:

- have a concern for the environment and have achieved greater integration of environmental issues in the planning process (Judge and Douglas, 1998);
- have a capability to implement pollution prevention technologies (Klassen and Whybark, 1999);
- have complementary assets—notably capabilities for process innovation and implementation—which can give rise to a cost advantage (Christmann, 2000);
- have a competence in environmental management which is driven by public policies and the values and beliefs of corporate decision-makers (Marcus, 2005);
- possess a range of other organizational capabilities including stakeholder integration, continuous innovation, superior management abilities, higher order learning, and green intellectual capital (Marcus and Geffen, 1998; Sharma and Vredenburg, 1998; Klassen and Whybark, 1999; Christmann, 2000; Sharma and Aragón-Correa, 2005; Chen, 2008).

As indicated above, research by Aragón-Correa et al. (2008) suggests that, contrary to conventional wisdom, even SMEs can adopt proactive environmental practices that can give rise to superior financial performance via specific firm-level capabilities that are rooted in the unique strategic characteristics of SMEs. Whether most small businesses are aware of, and deliberately seeking to leverage, these competitive capabilities still remains open to question and is worthy of further investigation (Patton and Worthington, 2003; Simpson et al., 2004; Worthington and Patton, 2005).

Implicit in some of the studies identified above is the idea that the development of organizational resources and capabilities cannot be divorced from influences in a firm's broader external context. In recognition of this fact, Aragón-Correa and Sharma (2003) have put forward a contingent resource-based view of proactive corporate environmental strategy which combines perspectives from the literature of contingency theory, dynamic capabilities, and the natural-resource-based view of the firm. The core of their argument is that certain features of a firm's business environment—complexity, uncertainty, and munificence—moderate the relationship between the dynamic capability inherent in the organization's beyond-compliance approach and its competitive advantage. These moderating effects—which can be either positive or negative—may explain why firms with similar characteristics (e.g. capabilities) develop different approaches to environmental protection and why proactive environmental strategies appear beneficial in certain circumstances but not necessarily in others.

Case Study: Walkers PLC[1]

Walkers PLC is part of Pepsico UK and Ireland and is the UK's largest snackfoods manufacturer with brands such as Walkers, Quavers, Doritos, and Wotsits. Its Leicester-based manufacturing facility is the largest crisp factory in the world, and it is estimated that over 10 million people eat one of its products every day.

In 2002, Walkers began working with the UK government-funded environmental consultancy, the Carbon Trust, on energy efficiency and carbon management schemes which helped it to achieve substantial savings through significant reductions in energy use at its factories. Through its work with the Carbon Trust, the company began to appreciate more fully that a great deal of its carbon impact came from activities in its supply chain and consequently in 2006/7 agreed to participate in a pilot study with the Trust aimed at analysing the carbon footprint of one of its products (cheese and onion crisps) across the entire product life cycle, from raw materials to manufacture and packaging to ultimate disposal of the packaging.

Working with the Trust, and with different organizations involved in its supply chain (e.g. potato and corn producers, cardboard and other packaging manufacturers), Walkers collected data on carbon emissions at each stage of the product's life cycle. The findings from this exercise confirmed the company's belief that a majority of the carbon emissions associated with the product lay outside its direct control, most notably in the production of the raw materials—potatoes, sunflowers, and seasoning. Other large contributors to the product's carbon footprint were cooking and processing and packaging, with smaller contributions from transport and disposal, the latter two using national averages to calculate emissions. Since consumer use of the product was deemed to have only a negligible impact on energy demand, this phase of the life cycle was excluded from the calculations.

As a consequence of the exercise, early in 2007, Walkers cheese and onion crisps became the first product in the United Kingdom to display the Carbon Trust's Carbon Reduction Label on its pack, a development it was hoped might appeal to environmentally conscious consumers. The exercise also revealed a number of areas where further savings could be made across the supply chain. For example, the company's practice of buying potatoes by gross weight had encouraged farmers to humidify them in order to add more water content (and therefore weight), thus making them more valuable to the producer. By switching to a policy of rewarding farmers for producing potatoes with lower water content, Walkers realized it could reduce its own energy use in the processing phase and that this, together with the reduced energy use by farmers, would lead to additional cost savings and emissions reductions within the supply chain.

By 2009, the company estimated that it had achieved a 7 per cent reduction in the carbon footprint of its product and had made associated savings of £400,000, which were reinvested in the business. It had also put in place a series of Supply Chain Summits which brought together key suppliers of raw materials and packaging in order to identify further emission reduction opportunities and had identified further energy saving measures at its Leicester factory. As for consumer reactions to the initiative, initial research by the company indicated a generally positive response to the idea of carbon labelling and to the Walkers brand. How far this has influenced/will influence consumer choices is still far from clear, although it is worth noting that a number of other leading brand names (e.g. Tesco, Dyson) have subsequently worked with the Carbon Trust on carbon labelling of some of their products.

■ **NOTE**

1. A shorter version of this case study first appeared in Worthington et al. (2005).

7 SMEs and the environment

Small and medium-sized enterprises (SMEs) are the most important sector of a nation's economy. They provide and create jobs, especially during times of recession; they are a source of innovation and entrepreneurial spirit; they harness individual creative effort, and they create competition and are the seedbed for businesses of the future. In short, small and medium-sized firms are vitally important for a healthy, dynamic market economy.

(Hillary, 2000)

While there is empirical evidence to indicate that larger companies are increasingly seeing environmental performance as a strategic issue, our knowledge of the factors shaping decisions and actions of small and medium enterprises (SMEs) is relatively under-developed.

(Worthington and Patton, 2005)

…strategic differences between big and small firms, the scope of SMEs' impacts on the global economy and on the natural environment, and the absence of previous analysis all suggest the importance of giving detailed attention to the issue of the strategic behaviour of SMEs in their interface with the natural environment.

(Aragón-Correa et al., 2008)

Introduction

Constituting over 90 per cent of all businesses worldwide, small and medium-sized enterprises (SMEs) are indisputably important in social, political, and economic terms. As major engines of economic growth—albeit on a more modest scale than their larger counterparts—SMEs also clearly have adverse impacts on the natural environment by dint of their wealth-creating activities. While it is widely accepted that the negative ecological effect of an individual small business will tend to be both limited and localized, the sheer number and distribution of SMEs suggest that their aggregate impact is likely to prove substantial (Rowe and Hollingsworth, 1996; Hillary, 2000; Petts, 2000; Biondi et al., 2002; Lawrence et al., 2006; Revell and Blackburn, 2007). Accordingly, any discussion of the greening of business organizations merits a detailed examination of the relationship between small firms and the environment (Rutherfoord and Spence,

1998; Tilley, 1999), not least since firm size has been highlighted as an important factor in explaining how and why some businesses choose to make environmental improvements (Baylis et al., 1998*a*; Aragón-Correa et al., 2008; see also Chapter 4).

Attempts to gauge the environmental impact of the small-firm sector tend to present a varied picture. Hoevenagel and Wolters (2000), for example, estimated that Dutch SMEs were responsible for 14 per cent of carbon emissions, 36 per cent of CFCs, and 24 per cent of waste in 1995. Figures for UK small businesses suggest a much larger environmental footprint, with SMEs thought to have been responsible for as much as 60 per cent of total business carbon emissions, 60 per cent of commercial waste, 70 per cent of pollution, and 80 per cent of pollution incidents in the mid- to late 1990s (Hillary, 1995; Marshall Report, 1998; Smith et al., 2000; Williamson et al., 2006). In reality, the total environmental impact of the small business community remains largely uncertain and is probably incalculable in most, if not all, cases (Hillary, 2000). This situation is echoed in the perceptions of small businesses regarding the extent to which they contribute to environmental damage, with survey evidence suggesting that confusion and/or denial frequently typify the stance of many small firm owner-managers (see below).

In focusing on the relationship between scale and environmental attitudes and practices, the discussion below picks up many of the key themes examined in previous chapters. Specifically, it investigates:

- small firm environmental attitudes and behaviour;
- the drivers of and barriers to environmental responsiveness by SMEs; and
- small firm perceptions of the competitive benefits of green performance.

In truth, much of the existing research on business and the natural environment is based on the experiences of larger organizations, including multinational enterprises. Differences in the scale, structure, management, resources, goals, and context of small and larger businesses suggest that the theories and research on the latter are not necessarily completely applicable to the former (Aragón-Correa et al., 2008). As such, the issues mentioned above deserve further examination.

What is an SME?

Definitions of SMEs tend to be either general or specific; either way, they are often imprecise, vague, and/or debatable. Over forty years ago for instance, the Bolton Report (1971) defined a small firm as an independent business, managed in a personalized way by its owner(s) and with a small share of the market for its products. Almost three decades later, Spence (1999) adopted a similar characteristics approach, arguing that small firms are generally independent and owner-managed, faced with multi-tasking, cash-limited, often involved in 'fire-fighting', built on personal relationships, controlled by informal mechanisms and largely mistrustful of bureaucracy.

Alongside these broad characterizations of the small firm community are the more technical definitions that are usually applied when official statistics are collected and/or grants are being awarded by public sector agencies or financial institutions. These definitions use criteria such as number of employees, assets, annual turnover or balance sheet totals, and ownership as the means of classifying enterprises. Despite a degree of convergence in technical definitions in Europe with the introduction of the EU SME definition in the mid-1990s (see e.g. Hillary, 2000), considerable variety still exists at a national level as evidenced by some of the research referred to in this chapter. In Lee's study (2008) of Korean businesses, SMEs are defined as employing between 21 and 499 people; the equivalents for Australia, New Zealand, and Spain are fewer than 200, fewer than 100, and fewer than 250, respectively (Collins et al., 2007; Aragón-Correa et al., 2008; Gadenne et al., 2009), with some writers distinguishing between micro, small, and medium-sized enterprises according to the number of employees (e.g. under the current official EU definition micro = 0–9; small = 10–49; medium = 50–249).

Given that there is no 'right' definition of what constitutes an SME and that this chapter draws from research undertaken in a wide range of sectors and national jurisdictions, the approach taken here reflects that of Parker et al. (2009), which is to define SMEs according to their national context. It is worth remembering that, as in the case of larger businesses, small firms are far from homogeneous and we should expect to find differences in the way in which small firm owner-managers think about and react to environmental issues and imperatives. In the real world, SMEs are extremely diverse and operate under differing market, social, and regulatory conditions, and they are therefore likely to adopt quite different business models and levels of environmental commitment in response to external demands for higher levels of green performance (Parker et al., 2009).

Small firm environmental attitudes, beliefs, and practices

For many smaller business owners and/or managers, the environment is seen as important at both a personal and a business level (Groundwork, 1998; Petts et al., 1999). Research into small firm attitudes and beliefs indicates that SMEs often express concern for the environment and have a largely positive attitude where environmental protection is concerned (Quentin Merritt, 1998; Lloyds/TSB, 1999; Tilley, 1999; Schaper, 2002; Hitchens et al., 2005; Redmond et al., 2008). When questioned, small businesses frequently claim to be generally aware of environmental issues and problems (Pedersen, 2000; Williamson and Lynch-Wood, 2001) and many see themselves as ecologically friendly, with appropriate measures in place to prevent and/or reduce their impact on the natural environment (Lloyds/TSB, 1999; Smith et al., 2000; Environment Agency, 2003).

Somewhat paradoxically, there appears to be a widespread belief among owner/managers that their own organizations have little or no adverse ecological impact (Rowe and Hollingsworth, 1996; Gerrans and Hutchinson, 2000; Smith et al., 2000; Friedman and Miles, 2002; McKeiver and Gadenne, 2005; Environment Agency, 2009). A common view appears to be that environmental damage is caused primarily by larger organizations and by the consumer society, with some managers attributing current problems to deep-rooted causes beyond their control, including rising living standards, global poverty, and overpopulation (Anglada, 2000). For firms that hold such opinions, the issue of the environment tends to be well down on the business agenda and consequently there is likely to be little incentive to invest in environmental protection measures or to respond to demands for improved environmental perform-ance within the small firm sector as a whole (Hillary, 1995; Holland and Gibbon, 1997; Groundwork, 1998; Rutherfoord et al., 2000; Revell and Blackburn, 2007; Redmond et al., 2008).

Managerial perceptions of limited environmental impact are, of course, by no means universal among SMEs and have been shown to vary according to circumstances. Regular surveys of small businesses by the UK Environment Agency indicate that awareness rises as the size of the firm increases, with larger SMEs accepting responsibility for environmental damage more readily than micro-enterprises (see e.g. Environment Agency, 2009). Awareness also seems to be influenced by variables such as sector (Patton and Worthington, 2003; Worthington and Patton, 2005), institutional context (Rutherfoord et al., 2000; Revell, 2003), and information, with prompted questioning on hazardous activities increasing managers' appreciation of environmental damage (Environment Agency, 2009). Notwithstanding these variations, the picture on the whole can probably best be summarized as one of limited understanding and awareness of environmental issues and problems among smaller businesses and a relatively wide-spread view that their impact at worst is insignificant and limited in scope (Anglada, 2000; Gerrans and Hutchinson, 2000; Studer et al., 2008).

With respect to the merits or otherwise of environmental protection measures, the default position adopted by many small firm owners and managers is that protecting the environment imposes a cost on businesses that can rarely be fully recaptured in the form of higher prices for consumers (Rutherfoord and Spence, 1998; Gerrans and Hutchinson, 2000; Rutherfoord et al., 2000; Taylor et al., 2003). In the language of strategic management, many small firms see environmental protection as a threat rather than a business opportunity, with notions of leveraging benefits from environ-mentalism evidently limited within the small business community (Anglada, 2000;

Worthington and Patton, 2005; also see the discussion below on the benefits of green performance).

One interesting exception to this perspective can be seen in the notion of 'ecopreneurship'; this is the idea that some individuals deliberately adopt environmentally responsible business practices and establish the so-called 'green-green' organizations in order to radically transform the sector in which they are operating (Isaak, 2002; Masurel, 2007). Compared to 'green' businesses, which are regarded as those that have seen the potential benefits of enhanced environmental performance, 'green-green' businesses represent a move towards more sustainable forms of entrepreneurship, with the intention being able to make a living and at the same time solve environmental problems (Bennett, 1991; Masurel, 2007). As Schaper (2002) points out, discussions of the concept of environmental entrepreneurship have spawned an evolving terminology; unsurprisingly, this has been accompanied by the development of typologies of green entrepreneurs, including Walley and Taylor's notions (2002) of (a) 'innovative opportunists' (financially orientated, having spotted a green niche); (b) 'visionary champions' (embracing a transformative, sustainability orientation); (c) 'ethical mavericks' (influenced by friends, networks, and post experiences with a sustainable orientation); and (d) 'ad hoc enviropreneurs' (accidental green entrepreneurs).

Despite the phenomenon of green entrepreneurship, extant research points to a substantial measure of commonality in the attitudes, beliefs, and perceptions of SME owners and/or managers regarding their relationship with the natural environment. The same could be said for small firms' responses to demands for improved environmental performance by smaller businesses. Generally, sceptical of self-regulatory approaches and unfavourably disposed to environmental legislation (Smith et al., 2000), most small firms appear to adopt an essentially reactive and compliance-based posture vis-a-vis regulatory intervention (Azzone et al., 1997; Bianchi and Noci, 1998; Petts et al., 1999; del Brío and Junquera, 2003; Patton and Worthington, 2003). This response has been linked to a variety of factors, including fear of prosecution, avoidance of adverse publicity, the ethical stance of managers and non-managers, and a range of other barriers to environmentalism which are discussed in more detail below (see also Petts et al., 1998; Tilley, 1999; Revell and Rutherfoord, 2003).

In terms of specifics, the available evidence indicates that small firm environmental practices often tend to be relatively limited and focused on attempts to improve energy usage and efficiency and on recycling of materials and other business inputs (Quentin Merritt, 1998; Gerrans and Hutchinson, 2000; Schaper, 2002; del Brío and Junquera, 2003; Redmond et al., 2008). That said, some more recent studies have suggested mixed levels of awareness and environmental actions even among micro-enterprises (Mir, 2008) and have pointed to a range of responses from reactivity to environmental leadership that appears to be linked to the type of firm and their organizational capabilities (Aragón-Correa et al., 2008).

GREEN SNAPSHOT: SMALL FIRMS AND GREEN TECHNOLOGY

While academic and practitioner research generally indicates that smaller firms are less environmentally pro-active than larger organizations, the overall picture presented in these studies does not always reveal the full story. A study funded by the US Small Business Administration's Office of Advocacy (2011) indicates that in relation to patent activity in green technologies and industries, innovative small firms tend to be sixteen times more productive than their larger counterparts in terms of patents per employee. Moreover, although four times as many large businesses as small innovative firms have at least one green patent, the latter are more likely than the former to have green technologies as a core part of their business. The study also suggested that small enterprises outperform larger businesses in patent originality, generality, and growth, being particularly active in patent registration in smart grids, solar energy, batteries, and fuel cells.

While not denying that some SMEs have demonstrated a more proactive approach to environmental protection, the evidence from international research still suggests that, for smaller firms in particular, this tends to be the exception rather that the general rule. Studies of investment in voluntary self-regulatory initiatives such as ISO14001 and EMAS (Eco-Management and Audit Scheme) for example, show that uptake among small business tends to be patchy at best as indicated in the case study at the end of this chapter (Groundwork, 1998; Johansson, 2000; Environment Agency, 2009). Given the numerous barriers to the adoption and implementation of a formal environmental management system (EMS) and the perception among smaller firms that their environmental footprint is negligible, most SMEs are naturally sceptical of the benefits of investing in managing their environmental performance (KPMG, 1997; Bianchi and Noci, 1998; Miles et al., 1999; Hillary, 2004; Halila, 2007). For the relatively small number of firms willing to undertake such an investment, factors such as the size of the firm, sector, degree of external pressure, inter-firm collaboration, and experience with quality management systems seem to be important influences in encouraging beyond-compliance managerial decisions (Patton and Worthington, 2003; Hillary, 2004; Halila, 2007).

Drivers of small firm environmental performance

As in the case of larger organizations, SME environmental practices are shaped by both external and internal influences. Following Bansal and Roth (2000), and in keeping with the analysis undertaken in Chapter 4, we examine four such factors in turn: legislation/ regulation, stakeholder pressures, economic opportunities, and ethical influences.

LEGISLATION/REGULATION

Studies of SME environmental practices in different industries, sectors, and national contexts point to government legislation/regulation as a key driver of organizational behaviour (Rowe and Hollingsworth, 1996; KPMG, 1997; Baylis et al., 1998*a*; Bianchi and Noci, 1998; Tilley, 1999, 2000; Anglada, 2000; Patton and Worthington, 2003; Worthington and Patton, 2005; Clemens, 2006; Studer et al., 2006; Williamson et al., 2006; Revell and Blackburn, 2007; Lee, S.-Y., 2008; Parker et al., 2009). Gadenne et al. (2009) claim that regulatory intervention by government helps to raise small firm environmental awareness and this predisposes owners and managers to change their business processes and environmental strategies. Williamson et al. (2006) have reached a similar conclusion, arguing that environmental regulation leads to better environmental procedures and practices within manufacturing SMEs, with regulatory compliance identified as the dominant response as suggested in a number of other studies of SMEs (see e.g. Petts et al., 1999; Patton and Worthington, 2003).

In practice, the relationship between environmental legislation/regulation and small firm behaviour is far more complex than might be initially presumed. Reference has already been made to the fact that many small businesses appear ignorant of existing regulations (Groundwork, 1998; Petts et al., 1999; Gerrans and Hutchinson, 2000; Hillary, 2000), rendering their claim to be compliant open to challenge. There are also questions concerning how far regulations are enforced by the relevant authorities (KPMG, 1997; Petts, 2000; Mir and Feitelson, 2007; Revell and Blackburn, 2007) and whether they are sufficiently extensive and robust as to require SMEs to engage in environmental improvements for fear of regulatory, market, and/or social sanction (Pimenova and van der Vorst, 2004; Studer et al., 2006; Parker et al., 2009).

Small firm responses to governmental regulation have also been linked to a range of other factors including business reactions to environmental support programmes and awards (Clement and Hansen, 2003; Studer et al., 2008), lack of management confidence in the efficacy of a regulatory approach (Petts et al., 1999), information deficiencies (Tilley, 1999; Williamson and Lynch-Wood, 2001), and differences in governance structures and institutional arrangements at a national level (Rutherfoord et al., 2000; Revell, 2003). In this context, the observation that small firms need to be distinguished on the basis of different internal responses to environmental commitment and business performance commitment is a useful contribution (Parker et al., 2009), given that it highlights the fact that governments may need to employ a variety of regulatory intervention strategies when seeking to encourage SMEs to make environmental improvements.

STAKEHOLDER PRESSURES

Like their larger counterparts, SMEs can face pressures from a variety of external and internal stakeholders in carrying out their day-to-day activities. Customers, suppliers, trade associations, financial institutions, larger organizations, NGOs, employees, and government bodies have all been suggested as possible sources of influence on small firm environmental awareness and behaviour. Alongside regulatory demands, social and market pressures clearly have the potential to influence the environmental practices of smaller enterprises and are thought to have been a significant driver of EMS adoption in the relatively limited number of small firms seeking certification to EMAS or ISO14001 (Gerstenfeld and Roberts, 2000; Hillary, 2000).

GREEN SNAPSHOT: GREENING SMALLER BUSINESSES

The UK small business advocacy group, the Federation of Small Businesses (FSB), claims that a major obstacle to the greening of smaller firms is that small business owners need to be convinced that going green makes economic and commercial sense. In a report published in 2010, entitled 'Making Sense of Going Green', the FSB called upon the UK government to put in place a range of measures aimed at incentivizing green behaviour in the small firm community. These included increased financial help for firms willing to install energy efficient equipment; the introduction of a smart metering system; further targeted action on a Feed-in-Tariff aimed at encouraging the take-up of renewable energy; and changes to the landlord–tenant relationship to promote the greening of business premises.

To support the move towards a low-carbon economy, the FSB argued that it was also necessary for the government to play a key role in establishing a number of long-term drivers of green growth. These should include public support for innovation, research and development, and a public procurement process aimed at promoting more sustainable behaviour (e.g. by sourcing locally) in a way that would be more small business friendly.

How far stakeholder groups shape small firm environmental attitudes and behaviour in practice, however, has been the subject of some disagreement between academic researchers and practitioners (see Box 7.1). Some studies suggest that, at present, small firms face little, if any, pressure within the supply chain or from end-consumers and this can act as a disincentive to engage in beyond-compliance voluntary environmental activities (see below). Others claim that stakeholder pressures either play, or have the potential to play, an important role in encouraging SME environmental proactivity, with customers and the supply chain seen as frequently prominent in driving environmental improvement within small businesses.

BOX 7.1 STAKEHOLDER PRESSURES ON SME ENVIRONMENTAL BEHAVIOUR

Indicative authors	Key argument(s)
Baylis et al., 1998a, 1998b; Quentin Merritt, 1998; Williamson and Lynch-Wood, 2001; Patton and Worthington, 2003; Revell and Rutherford, 2003;	There is little, if any, perceived pressure on small firms from key stakeholder groups such as customers or within the supply chain. This is particularly true in

Worthington and Patton, 2005; Lawrence et al., 2006; Kasim, 2007; Masurel, 2007; Mir and Feitelson, 2007; Revell and Blackburn, 2007; Mir, 2008; Studer et al., 2008	the case of microfirms and applies to different industries, sectors and national contexts.
KPMG, 1997; Groundwork, 1998; Lloyds/TSB, 1999; Bianchi and Noci, 1998; Noci and Verganti, 1999; Friedman et al., 2000; Álvarez Gil et al., 2001; McKeiver and Gadenne, 2005; Halila, 2007; Lee, S.-Y., 2008; Mir and Sanchez, 2009	Small firms are facing/will face increased pressures from stakeholder interests to improve on their environmental performance. Such influences include supply chain pressures, customers, shareholders, larger firms, and trade associations. Socio-economic factors at local level can also play a part in determining the degree of responsiveness.

Explanations as to why stakeholders do or do not exercise influence over SME responses are equally diverse. The pro-influence argument generally focuses on the role of different interests in raising small firm awareness of environmental issues and in providing support, collaborative opportunities, additional resources, and knowledge about the potential benefits of environmental action (Verheul, 1999; Aragón-Correa and Matías-Reche, 2005; Masurel, 2007; Roy and Therin, 2008; Gadenne et al., 2009). Small firms are also thought by some to be more susceptible to stakeholder pressures, with organizational flexibility seen as an important attribute in facilitating organizational change (Gerstenfeld and Roberts, 2000; Condon, 2004; Aragón-Correa and Matías-Reche, 2005; Masurel, 2007; Redmond et al., 2008).

GREEN SNAPSHOT: PARTNERING FOR GREEN ACTION

Financial initiatives and technological support aimed at encouraging green behaviour by SMEs are becoming increasingly evident and often involve collaboration between organizations from both the state and non-state sectors at both national and international levels. Three recent examples illustrate this development:

- In summer 2011, the Small Industries Development Bank of India (SIDBI) joined together with the Bureau for Energy Efficiency (BEE) in a scheme designed to promote greater energy efficiency by micro, small, and medium-sized enterprises via the use of targeted investments in energy efficiency technologies. SIDBI has also been involved in promoting renewable and clean technologies—via the use of soft loans—using financial support from agencies including KfW in Germany and the Japanese International Cooperation Industry.
- In autumn 2011, the Multinational Investment Fund (MIF)—part of the Inter-American Development Bank (IDB) Group—announced the establishment of a partnership with the Nordic Development Fund (NDF) to provide green microfinance products aimed at micro, small, and medium-sized businesses in Latin America and the Caribbean. The four-year project, which is known as the Ecomicro Program, is designed to help smaller firms to gain access to clean energy, energy efficiency technologies, and products aimed at adaptation to the impact of climate change.
- A Green Energy Efficiency Fund aimed at providing competitive green loans for small South African firms was also announced in autumn 2011. Designed to encourage investments in both energy efficiency measures and renewable energy generation, the fund is a joint venture between the South African Industrial Development Corporation and the German development bank KfW.

In contrast, the anti-influence case stresses how firm size may actually inhibit managerial responses. Small firms are said to be less visible and less susceptible to external influences compared to larger organizations and are perceived as having very little adverse impact on the natural environment either relatively or absolutely (Hillary, 2004; Aragón-Correa and Matías-Reche, 2005; Masurel, 2007). Being largely free from external scrutiny, frequently under-resourced, and often convinced that they have a negligible environmental impact, SMEs may be disinclined to engage in beyond-compliance behaviour, particularly if it is difficult for them to publish their efforts to the key stakeholder groups which are part of their institutional environment (Bianchi and Noci, 1998).

While some have questioned whether SMEs are less visible than larger organizations where environmental issues are concerned (Bowen, 2000*a*), many writers see some of the consequences of firm size (e.g. lack of time, resources, and information) as important moderators of, or barriers to, pro-environmental behaviour in small enterprises (see e.g. Gadenne et al., 2009). This issue is explored in the next main section of this chapter, following a discussion of the remaining two drivers of small firm environmental responsiveness.

ECONOMIC OPPORTUNITIES

In principle, there is no reason why smaller enterprises should not be able to gain commercial and economic benefits through higher levels of environmental performance. On the supply side, cost savings could be achieved, for instance, through better waste management, reduced resource usage, lower future liabilities (e.g. environmental taxes, insurance premiums), and improved product quality (Greenan et al., 1997; Friedman et al., 2000). On the demand side, SMEs may find that higher levels of environmental performance can open up new market opportunities and help to improve stakeholder relationships, thus contributing to improved organizational competitiveness (Groundwork, 1998; Álvarez Gil et al., 2001; Halila, 2007; Masurel, 2007; Gadenne et al., 2009).

While there is some evidence in the literature that some SMEs accept there can be gains from environmentalism (Groundwork, 1998; Gerrans and Hutchinson, 2000; Hillary, 2004), most studies of smaller enterprises indicate a less sanguine view among small firm owner-managers. For many, beyond-compliance environmental practices are regarded as peripheral, an unnecessary drain on organizational resources, and a cost to the firm that has, at best, questionable business benefits (Rutherfoord and Spence, 1998; Tilley, 1999; Simpson et al., 2004; Worthington and Patton, 2005; Studer et al., 2006; Parker et al., 2009). In short, the idea of win-win has little resonance for many small business owners, with few appearing far from convinced that there is a strong business case for engaging in pro-environmental activities that are not mandated by law (Drake et al., 2004; Revell, 2007; Revell and Blackburn, 2007; Gadenne et al., 2009).

This apparently widespread perception that there is likely to be a trade-off between business and environmental performance is not difficult to rationalize. Many owner-managers appear to believe that devoting organizational resources to higher levels of environmental protection:

- is not a business issue or business priority (KPMG, 1997; Rutherfoord and Spence, 1998; Rutherfoord et al., 2000);
- threatens to reduce a firm's competitiveness (Studer et al., 2006);
- is an issue of social responsibility rather than a market imperative (Williamson et al., 2006);
- does not add value to the organization either by reducing overall costs or generating extra customers (Rutherfoord and Spence, 1998; Patton and Worthington, 2003; Taylor et al., 2003; Revell, 2007);
- does not allow firms to recapture environmental expenditures through higher prices (Bianchi and Noci, 1998; Simpson et al., 2004); and
- offers few niche opportunities (Mir and Feitelson, 2007).

On the whole, most SMEs tend towards the view that the additional short-term costs of engaging in environmental improvements outweigh the future, longer-term, and often imprecise benefit said to be associated with such actions. Notions of 'eco-efficiency', 'ecological modernization', and the 'double-dividend' currently appear to have only limited purchase within the small firm community, although this could change over time as market and social conditions evolve (Lefebvre et al., 2003; Mir, 2008; Mir and Sanchez, 2009).

ETHICAL INFLUENCES

The observation that economic opportunities do not as yet appear to be a major driver of environmental performance within many SMEs does not imply that small firm behaviour simply reflects market conditions and imperatives. Business decisions and practices can also be shaped by moral and ethical considerations, as indicated by concepts such as corporate social and environmental responsibility, sustainable entrepreneurship/ecopreneurship, and environment-driven SMEs (Lepoutre and Heene, 2006; Masurel, 2007; Parker et al., 2009).

As the previous discussion on small firm environmental attitudes and beliefs indicates, SME owner-managers often express concern for environmental protection and this has been seen as indicative of a positive moral stance by organizational decision-makers (Petts et al., 1998, 1999; Studer et al., 2006). How far this translates into environmental action, however, is something of a moot point. Studies that suggest that some SMEs may be driven by duty or moral obligation to make environmental improvements tend to be relatively few (Naffziger et al., 2003; Masurel, 2007; Parker et al., 2009), while those pointing to a gap between positive environmental attitudes and actual behaviour tend to be more common (Tilley, 1999; Schaper, 2002; Hitchens et al., 2005; Mir and Feitelson, 2007; Redmond et al., 2008) and arguably more pragmatic regarding the relative balance between the various drivers of SME environmental practices (Masurel, 2007). According to some observers, most small firms do not recognize specific social responsibility issues and generally find it difficult to translate them into day-to-day practices that are consistent with the commercial goals of the enterprise (Lepoutre and Heene, 2006; Studer et al., 2008). If Tilley (2000) is correct, the fact that ethical considerations in business operate within a broader social-economic context makes it likely that a majority of smaller enterprises will favour a more 'shallow ecology' perspective to the notion of environmental protection.

Barriers to improved environmental performance

As the discussion in the previous section has illustrated, the distinction between the drivers of, and barriers to, small firm environmental behaviour is to some extent artificial in that their influence on the organization can often depend on the degree to which they exist and operate on a continuum that ranges from weak to strong. Box 7.2 highlights that key resistant forces identified in the literature include cognitive barriers, organizational deficiencies, a relative absence of external pressures, and owner-manager perceptions of the benefits of investing in environmental improvements, with small firms often lacking the capacity, capability, and/or willingness to engage in beyond-compliance environmental behaviour. That some choose to look beyond their core concerns of production, selling, and business continuity and invest in environmental improvement serves to re-emphasize that variety, as well as considerable uniformity, exemplifies business responses to the environmental agenda across all spatial levels, from the local to the global.

BOX 7.2 KEY BARRIERS TO SME ENVIRONMENTAL IMPROVEMENT

Barrier	Indicative evidence from the literature
Level of understanding and awareness	Small firm owner-managers often have a low level of awareness of environmental issues, problems, solutions, and legislative requirements (Gerrans and Hutchinson, 2000; Smith et al., 2000; Taylor et al., 2003; Bradford and Fraser, 2008). They lack knowledge, are not very eco-literate, and believe their organizations have little, if any, environmental impact (Tilley, 1999; Holt et al., 2000; Friedman and Miles, 2002; Perez-Sanchez et al., 2003; Lepoutre and Heene, 2006; Revell and Blackburn, 2007).

Organizational considerations	Environmental protection is not a priority for most small firms which are pre-occupied with other issues and have a short-term view (Tilley, 2000; Patton and Worthington, 2003; Revell and Blackburn, 2007; Redmond et al., 2008). SMEs tend to lack finance and other resources to invest in environmental improvements; have insufficient time, training, managerial expertise to invest in environmentalism (Petts et al., 1999; Friedman et al., 2000; Holt et al., 2000; del Brío and Junquera, 2003; Patton and Worthington, 2003; Drake et al., 2004; Pimenova and van der Vorst, 2004; Hitchens et al., 2005; Studer et al., 2006; Revell, 2007; Revell and Blackburn, 2007; Parker et al., 2009).
Lack of advice and support	Small firms believe they have insufficient help, advice, and support from external bodies and feel that there is inadequate infrastructure to sustain environmental improvement (KPMG, 1997; Groundwork, 1998; Tilley, 1999; Friedman et al., 2000; Williamson and Lynch-Wood, 2001; Halila, 2007; Revell and Blackburn, 2007; Gadenne et al., 2009).
Relative absence of external drivers of change	There is relative lack of external pressures on SMEs from the regulatory market and social domains (KPMG, 1997; Studer et al., 2006, 2008). Institutional and policy deficiencies can mean that small firms are often marginalized and they can become difficult to reach, mobilize, and encourage in environmental improvements (Rutherfoord and Spence, 1998; Hillary, 2000; Rutherfoord et al., 2000). The voluntary approach favoured by government can give the idea that environmental protection is a peripheral issue (Revell, 2007).
Attitudes to the business case for environmentalism	Environmental protection tends to be seen as a cost and threat to the firm (Hillary, 2000; Rutherfoord et al., 2000; Patton and Worthington, 2003; Taylor et al., 2003; Condon, 2004; Lawrence et al., 2006; Revell and Blackburn, 2007). Firms often remain unconvinced of the business case for environmentalism and perceive their size can limit the opportunity for cost savings and other benefits (Patton and Worthington, 2003; Drake et al., 2004; Simpson et al., 2004; Worthington and Patton, 2005; Revell and Blackburn, 2007).

Competitive advantage and environmental protection

For firms that are prepared to redirect organizational resources towards further environmental improvements, the question arises as to whether they do so in order to leverage an advantage over their rivals in the market place. Are they, in Bansal and Roth's terms (2000), motivated by a desire to improve their competitiveness?

Current evidence on the links between actual or perceived competitive advantage and environmental protection at firm level once again presents a mixed picture. On the negative side, several studies have suggested that SMEs on the whole see few competitive benefits to be gained from environmentalism (Taylor et al., 2003; Simpson et al., 2004;

Worthington and Patton; 2005; Studer et al., 2006; Revell, 2007), with Hitchens et al. (2005) arguing that there appears to be no substantial link between a firm's environmental performance and its competitive strengths measured in terms of above-average profitability, growth rates and R&D, skill, and the modernity of its plant and equipment. On the positive side, some researchers have pointed to an actual or theoretical relationship between a firm's competitive position and its environmental responses. Echoing Porter and van der Linde (1995a, 1995b), Noci and Verganti (1999) have argued that concern for the environment could stimulate innovation within SMEs and this could give rise to strategic benefits within beyond-compliance organizations. Others have linked more advanced strategies for environmental protection to higher levels of export intensity (Martín-Tapia et al., 2010) and to a firm's superior financial performance (Clemens, 2006), with the latter seen by some to be a consequence of the generation of organizational capabilities that are competitively valuable for smaller businesses (Aragón-Correa and Matías-Reche, 2005).

With regard to this contention, recent research by Aragón-Correa et al. (2008) calls into question the view that resource deficiencies in smaller organizations act as a disincentive to investment in environmental protection. Using a resource-based view (RBV) perspective, the authors argue that the unique strategic characteristics of SMEs (e.g. shorter lines of communication; the founder's vision; closer interaction; flexibility in managing external relationships; an entrepreneurial orientation) enable them to develop and deploy certain organizational capabilities (i.e. shared vision; stakeholder management; strategic proactivity) and these can give rise to more proactive environmental strategies. When tested empirically in SMEs in the automotive repair sector in Southern Spain, the researchers found that firms with the most environmentally advanced practices exhibited a significantly positive financial performance consistent with similar, although contested, findings obtained for larger organizations (see Chapter 6).

Support for the view that environmental performance can impact favourably on business performance is also evident in a cross-industry study of environmentally responsive Canadian SMEs (Lefebvre et al., 2003). In all four industries examined (wood products; printing; metal production; electrical/electronic products), the authors found a positive and significant relationship between environmental performance and product, process, and managerial innovations. With regard to the impact on overall competitiveness, however, the study suggests that greening the firm appears to involve different types of competitive advantage in different industries as a result of variations in market conditions. Where market conditions are favourable, they argue, firms are able to differentiate their product on the basis of environmental friendliness and can normally command a premium price as a result of enhanced product value. As market conditions become more adverse, they suggest, small firms find it more difficult to turn environmental initiatives into a profit, an observation that might help to explain why managers of small firms in some industries may find little resonance with the idea that greening the enterprise can pay (Revell, 2007).

Case Study: Environmental management systems and the smaller enterprise

EMSs are discussed in detail in Chapter 9. In this case study, the aim is to apply a driver/barrier analysis to the adoption of formal EMSs (e.g. ISO4001 and EMAS) within the small firm sector.

In broad terms, an EMS is a means by which a firm can measure, manage, and improve the environmental aspects of its operations. The two formal EMSs widely known are the EU-developed EMAS and the international standard ISO14001. The evidence indicates that where small firms are concerned, the uptake of both of these systems remains very limited (Groundwork, 1998; Johansson, 2000; Hillary, 2004; Studer et al., 2006). Compared to larger businesses, small firms appear generally reluctant to invest in an EMS, despite apparent commercial benefits and/or a degree of inducements by some national governments (Hillary, 2004; Studer et al., 2006, 2008). Why should this be the case?

In examining the issue of EMS adoption and implementation by smaller businesses, we draw on the work of Ruth Hillary (2004) who has used a combination of original research and a meta-analysis of over thirty published studies to explore questions relating to the sector's use of EMSs. The overall picture presented is one of relatively limited external pressures for EMS adoption/implementation compared with substantial internal and external barriers confronting organizational decision-makers considering the adoption of a formal system.

With regard to the drivers of EMS adoption, Hillary's research suggests that most of the pressure felt by small firms comes from external stakeholders, prominent amongst which are customers, particularly larger firms operating in an SMEs supply chain (see Table 7.1). As a number of other studies have indicated (Miles et al., 1999; Johansson, 2000; McKeiver and Gadenne, 2005), larger businesses can be a key driver of change in small firms by dint of their purchasing power and can use this to achieve 'voluntary' environmental improvements within SMEs; in effect EMAS or ISO4001 registration becoming a necessary condition for SMEs selling within the supply chains of larger businesses, especially multinational corporations (Miles et al., 1999).

Table 7.1 Drivers of EMS adoption by SMEs: a stakeholder approach

Key stakeholders	Other important stakeholders
Customer/supply chain	Insurers
Local authorities	General public
Local community	Suppliers
Regulators	Larger businesses
Own employees	Banks

Source: Adapted from Hillary (2004).

Table 7.2 Barriers to EMS adoption/implementation by SMEs

Internal barriers	Examples
Resource issues	Lack of time; lack of managerial skills for implementation; lack of training; requirement for capital expenditure
Understanding and perception	Lack of awareness of benefits; perception of overly bureaucratic approach; uncertainty of process of registration/de-registration; lack of knowledge
Problems of implementation	Inability to understand relevance of various stages; doubts over effectiveness of EMSs in relation to objectives; problems of internal auditor independence
Attitudes and firm culture	Lack of consistent top management support; inertia and resistance to change; lack of internal promotion of EMS
External barriers	Examples
Certifiers and verifiers	Lack of experienced verifiers; high cost of certification/verification; inconsistent approaches to process
Institutional weaknesses	Lack of promotion of EMSs; lack of financial support; inadequate institutional/legislative framework
Support and guidance	Lack of experienced consultants; relative lack of support from networks, trade associations etc.; poor quality information and guidance

Source: Adapted from Hillary (2004).

Hillary's analysis of countervailing influences accords with that of a number of other studies (e.g. Drobny, 1997; Miles et al., 1999; Williams et al., 2000; Pimenova and van der Vorst, 2004; Halila, 2007) in that it identifies both internal and external obstacles to change (Table 7.2). Internally, the key barrier to EMS adoption/implementation is thought to be human rather than financial, with lack of knowledge, negative attitudes among managers, and the general culture of the firm seen as significant issues faced by SMEs. On the external side, Hillary identifies four key barriers relating to certification verification/procedures, economic considerations, institutional weakness, and problems of inadequate support and guidance. For many smaller businesses, the perceived high cost of certification/verification, coupled with uncertainties over the benefits from adoption and the value of EMSs in the market place, appears to be a disincentive to invest. When combined with relatively limited external and/or internal pressure felt by many smaller firms, it is not surprising that uptake rates are low or that the early adopters among SMEs tend to be the larger, more mature firms operating in competitive global markets and/or those that are more ethically orientated (Miles et al., 1999).

Overall, Hillary's study suggests that any initial progress towards adopting an EMS tends to be impeded by negative attitudes within many SMEs and these may be a reflection of a broader antagonism towards environmental improvements in smaller businesses. The forces driving change may be less formidable that those resisting it and in the absence of a convincing business case are likely to prove the decisive influence where EMS adoption/implementation is concerned.

Section Four

Greening Business in Practice

8 Green strategies

…corporations are still far from the attainable goal of a comprehensive environmental strategy. But simultaneously, it is clear that a majority of corporations are moving towards this goal.

(Steger, 1993)

Fundamentally, engaging in competitive environmental strategy involves merely responding to a changing environment. Corporate decision makers who fail to do so are irresponsibly ignoring important market indicators, environmental protection today, and sustainable development tomorrow.

(Hoffman, 2000)

…the effects of climate change on companies' operations are now so tangible and certain that the issue is best addressed with the tools of the strategist, not the philanthropist.

(Porter and Reinhardt, 2007)

Introduction

In the strategic management literature, the strategy process is often portrayed as incorporating three main chronological elements: strategic analysis, strategic choice, and strategy implementation (Thompson, 2001; Lynch, 2006). Strategic analysis involves gathering information for organizational decision-makers which helps them understand and predict the current and future situation of the business, in particular in respect of its internal and external environment, including the expectations of its stakeholders. Strategic choice is about choosing between alternative courses of action available to the organization in light of the circumstances revealed by the initial analysis, in effect, generating strategic options, evaluating the different options available, and selecting a strategy (or strategies) from the alternatives being considered. Strategy implementation, as the name suggests, is the process of putting the chosen course of action into effect and includes issues related to resource allocation and organizational structure and design.

Leaving aside the question of whether the strategic management process is as planned and sequential as suggested by the implied linear model described above (see e.g. Mintzberg et al., 1998), strategy-making in organizations is clearly a multi-stage process involving numerous individual decisions that are influenced by both internal and external considerations, and which involve contested positions between the key actors involved. This is no less evident in the field of corporate greening as in other areas of organizational decision-making.

In this chapter the main focus is on some of the key strategies available to businesses in managing their relationship with the natural environment, with particular emphasis on different strategic postures and on the generic environmental strategies discussed in the literature. Since much of the research undertaken by academics has been conducted at the industry level, in the analysis below, the discussion on theoretically or empirically derived generic green strategies is supplemented by various cross-national examples of strategies that have recently been pursued by business organizations of different sizes and from different industry sectors.

What is strategy?

Dictionary definitions usually describe strategy as a plan or methodology designed to achieve predetermined objectives, its purpose being to provide the future direction and goals of the organization and to identify and gather the resources necessary in order to achieve the firm's objectives (Worthington and Britton, 2009). Andrews (1971) talks of strategy as being a rational decision-making process by which the organization's resources are matched with the opportunities arising from its competitive environment, achieving in effect a 'fit' between the firm's internal and external contexts. Johnson et al. (2005: 9) offer a similar definition, describing strategy as 'the direction and scope of an organisation over the longer term which achieves advantage for the organisation through its configuration of resources within a changing environment, to meet the needs of markets and to fulfil stakeholder expectations'. Under this definition, strategy is a complex concept involving questions of:

- *Direction*—where is the firm seeking to get to over the long term?
- *Scope*—in which markets should the organization compete and by what means?
- *Advantage*—how can the business outperform its rivals?
- *Resources*—what resources are required and how should they be deployed to achieve a competitive advantage?
- *External environment*—how do external factors affect the organization, for example by creating opportunities or posing risks?
- *Market and stakeholder requirements*—what is expected of the firm by the relevant actors in the organization's regulatory, market, and social domains?

Within an organization, a distinction is normally made between strategy at the corporate, business, and functional levels. Corporate strategies are concerned with decisions that apply to the organization as a whole and in particular where it is going and the scope of its activities. Key questions include which industries and markets a firm should compete in; should it enter into alliances with other organizations; and how should resources be allocated between the different parts of the business? At the business level, an organization's business (or competitive) strategies focus on how it competes successfully within a particular market or industry, and how it gains an advantage over its main competitors through its choice of products and by meeting the needs of its customers. At the functional level, its functional (or operational) strategies relate to the major functional areas of the organization such as marketing, production, finance, and purchasing and how these should be organized to achieve the firm's business and corporate strategies. These three well-established levels of strategy are sometimes augmented by a fourth, the firm's 'enterprise strategy', which is said to concern the role the organization plays in society, including its fundamental mission and its relationship with other social institutions (Carroll and Buchholtz, 2009).

The strategy process: issues of choice and integration

An environmental strategy has been defined as 'a pattern in action over time that is intended to manage the interface between business and the natural environment' (Sharma, 2000: 682). Such strategies are said to concern the manner in which a firm addresses issues concerning its ecological impact and to involve its selection of both the width and depth of environmentally friendly practices and activities (Clemens, 2001; Lee and Rhee, 2007). As indicated above, the term can be applied at different levels within the organization and ideally requires a firm to consider how its responses can be tailored to the needs of the enterprise, including its overall strategic requirements (see below).

An illustration of how the idea of different strategy levels can be applied to the choice of a firm's environmental strategies is provided in Box 8.1. According to Banerjee (2001), organizations have options when deciding how to integrate environmental concerns into their strategies, with the range of choices tending to move from a reactive/compliance-focused approach at the functional level to a more proactive stance at the business and corporate levels. His contention is that few, if any, firms show evidence of integrating the environment into their strategy at enterprise level, although environmental groups such as Friends of the Earth, Greenpeace, and World Wildlife Fund (WWF) manifestly have environmental protection as their core mission.

BOX 8.1 LEVELS OF ENVIRONMENTAL STRATEGY

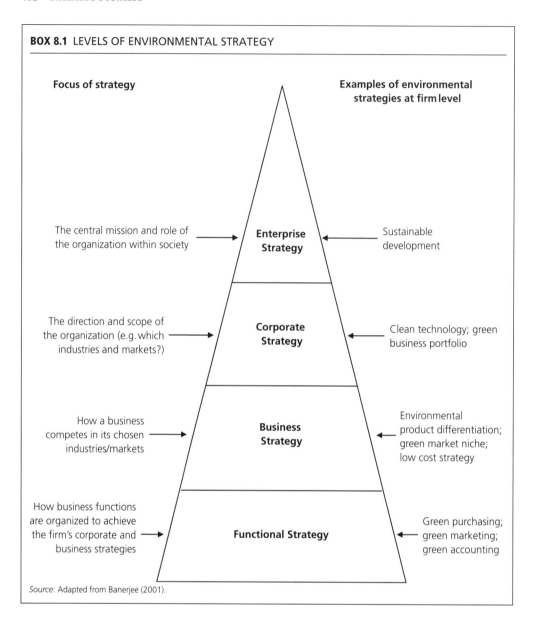

Focus of strategy

Examples of environmental strategies at firm level

The central mission and role of the organization within society → **Enterprise Strategy** ← Sustainable development

The direction and scope of the organization (e.g. which industries and markets?) → **Corporate Strategy** ← Clean technology; green business portfolio

How a business competes in its chosen industries/markets → **Business Strategy** ← Environmental product differentiation; green market niche; low cost strategy

How business functions are organized to achieve the firm's corporate and business strategies → **Functional Strategy** ← Green purchasing; green marketing; green accounting

Source: Adapted from Banerjee (2001).

With regard to a firm's choice of environmental strategy, the chronological strategy process model alluded to in the introduction to this chapter is well represented in the environmental management literature. In his paper on developing environmental management strategies, Roome (1992: 16) portrays the strategy process as involving the managed evolution of a business in reaction to its changing external context; a 'planned and programmed adjustment of the structures, systems and activities of business in response to perceived and anticipated changes in the business environment' involving the processes of strategic analysis, choice, implementation, review, and control. Aragón-Correa and Rubio-López (2007) adopt a similar stance, arguing that the processes of analysis, selection, implementation, performance measurement, and control evident in a firm's environmental strategizing are parallel to those followed in its general business strategy process.

The central message of the standard strategic management model is that a firm's choice of environmental strategy should be based on prior analysis of both its internal and external context. Kolk (2000), for example, has recommended that a business should examine its position from three points of view: outside/in, inside/in, and inside/out. Outside/in relates to influences external to the firm, including factors such as stakeholder pressures, industry structure, and market conditions. Inside/in concerns are those relating to the internal characteristics of the firm such as its existing practices, skills, resources, and capabilities, whereas inside/out considerations refer to the network of organizations of which the firm is a part and concern its relationships and patterns of dependencies with firms involved in its value chain.

In arguing for prior analysis of this kind, Kolk (2000) and others are pointing to the simple fact that environmental strategy formulation does not take place in a vacuum but needs to be based on the contingent requirements of a firm's internal and external environments (Hoffman, 2000; Aragón-Correa and Rubio-López, 2007). As noted previously, Angell and Rands (2002) see external pressures as the main driver of strategic formulation and implementation of environmental initiatives in manufacturing businesses, with the organization's context—including characteristics such as firm size and industry—acting as a filter that shapes managerial interpretations of the external environment. Aragón-Correa and Rubio-López (2007), in contrast, tend to place more emphasis on internal influences, arguing that strategy choice should be based on a firm's resources and capabilities, thereby stressing the fact that there can be several environmental approaches available for any organization according to its particular circumstances at a given point in time.

Whether environmental strategy formulation is a top-down or bottom-up process has also been the subject of some dispute (Winn and Angell, 2000); the balance of opinion, however, tends to favour the former, with senior managers and executives seen as central to the decision-making process (see e.g. Prakash, 2000a, 2001), particularly at the corporate and business levels. In making choices between alternative types of response, decision-makers will be influenced by a variety of considerations, including the nature and source of external pressure, corporate perceptions of risk and/or market opportunity, the degree of internal resistance to change, path dependencies, and the question of the ease of strategy implementation (Ghobadian et al., 1995; Hart, 1995; Roberts, 1995; Maxwell et al., 1997; Hoffman, 2000). When uncertainties over future regulations, competitor and market responses, and bottom line impact are added into the mixture, it is perhaps not surprising that some businesses tend to favour either a reactive, compliance-based approach or decide to make incremental adjustments to their existing practices rather than pursuing more environmentally proactive strategies (Roberts, 1995).

Apart from the issue of strategy choice, a firm's decision-makers have also to consider the equally important question of implementation and in particular how far to integrate the chosen environmental strategy into its existing policies, structures, practices, and procedures. Hoffman (2000) rightly points out that an organization's environmental strategy normally touches on many of its central objectives including its goals vis-à-vis corporate reputation, market growth, risk management, product development, and operational efficiency. It can also impact on the firm's day-to-day activities such as capital budgeting, product design, costing, and human resource management (Epstein, 1996; Banerjee, 2001). While some organizations make minimal attempts to embed their environmental actions into their existing business strategies and activities, others may seek to align them with their current operating context and characteristics including their resources and capabilities (Maxwell et al., 1997). The latter approach requires the organization to consider a variety of other related issues including the timing, scope, and consistency of change across business units and/or geographical boundaries; the need for supporting shifts in business culture, structure, reward systems, and job responsibilities; future capital investment programmes; and the question of identifying, measuring, and communicating the business value derived from environmentalism both internally and externally (Roberts, 1995; Starik et al., 1996; Maxwell et al., 1997; James et al., 1999; Hoffman, 2000).

Three ways in which a firm may address the complexities of the strategy implementation/integration process are illustrated in Box 8.2. All three schemes see implementation as a multi-stage issue, ideally requiring a systematic approach tailored to the needs and requirements of the organization. As with strategic choice, firms have alternatives where implementation is concerned and the processes of choice and implementation are interrelated rather than sequential as suggested by strategy models. A decision to move from compliance to a more proactive environmental strategy will invariably require the firm to adapt its existing management structures or create entirely new ones, a development which can prove a source of conflict and resistance, especially within organizations operating across multiple business divisions, diverse geographic markets, and under different social, market, and regulatory conditions (Maxwell et al., 1997).

BOX 8.2 APPROACHES TO ENVIRONMENTAL STRATEGY IMPLEMENTATION

Epstein (1996) suggests eight steps to implement a corporate environmental strategy. These are:

1. Strategic development and organization of corporate structure.
2. Identification and measurement of environmental effects of the firm.
3. Preparation of inventory of current environmental activities and their impact.
4. Integration of all current and future environmental effects into corporate decisions (e.g. on pricing, product design, investments).

(continued)

BOX 8.2 (CONTINUED)

---

5. Integration of financial analysis and control systems into environmental decisions.
6. Establishment of both internal and external reporting systems.
7. Integration of corporate environmental performance to performance evaluation systems.
8. Gathering feedback, reviewing, and revising strategy as required.

Starik et al. (1996) propose a three-step approach they call MOSAIC, an acronym for Mission, Objectives, Strategic orientation, Action plan, Implementation, and Controls. Step 1 requires a firm to examine its current MOSAIC to ascertain the organization's existing relationship with the natural environment. Step 2 comprises an analysis of the firm's relationship with its stakeholders and what it regards as important in its various environments. Step 3 is the combination of the first two steps to provide a revised MOSAIC aimed at developing a strategic environmental response that is relevant both now and in the future.

Like Epstein, Maxwell et al. (1997) have developed a programmed approach which they use to compare environmental strategy implementation at three firms: Volvo, Polaroid, and Procter and Gamble. Since firms have options under the different steps being examined, the authors refer to these as 'programmatic alternatives'.

The six steps comprise:

1. Establishment of structures for environmental goal setting.
2. Development of mechanisms to monitor and review environmental performance (e.g. environmental auditing procedures).
3. Establishment of incentives and controls to encourage environmental achievement (e.g. by employees).
4. Creation of guidelines and tools for environmental investments (e.g. financial and management systems).
5. Development of methodologies and tools to assist in environmental decision-making (e.g. risk management procedures; environmental impact approaches).
6. Guidelines for communication and negotiation with stakeholders.

Maxwell et al. suggest that a firm needs to find its own style of implementation according to its personal circumstances and contexts.

Strategic postures

Research suggests that firms often adopt particular strategic postures or generic responses where environmentalism is concerned. In the literature, such postures are frequently presented in the form of typologies or taxonomies and encapsulate a variety of responses of both a market and a non-market kind, including the lobbying of governmental decision-makers responsible for environmental regulations and legislation (see e.g. Lyon and Maxwell, 1999, 2003).

Most attempts at modelling alternative strategic postures revolve around the idea that a firm's environmental responses can be linked to its perceptions of the risks posed by its activities and/or the opportunities that could potentially be leveraged from embracing emvironmentalism. Steger's environmental strategy framework (1993)—discussed extensively in Chapter 5—suggests that an organization's overall strategic response is likely to reflect its calculation of the scale of both the environmental risks associated with its environmental actions and the potential market opportunities available from environmental protection; the resultant four postures of the firm—indifferent, defensive, offensive, or innovative—being presented in the form of a matrix (see Figure 5.3). Vastag et al. (1996) argue that the management of environmental risks (both internal and external) is the primary criterion a business needs to adopt when designing its environmental management approach; their four generic responses—reactive, proactive, strategic, crisis preventive—indicating how companies are likely to respond to these risks. When this framework was tested via a survey of Hungarian company representatives, the authors claim that the data indicated a relatively well-defined relationship between a firm's strategic posture on environmental management and the risks it faced, with industry and location key variables in shaping corporate responses.

While the above two examples illustrate how a firm's responses may be related, at least in part, to the threats arising from its interaction with the natural environment, some classification schemes place more emphasis on the different opportunities a business has to benefit from environmentalism. In Starik et al.'s matrix (1996) of strategic environmental postures, corporate responses are linked to the firm's change orientation and its approach to value creation for its green customers. Their contention is that organizations that have a more proactive approach towards environmental protection will tend to adopt a stance that is more innovative or aimed at preventing pollution at source, whilst the more accommodative organizations tend to be orientated towards compliance or minor improvements in a product's environmental performance (Box 8.3). This notion

---

BOX 8.3 TYPES OF ENVIRONMENTAL STRATEGIC POSTURE

		Firms attitude to value creation	
		Benefit enhancement	Cost reductions
	Proactive approach	Green product innovation (major modification	Beyond compliance pollution prevention
Firm's approach to change			
	Accommodative approach	Green product differentiation (minor modification)	Compliance focused pollution prevention

Source: Adapted from Starik et al. (1996).

that strategic decision-makers differ in their stance towards environmental protection also finds expression in Winn and Angell's factor-based model (2000) which, as indicated previously, focuses on the internal aspects of the corporate greening process (see Chapter 5 for a fuller discussion).

Further examples of theoretically and empirically derived schemes of strategy classifications are illustrated in Table 8.1. As these examples show, researchers frequently adopt schemes from the strategy and organizational management literature and apply them to a firm's environmental orientation in general or to its responses to particular environmental issues (e.g. climate change) or contexts (e.g. environmentally regulated industries). Common to most of the examples shown in Table 8.1 is the idea that a firm's environmental strategy and its underlying strategic posture can be neatly categorized along a continuum that ranges from the basically reactive/passive form of response to the more proactive, innovative and leadership-based approach said to be evident in some organizations. How far this is possible in practice, however, is open to question, given that an organization's environmental strategies (and tactics) are likely to vary according to the issue at hand and over time and can be simultaneously defensive in some contexts (e.g. in response to proposed environmental regulations) while offensive in others (e.g. in response to perceived market opportunities via environmentalism).

Table 8.1 Environmental strategy classification schemes

Author(s)	Scheme(s) for classifying environmental postures
Tsai and Child (1997)	The authors identify two models. The first is Oliver's[1] typology of strategic responses, which are acquiesce, compromise, avoid, defy, manipulate. They suggest a sixth option, namely cooperation. They then examine Kirchgeorg's[2] study of environmental strategy alternatives which comprises five options: innovation, retreat, resistance, adaptation, passivity.
Aragón-Correa (1998)	Aragón-Correa's analysis draws initially from Miles and Snow's[3] typology which identifies firms as 'prospectors', 'analysers' or 'defenders'. From this he developed five natural environment clusters which he termed 'environmental excellence', 'leading edge', 'compliance', 'compliance plus', 'non-compliance'. He described these as postures based on the three approaches to the natural environment derived from Miles and Snow.
Clemens (2001)	Clemens also sees Oliver's typology as a useful way of understanding a firm's environmental strategies and their associated tactics in relation to environmental regulation.
Bussye and Verbeke (2003)	Building on Hart's resource-based environmental approaches (end-of-pipe; pollution prevention; product stewardship and sustainable development), the authors suggest three resource-based environmental strategy profiles: a reactive strategy, pollution prevention, environmental leadership.
Lee and Rhee (2007)	Like Bussye and Verbeke, the authors use cluster analysis to distinguish different environmental strategy groupings. The four identified types were 'reactive', 'focused', 'opportunistic', and 'proactive'.

Notes: [1] Oliver (1991).
　　　[2] Kirchgeorg (1993).
　　　[3] Miles and Snow (1978).

Reactive versus proactive environmental strategies

As both the analysis in Chapter 5 and above illustrate, much of the early literature on the greening of business has produced typologies and taxonomies of environmental strategies and/or green organizations. For the purposes of empirical investigation, these systems of classification have often been collapsed into two groups: reactive versus proactive or compliance versus beyond-compliance behaviour (Sharma, 2002).

Slater and Angel (2000) have argued that reactive strategies are essentially non-strategic and involve firms responding to environmental problems or demands after an event has occurred, whereas proactive strategies involve a company strategically anticipating change in order to gain competitive benefits. Reactivity, in other words, is the idea that firms only take action when mandated to do so and their responses are often directed towards compliance with government regulations and widely accepted industry practice (Sharma and Vredenburg, 1998; Sharma et al., 1999). Proactivity, by way of contrast, is said to involve systematic patterns of voluntary, beyond-compliance behaviour; a commitment to environmentalism as an integrated part of a firm's overall strategy and operation; and a tendency of an organization to initiate changes in its various strategic policies, to cooperate with government and anticipate evolving regulatory trends, and to be ahead of the curve where regulatory, market, or social demands for improved environmental performance are concerned (Dechant and Altman, 1994; Andrews, 1998; Aragón-Correa, 1998; Sharma and Vredenburg, 1998; Bussye and Verbeke, 2003; Aragón-Correa and Rubio-López, 2007).

There is broad agreement in the literature that it is possible to differentiate between reactive and proactive approaches to environmental strategy-making and management via an examination of corporate attitudes, structures, and processes. Under Roome's strategic options model (1992) (see Chapter 5), firms that pursue reactive, compliance-based environmental strategies tend to take a piecemeal approach in response to legislation, public concern, or scientific evidence and consequently do not see environmentalism as a source of competitive advantage nor seek to embed it into the fabric of the organization (see Chapter 11). As an enterprise becomes more proactive (e.g. as in Roome's notions of 'compliance plus', 'commercial and environmental excellence', and 'leading edge'), its environmental strategy becomes increasingly integrated into its day-to-day operations and decisions, with senior managers adjusting core managerial practices and values and developing and utilizing management systems to challenge existing conventions and encourage organizational change.

Roome's implicit (and sometimes explicit) assumption that environmental proactivity requires a change in managerial mindsets, operational procedures, and resource commitments also finds expression in other studies. Slater and Angel (2000), for example, claim that proactive firms see environmental regulation as a strategic concern and give corporate status to environmental issues, with resources devoted to appropriate systems of environmental management and control (see Chapter 9) and to staff training and development. Vastag et al. (1996) reach a similar conclusion, arguing that a proactive and strategic approach to environmental management is typified by a management focus on outstanding performance, a commitment of resources to corporate-wide management training and education, and the location of environmental issues and responses within the most senior levels of the organization.

Whilst considerable effort has been devoted to debating the benefits to firms of moving from a reactive to a more proactive environmental strategy (see the discussion in Chapter 6 and Aragón-Correa and Rubio-López, 2007), rather less analysis has occurred concerning how organizations get from one to the other, including the question of how they can acquire capabilities in areas such as pollution prevention or green product development which allow them to achieve higher levels of environmental performance (Sharma, 2002). Is it simply that businesses are responding to the drivers of change discussed in Chapter 4 or that organizational decision-makers become convinced that corporate greening pays, or is the process more gradual, subtle, and developmental and influenced by existing capabilities and practices which provide a platform for organizational change and higher order learning (Shrivastava, 1995c; Lober, 1998; Sharma and Vredenburg, 1998; Branzei and Vertinsky, 2002; Aragón-Correa and Sharma, 2003; Sharma and Aragón-Correa, 2005; Etzion, 2007)? Marcus (2005) suggests that the answer probably contains elements of both perspectives, with environmental capability acquisition linked to both public policies and the values and beliefs of corporate decision-makers and filtered through psychological and organizational processes including perception, issue interpretation, and negotiation.

Firm-level green strategies

For firms wishing to reduce the impact of their activities on the natural environment, a range of strategies is available to organizational decision-makers. In the majority of businesses that are small or medium-sized and where ownership of the enterprise and the day-to-day management is usually in the same hands, the division between corporate and business-level strategy-making is effectively artificial, particularly when the firm operates out of one establishment and produces a single product or service. In larger firms—most notably multi-product, multi-business unit organizations—corporate environmental strategies will be formulated at corporate board level and include major decisions on the direction and scope of the firm's activities, its vision, allocation of resources, product portfolio, and targets for the organization as a whole and/or its constituent parts, while individual strategic business units usually determine the most appropriate competitive strategies to meet the overall corporate objectives. In practice, of course, a company's corporate environmental goals are often longer term, are frequently

Table 8.2 Hart's sustainability portfolio

Environmental strategy	Focus of green response	Focus of attention
Pollution prevention	Internal	Current position
Product stewardship	External	Current position
Clean technology	Internal	Future position
Sustainability vision	External	Future position

Source: Adapted from Hart (1997).

aspirational, and are usually closely linked to its objectives as a profit-making organization. How individual business units help to deliver these objectives can vary between the different component parts of the enterprise.

In his natural-resource-based analysis of corporate greening, Hart (1995) identified three interconnected strategies linked to competitive advantage: pollution prevention, product stewardship, and sustainable development (see Box 6.3). In a subsequent paper (Hart, 1997), he extended his analysis by including a strategy based on clean technology, with the resultant four approaches presented in the form of a sustainability portfolio, a simplified version of which is illustrated in Table 8.2. We examine each of these four strategies in turn.

POLLUTION PREVENTION

Firms adopting a pollution prevention strategy are essentially seeking to minimize or eliminate waste, effluents, and emissions associated with their activities. The introduction of the Toxic Releases Inventory (TRI) in the United States under which firms are required to provide information on emissions of toxic chemicals is a good example of this approach, with participating organizations encouraged to pursue pollution abatement measures for fear of negative stakeholder responses (Buchholz, 1998).

Pollution abatement can occur in two main ways: pollution control or pollution prevention (Hart, 1995). Pollution control—also often called an 'end-of-pipe' approach—essentially involves adopting measures to deal with pollution once it has occurred, for example by the recovery, storage, treatment, and disposal of pollutants via the use of pollution control technologies. As an environmental strategy, pollution control is normally portrayed as a short-term, reactive, and compliance-based response, requiring little, if anything, in the way of new skills and capabilities and generally thought to contribute nothing to value creation (Russo and Fouts, 1997; Sarkis and Cordeiro, 2001; Bussye and Verbeke, 2003; Claver et al., 2007).

Pollution prevention represents a more proactive, beyond-compliance approach, whereby emissions are reduced, prevented, or altered through changes to a firm's products and/or processes. Indicative measures include material substitution, recycling of waste products, process innovations, new housekeeping techniques, and system modification (Dieleman and de Hoo, 1993; Hart, 1995; Sarkis and Cordeiro, 2001) and this can necessitate substantial investments in environmental technologies aimed at generating future cost savings via environmentalism (Shrivastava, 1995b). A strategy of pollution prevention is generally held to require new capability-building in production and operations and has been associated with a different resource base than required under a pollution control logic (Hart, 1995; Russo and Fouts, 1997; Claver et al., 2007). This could explain why some firms appear to be reluctant to address pollution problems at source, despite the substantial benefits said to be associated with programmes such as 3M's Pollution Prevention Pays (3P) and Dow's Waste Reduction Always Pays (WRAP).

PRODUCT STEWARDSHIP

Product stewardship has been described as a form of product differentiation in that it focuses not merely on minimizing pollution within the production process, but more especially on all the environmental impacts generated within a product's life cycle (Bussye and Verbeke, 2003). According to Hart (1995, 1997), product stewardship requires a firm to integrate the 'voice of the environment' into product design and development processes through the use of such tools as Life Cycle Assessment or Analysis (LCA) and Design for the Environment (DfE). The former is used to assess the environmental impact of a product from the 'cradle to the grave', thereby allowing the firm to identify the environmental consequences throughout a product's life cycle, from material selection through to ultimate disposal, and to consider how it could achieve a lower environmental cost (Svoboda, 1999). The latter is a systematic way of including environmental thinking in product and process designs from the outset, thus allowing the creation of products that are easier to recover, reuse, or recycle, as exemplified by Rank Xerox's and Hitachi's approach in the 1990s (Hutchinson, 1996; Esty and Winston, 2006).

GREEN SNAPSHOT: HCL TECHNOLOGIES

HCL Technologies Ltd is a leading Indian IT services company, active in a variety of sectors including aerospace, defence, energy, healthcare, travel, and logistics. To achieve its objective of becoming a more environmentally sustainable organization, the company has established a 'Go Green Program' which is aimed at (a) reducing its environmental impact and (b) raising environmental awareness among its employees. The former includes efforts to reduce toxic and hazardous substances, minimize waste generation, reduce resource usage, and dispose of waste products in an environmentally friendly manner using authorized and certified contractors. The latter comprises corporate campaigns to inform employees of key environmental issues and initiatives aimed at providing opportunities for workers to contribute to environmental causes. HCL is also active in a number of economic and environmental fora (e.g. the Indian Council for Sustainable Development; the World Economic Forum) and is recognized as one of India's leading green businesses.

Within an organization, a product stewardship strategy can find expression in a firm's decision to exit an environmentally damaging business; to develop new, environmentally friendly products; and to redesign its existing products in order to reduce their environmental impact. Hart (1995), for instance, quotes the case of Proctor and Gamble's efforts to reduce the use of solvents and phosphates in its cleaning and detergent products and BMW's design-for-disassembly process aimed at pre-empting the German government's proposed 'take-back' law. Further examples include Indian IT company HCL Technologies' attempts to phase out hazardous materials in its products and Dutch carpet tile manufacture Desso's decision to adopt a cradle-to-grave philosophy as a key step towards a fully closed-loop system by 2020 (see Green Snapshots).

GREEN SNAPSHOT: DESSO CARPETS

The Dutch company Desso is one of Europe's largest producers of commercial grade carpet and carpet tiles used in a wide range of applications in offices, hotels, sporting venues, banks, schools, public buildings, universities, hospitals, and business premises. In 2007, the firm announced its intention of establishing a fully closed-loop system by 2020 based around a cradle-to-cradle (C2C)[1] philosophy. Working in partnership with the Environmental Protection Encouragement Agency (EPEA), Desso's aim is to produce products that are either entirely biodegradeable or are capable of being recycled in a way that provides the raw materials for new goods emerging from its operations. Key steps in the process include purchasing appropriate materials, using waste materials to provide a source of energy, reducing energy consumption, providing facilities for composting, recycling and product take-back, and completely modifying the way the firm does business (e.g. renting rather than just selling its products). The company already has a number of its carpet tile products certified to C2C and its intention is to extend this over the coming decade to its entire product range.

Note: [1]Information on C2C is available on the EPEA website.

CLEAN TECHNOLOGY

Hart's sustainability portfolio (1997) characterizes both pollution prevention and product stewardship as 'today's' strategies in that they seek to address current environmental issues in business without necessarily looking towards potential future vulnerabilities and imperatives. One way of achieving a forward-looking approach to the management of the firm's interface with the natural environment is to plan for and invest in clean technologies that are both more environmentally sustainable and strategically attractive.

Environmental technologies have been defined as 'production equipment, methods and procedures, product designs, and product delivery mechanisms that conserve energy and natural resources, minimize environmental load of human activities and protect the natural environment' (Shrivastava, 1995*b*: 185). Under this broad definition, they include both hardware (e.g. equipment) and operating methods (e.g. waste management practices) and can be seen as both a set of techniques and a management orientation that incorporates a variety of approaches to managing environmental problems, including manufacturing for the environment, design for disassembly, and total environmental quality management.

Where corporate responses are concerned, the last decade has seen a gradual increase in the number of companies researching into and developing cleaner and more sustainable technologies, often via the establishment of cross-border alliances or joint ventures (see below). In Denmark, Danfoss, a traditional producer of refrigeration and control components, has invested in the production of customized control boards for solar-powered inverters which facilitate connection to a country's electricity grid, allowing householders with solar panels to sell power directly to the central energy system. In Germany, Enercon, one of the world's largest producers of wind generators, and Q-cells—the world's largest producer of photovoltaic cells—have both capitalized on the country's push to become a leading player in clean technologies via incentivizing companies to develop more environmentally benign sources of power.

While the costs associated with investing in research and development, including the accumulation of new competencies, tend to suggest that a clean technology strategy will predominately be the preserve of larger corporations, the evidence suggests that even smaller businesses can exploit opportunities in this field. For example, an article in the *Financial Times* on 23 December 2010 reported that a small, unlisted UK company, Green Biologics, had signed a deal with two Chinese biochemical businesses—Guangxi Jinyuan Biochemical and Lianyungang Union of Chemicals—to provide fermentation technology that would be used in existing production facilities to produce biobutanol, a low-cost, advanced biofuel derived from sustainable feed stocks that can be used to replace petrol. Green Biologics' CEO suggested that, through its Chinese partners, the firm was able to build a platform for the introduction of the next generation of its products as part of its global strategy of offering advance plant designs and sustainable technologies aimed at reducing greenhouse gas emissions.

SUSTAINABLE DEVELOPMENT

The three environmental strategies discussed above are regarded by Hart as steps on the route towards sustainable development or what he subsequently called 'sustainability vision'. The concept of sustainable development has been examined in more detail in Chapter 2; here it is essentially used to denote an approach—or what Hart terms a 'road map'—aimed at minimizing the negative consequences associated with firm growth and development across all types of economies. Pursuing such a strategy requires a firm to consider the implications of all its decisions and interactions with other stakeholders and to examine the social, economic, and environmental impacts of its acquisitions of materials, design, and manufacturing processes, product distribution, consumption and disposal aspects, and market extension. For businesses seeking to move towards sustainability, what is required is a long-term vision and strong leadership and a willingness to invest substantially in R&D and in future market development (Hart, 1995, 1997; Bussye and Verbeke, 2003).

The idea of the sustainable business organization is discussed more fully in the final chapter; here it is sufficient to note that, as a strategy aimed at securing a firm's future position in emerging as well as developed markets, sustainable development is often an elusive and amorphous concept. Hoffman (2000) notes the increasing practice of corporate executives in companies such as Ford, DuPont, Dow, Nike, and Royal Dutch Shell to make proclamations on sustainability issues and questions whether a significant amount of progress has been made in this area. As the case study at the end of Chapter 11 indicates, a sustainability vision needs to be translated into practice at the corporate, business, and functional levels and even large multinational corporations can find this a considerable challenge nearly half a century after the idea first emerged.

Strategic environmental alliances

Companies engaged in pursuing more proactive environmental strategies may do so alone or in alliance with other organizations. Collaborations can range from the informal to the formal; may be loosely or tightly structured local, national, or international; and can involve organizations from one or more sectors of the economy. While some of these alliances may be formed with the aim of achieving greater operational efficiencies through a shared approach to environmental protection, others are more strategic in nature in that they seek to strengthen a firm's competitive position either via a market- or non-market-focused (e.g. by influencing legislation) approach to corporate environmentalism.

An example of firms working together to achieve a collaborative approach to environmental protection can be found in Holliday et al.'s examination (2002) of the business case for sustainable development, which discusses Nestlé's attempts to develop a greener supply chain by working closely with its many upstream business partners on the issue of environmental performance. Other examples are quoted by Biddle (2000), who notes how companies often establish strategic alliances in order to share green research and development costs and risks, exemplified by Coca Cola's partnership with Hoechst Celanese, the supplier of its recyclable bottles.

GREEN SNAPSHOT: PARTNERING FOR THE ENVIRONMENT

The growing importance of collaboration as a means of achieving corporate sustainability objectives is exemplified by Heinz's announcement (February 2011) of a strategic partnership with Coca Cola which enables the
former to produce its ketchup bottles using the latter's PlantBottle packaging technology. First launched in
2009, PlantBottle is a fully recyclable container that is partly made from renewable and sustainably sourced
plant-based material derived from sugarcane ethanol (see Green Snapshot on Braskem in Chapter 4) and which
has already helped Coca Cola to reduce its carbon impact. Through its switch to the new form of packaging,
Heinz hopes to contribute to its sustainability goals in areas such as waste production, energy and water use, and
greenhouse gas emissions.

In industries where research, development, and commercialization costs are huge, but
where potential for market development and penetration is also substantial, collaboration appears to make sense from a strategic point of view. Nowhere is this more evident
than in fields such as renewable energy and green car production. In early 2011, for
example, several Finnish companies (e.g. Switch) announced their intention to look for
partnerships with Indian firms in the development of renewables (including bio-fuels) in
an attempt to provide greater access to a rapidly emerging market. Some months earlier,
sixteen Chinese companies formed a national alliance aimed at jointly developing
electric vehicles and providing a supporting infrastructure for a rapidly growing customer base, while French and German auto manufacturers BMW and Peugeot/Citroen
announced their intention to establish an electric vehicle alliance to exploit the growing
demand for hybrid cars.

Apart from business to business (B2B) alliances of this kind, some firms have also
entered into strategic collaborative arrangements with environmental NGOs (non-
governmental organizations) to pursue mutually beneficial ecological goals; an arrangement generally described as a 'green alliance' (Stafford and Hartman, 1996; Hartman
et al., 1999; Stafford et al., 2000). Two well-known examples of such alliances are
McDonald's partnership with the Environmental Defense Fund (EDF) in the early
1990s aimed at establishing a waste reduction task force to address the company's
solid waste issues (Murphy and Bendell, 1997) and the alliance between Greenpeace
and the German company Foron Household Appliances to market an ozone-safe
refrigerator (Stafford et al., 2000). Collaborations of this kind can also occur at the
industry level, as in the case of WWF's partnership with the UK wood product trade,
established to promote trade in products from well-managed forests (Bendell and
Sullivan, 1996).

Although the potential benefits of a green alliance from a firm's point of view appear
to be less tangible than those normally associated with a B2B arrangement, there is
general agreement that businesses can gain political goodwill and credibility by engaging

with NGOs (Gunningham and Sinclair, 2002; Holliday et al., 2002). They may also uncover win-win technologies that improve the bottom line while protecting the natural environment, an outcome termed 'constructive engagement' (Rondinelli and London, 2003; Yaziji, 2004). Much the same line of argument can be put for cooperation between businesses and government agencies, whereby firms (or industries) achieve their regulatory goals at lower transaction costs via a business/government partnership, while the authorities can also claim a measure of enhanced environmental protection without the need to legislate or regulate corporate behaviour (see e.g. the discussion on 'negotiated agreements' in Chapter 3).

While the growth of cross-sector environmental partnerships can legitimately be seen as an indication of the changing role of the regulatory state (Gunningham and Sinclair, 2002) or an essential step on the route towards more sustainable forms of development (Hart, 1999), it also can be interpreted as evidence of an increasing acceptance by firms (and industries) that competitiveness can be advanced by companies engaging in more cooperative types of relationships with both regulators and environmentalists (Porter and van der Linde, 1995*a*, 1995*b*; Hoffman, 2001*b*). Observers claim that important synergies can arise from partnerships that merge the complementary capabilities of businesses, NGOs, and government agencies, and this can give rise to business opportunities by encouraging innovative approaches to environmental problems (see e.g. Holliday et al., 2002). That said, as the discussion in Chapter 6 has indicated, the precise nature of the link between proactive environmental strategies and business performance still remains a contested issue, as do the variables that are thought to influence this relationship.

Case Study: GE's Ecomagination initiative

GE (General Electric) is a multinational organization, operating across a range of business sectors from infrastructure and finance to the media. Headquartered in the United States, the company operates in over 160 countries and employs more than a quarter of a million people worldwide.

In 2005, the company launched its Ecomagination initiative, an environmentally focused business strategy aimed at producing profitable growth for the organization by providing solutions to the growing demand for cleaner and more efficient sources of energy, reduced carbon emissions, and increased access to cleaner sources of water. Launched with a multi-million dollar advertising campaign, the initiative emphasized the idea that being 'good' (i.e. socially and environmentally responsible) and being a successful business went hand-in-hand. GE's contention was that business opportunities could be exploited by providing solutions to the challenges associated with problems such as climate change and the need to move towards a reduced reliance on carbon-intensive products and services.

To qualify for inclusion in GE's Ecomagination portfolio, a product or service must be able to demonstrate measurable and significant improvement in operating and environmental performance or in value proposition. It must also provide value to investors as well as customers. Since the initiative began, products meeting these criteria have ranged from electric vehicles, aircraft engines, energy-efficient light bulbs, and water purification technologies to projects based on solar and wind energy.

According to GE's Ecomagination Annual Report in 2010, during the five years of the initiative, Ecomagination products and services had generated $85 billion for the business. The company had also been able to significantly reduce its own environmental footprint during this period. Its future aims include a commitment to achieving further reductions in environmental impact and to increased investment in clean technology research and development. It has also launched an Ecomagination Challenge fund aimed at stimulating innovative ideas that could contribute to GE's product development in the energy field.

While business benefits are difficult to quantify precisely, there is some evidence to indicate that GE has achieved an increase in revenue from its portfolio of environmentally sustainable consumer and industrial goods and services (see e.g. Ottman, 2010). It has also been suggested that its Ecomagination initiative has provided a number of other less tangible benefits such as creating customer trust in GE's brands and helping the business to attract and retain high-quality employees wishing to work for a socially responsible organization (see e.g. Esty and Winston, 2006; Laszlo and Zhexembayeva, 2011).

A sister programme, Healthymagination—aimed at promoting healthcare at lower costs to people around the world—was launched in 2008.

9 Environmental management systems

An effective environmental management system can help a company manage, measure and improve the environmental aspects of its operations. It can lead to more efficient compliance with mandatory and voluntary environmental requirements. It can help companies effect a cultural change as environmental management practices are incorporated into its overall business operations.

(Tibor and Feldman, 1999)

Small and medium-sized firms face internal and external barriers when seeking to address their environmental issues and adopt and implement EMSs, but it is the internal barriers that, initially, have the most significant role in impeding progress.

(Hillary, 2000)

… we do not agree with rejecting environmental standards altogether, as even imprecise standards may be better than none at all. However, firms seriously committed to environmental improvement need to be able to appeal to exigent standards which are clear and well publicized.

(Aragón-Correa and Rubio-López, 2007)

Introduction

Greening the firm is not simply a matter of devising appropriate corporate, business, and functional strategies but also requires an organization to consider what processes, procedures, and plans are required to enable it to manage and control its day-to-day operations and decisions in pursuit of its goals. Whether as a system of roles or as a process that is designed to assist the firm in achieving its objectives, the concept of management is normally taken to imply planning, organization, and coordination in key business areas such as staffing, resource deployment, finance, marketing, and operations. The term also equally applies to the way in which an organization manages its environmental impacts, including its internal responses to stakeholder demands for improved levels of corporate environmental performance.

In this chapter, we examine the role of the environmental management system (EMS) as a tool that can be used by an organization seeking to address issues relating to its environmental impact. While the term EMS applies to practices and processes that are to some degree unique to each organization by dint of differing management structures, procedures, priorities, and contextual influences (Stainer and Stainer, 1997), in the analysis below we focus on two major, internationally recognized systems of environmental management adopted by a growing number of business organizations: EMAS (the EU Eco-Management and Audit Scheme) and ISO14001. These systems represent what has been termed the bureaucratization of environmental management and are examples of voluntary, beyond-compliance policies adopted by firms seeking to demonstrate their environmental credentials (Kollman and Prakash, 2001; Takahashi and Nakamura, 2005). Given their emergence in the closing decade of the twentieth century, they have been linked to the increasing trend to self-regulation discussed in previous chapters and have been heralded as an example of regulatory flexibility (Steger, 2000; Gunningham and Sinclair, 2002), what Coglianese and Nash (2001) refer to as 'regulating from the inside' whether for operational or strategic reasons.

What is an EMS?

EMSs have been variously described as 'practices', 'processes', 'tools', 'programmes', 'frameworks', 'efforts', or 'policies' aimed at improving a firm's environmental performance. A selection of definitions by recent writers in the field is given in Table 9.1. As these definitions indicate, the term EMS is generally taken to mean a multi-faceted process of internal change that is designed to identify, measure, and control a firm's environmental impacts (Bansal and Hunter, 2003). Like the notion of quality systems with which they are most readily associated, EMSs aim towards improvement in a firm's performance through the establishment of structures, processes, and procedures capable of providing information, articulating goals, monitoring achievement, and undertaking corrective action where necessary. They are generally held to provide a means of ensuring organizational compliance with existing laws and regulations and to offer an opportunity to gain potential benefits for both the firm and the wider society (Coglianese and Nash, 2001; Schaltegger et al., 2003).

In practice of course, EMSs can vary substantially across firms. They may be informal or formal; externally accredited or non-accredited; rigorous or relatively loose in their application; internally devised or based on standards developed by trade associations (e.g. Responsible Care), national governments (e.g. BS7750), regional bodies (e.g. EMAS), or international organizations (e.g. ISO14001). They can also differ in terms of the number and mix of elements involved, the comprehensiveness of their coverage, and the ambitiousness of their objectives in relation to environmental improvements (Khanna and Anton, 2002b; Bansal and Hunter, 2003; Anton et al., 2004). In some cases, firms use recognized standards to develop a new in-house EMS or adapt existing

Table 9.1 Definitions of an environmental management system

Author(s)	Definition
Tibor and Feldman (1999: 257)	'An effective environmental management system can help a company manage, measure and improve the environmental aspects of its operations.'
Kolk (2000: 103)	'An EMS is that part of the overall management system which includes the organisational structure, responsibilities, practices, procedures, processes and resources for determining and implementing the firm's overall aims and principles of action with respect to the environment.'
Steger (2000: 24)	'An environmental management system is broadly defined (here) as a transparent, systematic process known corporate-wide, with the purpose of prescribing and implementing environmental goals, policies and responsibilities, as well as regular auditing of its elements.'
Coglianese and Nash (2001: 1)	'An EMS represents a collection of internal efforts at policymaking, planning, and implementation that yields benefits for the organisation as well as potential benefits for society at large.'
Florida and Davison (2001: 64)	'Like other management systems, an EMS is a formal system for articulating goals, making choices, gathering information, measuring progress and improving performance.'
Morrow and Rondinelli (2002: 1)	(An EMS is) '. . . a process for integrating corporate environmental policies and programmes . . . .'
Gunningham and Sinclair (2002: 111)	'. . . an EMS is a management tool intended to assist the organisation in achieving environmental and economic goals by focusing on systemic problems rather than individual deficiencies.'
Khanna and Anton (2002b: 409–10)	'EMS represents an organizational change within firms and self-motivated efforts at internalizing environmental externalities by adopting management practices that integrate environment and production decisions, which identify opportunities for pollution reduction and enable the firm to make continuous improvements in production methods and environmental performance.'
Schaltegger et al. (2003: 296)	'An EMS is a set of management processes and procedures that allow an organisation to analyse, control and reduce the environmental impact of its operations and services and to achieve cost savings, greater efficiency and oversight, and streamlined regulatory compliance—hence, it is closely linked with the notion of eco-efficiency.'
Anton et al. (2004: 633)	'EMSs represent an organizational change within corporations and an effort for self-regulation by defining a set of formal environmental policies, goals, strategies and administrative procedures for improving environmental performance.'

practices to such a standard without formally certifying their EMS (Rondinelli and Vastag, 2000). In others, the preference is to seek certification to a widely recognized standard at the plant, firm, or corporate level in the belief that this will bestow a higher level of legitimacy in the eyes of external stakeholders than a system that is internally devised and not externally accredited.

Notwithstanding the wide variations that can occur in EMSs at the firm level, many systems tend to be based around common features. Typically, these include the establishment of an environmental policy or plan; an implementation process involving the assignment of responsibility for carrying out the plan, together with any necessary

---

GREEN SNAPSHOT: NESTLÉ'S ENVIRONMENTAL MANAGEMENT SYSTEM (NEMS)

The huge Swiss-based food, beverage, and nutrition company Nestlé introduced a corporate-wide environmental management system (NEMS) in 1996 which was designed to be an important driver of environmental improvement and a means of ensuring that the organization's practices were compliant with legal obligations and with internal policies and programmes. Based on the traditional cycle of environmental policy formulation, through target setting and performance measurement, to management review and improvement, NEMS was mandatory throughout the business. Subsequent analysis suggested that it had proved instrumental in helping Nestlé to make significant reductions in environmental impact and in raising awareness of environmental issues among company personnel (see e.g. Holliday et al., 2002).

In May 2006, the company's executive board decided to adapt the existing system to be fully compliant with ISO14001 and to certify all Nestlé factories against this international standard. The company believed that this would provide it with worldwide external recognition of its efforts in environmental management and would help to build trust among its external stakeholders in its bid to become the world's leading recognized nutrition, health, and well-being business.

By the end of 2010, Nestlé reported that 91 per cent of its factories had achieved certification to ISO14001 and that the remaining plants were in the process of preparing for certification. It also indicated its intention of extending its certification programme to its distribution centres and research and development facilities and of encouraging its business partners to do likewise.

---

training and resource commitment; the checking of progress via the application of a systematic auditing process; and the use of procedures to correct for any deficiencies or system inadequacies (Coglianese and Nash, 2001). Kolk (2000) and Matthews (2003) describe these various elements as a cycle of 'plan', 'do', 'check', and 'act', stressing the behavioural aspects of an EMS. Florida and Davison (2001) emphasize the similarity between an EMS and other management systems given the focus on articulating goals, making choices, gathering information, measuring progress, and improving performance.

As will be evident from the discussion above, the establishment of a dynamic EMS aimed at achieving continuous improvements in a firm's environmental performance will almost invariably imply the need for an organization to make changes in its structure, processes, practices, and relationships (Jørgensen, 2000). A critical determinant of whether such changes occur and how far an EMS is integrated into day-to-day business practices and processes will be the commitment of an organization's top management (Welford, 1995; Monaghan, 1997; Prakash, 1999; Coglianese and Nash, 2001), an observation that echoes the findings of studies of environmental proactivity in general. Such commitment is likely to prove harder to achieve in smaller organizations and may account in part for the negative corporate attitudes and perceived stop-start approach to EMS implementation evident in studies of small and medium-sized enterprise (SME) environmental responses (Hillary, 2000).

The issue of certification

One of the choices confronting a business when establishing an EMS is whether to opt for a scheme that is certificated by an external body. The main options available to firms in this regard are to model their EMS on an existing standard but not seek certification; self-certify to a standard (where this is possible); certify via a non-accredited verifier; or seek official certification through an accredited certification body.

The idea of seeking certification of one's EMS has been linked to the emergence of the British Standard 7750 in the early 1990s (Morrow and Rondinelli, 2002) and the subsequent development of EMAS and ISO14001 in the same decade. These standards provided for a system of certification that essentially involves the use of an external, accredited body to confirm that an organization's EMS meets the requirements of a given standard and has been effectively implemented. Firms seeking certification can do so to one or more of the nationally or internationally recognized schemes available, with some organizations using standards established at the national level as a stepping stone to either EMAS or ISO14001 (see below). In the latter case, it is worth noting that certification is not mandatory, though some governments actively encourage it (e.g. Japan) by supporting registration agencies (Kolk, 2000).

Table 9.2 provides a snapshot of ISO14001 and EMAS certifications in selected countries in recent years. The statistics indicate that ISO14001 is a more popular standard than EMAS even in EU countries, with the total (estimated) worldwide number of certifications in 2006/7 in excess of 125,000 compared to around 5000 for EMAS during the same period. ISO certifications appear to be particularly favoured by Chinese and Japanese organizations, with significant numbers also found in Spain, Italy, the United States, and the United Kingdom. Problems of data collection, together with the possibility of self-certification in some cases, make it highly likely that the figures shown in Table 9.2 significantly underestimate the true extent of certification, particularly where the ISO standard is concerned.

For organizations, the certification decision involves a calculation of the perceived costs and benefits. On the upside, it is argued that certification provides a signal of a firm's commitment to environmental improvement; increases confidence that its EMS conforms to a recognized standard; appeals to external stakeholders; drives continuous environmental improvement; and provides access to markets where purchasing organizations require suppliers to have certification to a recognized standard such as EMAS or ISO14001 (Kolk, 2000; Rondinelli and Vastag, 2000; Morrow and Rondinelli, 2002; Vastag, 2004; González-Benito and González-Benito; 2005). On the downside, critics point to the costs, complexity, and bureaucratic demands associated with certification which are felt to act as a particular disincentive to smaller businesses that might be considering the possibility of establishing an EMS (Miles et al., 1999; Kolk, 2000; Kollman and Prakash, 2001; Perez-Sanchez et al., 2003).

Table 9.2 EMAS and ISO14001 registrations (selected countries)

	ISO14001	EMAS
Austria	550	675
Argentina	543	0
Australia	1964	0
Brazil	2510	0
China	18979	0
Denmark	808	392
France	3629	21
Germany	5800	823
India	1500	0
Italy	9825	1710
Japan	21779	0
Malaysia	598	0
Netherlands	1132	7
Norway	475	26
Russian Federation	223	0
South Africa	406	0
Spain	11205	1527
Sweden	4865	134
United Kingdom	5400	342
United States	8081	0

Notes:
1. The statistics for ISO14001 were collated by Rienhard Peglau and relate to the period December 2006–January 2007. More recent data does not appear to be available.
2. The statistics for EMAS were extracted from the EMAS website in November 2011. The figures for the number of registrations are updated on a regular basis.

Arguably, one of the most substantial criticisms of certification is that it does not guarantee that firms with a recognized international standard such as ISO14001 are achieving satisfactory levels of environmental performance. As has been pointed out, organizations that are ISO-certified may still have a level of environmental perform-ance which is below the average for their sector and may not even be conforming to local environmental laws (Aragón-Correa and Rubio-López, 2007). In reality, certification to a given standard tends to ensure that a firm is using a consistent environmental manage-ment process, not that it is achieving environmental compliance or a given and continu-ous level of environmental performance (Rondinelli and Vastag, 2000). We revisit this and other aspects of certification in the concluding section on the empirical research on EMSs.

Establishing an EMS: some initial considerations

Given the wide range and sources of environmental impacts within any business, it is inevitable that the design of an effective EMS will cut across traditional areas of responsibility, organization, and function within the firm. Roberts (1995) argues that there are three broad approaches to developing an EMS: 'incremental improvement' (i.e. small changes to existing procedures); 'redesign' (i.e. changing one or more of existing operations and procedures); and 'rethink' (i.e. looking at the entire operation and deciding how it can be improved). While Roberts suggests that each approach has its merits, he argues that the latter is likely to provide a superior solution to the problem of ensuring that the system is able to pull potentially disparate elements into an integrated and organizational whole.

From an entirely instrumental point of view, an EMS should allow an organization to achieve the objectives set out in its environmental policies and provide a means of adjusting the system and/or policies as appropriate. This requires the firm's decision-makers to give consideration to issues such as the most appropriate organizational structure, the role of individuals and their responsibilities, training needs, the design of the decision-making process, documentation, reporting and review procedures, and so on. Welford and Gouldson (1993) have suggested that to be effective an EMS should be:

- 'comprehensive'—that is, covering all organizational activities including implementation and the responsibilities of individuals;
- 'understandable'—that is, people should know their duties and responsibilities and these should be regularly monitored;
- 'open'—that is, open to review and with a commitment to a continuous cycle of improvement and a tendency towards a participatory style of management.

In their opinion, Total Quality Management (TQM) systems provide a potential model for the design and implementation of an EMS, with their emphasis on teamwork, commitment, communications, organization, planning, monitoring, and control.

The need for top management commitment to the process of establishing and operationalizing an organization's EMS has already been alluded to; Welford and Gouldson (1993), Roberts (1995), Monaghan (1997), and Kolk (2000) amongst others see this as a necessary, though not sufficient, condition for the building of an effective EMS. In addition, it has been suggested that system effectiveness is enhanced through ensuring that the EMS is seen as part of the mainstream management of the firm; covers all aspects of the organization's activities; is formalized rather than ad hoc; open to external verification; and properly documented and published (Monaghan, 1997). In short, it should ideally 'encompass the totality of organisational, administrative, and policy provisions to be taken by a firm to control its environmental influences' (Kolk, 2000: 103–4). Whether this is a realistic proposition—particularly in smaller organizations— remains open to question (O'Laoire and Welford, 1996; Hillary, 2000, 2004).

The EMS cycle

No two firms will have identical EMSs. That said, most EMSs tend to have a number of basic elements particularly if they are modelled on existing standards such as EMAS and ISO14001. These two widely known systems are examined in detail in later sections of this chapter. Here we discuss in broad terms the common components found in systems that operate in most organizations. Following Kolk (2000), the discussion is structured around the plan-do-check-act cycle of environmental management. This cycle and its sub-component parts are depicted in Figure 9.1.

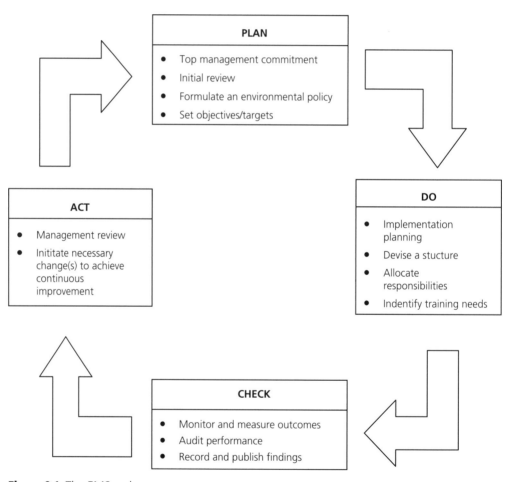

Figure 9.1 The EMS cycle

Source: Adapted from the EU Eco-Management and Audit Scheme (EMAS), available at ec.europa.eu/environment/emas

PLAN

The planning phase of the environmental management process normally begins with an initial review or baseline study, often carried out by a small management team or project group appointed to gather information on the organization's current position and practice. A review of this kind tends to focus on the firm's activities and their environmental impact; current knowledge, policies, and operations; existing legislative and regulatory requirements; problems to be addressed; and the existence of any structural components that could form the basis of a future EMS. Armed with this information, including any gaps in knowledge and provision, an organization is better placed to formulate its environmental policy and its future objectives and targets for improved environmental performance.

An environmental policy has been defined as 'a statement of intent that conveys the commitment of a company to achieving and maintaining a specified standard of environmental performance' (Roberts, 1995: 102) or as 'an organisational-based statement of objectives which [must] clearly outline the firm's commitment to environmental improvement' (Welford and Gouldson, 1993: 51). As these definitions indicate, the main components of an environmental policy tend to be:

- a statement of intent relating to environmental performance;
- the underlying principles and objectives governing this declaration; and
- an implied commitment to comply with existing laws and regulations.

Environmental policies in effect identify what the organization is seeking to achieve; set the direction for future action; underscore the organization's commitment to compliance and to continuous environmental improvement; and provide a framework for the setting of environmental objectives and targets. In practice, of course, real-world environmental policy statements can vary substantially in terms of their specificity, scope, and degree of commitment (see Green Snapshot: Environmental policy statements). While such voluntary declarations often signal a serious intent to greater environmental sustainability, it does not follow that public commitment to a policy will inevitably translate into corporate greening actions or that a policy will be religiously implemented in all its dimensions (Winn and Angell, 2000; Ramus and Montiel, 2005).

As Monaghan (1997) has noted, there is no right or wrong way to draft an environmental policy statement; these tend to be unique to each organization and clearly ought to address the specific needs of the firm including its financial, operational, and business imperatives. Guidelines produced by industry bodies or international organizations (e.g. the International Organization for Standardization (ISO)) generally recommend that statements of this kind should be relatively transparent, open to inspection by external stakeholders, and realistic in their objectives. Being an integral part of an EMS, an environmental policy, along with an environmental audit, can be seen as an indicator of corporate environmental commitment (Zeffane et al., 1995) or what Dion (1998) calls

---

GREEN SNAPSHOT: ENVIRONMENTAL POLICY STATEMENTS

Variations in corporate environmental commitments, policies, or codes are illustrated by the following three examples of well-known organizations.

easyJet—to be environmentally efficient in the air and on the ground and to take the lead in shaping a greener future for aviation (e.g. via carbon offsetting and through aircraft design). The company states that its goal is to be as efficient as possible and to strive to find ways to minimize its future environmental impact (e.g. emissions, waste, noise).

JCB—to reduce the company's direct greenhouse gas impact by 35–40 per cent by 2020; ensure legislative compliance; promote high standards of energy efficiency; ensure minimal visible and audible nuisance to the public; undertake comprehensive waste management programmes worldwide; and invest in the development of new technologies to reduce carbon emissions and exploit sustainable energy sources. The organization is also committed to reporting annually on its environmental performance.

Tata Steel—the company states that it is committed to identifying, assessing, and managing its environmental impacts; developing and rehabilitating abandoned sites (e.g. through afforestation programmes); protecting and preserving biodiversity throughout its operations. Its policies include making efficient use of natural resources; reducing and preventing pollution; engaging in waste reduction and recycling; monitoring, managing, and reporting on its environmental impact and performance; and protecting biodiversity. It also aims to go beyond compliance with regulatory requirements and to pursue a goal of continuous improvement in its environmental performance.

---

a manifestation of the philosophical viewpoint of the firm concerning the relationships between humans and the natural world (see Box 9.1). A less generous interpretation is that the growing use of corporate environmental policy statements by business organizations is not necessarily a sign of increasing environmental proactivity, but more an attempt at 'greenwashing' aimed primarily at establishing an environmentally responsible public image (Ramus and Montiel, 2005).

BOX 9.1 DION'S TYPOLOGY OF ENVIRONMENTAL POLICIES

On the basis of a national survey of thirty Canadian manufacturing companies in the early 1990s, Dion argues that environmental policies tend to vary in content according to their emphasis either on technical rationality and technocentrism/technocracy or on ecological rationality and ecocentrism/ecocracy. His analysis of policy content results in a four-fold typology, with two of his categories classified as exhibiting strong anthropocentrism (Types 1 and 2 below) while the other two indicating weak anthropocentrism (Types 3 and 4 below).

   Dion's typology is as follows:

1. *The Neo-Technocratic Enterprise*—firms that exploit nature for its own sake and that apply a technocratic approach to their relationship with the natural environment. Typical policy features include regulatory compliance, corporate transparency, collaboration with external stakeholders on environmental solutions, and an emphasis on individual responsibility.

(continued)

BOX 9.1 (CONTINUED)

2. *The Techo-Environmentalist Enterprise*—businesses that attempt to both protect the environment and achieve increased levels of short-term profitability. In addition to the above policy features, this type of enterprise also invests in environmental programmes, training of personnel, support for innovative solutions to environmental protection, and quasi-legal mechanisms (e.g. audits).

3. *The Pseudo-Environmentalist Enterprise*—firms that seek to adopt a socially responsible approach to resource exploitation for long-term as well as short-term reasons. Additional features to those exhibited in Types 1 and 2 include an emphasis on recycling, source reduction, reuse of products, safe waste disposal, and preventative methods.

4. *The Quasi-Environmentalist Enterprise*—is an organization committed to ecological ideals and the strategies needed to achieve them (e.g. investment in research and development related to environmental protection). Nature is seen as important in its own right, though not to the extent that it takes precedence over humans. This type of enterprise has policies that exhibit the characteristics of the three previous types but which additionally include support for green R&D, a proactive approach to environmental protection, and a commitment to stakeholder education and environmental issues.

Dion gives some examples of firms in each category, while recognizing that his classifications are to a large extent 'ideal types'. Thus, he suggests that:

- Type 1 policies are said to be exhibited by the Canadian Pacific Railway;
- Type 2 policies by Alcan;
- Type 3 policies by TetraPak; and
- Type 4 policies by Colgate-Palmolive and IBM Canada.

Sensibly, he reminds us that an organization's environmental policy may look attractive on paper, but does not necessarily tell us anything about its actual implementation or the firm's respect for its own stated norms and objectives.

Source: Based on Dion (1998).

Alongside the formulation of an environmental policy, the planning phase of the EMS cycle usually involves establishing a programme for achieving the firm's environmental objectives. Some of the key questions an organization needs to address include what resources are necessary to implement the policy; where the various responsibilities lie; what methods and actions are required to meet the policy objectives/targets; what are appropriate timeframes; and what needs to be put in place to ensure that effective communication occurs with both internal and external stakeholders. In an ideal world, organizations should integrate their plans and programmes with other areas of management; if necessary, this may require new structures to be established in order to facilitate the simultaneous achievement of the firm's environmental and broader business and corporate objectives (Kolk, 2000).

DO

The 'plan' and 'do' phases of environmental management tend to overlap, with the latter focusing essentially on questions relating to policy implementation. These usually revolve around issues of structure, role, and responsibility, training needs, documentation, communication systems, and resource allocation processes.

In putting its plan into effect, a firm needs to ensure that subsequent phases of the cycle—especially the audit process (see below)—have been given due consideration and that the structures and processes are in place to allow the organization to gather information on its performance within the agreed time frame. Other considerations include questions of liaison between different parts of the organization over issues such as training requirements; methods of gathering and recording information; the possible integration of environmental management into reward and appraisal systems; and mechanisms for developing employee motivation and for demonstrating organizational commitment to environmental improvement. With regard to the latter, some organizations may prefer to designate an 'environmental champion' who through her/his formal role and/or personal activism promotes the process of environmental management within the organization and acts as an instrument for change, as the firm seeks to incorporate environmental issues into its day-to-day operations and decisions (Andersson and Bateman, 2000).

CHECK

This phase of the environmental management cycle focuses on the question of organizational performance in relation to a firm's stated environmental policy, objectives, and targets. The aims in essence are to analyse how far the business has achieved its environmental goals, identify any discernable problems and their cause(s), highlight possible areas for improvement, and begin to put in place procedures for problem-solving and improved performance. A key element of this stage of the process is the environmental audit, which is basically a mechanism for checking outcomes against the standards set down by legislation and regulation; the organization's own stated objectives; and best practice elsewhere, including the firm's competitors (Welford and Gouldson, 1993).

A useful description of the different phases of the audit process (i.e. pre-audit, audit, post-audit) and its underlying principles can be found in Welford and Gouldson (1993). They note that—whether conducted internally or carried out through the use of external consultants—an environmental audit is a multistage process involving, *inter alia*, the examination of company documents, record checking, on-site inspections, staff interviewing, investigation of management processes and systems, and the subsequent evaluation of findings. The culmination of this process is usually some form of report which often contains an action plan designed to address any identified deficiencies, suggest alternative solutions, set out a timetable for implementation, and indicate the individuals responsible for undertaking corrective action. This report naturally provides the basis for the management review, which is a central component of the final step in the EMS cycle.

ACT

Armed with information provided through the check phase of the EMS cycle and from other sources (e.g. proposed new legislation, analysis of competitor behaviour), a firm's management is in a position to establish what changes, if any, need to be undertaken to the organization's policies, objectives, targets, systems, and/or processes to achieve the desired outcomes and to demonstrate a commitment to continual improvement in environmental performance. Key issues requiring consideration at this stage of the process can include potential changes to the organization's environmental policies, operations, use and acquisition of materials, supplier relationships, training, structure, procedures, communication strategies, and so on. Roberts (1995) asserts that the most important feature of an effective EMS is its circular and all-embracing form, with the 'act' phase starting the whole planning process off again. In the last analysis, however, it is worth remembering that a well-designed and implemented EMS is no guarantee that an organization will achieve a high level of environmental performance, nor that it will necessarily help to create and embed the kind of cultural commitment to environmental improvement associated with the notion of a 'greened' business.

Environmental management systems in practice: EMAS and ISO14001

For firms seeking to establish an EMS, there is a broad spectrum of schemes from which they can choose. Some of these involve environmental management standards devised at national level by government and other agencies and which, as indicated above, may be used as a stepping stone to EMAS and/or ISO14001. Examples of such schemes currently in operation in selected EU countries are described briefly in Table 9.3; they include schemes that apply to both private and public sector organizations, are sometimes sector specific, and may be targeted at SMEs. Unlike the two EMS standards described in detail below, they have not generally stimulated the same degree of interest among academic researchers, but should still be seen as an important indicator of the desire by national governments and others to encourage a structured approach to environmental management among organizational decision-makers.

Table 9.3 National EMS schemes in selected EU countries

Country	Scheme	Description
Finland	EcoStart	Launched in 2006 as a way of helping SMEs to develop a less formal type of EMS. The focus is on eco-efficiency and environmental performance and it can serve as a stepping stone to EMAS/ISO14001.
France	Environnement	A three-stage model developed by a cross-sector partnership to assist firms to implement an EMS. It can facilitate the achievement of ISO14001 or EMAS accreditation by SMEs.
Germany	EcoStep	A cross-sector initiative developed between 2001 and 2004 that was designed to encourage SMEs to establish an EMS by integrating the basic requirements of different management systems (e.g. ISO9001; EMAS) into one scheme.
Spain	Ecoskan	A scheme first established in 1998 that assists firms to systematize their approach to environmental management and to ensure legislative compliance. In 2004 it became a certifiable environmental management standard.
United Kingdom	BS8555/IEMA Acorn Scheme	The Acorn Scheme is an officially recognized EMS standard that is based on British Standard BS8555. It has six levels of performance and is supported by the UK government.

Source: Adapted from 'Step up to EMAS: Study on Guidelines for Transition from Non-Formal EMS and ISO14001 to EMAS', available at ec.europa.eu/environment/emas/documents/StepUp_2

THE ECO-MANAGEMENT AND AUDIT SCHEME: EMAS

Like ISO14001 and British Standard 7750, the European Union Eco-Management and Audit Scheme emerged in the 1990s and has been described as a 'consciously crafted supranational regime' whose origins lie in the process of economic globalization and in the increasing acceptance by businesses that there was a need to address their environmental impact (Kollman and Prakash, 2001). Stage 1 of the scheme (EMAS I) became operative in 1995 and was originally restricted to company sites in industrial sectors under European Council Regulation No. 1836/93. In 2001, a further EC regulation opened up EMAS to all economic sectors, including both public and private services, and the revised scheme (EMAS II) continued using ISO14001 as the environmental standard required by EMAS, thereby providing for the possibility of a fast track to EMAS registration for ISO14001-certified organizations (Schaltegger et al., 2003). Under the latest revision to the scheme (EMAS III), which came into effect in January 2010, steps were taken to improve the applicability of EMAS (e.g. by adopting core environmental indicators through which environmental performance can be compared and documented) and to strengthen the scheme's visibility and outreach (e.g. introducing a single EMAS logo and by encouraging global uptake of the scheme by allowing organizations outside the European Union and the European Economic Area to apply for EMAS certification). These new regulations contained a number of permissive provisions which allowed member states to decide whether or not certain features of the scheme should be implemented within their national jurisdiction.

In simple terms, EMAS is an EU-regulated voluntary EMS which is designed to allow firms and other organizations to evaluate, manage, and continuously improve upon their environmental performance. To achieve its objectives of continuous improvement, the scheme provides a framework through which organizations can establish an EMS, gather information on their environmental performance, seek independent verification of their achievements, and report their progress to external stakeholders. According to the *Europa* website (see e.g. http://ec.europa.eu/environment/emas), the core elements of EMAS are 'performance', 'credibility', and 'transparency'. Performance is achieved by carrying out annual updates of the firm's environmental policy and via actions which both implement and evaluate the organization's achievements. Credibility is said to come from third-party verification by independent external verifiers, while transparency is a function of the requirement to provide an environmental statement that is open to public scrutiny as a necessary condition for EMAS registration.

In order to qualify for EMAS registration, firms are required to undertake a number of steps that focus on the process of ensuring that a credible EMS is in place and functioning effectively (Schaltegger et al., 2003). In keeping with the plan-do-check-act approach to environmental management discussed above, a firm is required to:

- undertake an environmental review that establishes its baseline situation, its environmental impacts, regulatory context, and existing practices;
- formulate and adopt an environmental policy that contains a commitment to comply with existing environmental laws and regulations and to seek continuous improvements in environmental performance;
- establish an environmental programme and management system aimed at achieving the organization's stated environmental policy and objectives, including questions of individual responsibility, training needs, operating procedures, monitoring, and communication systems;
- carry out an environmental audit that examines the firm's achievements and the efficacy of its EMS; and
- produce an environmental statement which sets down how well the organization has performed against its objectives and policies and what future steps need to be undertaken to ensure that continual improvement in environmental performance occurs.

In order to become registered, an organization's review, EMS, audit process, and environmental statement must be approved by an accredited EMAS verifier, while its environmental statement needs to be sent to the EMAS Competent Body for registration and made publicly available before the firm is given permission to display the EMAS logo on its letterheads.

Built into the EMAS cycle is the need for a declaration of top management commitment to environmental improvement; proof of full legal compliance; active employee participation in all stages of the process; appropriate training and education of all employees; procedures to ensure effective internal and external communication; and evidence of corrective action and of regular management review of its EMS. In the majority of cases, these requirements are in addition to those needed for registration to ISO14001 and, consequently, EMAS is generally seen as a more demanding environmental management standard than its international counterpart.

ISO14001

The internationally recognized standard ISO14001 is one of a family of standards that address various aspects of environmental management and which emerged in the wake of the United Nations Conference on Environment and Development in the early 1990s (Bansal and Hunter, 2003). Other standards in the series cover issues such as environmental auditing, environmental performance evaluation, environmental labelling, and life cycle assessment (see e.g. Curkovic et al., 2005).

Whereas EMAS could be said to revolve around voluntary participation in a regulated system, ISO14001 has been described as being based on certification shaped by industry bodies under the auspices of the International Organization for Standardization (Steger, 2000). First published in 1996, and updated in 2004, the standard sets out the generic requirements for an EMS, with the aim of providing a framework to assist an organization to address its environmental performance in a holistic and systematic way (Morrow and Rondinelli, 2002; Esty and Winston, 2006). Guidelines on the different elements of an EMS and its implementation, together with discussion of the principal issues involved, are provided under its sister standard ISO14004.

According to Bansal and Hunter (2003), ISO14001 is founded on three underlying principles: pollution prevention, voluntary participation, and continuous improvement. As with EMAS, its component elements follow the plan-do-check-act cycle, with organizations having to undertake a number of steps in order to comply with the ISO standard. These involve:

- the development of an environmental policy to which senior management is committed;
- the identification of the firm's impact on the natural environment (e.g. through its products, services, and activities) and of its legislative and regulatory obligations;
- the establishment of the firm's priorities and the setting of targets and objectives for reducing its environmental impacts;
- the realignment of the firm's structure and processes in order to achieve its objectives; and
- the checking of the organization's performance and the subsequent correction of its EMS (Rondinelli and Vastag, 2000; Bansal and Hunter, 2003; González-Benito and González-Benito, 2005).

Boiral (1998) presents these different stages in the form of a linear diagram, with commitment and policy leading to planning; followed by implementation, measurement, and checking; and, finally, management review and continual improvement, with the latter starting the whole process off again through the setting of the firm's revised environmental policy.

As a process-based rather than a performance-based standard (Tibor and Feldman, 1999; Bansal and Hunter, 2003; Schaltegger et al., 2003), ISO14001 is generally held to offer considerable flexibility to aspirant organizations, since it can be implemented by a wide variety of enterprises irrespective of their existing level of environmental maturity. Achieving ISO14001 conformity signifies that a firm has implemented an EMS with the component elements indicated above; the standard does not specify how the requirements should be met, nor does it provide an indication of what might be desirable environmental objectives (Bansal, 2002; Bansal and Hunter, 2003; Schaltegger et al., 2003). It is also possible to self-declare conformity to the ISO standard, certification being an option but by no means obligatory under existing arrangements.

Material produced by the International Organization for Standardization and available through its website (www.iso.org) indicates that the underlying philosophy behind ISO14001 is that 'whatever the organization's activity, the requirements for an effective EMS are the same'. By providing a template for the establishment of an EMS, the assumption appears to be that better environmental management will inevitably result in better environmental performance (Tibor and Feldman, 1999; Montabon et al., 2000). This is not a view that can claim to have universal support (see e.g. Krut and Gleckman, 1998; Aragón-Correa and Rubio-López, 2007).

Comparing EMAS and ISO14001

Given that EMAS is modelled around ISO14001, the two systems clearly have a great deal in common. Nevertheless, there are a number of important differences between the two standards which are worth emphasizing.

Table 9.4 provides a comparison of the two schemes. Apart from differences in the geographical focus of EMAS and ISO14001, the former tends to be more stringent than the latter at the planning, implementation, and follow-up stages of the EMS cycle. Employee participation, for example, is a requirement under EMAS as is the need to provide proof of legal compliance and to undertake an initial environmental review. Perhaps most significantly, firms seeking to certify under EMAS have to produce an environmental statement which must be checked and validated by an officially approved certifier and must be made available for scrutiny by the public and other stakeholders, whereas no such statement is required under ISO14001. Whether any of these differences might ultimately give rise to

Table 9.4 Comparing EMAS and ISO14001: some key differences

Dimension	EMAS	ISO14001
Geographical focus	European focus, but with the possibility of outreach under EMAS III	Internationally focused standard, available in all countries
Environmental review	Firms need to undertake an environmental review.	An environmental review is recommended
Legal compliance	Evidence of legal compliance is obligatory	No requirement to provide evidence of legal compliance, simply a commitment
Employee involvement	Employee participation required at all levels	Employee participation is encouraged
Communication aspects	Firms need to establish transparent and open dialogue with the public and provide information on a periodic basis	Firms only need to provide information on their environmental policy
Environmental statement	Independently verified public statement is required	No requirement to provide an environmental statement

different standards of environmental performance under the two schemes is far from clear (Kollman and Prakash, 2001); nor is it evident whether the relative popularity among firms of ISO14001 over EMAS is related to the additional demands of the latter, or, as del Brío and Junquera (2003) have suggested, is mainly due to the former's worldwide recognition as an international standard of environmental management.

The advantages and disadvantages of EMSs

An assessment of the pros and cons of EMSs can be conducted at either a societal or organizational level. From a societal point of view, as a form of voluntary self-regulation, EMSs are generally held to be more flexible and less constraining than legislation as an approach to tackling environmental problems and are thought to be less distorting of the competitive dynamics of markets than either taxes or pollution permits (Bansal and Hunter, 2003; Curkovic et al., 2005). On the downside, critics argue that they focus on means (i.e. process) rather than ends (i.e. performance); are costly and document-driven; adopt questionable certification processes; tend to favour larger businesses; and can be used by purchasing organizations as a form of non-tariff barrier (Prakash, 1999; Rondinelli and Vastag, 2000; Steger, 2000; Curkovic et al., 2005; Aragón-Correa and Rubio-López, 2007; Halila, 2007). Overall, it would be fair to say that, notwithstanding their imperfections, EMSs are a useful weapon in the fight against further environmental degradation; they may help to sensitize the corporate sector to the need to consider the issue of environmental protection alongside the pursuit of profits and organizational growth.

At the firm level, the case for establishing an EMS largely focuses on the contribution it can make to the operational, managerial, and competitive position of the enterprise. These claimed advantages tend to be particularly associated with systems that are certified to standards such as EMAS and ISO14001. By possessing a certified EMS, it is argued that organizations can:

- identify potential savings and reduce waste (Tibor and Feldman, 1999; Kollman and Prakash, 2001; Bansal and Bogner, 2002; Morrow and Rondinelli, 2002);
- reduce overheads, risks, and compliance costs (Steger, 2000; Curkovic et al., 2005);
- improve internal management processes and organizational efficiency (Rondinelli and Vastag, 2000; del Brío and Junquera, 2003);
- generate a positive image (Boiral, 1998; Kollman and Prakash, 2001; del Brío and Junquera, 2003);
- enhance external relationships and reduce institutional pressures (Boiral, 1998; Tibor and Feldman, 1999; Bansal and Bogner, 2002);
- create a culture of environmental protection among employees (Kolk, 2000; Kollman and Prakash, 2001; Morrow and Rondinelli, 2002); and
- gain access to markets where environmental management standards are a pre-requisite (Kolk, 2000; Bansal and Bogner, 2002).

As Morrow and Rondinelli (2002) have cautioned, however, claims of putative benefits such as these are often based on anecdotal evidence or on single case studies (e.g. Ford, IBM, Alcoa) where self-reported gains are not always easy to verify.

The case against the adoption of an EMS centres primarily around the issues of cost and complexity. The expense and difficulties involved in creating a new management system or modifying an existing one, together with the additional costs incurred in implementation, documentation, education and training of staff, and so on, are seen as a

---

GREEN SNAPSHOT: A STUDY OF EMAS

A European Commission study (2009) of the costs and benefits of EMAS registration to firms of all sizes found that the three most commonly identified advantages of registration were:

- increased efficiency savings (in energy and resources);
- reduced negative incidents; and
- improved stakeholder relationships.

The least important benefits cited by participants in the study were increased market opportunities, financial savings, and staff recruitment and retention. These findings largely mirror the results of previous academic research on EMSs cited in this chapter.

The EC study also pointed to a lack of clarity among firms regarding the measurable benefits of EMAS registration and the costs of implementation as important barriers likely to discourage organizations from considering registration to a recognized standard such as EMAS.

potential disincentive for some organizations contemplating a certified system (Prakash, 1999; Kolk, 2000; Kollman and Prakash, 2001; Bansal and Bogner, 2002; Khanna and Anton, 2002*a*). SMEs, in particular, appear to be reluctant to go down the EMS route (see e.g. the case study in Chapter 7) and are often thought to lack the necessary skills, aptitudes, resources, and managerial commitment to invest in managing their environmental performance in a structured and comprehensive manner (Miles et al., 1999; Perez-Sanchez et al., 2003; Halila, 2007).

Critics also argue that the introduction of an EMS can expose environmental risks that cannot be addressed economically by the organization and may attract rather than deflect unwelcome scrutiny of the firm by external stakeholders (Bansal and Bogner, 2002). The fact that some businesses may seek certification of their EMS for public relations rather than environmental performance reasons is also seen as a potential weakness of this approach to business self-regulation, especially given the focus of EMSs on process rather than outcome (Rondinelli and Vastag, 2000).

In relation to the question of perceived advantages and disadvantages of EMSs, it should be noted that some analyses tend to conflate the establishment of a system with the process of certification, which undoubtedly adds an additional dimension to the question of costs versus benefits. Overall, there appears to be widely diverging views concerning the desirability and pros and cons of standards such as EMAS and ISO14001, with the former seen as either more bureaucratic or more sophisticated and the latter as either vaguer or more flexible by different observers (Kolk, 2000).

EMSs: the empirical evidence

To complete the discussion of EMSs, it is useful to investigate the empirical findings of recent researchers in the field. A majority of the studies that have been undertaken relate to ISO14001 and broadly fall into three main categories: the reasons for adopting an EMS; the reasons for EMS certification; and possible links between EMSs and firm-level performance. We examine each of these issues in turn.

REASONS FOR EMS ADOPTION

Studies carried out following the establishment of EMAS and ISO14001 indicate that decisions on EMS adoption can be influenced by a variety of factors. In an early survey of high adopters verses non-adopters, Florida and Davison (2001) identify business-driven reasons (e.g. commitment to environmental improvement; corporate goals; business performance) as key influences on a firm's decisions to engage in innovative environmental practices. In their analysis, high adopters generally tended to be larger plants, with more people engaged in green initiatives and with higher levels of resources committed to environmental protection measures. The local and national regulatory climate, together with achieving improvements in community relations, was also identified as significant influences on the adoption decision.

The idea that both internal and external considerations impact upon managerial responses also emerges in other studies. Morrow and Rondinelli's investigations (2002) of German firms identify questions of environmental performance, company image, the pursuit of savings, and the desire to pursue regulatory compliance as important factors motivating businesses to adopt corporate EMSs. Anton et al. (2004) emphasize the impact of liability threats and pressures from consumers, investors, and the public, while Alberti et al. (2000) suggest that national regulation has proved an important factor driving EMS implementation in several EU countries.

Issues of choice of the system and the degree of comprehensiveness of an organization's EMS are also examined in the literature, with Khanna and Anton (2002*b*) and Anton et al. (2004) noting that the mix and number of practices adopted by firms tend to be affected by the differential incentives they face (e.g. regulatory threats versus market opportunities), while del Brio and Junquera (2003) link the adoption of ISO14001 by Spanish industrial companies to its worldwide recognition as an environmental management standard and its applicability across sectors. The fact that adoption rates clearly vary across national jurisdictions has also attracted academic attention, with Kollman and Prakash (2001) arguing that cross-national variations in firms' responses in the United Kingdom, the United States, and Germany are influenced by an organization's institutional contexts, most notably the type of adversarial economy (i.e. adversarial legalism versus prescriptive interventionism) and the nature of the policy regime (i.e. procedural versus substantive) under which it operates.

REASONS FOR EMS CERTIFICATION

Given the perception that investing in an internationally recognized environmental management standard can be costly and may not offer any discernible advantage over an in-house system (Bansal, 2002; Bansal and Bogner, 2002), researchers have naturally been keen to investigate the reasons why some firms seek EMS certification. As in the case of adoption generally, empirical studies point to a variety of factors that could explain business behaviour.

Analysis of the literature suggests that certified firms tend to be:

- those that are seeking to reinforce rather than reorient their current strategies, that is, those that already have considerable environmental legitimacy and a strong international presence (Bansal and Bogner, 2002; Bansal and Hunter, 2003);

- experienced in the use of quality systems, including certification and the development of cross-functional management teams (Curkovic et al., 2005);
- concerned to achieve regulatory compliance and to establish a good external reputation (Fryxell and Szeto, 2002);
- motivated by ethical and competitive considerations (González-Benito and González-Benito, 2005); and
- managed by individuals who see external pressures as opportunities rather than threats (del Brío and Junquera, 2003).

While firm-level characteristics, including the size of the organization, figure in most of the studies undertaken, work by Chapple et al. (2001) identifies industry as a key influence, the authors arguing that firms are more likely to comply with ISO14001 in industries that have a high level of exports relative to turnover.

Complementing the various studies conducted at national level, Vastag (2004) has investigated the drivers of ISO14001 certification via an exploratory cross-national study of certification densities in selected countries. The main conclusion to emerge from the research was that, at a national level, certification patterns could be explained by two factors: the existing base of ISO9000 certificates, and the number of environmental treaties signed and ratified. The first factor points to the possibility that the overlap between the two ISO standards (i.e. quality management and environmental management) might predispose firms to seek certification to ISO14001 since prior experience might provide a relatively low-cost route to establishing an improved external image. The second suggests that certification decisions also need to be seen against the background of the political-economic climate of the time, including considerations of international trade and development and the role of government in influencing attitudes to environmental protection within the business community.

EMSs AND FIRM-LEVEL PERFORMANCE

As in the case of research into the business case for corporate greening generally (see Chapter 6), the findings on the impact of an EMS on firms' performance tend towards the positive although not exclusively so. In general, the possession of a formal certified system such as ISO14001 or EMAS has been linked to improvements in both environmental and corporate performance, in firms both large and small (e.g. see Hillary, 2000; Montabon et al., 2000; Rondinelli and Vastag, 2000; Melnyk et al., 2003). Somewhat more cautiously, Bansal and Bogner (2002) report that there appears to be no notable difference in the financial performance of certified and non-certified firms, raising the question of whether a recognized standard is any better than in-house arrangements (see e.g. Steger, 2000) or whether EMS certification can realistically provide a reliable basis upon which a firm can achieve a measure of differentiation from its competitors (Aragón-Correa and Rubio-López, 2007).

Case Study: EMAS experiences in selected firms[1]

Empirical research into EMS adoption indicates that firms often face several obstacles when deciding whether to implement a certificated EMS such as EMAS or ISO14001. These barriers are particularly acute for smaller enterprises (see Chapter 7). In this case study—produced from material available via the EMAS website—the focus is on four businesses that have overcome these barriers and have adopted the European system EMAS which, as mentioned previously, became operative in 1995 and is currently in its third iteration. As the four examples illustrate, the EMAS standard attracts firms of all sizes, in all industries and sectors, and across all European countries.

FRANZ DORNER AND PARTNER KEG, AUSTRIA

Franz Dorner and his wife operate a poultry farm and solar power plant in Austria. In 2009, this became the country's first farm to achieve registration under EMAS.

As an agricultural business, the firm has a number of environmental impacts, particularly energy and water use, issues of animal health and hygiene, and waste production. Reducing these impacts has formed key elements of the organization's environmental policy, along with the aim of becoming energy self-sufficient, contributing to biodiversity, and protecting the local landscape.

Having begun to invest in environmental protection measures when they took over the farm in the later part of the 1980s, the Dorners embarked on an ambitious plan to tackle the problems of resource use and waste production associated with their activities. A heating system based on wood chips sourced from their own forests was installed in 2001, and work was started on a photovoltaic power plant in 2004 which has subsequently resulted in the firm becoming a net energy producer. Against this background, and other initiatives, EMAS registration was the logical next step.

While the business has been successful in reducing its environmental impact, several problems have been encountered during the process, including a delay in receiving authorization for the solar power plant. Where EMAS registration was concerned, another key challenge was that no experience was available in EMAS consultancy in the agricultural sector in Austria and at the time there was only one Austrian verifier available for this sector.

VERALLIA, PORTUGAL

Unlike the previous organization which is a micro-enterprise, the Portuguese glass container manufacturer and distributor, Verallia, is a medium-sized firm employing over 200 workers. It is part of the French conglomerate, Saint-Gobain, which operates in around fifty countries and various industries. When it achieved EMAS registration in 2003, Verallia was the only EMAS-registered glass container manufacturer operating in Portugal out of five in total.

Given the nature of the business, the company's key social and environmental impacts related to questions of resource use and pollution, food safety issues, the health and safety of workers, and product disposal. The organization's overall policy goals were to reduce any adverse impacts, achieve continuous improvements, exceed shareholder expectations, encourage employee participation, and seek to become a more sustainable business. Technology and innovation were to play an important role in achieving these goals.

Where organizational benefits were concerned, the firm saw EMAS as a useful tool for evaluating its environmental performance, for identifying areas where it could do better, and for gaining external recognition by key stakeholders (e.g. customers, suppliers, government). It was also seen as a mechanism for ensuring compliance with environmental legislation, thereby reducing the risk of fines for non-compliance and the danger of adverse publicity and damage to its reputation.

The evidence indicates that Verallia encountered a number of significant challenges in meeting the EMAS standard, including the need to invest in new equipment; to undertake additional training of staff in environmental awareness; to encourage staff participation in environmental improvements and measurements, and the requirement to gather and analyse data for validation by an accredited verifier and for disclosure to external parties. On the plus side, since 2006, the firm has been able to cut its water consumption substantially despite a difficult external economic environment.

A S TALLINNA VESI, ESTONIA

A S Tallinna Vesi is Estonia's largest water utility company, operating out of three sites and providing waste water disposal services and drinking water to around one-third of the country's population. It employs around 300 workers and is a listed company with a high reputation for environmental performance.

As well as being concerned with its own environmental performance, the firm also sees its responsibilities as extending to its customers in areas such as water use and disposal. To minimize its environmental impact, the company decided to establish an EMS based on ISO14001 and this subsequently formed the basis of its involvement in an

EMAS pilot project in 2004/5 aimed at implementing a national EMAS system with the help of participating businesses. In 2005, A S Tallinna Vesi became the first company in Estonia to be EMAS-registered and it has continued to invest in environmental improvements in order to reduce its environmental impact.

In building on the existing ISO14001 foundation, the firm believes it has gained greater external credibility, particularly in the collection and presentation of independently verified data and information. The process, however, has not been entirely straightforward, with a lack of time and problems such as interpreting the requirements for EMAS compliance and for external reporting proving challenging at the outset.

AXEL SPRINGER AG, GERMANY

The printing firm Axel Springer was one of the first businesses to achieve EMAS registration at its three plants in the later part of the 1990s. In its first environmental statement in 1994, the company set out its environmental policy which was aimed primarily at reducing resource and energy use and at preserving biodiversity. The implementation of an EMS aimed at reducing its environmental impact and at raising environmental awareness among its stakeholders (e.g. employees, suppliers) was seen as an important step in achieving its objectives.

For Axel Springer, the establishment of EMAS in 1995 provided an opportunity to demonstrate its commitment to environmental protection, and the company believes it has benefitted in a variety of ways from EMAS certification (e.g. by improved operational efficiency; greater environmental awareness and actions among employees; enhanced public image). Among the improvements in environmental performance in recent years have been reduced water and gas consumption; reduction of waste and polluting products; lower emissions of greenhouse gases; and initiatives on green procurement and biodiversity enhancement. As with the other firms discussed in this case study, Axel Springer found the implementation of EMAS initially challenging, particularly with respect to the bureaucratic aspects of the certification process, although it still asserts that the benefits of implementing the system significantly outweighs the problems.

■ NOTE

1. The information used in this case study is based on material provided freely via the EMAS website and was accessed in 2011. For further case studies, see http://ec.europa.eu/environment/emas.index_en.htm

10 Greening business functions

Purchasing and supply chain managers are in a critical position to influence the size of the overall environmental footprint of a company. Their influence on activities such as supplier selection and evaluation, supplier development, and purchasing processes means that they can have a major impact on the ability of a company to establish and maintain a competitive advantage through EFP (i.e. environmental friendly practices).

(Walton et al., 1998)

Green marketing subsumes greening products as well as greening firms. Though normative concerns impact consumers' and firms' decision making, economic aspects of green marketing should not be neglected. Managers need to identify what ought to be greened: systems, processes or products?

(Prakash, 2002)

Accounting numbers can change corporate and investor behavior . . . accounting has the ability to define how the game is being played. If we want to change the rules of the game, then we first need to change accounting.

(Sherman et al., 2002)

Introduction

If a firm's stated environmental objectives are to be any more than mere rhetoric, then they need to be translated into action within—and often beyond—the organization. Chapters 8 and 9 have shown that an enterprise's environmental strategies, policies, and systems of environmental management can provide an indication of its commitment to improved environmental performance by giving us an insight into the firm's approach to managing its interface with the natural environment. Turning its plans and aspirations into reality, however, very much depends upon what goes on at an operational level, and how it seeks to reduce its environmental impact on a day-to-day basis, as it transforms inputs into outputs in pursuit of its economic and commercial goals (e.g. value creation).

The process of value creation within profit-seeking organizations can be conceptualized as a chain of inter-related activities (i.e. a value chain) which comprises core or primary activities such as inbound logistics, operations, marketing, sales, and service, together with support activities that include procurement, research and development, human resource management, and infrastructural arrangements (Porter, 1985). These different aspects of the value-creation process all provide opportunities not only for creating competitive advantage but also for addressing the firm's impact on the natural environment, linking as they do the creation, sale, and transfer of the organization's product(s) to the consumer at the end of its value chain (Worthington et al., 2005).

In this chapter, we focus on three main aspects or functional areas of an organization's value-creating process—purchasing, supply chain management, and marketing—and show how these can be used to demonstrate a firm's green credentials in pursuit of its corporate and business-level environmental strategies. While these are only some of the many areas in which firms can address their environmental impact, they represent key generic and boundary-spanning processes found in most organizations, irrespective of firm size, sector, or industry (Preuss, 2001; Vachon and Klassen, 2006). Moreover, the evidence indicates that green purchasing, green supply chain management, and green marketing activities have become more prevalent within organizations in recent years, and as a result these issues have attracted considerable academic attention, as the discussion below will indicate.

The chapter concludes with a brief discussion of green accounting.

Green purchasing

DEFINITION AND SCOPE

The term 'green purchasing' is often used synonymously with green supply, green sourcing, eco-procurement, and environmentally friendly or socially responsible buying (see e.g. Drumwright, 1994; Walton et al., 1998). Walton and Galea (2006) suggest that, at the highest level of abstraction, green purchasing refers to the buying of products or services that have a lesser or reduced effect on human health and the environment compared to rival products that serve the same purpose. Russel (1998) prefers the concept of 'greener' purchasing, defining it as the integration of environmental considerations into an organization's purchasing policies, programmes, and actions, while Handfield and Melnyk (1996) and Handfield et al. (2002) use the term 'environmentally conscious' purchasing to describe the process of formally introducing and integrating environmental concerns and issues to the buying process within an enterprise.

As a key and initial upstream process within an organization's supply chain, purchasing is in a pivotal position to influence a firm's response to environmental concerns (Zsidisin and Siferd, 2001). Purchasing decisions can be aimed at achieving resource reduction, product reuse, recycling, reclamation, energy efficiency, and so on, and these can become important criteria shaping organizational buyer behaviour (Green et al., 1996; Carter et al., 1998, 2000; Min and Galle, 2001; Vachon and Klassen, 2006). The question is not simply what a firm purchases, but from whom it buys its goods and services, with supplier selection based on vendor environmental performance increasingly becoming an integral part of the greener purchasing process within many larger organizations in both the private and public sectors (Green et al., 1996; Min and Galle, 1997; Russel, 1998; Walton et al., 1998).

The involvement and support of suppliers in helping an organization to achieve its environmental goals is well recognized in the literature (Rao and Holt, 2005). In studies of green supply chain management in Chinese enterprises, Zhu and colleagues (2004, 2007*a*, 2007*b*) place supplier/buyer relationships at the heart of green purchasing, with cooperation over environmental objectives, supplier ISO14000 certification, and environmental audits of suppliers' internal management processes representing key indicators of environmentally friendly procurement practices. Similar conclusions are reached in Lamming and Hampson's literature review and study (1996) of five major UK companies, with collaboration and relationships, product stewardship, life cycle assessment, the use of environmental management systems, and vendor questionnaires identified as five basic types of strategy used by companies engaged in green purchasing.

At its essence then, green purchasing or green supply can be said to comprise those supply management activities that seek to improve the environmental performance of purchased inputs or of the organizations that supply them (Bowen et al., 2001, 2006). While some definitions focus primarily on the purchasing function's involvement in facilitating internally driven environmental initiatives such as source reduction or recycling (Vachon and Klassen, 2006), others give equal weight to what can be described as greening the supply process and joint vendor/buyer development of new environmental products, processes, or technologies (Rao, 2002; Bowen et al., 2006). Rao and Holt (2005), for example, emphasize the need for buyers to manage the environmental performance of suppliers through the use of evaluation and mentoring techniques in order to address such issues as reduction of waste produced, material substitution, and waste minimization of hazardous materials. Hamner (2006) identifies eleven strategies that can be used in green purchasing, ranging from the buyer specification of either desirable or undesirable product attributes (e.g. a product must have recyclable components or not use solvent-based materials) through vendor questionnaires and environmental management system certification to advanced forms of environmental collaboration, up to and including industrial ecology (see Box 10.1).

Implicit in Hamner's typology (2006) of green purchasing strategies is the idea that green purchasing/supply is something of an elastic concept that frequently overlaps with the notion of green supply chain management (see below). Moreover, it is clear that green purchasing initiatives require not only cooperation of some kind with suppliers but also collaboration with other functional areas within the organization (see e.g. Sarkis

---

BOX 10.1 THE CONCEPT OF 'INDUSTRIAL ECOLOGY'

Lowe (1990) defines industrial ecology as a systematic organizing framework for the many facets of environmental management which views the industrial world as a natural system, a part of the local ecosystems, and the global biosphere. According to Graedel (1994), it is an 'ensemble concept' which studies all the interactions between industrial systems and the environment. As applied to industry, it aims to optimize the total materials cycle from the virgin material phase to the ultimate disposal of waste products.

   Industrial ecology (ecosystems) has been described on three levels, characterized by the ability of the system to recycle or reuse material or the system's openness (Sarkis, 2001). At level one, the system is portrayed as a linear flow system where unlimited energy and materials flow into and subsequently out of the system. The second level involves an element of energy and material reuse within the system, while level three conceives of ecosystem components linked together and no waste outflows from the inputs entering the system. As Sarkis (2003) has noted, some partial industrial ecosystems (level two) are currently in operation, the Kalunborg industrial ecosystem in Denmark being perhaps the best known example. See also Zhu and Cote's (2004) case study of the Guintang Group in China.

---

and Rasheed, 1995; Sarkis, 2001) and often need considerable effort devoted to promoting starting, managing, and maintaining such initiatives internally (Russel, 1998). Integrating environmental criteria into purchasing decisions is manifestly a challenge for many organizations, particularly small and medium-sized enterprises operating in resource-restricted environments and with relatively limited levels of environmental awareness and eco-literacy (Baylis et al., 1998*a*). As in other areas of environmental management, green purchasing programmes are likely to be judged not simply on whether they improve a firm's environmental performance but also in terms of their impact on the bottom line (Hutchison, 1998). Untangling purchasing's contribution to a firm's economic performance is by no means a simple task from either a theoretical or methodological point of view (e.g. is buying more environmentally friendly inputs to improve a firm's image a purchasing or marketing issue?).

GREEN PURCHASING: DRIVERS, BARRIERS, AND CLAIMED BENEFITS

Studies of organizations involved in green purchasing (and green supply chain management) initiatives largely support Bansal and Roth's (2000) assertion that regulation, stakeholder pressures, economic opportunities, and ethical influences are important drivers of firm-level behaviour in this domain (Green et al., 1996; Lamming and Hampson, 1996; Carter et al., 1998; Roberts, 2003). Purchasing decisions provide a means through which an organization can demonstrate legislative compliance (e.g. in areas such as mandated product disposal, recycling, or packaging reduction); meet stakeholder demands for more environmentally focused buying activities (e.g. World Wildlife Fund's (WWF) lobbying of Do-It-Yourself (DIY) retailers in the United Kingdom over sustainable timber products); increase business performance (e.g. by reducing disposal and liability costs); and indicate its commitment to socially responsible buying behaviour (e.g. by seeking out green products or services). The degree to which any individual business responds to these pressures will vary between organizations, as well as across industries and different national jurisdictions; it will also tend to reflect variations in organizational context, including business objectives and capabilities and the degree to which environmentally driven purchasing behaviour has managerial support and advocacy (Drumwright, 1994; Carter et al., 1998; Rao, 2002).

The crux of the business case for greening the purchasing function revolves around the claim that it can create economic value for an organization. Working with green suppliers, it is argued, can reduce a firm's operating costs, improve its public image, enhance stakeholder relationships, lower risks and future liabilities, and may help it to differentiate its products in the eyes of consumers (Lamming and Hampson, 1996; Russel, 1998; Carter et al., 2000; Min and Galle, 2001). Gains may also arise as a result of integrating suppliers into a collaborative decision-making process, with environmental signals in a firm's purchasing policies helping to stimulate suppliers to innovate, either on their own or in a partnership arrangement with the buying organization (Green et al., 1996; Bowen et al., 2001; Rao and Holt, 2005).

In practice, of course, building environmental criteria into a firm's purchasing policies is not necessarily straightforward; nor is it guaranteed to garner widespread support within the component parts of a business. For most, if not all, buying organizations, purchasing decisions will be influenced by a range of factors including price, quality, performance, and security of supply as well as by the needs of internal and/or external consumers. Insofar as environmental considerations compromise other purchasing objectives or a firm's functional, business, and corporate imperatives, this can create substantial resistance to greening the purchasing process, particularly among those who believe that such an initiative will prove expensive to develop and implement or may impact adversely on the organization's overall competitiveness (Min and Galle, 1997, 2001).

Evidence from empirical studies of green purchasing tends to suggest that the sceptical view of its contribution to business performance has been relatively common within organizations for much of the last two decades, with firms often adopting a reactive stance based around legislative compliance (Min and Galle, 1997; Russel, 1998). Where firms have introduced green purchasing strategies, this has been linked to the ability to achieve economies of scale via large purchasing volumes (Min and Galle, 2001), environmental actions in other parts of a business (Green et al., 1996), perceptions that green purchasing can pay (Carter et al., 2000), and the presence of a skilful policy entrepreneur who champions the case for socially responsible buying (Drumwright, 1994). While the moral case for using environmental criteria in the buying decision will be important for some organizations, business logic suggests that private sector purchasing strategies are likely to be evaluated on economic and commercial grounds by most firms. In this regard, the strength of external demands on profit-seeking enterprises—not least from large public sector consumers of goods and services—seems destined to play an increasingly important role in the coming years in pushing green purchasing higher up the corporate agenda.

Green supply chain management (GSCM)

DEFINITION AND SCOPE

Opportunities to improve a firm's environmental performance at an operational level go beyond greening the purchasing function and apply to the whole of what is known as an organization's supply chain. At its simplest and most basic, a supply chain can be conceived of as a triadic relationship in which a single firm purchases its inputs from one supplier and sells its product to a single customer who is the end-user of its good or service. In reality, few, if any, supply chains are this simple; large multi-product firms in particular are often members of multiple, highly complex, and extended networks of suppliers, distributors, and consumers, and these will vary according to the product and/or market concerned and can also vary over time and geographical location (Hervani et al., 2005).

Like many other concepts in the field of corporate greening, GSCM definitions vary substantially in the academic literature according to the interests and concerns of researchers (Zhu et al., 2008a). Early conceptualizations tended to equate GSCM largely with green purchasing behaviour that was aimed at addressing environmental issues through the supplier/buyer relationship (see e.g. Green et al., 1996; Narasimhan and Carter, 1998). More recent contributions see green purchasing as just one element within the process of GSCM which is now taken to mean the integration of environmental thinking into a range of supply chain aspects, including materials sourcing and selection, product design and manufacturing, distribution, marketing, disposal, and research and development (Zsidisin and Siferd, 2001; Zhu and Sarkis, 2006; Srivastava, 2007; Zhu et al., 2007b).

Under this broader definition, GSCM can be analysed from a variety of viewpoints (e.g. Srivastava's literature review links it to 'green design' and 'green operations', while Zsidisin and Siferd focus on purchasing, operations management, and logistics) that incorporate a wide range of practices and activities including green purchasing; life cycle analysis; eco-design; inbound, outbound, and reverse logistics; and waste management (see e.g. Box 10.2). While detailed discussions of these different aspects is beyond the purpose of this chapter, the essential point to stress is that numerous opportunities and approaches exist within a firm's supply chain to address environmental concerns relating to its activities, of which green sourcing is just one option at the inbound end of the process.

BOX 10.2 GSCM—SOME ASSOCIATED CONCEPTS

---

1. Reverse logistics—has been defined by Elkington (1999) as the use of logistical and distribution systems to recover products or materials that are destined for recycling or remanufacturing, that is, effectively returning items to the forward supply chain. For a literature review see Carter and Ellram (1998).
2. The '4Rs' refer to the concepts of reduction, remanufacturing, reuse, and recycling and are part of what Sarkis and Rasheed (1995) call environmentally conscious manufacturing. In essence the basic meaning of each of the terms is as follows:
   - *Reduction*—efforts to minimize waste, particularly via source reduction (e.g. through changes in inputs or processes)
   - *Remanufacturing*—the repair, refurbishment, or reworking of components and equipment for either internal use or sale (e.g. through disassembly and subsequent reassembly)
   - *Reuse*—using a material with minimum or no further treatment (e.g. reusing wooden pallets or rewashed bottles)
   - *Recycling*—reuse (sometimes in a different form) following further treatment (e.g. building waste turned into road materials)

The extent to which an enterprise is able to exploit such opportunities depends to a large degree on its ability to manage and coordinate the complex network of activities within its supply chain and the associated material and information flows involved in delivering a finished product to the end-user or customer (Hervani et al., 2005; Preuss, 2005*a*, 2005*b*; Seuring et al., 2008). Consideration needs to be given not only to intra-organizational relationships but also to those activities in a firm's supply chain which involve managing the organization's environmental performance beyond its own boundaries (Sinding, 2000). Examples of the former include cross-functional cooperation on product design and environmental and quality control mechanisms. The latter can involve such areas as cooperation with suppliers (e.g. first and possibly second tier and beyond) on environmental objectives; with customers on product design and packaging; and with waste recovery organizations on questions of recycling, waste management, and reduction (Zhu and Sarkis, 2006; Zhu et al., 2007*a*, 2008*b*).

GSCM: BARRIERS AND OPPORTUNITIES

As an approach to improving the environmental performance of an organization, GSCM initiatives often encounter considerable obstacles to both their development and implementation. Concerns among organizational decision-makers include questions of cost, complexity, efficacy, impact on operational and economic performance, and a general perception that integrating environmental considerations into supply chain practices may result in a trade-off between environmental and business imperatives (Handfield et al., 2005; Hervani et al., 2005; Simpson and Power, 2005). Preuss (2005*a*) has claimed that there is a significant gap between the rhetoric and reality of corporate greening when viewed from the supply chain management function, with firms achieving suboptimal performance in all three areas of GSCM: the management of transformation of materials; the management of information flows; the management of supply chain relationships. Much of this gap he attributes to structural constraints, including scepticism over the benefits of greening the supply chain; inadequate resources to try new approaches; the position of supply chain personnel in the decision-making hierarchy; a performance-driven culture among purchasing professionals; and the generally reactive, non-strategic nature of the role of supply chain personnel.

The more optimistic view of GSCM practices is that numerous opportunities exist in the management of a firm's supply chain to achieve environmental, operational, and economic improvements simultaneously (see e.g. Russel, 1998; New et al., 2000; Bowen et al., 2001; Preuss, 2001, 2005a, 2005b). In studies of GSCM activities in Chinese businesses, Zhu and associates argue that inter-firm collaboration can improve an organization's environmental performance and that this can ultimately have a positive impact on operational and economic outcomes (Zhu and Cote, 2004; Zhu et al., 2005). A central plank of the win-win-win perspective is the claim that the establishment of long-term buyer/supplier relationships—involving practices such as supplier screening and evaluation, buyer training, mentoring, and general capacity building of suppliers—can yield strategic gains for participating businesses. Needless to say, how far this is always true in practice has been the subject of some debate (Rao and Holt, 2005; Zhu et al., 2007a, 2007b).

GREEN SNAPSHOT: PATAGONIA

The US outdoor clothing company Patagonia, is generally held to be one of the world's leading green and socially responsible businesses (see e.g. Esty and Winston, 2006). Part of this reputation comes from its actions in the supply chain where it aims to ensure that its products are produced under safe, fair, legal, and humane conditions and, where possible, materials are used that have a reduced environmental impact and are recyclable. To share information with customers on the environmental impact of its products, the company has developed its Footprint Chronicles which seek to quantify the environmental impact of Patagonia's supply chain. Information is provided on the distances travelled by particular products and on carbon dioxide emissions, the amount of waste generated, and the amount of energy used in producing each item. There is also information on the bad as well as the good aspects of the manufacturing process, including the use of environmentally hazardous materials.

In addition to monitoring its own performance, Patagonia has also shared its knowledge and experiences on supply chain issues and sustainability generally with other large businesses, including Nike, Gap, Ikea, Marks and Spencer, and Wal-Mart. An article in *Forbes Magazine* on 24 May 2010 describes how the company had begun sharing its experiences with Wal-Mart for free in 2008/9 and had helped the giant retailer to calculate how much water it consumed in the manufacture of its garments, and whether pesticides were used. It had also provided assistance with the development of Wal-Mart's supplier sustainability questionnaire which is used to evaluate the social and environmental performance of its suppliers.

While much of the attention has naturally been focused on the benefits gained by those buying organizations that engage in GSCM practices, Preuss (2001, 2005*a*, 2005*b*) has drawn attention to the existence of what he calls a 'green multiplier'. Like its namesake in the field of economics, the multiplier concept basically refers to the ripple effect that can occur—in this case in the field of environmental protection—from a firm's pro-environmental activities within its supply chain. Faced with customer demands for improved environmental performance in its products, a firm may pass these demands down to its first-tier suppliers who in turn pass these on to their suppliers, and so on. In this way, the supply management function can be instrumental in initiating a green multiplier effect through the supply chain, which can provide new business opportunities for all the participant organizations and might ultimately prove an important agent for change at both the organizational and the wider society level (Russel, 1998; Preuss, 2005*a*).

Green marketing

DEFINITION AND SCOPE

The term 'marketing' has been defined in a wide variety of ways, ranging from Kotler's essentially economic notion of an activity directed at satisfying human needs and wants via exchange processes, to the more managerial approaches adopted by professional bodies such as the Chartered Institute of Marketing (Worthington and Britton, 2009). Central to most definitions is the idea that as a core business function, marketing is concerned with meeting the needs of the consumer in a way that proves beneficial to the enterprise: creating value for the organization through creating value for its customers. Accordingly, key marketing activities include:

- identifying customer needs and wants (e.g. via marketing research);
- designing 'offerings' to meet the specific needs of different types of customers (e.g. via market segmentation);
- choosing products, prices, promotional techniques, and distribution channels that meet the needs of a particular market segment (e.g. via targeted marketing mix strategies);
- undertaking market and product planning (e.g. via integration with other business functions);
- responding to changing market conditions (e.g. via the establishment of a marketing information system).

Although the natural environment received some consideration in the marketing literature in the 1970s (e.g. Fisk, 1973; Kinnear et al., 1974), Peattie and Crane (2005) claim that it was only in the late 1980s that the idea of 'green marketing' emerged, largely in response to growing consumer demands for greener products. In the inevitable flurry of academic activity which greeted this new development, numerous articles and books began to appear on the topic of what was termed variously as 'green marketing', 'greener marketing', 'environmental marketing', 'ecological marketing', 'enviropreneurial marketing', 'sustainable marketing', and even 'socially responsible marketing'. Examples of definitions from a sample of the literature published over the last two decades can be found in Table 10.1.

Despite Polonsky's recent assertion (2011) that the focus of all definitions is essentially on exchange processes that minimize environmental harm, what green marketing actually is or how broadly its boundaries can reasonably be drawn is arguably less precise (Grant, 2007; Priebe, 2010). El Dief and Font (2010), for example, suggest that the green marketing process covers a wide range of activities in which a firm is involved, including new product development, logistics, production, pricing, packaging, distribution, and promotion, thereby linking green marketing to other activities in an organization's value chain (e.g. green purchasing and supply chain management). Narrower definitions in contrast have often associated the term with the greening of the different aspects of traditional marketing and have frequently focused on the production of 'green' products for sale to 'green' consumers (Kilbourne, 1998), including the promotion of a good's environmentally friendly characteristics.

While the debate over what constitutes green marketing might seem something of a semantic diversion, it has been suggested that the term is often attached to activities that

Table 10.1 Selected definitions of green marketing

Author(s)	Definition
Polonsky (1994, 1995)	'Green or Environmental marketing consists of all activities designed to generate and facilitate any exchanges intended to satisfy human needs and wants, such that the satisfaction of these needs and wants occur, with minimal detrimental impact on the natural environment.'
Peattie (1995) and Peattie and Charter (1997)	'The holistic management process responsible for identifying, anticipating and satisfying the needs of customers and society, in a profitable and sustainable way.'
Crane (2000)	'Green Marketing is . . . taken to mean the incorporation of environmental dimensions into marketing activities.'
Peattie (2001b)	' . . . marketing activities which attempt to reduce the negative social and environmental impacts of existing products and production systems, and which promote less damaging products and services.'
Polonsky and Rosenberger (2001)	' . . . is a holistic, integrated approach that continually re-evaluates how firms can achieve corporate objectives and meet consumer needs while minimizing long-term ecological harm.'
Ottman et al. (2006)	'Green marketing must satisfy two objectives: improved environmental quality and customer satisfaction.'
Ward (2011)	'Green marketing refers to the process of selling products and/or services based on their environmental benefits. Such a product or service may be environmentally friendly in itself or produced and/or packaged in an environmentally friendly way.'

are underpinned neither by a marketing nor an environmental philosophy (Peattie and Crane, 2005). Reviewing the history of green marketing since the 1990s, Peattie and Crane (2005) have identified five types of misconceived marketing behaviour which they believe have hampered progress towards greater sustainability: 'green spinning', 'green selling', 'green harvesting', 'enviropreneur marketing', and 'compliance marketing'. Green spinning, for example, involves the use of public relations (PR) techniques by firms seeking to manage their reputation and to reduce the risk of negative stakeholder reactions to the organization's activities (e.g. oil companies). Compliance marketing relates to the practice of promoting one's green credentials simply on the basis of complying with existing environmental regulations (e.g. chlorofluorocarbon (CFC) free products) or of demonstrating a willingness to undertake environmental actions while simultaneously lobbying against any further legislation.

If Peattie (2001*b*) is correct, the definitional problem is further complicated by the tendency for our views of what might constitute green marketing to change over time as our understanding of the interaction between the economy and environment develops. Initial perspectives he describes as 'ecological marketing' with its limited focus on reducing consumer dependence on particularly damaging products (e.g. pesticides such as DDT). By the late 1980s, 'environmental marketing' had emerged with its emphasis on exploiting green consumer demand, with firms using this as a basis for gaining a competitive advantage. Peattie calls his third phase or age 'sustainable marketing' which he describes as a more radical approach to markets and marketing in which attention is paid to meeting the full environmental costs of production and consumption; focusing in other words on the 'the way we live, produce, market and consume' (p. 144). This phase, he suggests, is still far from established and is likely to prove a significant challenge to the practice of marketing if products and the processes of production and consumption are to become more sustainable in the broadly accepted sense of the term (e.g. Brundtland).

THE IDEA OF THE 'GREEN CONSUMER'

Whether defined broadly or narrowly, environmentally focused marketing claims have become evident in a growing number of businesses. Why is this the case?

Given that the satisfaction of human needs and wants is central to the idea of marketing, it seems reasonable to assume that a significant driver of green marketing activities within profit-seeking businesses has been growing customer demands for more environmentally friendly products, what Peattie terms the age of 'environmental marketing' (see above). Alongside the other factors that predispose organizations to 'go green' (see Chapter 4), the green marketing literature regularly highlights the importance of consumers to the development and commercialization of greener products and to the increasing incorporation of environmental issues into marketing communications (Lampe and Gazda, 1995; Mendleson and Polonsky, 1995; Langerak et al., 1998; Peattie, 2001a). Expressions of public concern over the environmental performance of firms and their products, the publication of green consumer guides, the emergence of new markets for the introduction of environmentally orientated goods and services (e.g. eco-tourism), indicators of reduced environmental impact (e.g. eco-labels), and other customer-focused developments all seem to support this idea of a consumer-led green revolution (Peattie, 2001a, 2001b). To what extent has this been the primary influence on firm behaviour?

While it is undoubtedly true that growing environmental awareness has provided opportunities for businesses (e.g. the Body Shop, Patagonia) to exploit the apparent preference of some consumers for less environmentally damaging products, current evidence does not support the idea of a predominant and widespread customer-driven corporate greening process. Research suggests that consumers' positive attitudes towards environmental products are not always translated into purchasing behaviour because of factors such as higher prices for green products, consumer confusion or cynicism over green claims, concerns over the relative performance of greener offerings, and the tendency of most consumers to choose a product on the basis of various attributes, of which environmental performance, if important at all, occupies a minor position (Mendleson and Polansky, 1995; Kalafatis et al., 1999; Follows and Jobber, 2000; Gurau and Ranchhod, 2005; Litvine and Wüstenhagen, 2011). As Ginsberg and Bloom (2004: 79) succinctly put it, while customers generally 'prefer to choose a green product over one that is less friendly to the environment when all other things are equal, those "other things" are rarely equal in the minds of consumers'.

In taking up this theme to understand environmental purchasing behaviour, it is necessary to take account of the perception that all other things are not equal. Peattie (2001a, 2001b) argues that firms should focus on the purchase decision rather than the purchaser. In his opinion, the likelihood of an individual being influenced by a product's environmental performance when making a purchase will be shaped by the degree of consumer compromise involved (e.g. over relative price, performance, convenience of purchase) and the degree of confidence a customer has in the environmental benefits of a particular product choice (e.g. will it make a material difference or does it address an important environmental problem?). These two influences on the green purchasing decision form the basis of the author's green purchase perception matrix (see Table 10.2), which shows how a consumer's reactions to the purchase of specific products can vary according to their confidence and willingness to compromise, with some green products likely to occupy stronger positions in the market place than others based on these two variables.

Although Peattie (2001a) warns that a preoccupation with the purchaser rather than the purchase decision might result in something of a wild goose chase, some marketers believe that identifying different groups of green consumers on the basis of different levels of response to environmental concerns is both informative and helpful in the design of most targeted green marketing strategies. Referring to a survey of US consumers in 2002,

Table 10.2 Peattie's green purchase perception matrix

Degree of consumer compromise relative to conventional purchases (e.g. over price, performance, or availability)

	High	Low
Degree of consumer confidence in the environmental benefits of a purchase — High	'FEELGOOD PURCHASES (e.g. organic cotton clothing)	WIN-WIN PURCHASES (e.g. recycled paper or green investments)
(e.g. will the purchase make a material difference) — Low	WHY BOTHER? PURCHASES (e.g. electric cars)	WHY NOT? PURCHASES (e.g. unleaded petrol)

Source: Adapted from Peattie (2001*a*: figure 1).

Ginsberg and Bloom (2004) provide an example of how a consumer market can be segmented into different shades of green according to an individual's attitudes, predispositions, and habits. The consumers most receptive to green appeals are described as 'true blue green' (9 per cent) and 'greenback greens' (6 per cent), while the least or non-receptive are known as 'grousers' (19 per cent) and 'basic browns' (33 per cent). In between is a group referred to as 'sprouts' (31 per cent) whose purchasing decisions tend to be driven by price, but who can be persuaded to buy green if appealed to appropriately. On these calculations, consumers receptive to a green appeal (in the United States) number somewhere between 15 and 46 per cent of the overall consumer market, a spread which might go some way towards explaining why some businesses remain sceptical (or unconvinced) that investing in higher levels of green performance is worthwhile, at least in the short term, and why others—including leading companies such as Procter and Gamble, McDonald's, Wal-Mart, and Coco-Cola—appear to have engaged in green marketing largely for financial reason (e.g. lower costs) rather than in response to consumer demand (Kassaye, 2001; Nair and Menon, 2008).

GREEN MARKETING STRATEGIES

What goes on in marketing departments cannot realistically be separated from decisions taken at business and corporate levels. Issues such as the design, price, promotion, and distribution of products are influenced by the firm's choices concerning how it wishes to portray itself, what markets it wants to compete in, and how it intends to compete in those markets against its rivals (see Chapter 8). In short, the idea of a green marketing strategy can be applied at all levels of the organization and can be related as much to a firm's overall strategic posture as it can to its actions at a tactical level (see below).

Corporate responses to the opportunities provided by the emergence of the green consumer can, of course, vary substantially as the discussion in Chapter 5 has clearly indicated. In the context of green marketing, Ginsberg and Bloom (2004) have argued that a firm's strategy should be related to the likely size of the green market in its particular industry and to its ability to differentiate its product(s) on environmental grounds from those of its competitors. Using these two dimensions, the authors identify four potential strategic responses: 'lean green', 'shaded green', 'defensive green', and 'extreme green'. The major characteristics of each strategy are illustrated in Box 10.3.

BOX 10.3 GINSBERG AND BLOOM'S GREEN MARKETING STRATEGY MATRIX

Ability to differentiate product on the
basis of relative greenness

	High	Low
High	EXTREME GREEN	DEFENSIVE GREEN
Low	SHADED GREEN	LEAN GREEN

Potential size of green market segments

Lean Green: Where pro-environmental activities are used to reduce costs and improve efficiencies, but where the firm is reluctant to publicize or market its green initiatives for fear of raising public expectations (e.g. Coca Cola).

Defensive Green: Where green marketing is used defensively in response to a crisis or a competitor's behaviour. Often involves support for environmentally friendly events and programmes (e.g. Gap).

Shaded Green: Involves investing in long-term, organization-wide environmentally friendly processes in an attempt to gain a competitive advantage by meeting consumer needs through innovative products and technologies (e.g. Toyota).

Extreme Green: Where environmental issues are fully integrated into the organization in all areas. Environmental concern is often a major driving force from the very beginning of the organization (e.g. The Body Shop).

Source: Ginsberg and Bloom (2004) © MIT Sloan Management Review/Massachusetts Institute of Technology. All rights reserved. Distributed by Tribune Media Services.

While Ginsberg and Bloom's analysis suggests that a firm should base its strategic response on *ex ante* research into the opportunities afforded by prevailing market and competitive conditions, green marketing strategies can also be shaped by *ex post* perceptions that a changing business and competitive environment might prove problematic or threatening. Researching the strategic responses of firms in the wake of a perceived consumer backlash against green products, Crane (2000) also identifies four general strategic approaches adopted by managerial decision-makers: 'passive greening', 'muted greening', 'niche greening', and 'collaborative greening'. Firms pursuing a passive approach do not regard the environment as important for branding and positioning purposes and consequently do not actively seek out green markets nor engage in across the board environmental improvements unless pressured to do so by key influential stakeholders (e.g. regulators, business customers). Muted greeners in contrast tend to adopt an incremental approach to environmental product improvement in the hope of protecting the organization's reputation against negative reactions by external parties.

Crane's third green marketing strategy, 'niche greening', represents an approach in which the firm deliberately targets consumers with strong environmental preferences and accordingly sees the environment as critical to its positioning and branding of products and as a source of competitive advantage. Whereas this approach places emphasis on the ability of the organization's decision-makers to identify and exploit opportunities by adopting a narrow strategic posture, collaborators believe that creating value is best achieved by working with other organizations in the firm's supply chain and beyond (e.g. with competitors and/or environmental NGOs), a strategy based on the recognition that many of the organization's green marketing problems are often located outside its own boundaries. As Crane rightly observes, a collaborative approach to greening the firm and its products can coexist with one of the other three strategic orientations, with inter-organizational alliances or partnerships helping a firm to respond reactively to stakeholder demands (passive greening), enhance its image (muted greening), or retain and promote its green credentials in the market place (niche greening).

GREEN SNAPSHOT: GREEN ENDORSEMENT

Chinese PC maker Lenovo's claim to be a socially and environmentally responsible business received a considerable boost when it was placed first in the 2007 Greenpeace ranking of electronic manufacturers' recycling and toxic content policies. Other companies in the top five that year were Nokia, Sony Ericsson, Dell, and Samsung, while Apple occupied last place in the ranking.

Lenovo, which purchased IBM's consumer electronics division in 2005, achieved its ranking on the basis of its e-waste policies and practices, which included reporting on the amount of e-waste it recycled as a proportion of sales and offering product takeback and recycling facilities in all the countries where its products were sold.

Greenpeace suggested that major factors in driving improvement in the green performance of the electronic companies included in its quarterly rankings had been a combination of consumer expectations, competitive pressures, and regular dialogue between Greenpeace campaigners and the organizations concerned.

LEVELS OF RESPONSE

The needs and wants of consumers tend to be only one factor influencing a firm's decisions concerning how far, if at all, it wishes to demonstrate and promote its green credentials. Considerations of the financial bottom line, the expectations of other key stakeholders, problems of implementation, the impact on internal structures and processes, and consistency with the organization's overall strategic objectives are just some of the other concerns likely to affect managerial attitudes and actions (McDaniel and Rylander, 1993; Mendleson and Polonsky, 1995; Polonsky, 1995, 2011; Rivera-Camino, 2007). The issue of the level or scope of responses is also one that the enterprise needs to address when formulating and implementing a green marketing strategy.

In relation to what they term 'enviropreneurial' marketing strategies, Menon and Menon (1997) identify three levels at which green marketing activities can occur within the firm: tactical, quasi-strategic, and strategic. Tactical green marketing relates to decisions at the functional level and involves the use of organizational resources to achieve specific marketing objectives (e.g. promoting a green image). Quasi-strategic responses concern the use of changes in business practices aimed at furthering the organization's competitive position in existing businesses and markets (e.g. development of a green brand). Strategic greening connotes a fundamental change in corporate philosophy, an irreversible commitment to the principles of sustainability that is reflected in decisions relating to market participation and development (e.g. entering new businesses or markets or exiting others).

A useful example of how strategic, quasi-strategic, and tactical green marketing activities might be undertaken across a range of functional marketing areas (e.g. targeting, pricing, promotion) has been suggested by Polonsky and Rosenberger (2001). A shortened and revised version of their analysis is provided in Table 10.3, for illustrative purposes. As the authors point out, in an ideal world, external coordination should occur across functional areas if a firm's green marketing strategy is to be effective, in short, achieving integration in aspects such as promotion, positioning, and targeting at a tactical, quasi-strategic, and strategic level. As Peattie and Crane (2005) have shown, however, some manifestations of green marketing activity within organizations can involve essentially tactical approaches to corporate positioning or promotion (e.g. the authors' concepts of 'green spinning', 'green selling', and 'compliance marketing') that have the effect of creating cynicism and distrust among consumers who become increasingly resistant to claims about green products and to the businesses that produce and/or sell them.

GREENING THE 'MARKETING MIX': SOME KEY ISSUES

Green marketing activities can be directed at both the organization and its product(s), and normally encapsulate what marketers refer to as the 4Ps of the marketing mix:

Table 10.3 Level of green marketing response by activity

	Tactical greening	Quasi-strategic greening	Strategic greening
Targeting	Advertising green credentials in green-focused media	Green brand development as part of overall portfolio	Development of new strategic business unit focusing on green market
Product design	Supplier selection on environmental performance basis	Use of life cycle analysis to reduce environmental impact	Environmentally focused product design at the outset
Positioning	PR campaign to highlight green practices	Change in corporate logo to imply future direction of organization	Organization founded on environmental ideals
Promotion	Use of PR to overcome bad press over environmental performance	Policy of promoting environmental benefits of firm's offerings	Regular support for environmental campaigns as part of organization's *raison d'être*
Pricing	Linking higher price with cost savings through using a green product	Switch of pricing method to link product use to price paid	Change in approach to meeting consumer needs e.g. renting rather than selling

Source: Adapted from Polonsky and Rosenberger (2001: figure 2).

product, price, promotion, and place (Table 10.3). These are essentially a set of controllable variables which a business can manipulate to influence a buyer's response, in this case by highlighting the organization's and/or product's green credentials in the hope that this will prove attractive to consumers for whom environmental concerns are an important part of the buying decision. As Ottman and colleagues (2006) have warned, however, a focus on products and production processes rather than on consumer needs can give rise to what they term 'green marketing myopia', a perception that green products will sell themselves irrespective of the value sought by targeted customers.

Product

A green product has been defined as one whose 'environmental and societal performance in production, use and disposal is significantly improved and improving in comparison to conventional or competitive offerings' (Peattie, 1997: 201). Based on this definition, higher levels of environmental performance may be the result of changes in product design, product characteristics, production processes, packaging, product use, product disposal, or, in some cases, even product redefinition. These in turn may involve activities aimed at waste minimization, material substitution, the promotion of efficient product use, the modification or redesign of production processes, changes in technology and issues relating to packaging, and so on (Bridges and Wilhelm, 2008). The greening of products also requires a considerable degree of intra-organizational coordination between the marketing function and areas such as product planning and development, design, manufacturing, purchasing, and distribution if the firm is to achieve an integrated approach.

In bringing a 'greener' product to the market place, a business needs to decide whether to target a specific market niche or to try to appeal to consumers generally by presenting a product's environmental performance as just one of its key attributes alongside consumer concerns such as price, quality, and service (Esty and Winston, 2006). Equally, it needs to consider how it can best provide potential customers with information about the product's green credentials/performance. One way of doing this is via its promotional activities (see below); another is by achieving external certification from a recognized and reputable body (e.g. the Forest Stewardship Council) or by qualifying for the display of an eco-label which certifies that a given product is environmentally safe or friendly (Lampe and Gazda, 1995; Rex and Baumann, 2007). Examples of the latter include the Blue Angel (Germany), the White Swan (Nordic Countries), the Green Seal (the United States), the EU's European Eco-Label, and the Eco-Mark (Japan).

Pricing

The pricing of green products can prove something of a dilemma for an organization. On one hand, the claim that one's offering delivers additional benefits over and above conventional products, coupled with the likely additional costs of production, tends to suggest that a firm should charge a higher price in the market place, particularly when targeting the green consumer, (e.g. the Toyota Prius). On the other hand, consumer resistance to price increases, coupled with a degree of cynicism over green claims, might suggest that any price rises should be kept to a minimum or alternatively absorbed by the business (e.g. by spreading additional costs across the firm's product range), especially if

---

GREEN SNAPSHOT: ABUSING GREEN LOGOS?

Ecolabels and other forms of environmental logo are meant to provide some form of assurance that a product meets certain predetermined environmental criteria, particularly if underwritten by a reputable body such as a renowned environmental or conservation organization. Policing such schemes, however, is by no means an easy task.

According to a 2011 report by the investigative group Global Witness, some companies which are members of WWF's Global forest and trade network (Gftn) and use its panda logo to denote that timber products have been acquired sustainably have been involved in either the clearance of biologically rich and diverse rainforests or in purchasing wood from potentially illegal sources. The claim is that lax membership and participation rules mean that some firms in the Gftn may not always abide by its core principles. Needless to say, WWF has challenged the allegations and claims that the Gftn has made a major contribution to conservation through positive engagement with the industry at both producer and retailer levels.

the firm's green image might be undermined by suspicions of profiteering (Peattie and Charter, 1997).

While a 'cost-plus' based approach to pricing would tend to favour a premium pricing strategy, larger organizations usually take a more strategic view, with questions of competitor pricing and customer price sensitivity no less important influences in the pricing decisions of green products than for non-green alternatives. A willingness to absorb short-term cost increases might also prove strategically justifiable when the organization anticipates future savings and/or revenue contributions from eco-efficiency gains and other environmentally linked benefits (e.g. improved corporate image).

Promotion

Whereas pricing decisions relate to a firm's products, green promotional activities can apply to both its offerings or to the business itself. In the latter case, the organization becomes the brand, with its products bought (or in some cases, rejected) on environmental grounds (e.g. BP's image was severely dented following the oil spill in the Gulf of Mexico in 2010).

Green promotion can take a number of forms from advertising, sales promotion, and personal selling to sponsorship of an environmental cause or the publication of an environmental report available for key stakeholder groups interested in the organization's green performance. Ottman et al. (2006) have suggested that the marketing messages contained in a firm's promotional activities can prove beneficial for an organization by helping to connect the business and/or its green products with desirable customer value attributes such as efficiency, cost effectiveness, health and safety, and convenience (e.g. Proctor and Gamble's Tide Coldwater detergent). On the downside, green claims can often be confusing (e.g. the term 'recyclable' is often used in a variety of ways), appear little more than 'greenwash', and can backfire on firms whose claims are subsequently found to be misleading or at best only a partial picture. They may also encourage additional scrutiny of the organization that could highlight issues the firm would prefer to keep hidden and this could damage other brands in the enterprise's portfolio as well as the business generally (Polonsky and Rosenberger, 2001; Ginsberg and Bloom, 2004).

Place

Given that the distribution of physical products is a major contributor to a firm's environmental impact, an organization's green marketing decisions can also include considerations of the choice of distribution systems aimed at minimizing environmental costs and/or maximizing recycling opportunities, the siting of depots for distribution or of retail outlets to minimize customer travel, and a wide range of issues related to packaging, transport, and logistics. Centralized distribution systems, for example, can help to reduce the number of vehicle movements and the amount of transit packaging used by an organization, while changes in delivery methods (e.g. online shopping and/or home deliveries) can lead to a reduction in car usage by consumers and hence in carbon emissions and other environmental problems.

GREEN STRATEGIES AND THE MARKETING MIX

Ginsberg and Bloom (2004) argue that an organization's overall green marketing strategy can be linked to the way in which it utilizes the four elements of the marketing mix. A lean green strategy, they suggest, tends to be exhibited mostly in its choices concerning product design, development, and manufacturing, while a defensive approach also includes attempts to leverage benefits through the use of public relations, including sponsorship of environmentally focused events and causes (e.g. Gap). Shaded greeners, in contrast, pursue a strategy in which product and process innovations assume primary importance, while some emphasis may also be placed on green promotion and pricing, whereas under an extreme green approach, heavy use is made of all the marketing mix elements, including the choice of distribution systems and retailers on the basis of their putative green performance (e.g. Patagonia, The Body Shop).

In reality, of course, it is worth remembering that broad categorizations of generic green strategies of this kind are mainly heuristic devices and that organizations rarely, if at all, match all the dimensions suggested by academic researchers. Moreover, a firm's choices regarding the way it utilizes the marketing mix variables can vary between products and over time and space, with green attributes assuming greater significance in some geographical locations and markets than in others. In the final analysis, expressions or manifestations of greenness should not be regarded as an absolute but seen in relative terms; whatever marketers might claim, no product or firm can be entirely environmentally friendly and we should judge an organization's green credentials on its merits, not on the basis of clever terminology or self-professed achievements (e.g. according to an analysis of over 4,000 CSR reports carried out by researchers at Leeds University and the Euromed Management School in Marseilles, environmental claims by some of the world's largest companies routinely included incorrect statistics and omitted vital information. See for example *The Guardian*, 25 November 2011, page 44 for further details).

Green accounting

As the previous sections of this chapter have shown, a firm can demonstrate its green credentials in a variety of ways, including through its purchasing and supply chain activities and how it designs the various elements of the marketing mix. Concern for the environment can also be expressed via the way in which it seeks to integrate environmental considerations into its conventional accounting practices.

In an organizational context, green or environmental accounting can cover all areas of accounting that may be affected by a firm's responses to environmental issues (Gray and Bebbington, 2001). Greenham (2010: 335), for example, takes a sustainability-focused view of the concept, arguing that 'green accounting measures the impact of human activity on the earth's ecological systems and resources and not just the financial effects of such activity'. More managerialist approaches stress the incorporation of environmental concerns into existing business practices and paradigms, seeing accounting essentially as a management tool that is used for both internal and external purposes (United States EPA, 1995; Bennett and James, 2000; Yakhou and Dorweiler, 2004) and which supports organizations in their primary aim of transferring inputs into outputs in pursuit of conventional objectives such as growth and profitability (Gray and Bebbington, 2001).

When viewed as an aid to business decision-making, green accounting essentially involves the gathering, analysis, and presentation of both monetary and non-monetary data and information on a firm's environmental performance and impact, including the potential financial implications of management decisions (e.g. future risks and contingent liabilities). Activities aimed at producing information largely for internal use are referred to as 'environmental management accounting' (Bartolomeo et al., 2000); where the information is used primarily to provide a degree of accountability to external stakeholders, the term 'external environmental accounting' is frequently used (see e.g. Schaltegger et al., 2003) and includes the practice of reporting on a firm's environmental impacts to audiences outside the organization.

Internally orientated environmental accounting systems can be used to shed light on how environmental issues impact on a firm's economic situation and on how the organization's activities affect the natural environment (Schaltegger and Burritt, 2000). In the case of the former, monetary values can be attached to a firm's decisions and behaviour such as investing in cleaner technology or methods of production or incurring fines for non-compliance with environmental regulations. The latter, in contrast, involves the provision of information in a non-monetary form, including data on past, present, and estimated future material and energy consumption by product, site, division, or company as a whole (Schaltegger et al., 2003).

Where practised, green or environmental management accounting makes use of a range of accounting tools, including environmental cost accounting, environmentally focused capital and operational budgeting, environmental financial planning, and material and energy flow accounting. (For a useful description of the different tools, see Schaltegger et al., 2003: chapter 17; see also Bennett and James, 2000, and Burritt, 2004, for case studies of some of these approaches in real organizations.) Environmental cost accounting, for example, essentially concerns the identification and allocation of environmental costs to the material flows or other physical aspects of a firm's operations (Graff et al., 1998), in effect placing an environmental cost on the organization's products and processes. According to a report produced by the US Environmental Protection Agency (1995), uncovering and recognizing such costs alongside the normal costs of an organization's activities may generate savings and/or increased revenues (e.g. through the sale of waste products), aid firms in areas such as product pricing, design, and environmental management, and contribute significantly to improved business performance and competitive advantage.

Turning briefly to the notion of external environmental accounting, this too provides information that is recorded in both monetary and non-monetary forms and whose disclosure and presentation has frequently been influenced by a variety of external users including regulators, standard setting bodies (e.g. the International Accounting Standards Board), and other stakeholders (e.g. professional accounting bodies) interested in business performance (Marshall and Brown, 2003; Schaltegger et al., 2003; Huang and Kung, 2010). On the whole, the requirement for firms to provide readily accessible data and information on social and environmental impacts tends to apply predominately to large organizations and is usually voluntary, although some countries have certain elements of compulsion (e.g. Australia, France) where external accountability is concerned. International attempts to provide a more universal system of external accounting is exemplified by the Global Reporting Initiative (GRI), which first produced guidelines in 1999—subsequently revised in 2002 and 2006—setting out the principles and indicators that organizations can use to measure and report on their social, environmental, and economic performance (see e.g. Schaltegger et al., 2003, and Visser, 2009, for further details).

While it seems fair to suggest that external environmental accounting by businesses has been one important consequence of the rise of environmental awareness (Gray and Bebbington, 2001), some observers still see it as largely a marketing and PR exercise that falls far short of the triple bottom line philosophy advocated by John Elkington (1999) and others (e.g. Esty and Winston, 2006). Newton and Harte (1997: 92) have warned that organizational systems and processes can by their very design create 'an appearance of "objective" greenness which masks the social construction of environmental data'. In the final analysis, accounts of any kind are invariably partial and biased constructions of a complex world (Gray and Bebbington, 2000); the innate conservatism of the accounting professional makes it likely that what is revealed in environmental information analysis and disclosure is at best an incomplete view of an organization's impact on the natural environment.

Case Study: Puma

The German sports and leisure company Puma is part of the PPR group. In May 2011, under the leadership of its CEO Jocken Zeitz, the company became the first major corporation to publish the results of the economic valuation of its environmental impact as part of its plan to incorporate the social and environmental costs and benefits of its activities into its financial accounts.

Using an Environmental Profit and Loss Account methodology, developed in partnership with PriceWaterhouseCoopers and the environmental research group Trucost, the firm calculated that the impact of its water consumption and greenhouse gas emissions throughout its supply chain was equivalent to 94.4 million euros, split roughly 50/50 between the two types of impact. Its analysis showed that the activities of its suppliers accounted for around 87 million euros of the total impact, with the production of raw materials such as leather and cotton the largest single contributor at just over 41 million euros.

In announcing these results, Zeitz stressed the importance of recognizing that the use of ecosystem services was a key part of corporate performance and that, in future, businesses would be required to incorporate the true costs of these into their accounting and reporting procedures since they would impact on the bottom line (e.g. if firms were faced with additional costs because of charges/taxes imposed on resource usage or if insurance premiums increased because of higher risks). By acting now, Puma believes this will not only increase transparency and provide a benchmark for others to follow, but will also make the business more sustainable in the future and this could provide a competitive advantage both on the demand and supply side.

As part of its move to become a more sustainable business organization, Puma has set targets to reduce its waste, energy, and water use and its carbon footprint by 25 per cent by 2015 and it has recently introduced new environmentally friendly packaging for its footwear, replacing the traditional cardboard box with reusable, recyclable, and, eventually, biodegradable bags. It also aims to develop its environmental and social impact assessments further to include issues such as waste, land use, and acid rain and to calculate the economic benefits caused by its activities (e.g. jobs created, business growth) in keeping with the idea of a triple bottom line approach. While media coverage of Puma's plans and impact-assessments have been generally favourable, critics have pointed to its continued sponsorship of motorsports, including Formula 1 and Moto GP, activities with a discernible environmental impact that seems to run counter to its aim to become a more sustainable enterprise.

Section Five
Conclusion

11 Towards the ecologically sustainable business organization?

If goals of sustainability are to be achieved, corporations must be reformed, redesigned and restructured to minimise their negative ecological impacts.

(Shrivastava, 1995c)

The self-sustaining order of the modern organization is one of utilitarian-based techno-rationalism, a social architecture where the moral code is constructed around growth, consumption, profitability and personal success.

(Crane, 2000)

...achieving sustainability is a journey for businesses, and while many are on the path, no firm is sustainable.

(Sharma and Henriques, 2005)

Introduction

The closing decades of the twentieth century clearly witnessed a growing concern among business leaders over the impact of economic activity on the natural environment, alongside a gradual acceptance by many of the world's leading corporations that improved environmental performance and creating value for the organization were readily compatible (Laszlo, 2008). While the analysis in the previous chapters has shown that not everyone agreed (or agrees) that the greening of business will ultimately prove a source of competitive advantage, there can be little doubt that an increasing number of firms have taken steps to reduce their environmental impact, albeit with considerable variation in the nature, scale, and pace of individual responses to the pressures emanating from both internal and external stakeholders.

After four decades or more of discussions, analysis, theorizing, and empirical research into corporate environmentalism, it is fitting that the final chapter in this book seeks to assess the business community's current position in the journey towards more sustainable forms of development. Given that more and more organizations are beginning to regard environmentalism as a strategic business issue, have we reached a point where we can realistically talk of an ecologically sustainable business organization? What would such a business look like, how might it be defined, and what would be demonstrable indicators of corporate sustainability? These are some of the key issues addressed in the concluding section of this study.

It ought to be stated at the outset that the environmental dimension of business performance is only one aspect associated with the concept of sustainable development (see Chapter 2) and that strictly speaking sustainability in an organizational context applies to practices that 'contribute to sustaining and renewing the quality of life of their workforces and the community' as well as 'adding to the richness and diversity of the biosphere' (Dunphy and Benveniste, 2000: 3). While human or social sustainability is no less important than ecological sustainability, it is appropriate—given the focus of this book—to concentrate on the latter, while still recognizing that organizations can appear sustainable in some senses (e.g. human or ecological or economic) and not in others (e.g. ecological or economic or human) or may be achieving different levels of performance on each aspect of the concept.

What is a sustainable business organization?

Sustainable businesses are generally held to be organizations that subscribe to and practise the principles that underlie the notions of sustainability or sustainable development (see the discussion in Chapters 2 and 7). Precisely what this means in practice is not entirely clear; as Diesendorf (2000) has pointed out, both sustainability and sustainable development are contestable concepts that are often used interchangeably to refer to outcomes that are simultaneously economic, social, and environmental, the so-called 'Triple Bottom Line' (Elkington, 1994, 1999; Hart and Milstein, 2003). What should be included in this calculation and what issues a business organization could reasonably be expected to address are frequently vague and almost always a matter of some controversy (Jennings and Zandbergen, 1995; Lamming et al., 1999).

Lying at the heart of the definitional problem is the question of how far and in what ways a firm needs to configure its policies, practices, and products to address the kinds of broad issues and principles highlighted in both the Brundtland Report and the Earth Summit in Rio, if it is to be regarded as a sustainable enterprise. Some writers have suggested that global problems (e.g. worldwide food security, population growth and its impact on ecosystems) and/or key sustainability principles (e.g. social equity, environmental integrity) can/should be tackled in part through decisions at a corporate level (Shrivastava, 1995c, 1996; Shrivastava and Hart, 1995; Elkington, 1999; Dunphy and Benveniste, 2000; Bansal, 2005; Hahn and Scheermesser, 2006), in effect linking corporate activities to the fundamental problems highlighted in the sustainability debate. Hart and Milstein's assertion (2003) that a sustainable organization is one that is contributing to sustainable development by simultaneously creating economic, social, and environment benefits typifies this broad perspective. Dyllick and Hockerts (2002) have expressed a preference for a stakeholder view of corporate sustainability, arguing that it is concerned with meeting the needs of a firm's direct and indirect stakeholders both now and in the future through the maintenance and growth of its economic, social, and environmental capital base.

Within the debate over the meaning of corporate sustainability, some observers have focused on the notion of ecological or environmental sustainability, an issue that—as previously noted—formed the subject of a special edition of the *Academy of Management Review* in the mid-1990s (see Volume 20, No. 4, 1995). In an early contribution to the field, Shrivastava and Hart (1995) defined ecologically sustainable organizations as those that attempt to reduce their consumption of non-renewable energy and virgin materials and minimize their environmental hazards and emissions of pollutants, in short, pursuing their economic goals at the same time seeking to reduce their environmental impact (see also Dunphy and Benviste, 2000). Central to this definition is the idea that ecologically sustainable businesses are those that attempt to minimize the environmental damage caused by their operations and to reconfigure their relationship within the natural environment, by respecting the limits of its carrying capacity and avoiding degrading ecosystem services in order to protect their own long-term economic viability (Dyllick and Hockerts, 2002). This essentially organizational-focused view of sustainability has been challenged by Starik and Rands (1995: 909) who argue that, since organizations exist within a framework of relationships, 'the test of an organization's ecological sustainability is the degree to which its activities can be continued indefinitely without negatively altering the *limiting factors* that permit the existence and flourishing of other groups of entities, including other organizations'.

In calling for a multi-system, multi-level perspective of ecological sustainability, Starik and Rands are suggesting that the measures or indicators of an organization's progress will vary according to the level at which it is analysed, such that firms 'can achieve ecological

---

GREEN SNAPSHOT: RESENE PAINTS

In 2010, Resene Paints was named New Zealand's Sustainable Business of the Year because of its continued commitment to sustainable business practices and its efforts to encourage sustainable innovation in the paint industry. In addition to improving the environmental performance of its products through the removal and/or reduction of toxic and hazardous materials at all stages of their life cycle, Resene has also instituted a paint and paint packaging recovery service aimed at helping users to recycle and dispose of unwanted products and has established an Eco.Decorator programme designed to create a nationwide network of environmentally responsible painting contractors who have been assessed as meeting particular levels of environmental performance. Contractors successfully completing the programme can promote their business as a Resene Eco.Decorator, thereby giving them a potential advantage in bidding for projects that are based around sustainability principles.

sustainability by different means and in different configurations, consistent with the concept of equifinality' (p. 915). The more common-place approach—and the one adopted below for consistency's sake—is to focus on the organization as the unit of analysis, since firms are, in Shrivastava's words (1995c), the primary engines of economic development and have the financial resources, technological skills and knowledge, and the institutional capacity to implement ecological solutions. In choosing and putting these solutions into practice, we readily acknowledge that other factors will be at play, not least the role of both broader societal and individual influences in shaping organizational responses.

Indicators of ecological sustainability at firm level

Identifying appropriate indicators of sustainability at firm level is no easy task. Welford (1997b) has pointed out that definitions of sustainability/sustainable development can vary in terms of their focus (e.g. principles versus impact), thereby resulting in different views of how to assess a firm's achievements and strategies, including its choice of the most appropriate tools to move it along a more sustainable path. Claims that sustainable businesses are those that have a high level of performance in economic, social, and environmental terms or have an accounting system that adopts a Triple Bottom Line approach (Atkinson et al., 2000) do not add to our understanding to any great extent. They simply remind us that sustainability is a multi-dimensional construct that is open to significant interpretation and re-interpretation over time within both the academic and practitioner communities (Elkington, 1999).

Welford and Jones's approach (1996) to sustainability measurement has been to identify seven broad 'elements of sustainability' (e.g. general principles, equity, biodiversity and animal protection, life cycle impacts) and then to suggest more detailed measures firms need to adopt if they are to be consistent with the concept of sustainable development. Under biodiversity and animal protection, for example, they argue that activities such as habit regeneration; reporting on species and habitats and on organizational impact; the abandonment of animal testing; and the use of environmental impact assessments for new sites, processes, and products, are appropriate indicators of a firm's commitment to the sustainability agenda. To track an organization's progress along the road to sustainability, they suggest, requires not just recording what steps the firm is taking but also finding ways of measuring and subsequently reporting on its performance to both internal and external stakeholders.

GREEN SNAPSHOT: TOM'S OF MAINE

Tom's of Maine produces personal care products using natural ingredients (e.g. dental products, soap, deodor-ant). In 2006, a controlling interest in the company was purchased by Colgate-Palmolive.

The Company's claim to be seen as a sustainable business revolves around its approach to sourcing, manufacture, packaging, and product disposal. Using a 'stewardship model' which sets out its definitions of 'natural', 'sustainable', and 'responsible', the company has a policy of sourcing high-quality, naturally produced ingredients that have to meet strict social and environmental standards. Where possible, Tom's works with vendors who operate sustainable farming practices and its suppliers are subject to an audit to ensure that its stringent standards (e.g. no animal testing) are upheld.

On the manufacturing side, the firm aims to produce its products safely and sustainably, using energy-efficient lighting in its factory and warehouse; reusing materials where possible; operating a recycling system; and offsetting its electricity consumption by investing in renewable energy credits. The company also engages in sustainable practices in its offices and has donated land for green space for use by the local community.

Once produced, products are packaged using recycled and recyclable material, which helps to reduce the company's solid waste, waste water, consumption of electricity, and air pollution. Since 2011, Tom's has also begun to package its toothpaste in more easily recyclable plastic laminate tubes that help to reduce the use of energy in the manufacturing and distribution process. To help increase recycling opportunities, the firm has also established a number of partnership arrangements and has joined a recycling programme called Gimme 5 which collects Tom's plastic deodorant containers which were previously difficult to recycle.

While Welford and Jones's 'measures of sustainability' model places emphasis on the need to address the underlying principles of sustainable development and does not separate the social, economic, and environmental dimensions to any great degree, other contributors have sought to identify possible indicators of corporate ecological sustainability, while accepting that there is often considerable overlap between economic, social, and environmental performance. For Diesendorf (2000), potential measures could include rates of material flow and energy use, rates of greenhouse gas emissions, water and air pollution, and area of land degraded and polluted. Less specifically, Lamming et al. (1999) have suggested that what they term 'environmental soundness' can be judged by an organization's approach to issues such as the conservation and enhancement of the natural resource base and life support systems, technological reorientation, and the depletion of non-renewable resources: a mixture of predisposition and action.

This idea that measures of ecological sustainability should include both tangible and intangible indicators (e.g. corporate attitudes and acceptance of certain principles) is perhaps best illustrated by the suggestion that corporate performance ought to be judged from a systemic point of view (Shrivastava, 1995a, 1995c, 1996; Shrivastava and Hart, 1995). Using the basic systems model outlined in Chapter 1, the authors argue that an organization's progress towards sustainability should be assessed in relation to its vision and by its actions at the input, output, and throughput stages of the transformation process, what they call the vision, inputs, throughputs, outputs (VITO) elements.

Measured in this way, evidence of progress towards greater ecological sustainability would include more environmentally focused missions, goals, and strategies; action to reduce energy and raw materials usage; the design and development of more environmental products and packaging; cleaner and more efficient production systems; the minimization and management of waste and pollutants; and the development of green organizational structures, systems, cultures, and competencies (see e.g. Shrivastava, 1996).

When combined with a multiple levels of analysis approach, the systems framework understandably produces a much larger and broader range of characteristics, seen to be indicative of ecologically sustainable organizations, including corporate involvement in environmental partnerships, the commitment of resources to inter-organization and ecological cooperation, encouragement of pro-environmental policy instruments, and support for initiatives aimed at promoting eco-literacy (Starik and Rands, 1995). One inevitable consequence of this perspective is that achieving ecological sustainability status is destined to be beyond the reach of any organization in an absolute sense; corporate responses should be seen as progress along a road for which there is no ultimate and definable destination. Another implication is that to become more ecologically sustainable often requires various form(s) of cooperation with other organizations, including governments, environmental NGOs, and other businesses. To this extent, Roome and colleagues may be correct in arguing that the transition towards sustainable development cannot be achieved by any one organization acting alone (Clarke and Roome, 1999; Boons and Roome, 2005). This is a theme to which we return towards the end of this chapter.

Paths towards ecological sustainability

Accepting that ecological sustainability needs to be viewed as a relative concept, the next obvious question is: how can a business make progress on the sustainability front? Put differently, what needs to occur at firm level to move an organization along the path towards the elusive goal of environmentally sustainable development?

The greening of a business, its choice of strategies, policies, products, practices, and processes, is clearly seen as part of the answer to this question (see e.g. Box 11.1). Measures including the use of life cycle analysis, environmental auditing and reporting, waste reduction and recycling, the adoption of cleaner technologies, the switch from non-renewable to renewable resources, product redesign, green purchasing, and so on have all been advocated as ways in which an organization can engage in more sustainable forms of behaviour (Elkington, 1994; Starik and Rands, 1995; Diesendorf, 2000; Bansal, 2005). Where a firm's choice of strategies is concerned, it has been argued that these need to be inter alia:

- adopted and implemented at all levels within the organization (Starik and Rands, 1995);
- linked to the type of economy (e.g. market vs. survival) in which the firm is operating (Hart, 1997; Hart and Milstein, 1999);

BOX 11.1 DEVELOPING SUSTAINABLE PRODUCTS

For firms wishing to demonstrate their commitment to the idea of sustainability, one obvious approach is to develop and market green products. Writing in the *Harvard Business Review* in June 2010, Professors Unruh and Ettenson describe three broad strategies an organization can take to align its green aspirations with its capabilities: accentuate, acquire and architect. These strategies are depicted in the following table.

Strategy to align the firm's green goals with its capabilities	Brief description of strategic path to green growth	Firm's potential to leverage existing/ latent green attributes	Firm's existing green resources and capabilities
Accentuate	Highlight existing green attributes	High	Low
Acquire	Obtain a green brand	Low	Low
Architect	Build new offerings from scratch	Low	High

1. *Accentuate Strategy*—this essentially involves exploiting any existing or latent green attributes in a firm's current portfolio, for example by stressing the environmental characteristics of a particular product currently on sale. Unleaded petrol is a good example. As the authors point out, however, this strategy can backfire if the product concerned has some features that appear unsustainable (e.g. if the product is tested on animals) or if the other products in its portfolio appear significantly less green by comparison.

2. *Acquire Strategy*—as the name implies, this approach involves purchasing someone else's green brand. Two excellent examples are Unilever's purchase of Ben and Jerry's and Colgate-Palmolive's acquisition of Tom's of Maine. Adding an established and well-respected green brand name to one's portfolio is obviously attractive and can help to develop a firm's green capabilities in areas such as production, design, and supply chain management. One potential danger of such an acquisition is that the purchase is seen negatively by external stakeholders (e.g. by being regarded as tokenism or as a means of destroying a rival).

3. *Architect Strategy*—for firms with existing green development capabilities and attributes, an appropriate strategy may be to develop a green product from scratch. Unruh and Ettinson quote the example of the Toyota Prius which has had widespread market appeal and has caused competitors to respond by developing products to capture the growing level of consumer demand for more environmentally friendly vehicles. As with the other strategies, the authors warn that an organization needs to ensure that its green claims are credible and that the other products in its portfolio are not manifestly unsustainable for fear that they will be brought into focus by the new green offering. On the upside, the acquisition or development of green skills and abilities may be applied to other products and this might help the organization to gain a competitive advantage as consumers become more environmentally conscious.

- consistent with recognized sustainability principles such as the Business Charter for Sustainable Development (Shrivastava, 1995c); and
- forward-thinking and long-term (Shrivastava, 1995b; 160).

It has even been argued that practising sustainability at the corporate level would compel an organization 'to exit environmentally hazardous business and enter into environmentally friendly ones' (Hart, 1996: 160); to become, in Diesendorf's words (2000), a 'sustainability-promoting corporation'. Business leaders in industries such as petrochemicals, mining, and nuclear energy are unlikely to treat this suggestion seriously.

Whether greening a firm's operations and strategies is a sufficient measure of its sustainability has been called into question by those who believe that sustainability requires a much deeper level of organizational change than is evident in most corporate ecological responses (see e.g. Welford, 2000). Proponents of this view argue that, as well as seeking to limit the environmental damage caused by their existing operations, to become sustainable a firm needs to undertake a complete redesign of the business: the creation of a new style of corporation with a fundamentally different relationship with the natural environment (Shrivastava, 1995a, 1995c; Shrivastava and Hart, 1995). To address the problem of damage limitation, Shrivastava and Hart (1995) advocate the use of total environmental management based upon the systems perspective referred to above (i.e. the VITO elements). Issues to be addressed under this approach would include product design, technology choice, the use of renewables, waste management and recycling practices, and questions of product disposal, with life cycle analysis providing an organization with a way to achieve a holistic perspective.

With regard to the question of transforming the organization itself, Shrivastava and Hart propose a policy of sustainable organizational design in which all elements of a firm (e.g. mission, strategies, competences, structures, processes, culture, etc.) undergo a process of change. To approach sustainability, they argue that all these design elements must be focused on social and environmental performance and should be internally consistent and self-reinforcing. Key ways in which this might be achieved are illustrated in Table 11.1.

The assertion that a firm needs to address the issue of sustainability from a variety of perspectives, including the question of organizational design, is also evident in Griffith's call (2000) for the creation of new sustainability-inducing organizational architectures and in Elkington's claim (1999) that, to become more sustainable, an organization needs to undergo changes in its approach, thinking, mind-set, and culture. To achieve such a transformation, Elkington argues that firms need to adapt new paradigms in seven main areas, including corporate governance, life cycle technology, transparency, and values. Within each of these areas, he identifies various steps a business needs to take to achieve this paradigm shift. In all, he proposes thirty-nine steps or stepping stones towards organizational sustainability, which include the use of a Triple Bottom Line approach,

Table 11.1 Designing sustainable corporations

Focus	Change in approach	Examples
Mission	From short-term financial considerations to longer term global concerns (e.g. environmental impact). Strong sense of social–environmental purpose/ strategic intent; strong corporate norms and values and well-articulated principles to guide behaviour	Reforestation schemes; community development in the Third world
Corporate and competitive strategies	Environmental and social responsiveness must infuse corporate and competitive strategies	Leaving hazardous industries or entering environmentally friendly ones; reducing resource usage; trade not aid approach
Core competencies	Reconfiguration of technological capabilities to support strategies; audits of technical and human skills and reallocation towards technologies which meet criteria for environmental management	Collaboration/joint ventures to develop new environmental technologies especially with the developing world
Structure and systems	Design structure and systems to realize mission and execute strategies. Making organization sensitive to values and demands of environmentalism	Board level developments; 'champions' at top level; rewards for environmental performance
Organizational processes and culture	Ensuring organizational processes and values which encourage environmental awareness. Culture that emphasizes importance of natural world; integration of environmental into day-to-day processes; constructive involvement with external stakeholders	Green Teams to implement environmental programmes
Performance criteria	Viewing performance in holistic terms. Returns measured in more than commercial terms	Triple Bottom Line approach

Source: Based on Shrivastava and Hart (1995).

product stewardship, the creation of green business networks, greater transparency, and a focus on sustainable consumption rather than production growth. One suspects that corporate executives would find such a list not just convenient in a literary sense but also both daunting and unrealistic.

Whatever pathway to ecological sustainability an organization decides to pursue, all observers generally agree that progress is dependent on creating supportive internal systems and on garnering the commitment and enthusiasm of a firm's employees, particularly those occupying senior executive and management positions. Achieving transformational change is not simply a policy problem; it is also dependent on ensuring employee 'buy-in' and on adopting appropriate implementation and verification processes across the entire enterprise. On the whole, creating a sustainability-championing and focused workforce is likely to prove more of a challenge than designing an effective system of environmental management, particularly if—as is frequently the case—an organization's systems of incentives and compensation are not geared towards rewarding excellence in ecological performance (Landis Gabel and Sinclair-Désgagné, 1994).

GREEN SNAPSHOT: INTERFACE

Interface is a large, globalized manufacturer of modular floor coverings and upholstery fabrics, predominantly used for commercial applications. Its stated vision is to be the first company to become—by 2020—what it calls a sustainable and restorative enterprise through its actions on five dimensions: people, process, product, place, and profits. Its watchwords include respect for individuals, human dignity, product and process quality, superior value, environmental protection and restoration, and profitability. Under its late founder and CEO, Ray Anderson, the company has undergone a substantial transformation in an attempt to move it on to a sustainable path without sacrificing its core business goals.

Since its sustainability journey began in 1994, Interface points to the progress it has made in three main areas: its environmental footprint, the design and manufacture of its products, and its corporate culture. Key steps in its progress to 'Mission Zero' include:

- significant reductions in energy use, water use, and greenhouse gas emissions;
- increased use of renewable energy and bio-based raw materials;
- substantial cuts in the amount of waste sent to landfill;
- progress on the move towards closed-loop products;
- initiatives aimed at enthusing all the firm's stakeholders around its vision; and
- widespread focus on the social and environmental impacts of its operations, products, and processes.

It recognizes, however, that considerable obstacles still need to be overcome if it is to achieve its mission zero goal. Challenges include the need for further action on sourcing 100 per cent recyclable raw materials, sustaining an engaged culture among the company's stakeholders, and achieving a zero footprint on waste, energy use, and emissions.

Bolt-on versus embedded sustainability

Any assessment of a firm's claims to be an ecologically sustainable organization needs to consider the degree to which its actions do not simply pay lip service to the underlying principles of sustainable development, but indicate a step-change in its attitudes and behaviour. To paraphrase Laszlo and Zhexembayeva (2011), is sustainability 'embedded' into the DNA of the organization or is it more of an afterthought, a kind of 'bolt-on' sustainability that seeks to portray the business as environmentally and socially responsible but without any significant change to its core business activities and perceptions of value creation?

Laszlo and Zhexembayeva's central assertion (2011: 105) is that bolt-on versus embedded approaches to organizational sustainability represent 'two strikingly different ways to manage social and environmental pressures for business opportunity'. Under the former approach, green initiatives (e.g. green products, environmentally responsible practices) tend to lie at the margins of the business, existing alongside a firm's mainstream activities which may be far from sustainable in an ecological and/or social sense. Whilst this does not imply that efforts at greening (or corporate social responsibility) are of no value, it warns us of the need to judge a firm's claims (e.g. in its social and environmental reports or its corporate publicity and advertising) on its merits, by its overall actions and not just its words or symbolic gestures. In short, a healthy dose of scepticism and critical appraisal is likely to produce a more objective assessment of corporate ecological performance than one that is grounded in partial analysis and the use of clever marketing and communication strategies.

An embedded approach to sustainability starts from the conviction that creating value for a business can be achieved simultaneously to creating value for society and the environment, the idea that environmental, health, and social value can be incorporated into a firm's core business activities with no trade-off in price or product quality. To achieve what they call the 'next big competitive advantage', the authors argue that a firm needs to rethink its business and develop new competencies, practices, processes, and

Table 11.2 Bolt-on versus embedded sustainability

	Bolt-on	Embedded
Primary goal	Create shareholder value	Create sustainable value
Scope	Seek symbolic wins at the margin of the business	Transform the firm's core business activities
Attitude to customer	Offer 'green' or 'socially responsible' products at higher prices or reduced level of performance	Offer 'smarter' solutions without a trade-off in price or quality
Approach to capturing value	Reduce risk and improve organizational efficiency	Seek sustainable value creation in all areas of the business
Action within the value chain	Focus on the firm's own activities	Manage across the value chain throughout the life cycle
Approach to stakeholder relationships	Seek advantage within transactional relationships (e.g. customers, employees)	Build transformative relationships with all key stakeholders including regulators
Stance towards competitors	Zero-sum approach: firm's gain is competitor's loss	See cooperation with rivals as potential source of gain
Organizational response	Create a separate department to manage sustainability	Make sustainability everyone's job within the organization
Approach to competency building	Focus on traditional management skills, for example, planning, analysis	Add new competencies in areas such as design, inquiry and appreciation
Attitude to visibility	Make greening/corporate social responsibility (CSR) initiatives highly visible and manage any adverse reaction	Make sustainability performance largely invisible but widely acceptable

Source: Adapted from Laszlo and Zhexembayeva (2011).

perspectives, in effect to undertake a comprehensive business makeover. A way to conceptualize the difference between this approach to sustainability and the bolt-on variety is illustrated in Table 11.2.

If, by implication, embeddedness constitutes a meaningful test of organizational sustainability, few, if any, firms currently could be said to have achieved the status of a sustainable enterprise on all dimensions, although some could perhaps reasonably claim to be further along the path than many of their counterparts. Consistent with the central tenet of the win-win school, Laszlo and colleague argue that a critical first step on this journey is to move from seeing sustainability as a necessary business cost (and possibly unnecessary distraction), to regarding it as a vital source of business opportunity; a means of achieving a competitive advantage, whether by using embeddedness to strengthen an existing strategic position (e.g. low cost of differentiated product) or to pursue new and relatively uncontested market space (e.g. by an innovative solution to a difficult environmental problem). If this prescription is correct, then the inevitable questions are, why are some firms evidently reluctant to embrace the sustainability agenda, and what are some of the key obstacles to the emergence of the sustainable business organization?

Barriers to the creation of sustainable businesses

A recurrent theme in much of the literature discussed in this book has been the notion that the greening of business and the gradual move towards creating a more sustainable form of enterprise represents a win-win situation, a gain for the firm and a gain for the environment. Implicit (and frequently explicit) in this line of reasoning is the idea that any failure to exploit the claimed advantage of corporate environmentalism must be largely a question of a lack of imagination or possibly a problem of inertia on the part of business leaders. From this perspective, unsustainable business responses are seen as a manifestation of an unwillingness by corporate decision-makers to look much beyond 'business as usual', a failure to see the firm's relationship with the natural environment as a business opportunity rather than as an unwanted business cost that should be avoided as far as possible.

Explanations for this apparent antipathy to the idea that sustainability pays often point to business realities as a key obstacle to more environmentally progressive forms of behaviour. Faced with a plethora of day-to-day business imperatives and often with challenging microeconomic (for example, competition) and macroeconomic (for example, recession) conditions, many firms understandably take a defensive or at best incremental approach to greening the organization (Hart and Milstein, 1999; Steger et al., 2007). Appeals to a long-term vision rooted in the vague notion of sustainable development are likely to cut little ice with many hard-pressed business decision-makers whose main preoccupations are largely short-term and almost invariably focused on survival, growth, and profits, and on creating and enhancing shareholder (or owner) value.

While it is tempting to focus exclusively on current business pre-occupations and orthodoxies as the primary obstacle to the creation of sustainable enterprises, Pearce and Barbier (2000) are surely right when they recommend that we look beyond the agents of the problem and also consider the underlying causes of ecologically unsustainable forms of behaviour. Is the problem of ecologically damaging levels of production and consumption simply attributable to the choices made at an individual level in firms and in households, or are these choices underpinned (and possibly encouraged) by the existence of a largely growth-focused economic, policy, and institutional environment (Purser et al., 1995; Welford, 1997*b*; Pearce and Barbier, 2000)? To Pearce and his fellow contributors (1989, 2000), the source of most environmental problems lies in an economic system that fails to assess properly the true economic value of the contribution made by the natural environment and in the failure of markets, institutions, and governments to provide adequate incentives to manage environmental assets sustainably. If this analysis is correct, it would not be surprising if the pursuit of sustainable development was not at the top of most corporate agendas, unless it could be demonstrated beyond reasonable doubt that ecological sustainability invariably pays.

Although it has been beyond the scope of this book to undertake a detailed analysis of the cause of and solutions to global environmental problems, it is worth reiterating that businesses are not simply victims of their external context as the above line of reasoning appears to imply. How markets operate; what government policies are pursued, abandoned, and stifled; what incentives are introduced or removed; and so on are all influenced by inputs from the business community and from other vested interests within democratic systems of government. If, as appears to be the case, a growing number of the world's leading corporations are embracing the idea that they have an important role to play in building a more sustainable future (see Box 11.2), then this will ultimately be reflected not only in corporate decisions but also in policy and institutional developments at national level and beyond. While progress in this direction often appears painstakingly slow, signs that corporate sustainability goals may be becoming gradually more institutionalized within larger enterprises (Bansal, 2005) suggest that a cultural shift may be occurring that will help to move more and more firms on the path towards ecological sustainability in the coming decades. The challenge will be to persuade the sceptics and the doubters that this is a road worth taking; this will not be an easy task.

BOX 11.2 CEO ATTITUDES TO SUSTAINABILITY

The claim that business leaders are increasingly buying in to the idea that sustainability is becoming a business imperative is supported by a recent survey of over 750 United Nations Global Compact (UNGC)[1] CEOs published in 2010. The survey results show that 93 per cent of CEOs see sustainability as important to their company's future success, with 54 per cent rating it as very important: a significant increase overall on the results of a similar survey conducted three years earlier. Key concerns among respondents included access to education, the impact of climate change, the alleviation of poverty and hunger, and the provision of clean water and sanitation. The most commonly cited factors by CEOs in motivating them to take steps to address sustainability issues were the questions of the impact of brand, trust, and reputation, with many business leaders concerned about how the global downturn and financial crisis in recent years had tarnished the reputation of business among key stakeholders.

An interesting fact to emerge from the UNGC survey was that the commitment to sustainability varied according to region, with CEOs from the Asia Pacific (APAC) countries appearing the most committed (98 per cent compared to the survey average of 93 per cent) and those from the Middle East and North Africa the least committed (but still 79 per cent). One explanation for this level of support among APAC CEO's was that business leaders in emerging economies see sustainability in very local, personal, and immediate terms, exemplified by their concern over issues such as access to clean water and poverty alleviation. This finding adds weight to the argument by Hart (1997) that the idea of sustainable development varies according to the type of economy concerned.

The CEO survey also highlighted a shift in emphasis among corporate executives from sustainability as a moral imperative to its imperative as a strategic business issue, with business case arguments underpinning the commitment to sustainable development (e.g. sustainability as a means to reducing costs and/or increasing revenue). To gain such advantages, business leaders claimed that there was a need to integrate sustainability into the firm's day-to-day practices, to embed it into their strategies and operations. Despite the fact that a majority of respondents expressed confidence that such integration had occurred/was occurring, the survey notes that there was still often something of a mismatch between aspiration and reality, with problems in areas such as supply chain management and subsidiary performance. To embed sustainability further, the survey identifies five key enabling conditions/necessary actions, including the need for supportive market conditions (e.g. greener consumers), measures of corporate performance (e.g. remuneration packages linked to sustainability outcomes), regulatory developments (e.g. sponsoring collaborative approaches), and educational initiatives (e.g. training on sustainability issues for managers and employees).[2]

Notes: 1. The UNGC is the world's largest voluntary corporate responsibility initiative, with over 7,000 signatories (including thousands of businesses) across the globe. Launched in 2000, the Compact is a framework for businesses committed to aligning their activities with ten universally accepted principles in the areas of human rights, anti-corruption, labour, and the environment.
2. Accenture is a global management consultancy, outsourcing, and technology services organization. It can be accessed via its homepage www.accenture.com

A final comment

As has been demonstrated throughout this book, the forces pushing firms towards greener, more ecologically sustainable forms of behaviour lie both within and outside the organization, in developments (or lack of them) in the social, regulatory, and market domains of business. No firm can escape the context in which it operates, and its actions and decisions with regard to environmentalism will be shaped by a variety of factors including changing consumer attitudes to green products; the demand by large corporate buyers for a higher level of environmental performance by their suppliers; regulatory and fiscal initiatives by governments; shifts in public opinion; and the general economic and political climate facing business decision-makers at any point in time. Given that every firm's context will be unique to some degree, we should not be surprised that organizations will be at different points on the path towards sustainability, with some seeing it as central to the enterprise's mission (see the case study at the end of this chapter) while others act, if at all, only when forced to do so. In between these two positions probably lie the vast majority of businesses, committed to taking some steps, whether large or small, to improve on their environmental performance either for reasons of competitiveness, legitimacy, or social responsibility (Bansal and Roth, 2000).

In the final analysis, we should not forget that in a market-based, capitalist economic system, most businesses are privately owned, whether by the people who run them or by outside investors; they are first and foremost economic institutions driven by economic and commercial imperatives, and with performance largely measured on the basis of short-term value creation and risk management processes. In these circumstances, appeals to the business community to adopt the principles and practices associated with sustainable development tend to be judged in business case terms: do the benefits ultimately outweigh the costs? The evidence suggests that despite a general shift in business culture towards corporate environmentalism, large numbers of businesses across the globe—especially small and medium-sized enterprises (SMEs)—still remain to be convinced that greening the organization can pay. Only when this happens are we likely to see a step-change towards widespread and embedded corporate ecological sustainability, where reducing the organization's adverse environmental impacts is seen as a strategic issue and becomes part of the everyday process of doing business and making money for the overwhelming majority of profit-seeking enterprises. That day is still to dawn.

Case Study: Unilever's 'Sustainability Living Plan'

The Anglo-Dutch Consumer Goods Group, Unilever, is the world's second largest food and personal goods corporation supplying about 2 billion customers every day. Its products include Dove, Lynx, Persil, Flora, PG Tips, Marmite, Knorr, Bertolli, and Ben and Jerry's Ice Cream. Under its CEO, Paul Polman, the group launched its 'Sustainability Living Plan' in November 2010, which aimed at putting the idea of sustainability at the heart of its global operations. Focusing on sustainable growth and sustainable sourcing, the plan set the highly ambitious target of doubling the organization's sales while halving its environmental impact by 2020. These goals were announced in the wake of new pledges on sustainability by its larger rival Procter and Gamble that covered much of the same ground.

Polman's underlying philosophy is that firms need to take responsibility for the damage they are causing to the environment, not simply through their own operations but throughout their entire supply chain. With the increasing influence of the Internet and particularly social network sites such as Facebook, he believes that businesses will come under growing consumer pressure to behave responsibly and that customers will start to switch their spending towards products and organizations that meet their requirements in terms of environmental and social performance.

Central to Unilever's vision is the idea that organizational growth and reduced environmental impact are entirely compatible and that becoming a more sustainable organization will be the only way to do business in the long term. In Polman's opinion, firms that commit themselves to reducing their negative impacts will help to restore confidence in the business community and are likely to gain a competitive advantage over their rivals. Not undertaking such a commitment, he believes, is likely to prove a significant risk as the business environment changes.

Under its Sustainable Living Plan, Unilever aims to reduce its emissions of greenhouse gases, its use of water, and the amount of waste created. In addition to addressing these issues within its own production units, the group is also committed to reducing its impact across its entire supply chain, not least from its customers who consume large amounts of water in using its products (e.g. soap and shampoo) and receive considerable amounts of packaging that needs to be disposed of responsibly. With regard to its suppliers of agricultural products, the corporation aims to add half a million smallholder farmers and distributors in developing countries to its supply chain in order to improve their economic prospects and general well-being. It also aims to source all its agricultural raw materials from sustainable sources by 2015; improve the nutritional value of its products by reducing their calorific value and levels of salt, sugar, and saturated fat; educate consumers in developing countries in the hygienic use of its products to reduce illness; undertake initiatives to improve water quality and safety; and reduce reliance on non-renewable sources of energy.

While Polman admits that it is not entirely clear how Unilever will be able to achieve all its objectives within the next ten years, a number of specific measures have already been identified. These include developing washing powders that work at lower temperatures; reducing the amount of waste produced within the supply chain; schemes to reduce water usage; doubling the use of renewable energy; cutting truck mileage; and developing new products and innovative solutions to consumer needs in, as yet, unspecified ways. The organization also aims to develop its relationships with leading NGOs (e.g. the Rainforest Alliance and Oxfam) to help bring more small farmers into its supply chain and to achieve its goal of 100 per cent sustainable sourcing in the future. Progress towards all of these goals will be outlined in the group's annual reports.

While Polman is confident that Unilever can achieve its economic, social, and environmental targets over the next decade, some observers believe they may be less than popular with certain of the organization's stakeholders. Writing in *Marketing Week* on the 9th of December 2010, Stuart Smith argued that Unilever's plan could prove highly risky and potentially unattractive to City investors who tend to take a short-term view of a firm's performance. Smith suggests that the group's plans may appear overly ambitious to the markets, may prove difficult to stage-manage, and lack clarity over how the stated goals will be achieved. He believes that, for the time being, large institutional investors will give Unilever the benefit of doubt but that their opinion is likely to quickly change if its plans for revenue growth begin to stall.

■ REFERENCES AND FURTHER READING

ACCA (2002) *Environmental Taxes*. London: Association of Chartered Certified Accountants.

Alberti, M., Caini, L., Calabrese, A. and Rossi, D. (2000) 'Evaluation of the Costs and Benefits of an Environmental Management System', *International Journal of Production Research*, 38(17), pp. 4455–66.

Álvarez Gil, M.J., Burgos Jimeńez, J. and Céspedes Lorente, J.J. (2001) 'An Analysis of Environmental Management, Organizational Context and Performance of Spanish Hotels', *Omega*, 29, pp. 457–71.

Ambec, S. and Lanoie, P. (2008) 'Does It Pay to Be Green? A Systematic Overview', *Academy of Management Perspectives*, November, pp. 45–62.

Andersen, M.S. and Sprenger, R.-U. eds. (2000) *Market-based Instruments for Environmental Management: Politics and Institutions*. Cheltenham: Edward Elgar.

Andersson, L.M. and Bateman, T.S. (2000) 'Individual Environmental Initiative: Championing Natural Environmental Issues in U.S. Business Organizations', *Academy of Management Journal*, 43(4), pp. 548–70.

Andrews, C. (1994) 'Policies to Encourage Clean Technology', in Socolow, R., Andrews, C., Berkhout, F. and Thomas, V. eds. *Industrial Ecology and Global Change*. Cambridge: Cambridge University Press, pp. 405–22.

Andrews, C.J. (1998) 'Environmental Business Strategy: Corporate Leaders' Perceptions', *Society and Natural Resources*, 11(5), pp. 531–40.

Andrews, K.R. (1971) *The Concept of Corporate Strategy*. Burr Ridge, IL: Irwin.

Andrews, R.N.L. (1998) 'Environmental Regulation and Business Self-regulation', *Policy Sciences*, 31, pp. 177–97.

Angell, L.C. and Rands, G.P. (2002) 'Factors Influencing Successful and Unsuccessful Environmental Change Initiatives', in Sharma, S. and Starik, M. eds. *Research in Corporate Sustainability: The Evolving Theory and Practice of Organizations in the Natural Environment*. Cheltenham: Edward Elgar, pp. 155–86.

Anglada, M.L. (2000) 'Small and Medium-sized Enterprises' Perceptions of the Environment: A Study from Spain', in Hillary, R. ed. *Small and Medium-Sized Enterprises and the Environment: Business Imperatives*. Sheffield: Greenleaf, pp. 61–74.

Anton, W.R.Q., Deltas, G. and Khanna, M. (2004) 'Incentives for Environmental Self-regulation and Implications for Environmental Performance', *Journal of Environmental Economics and Management*, 48(1), pp. 632–54.

Apsan, H.N. (2000) 'Running in Nonconcentric Circles: Why Environmental Management Isn't Being Integrated into Business Management', *Environmental Quality Management*, Summer, pp. 69–75.

Aragón-Correa, J.A. (1998) 'Strategic Proactivity and Firm Approach to the Natural Environment', *Academy of Management Journal*, 41(5), pp. 556–67.

——Hurtado-Torres, N., Sharma, S. and García-Morales, V.J. (2008) 'Environmental Strategy and Performance in Small Firms: A Resource-based Perspective', *Journal of Environmental Management*, 86, pp. 88–103.

——Matías-Reche, F. (2005) 'Small Firms and the Natural Environment: A Resource-based View of the Importance, Antecedents, Implications and Future Challenges of the Relationship', in Sharma, S. and Aragón-Correa, J.A. eds. *Corporate Environmental Strategy and Competitive Advantage*. Cheltenham: Edward Elgar, pp. 96–114.

Aragón-Correa, J.A., Matías-Reche, F., Senise-Barrio, M.E. (2004) 'Managerial Discretion and Corporate Commitment to the Natural Environment', *Journal of Business Research*, 57, pp. 964–75.

——Rubio-López, E.A. (2007) 'Proactive Corporate Environmental Strategies: Myths and Misunderstandings', *Long Range Planning*, 40, pp. 357–81.

——Sharma, S. (2003) 'A Contingent Resource-based View of Proactive Corporate Environmental Strategy', *Academy of Management Review*, 28(1), pp. 71–88.

Arora, S. and Casson, T. (1995) 'An Experiment in Voluntary Environmental Regulation: Participation in EPA's 33/50 Program', *Journal of Environmental Economics and Management*, 28(3), pp. 271–86.

————(1996) 'Why do Firms Volunteer to Exceed Regulations? Understanding Participation in EPA's 33/50 Program', *Land Economics*, 72(4), pp. 413–32.

Arrow, K., Bolin, B., Constanza, R., Dasgupta, P., Folke, C., Holling, C.S., Jansson, B.-O., Levin, S., Maler, K.-G., Perrings, C.A. and Pimental, D. (1995) 'Economic Growth, Carrying Capacity and the Environment', *Science*, 268, pp. 520–1.

Arthur D. Little (1996) *Workshop Environmental Strategy: Creating Business Advantage*. Rotterdam, cited in Kolk and Mauser (2002).

Aspinwall, R. and Smith, J. (1996) *Environmentalist and Business Partnerships: A Sustainable Model?* Cambridge: The White Horse Press.

Atkinson, S., Schaefer, A. and Viney, H. (2000) 'Organizational Structure and Effective Environmental Management', *Business Strategy and the Environment*, 9, pp. 108–21.

Azzone, G. and Bertele, U. (1994) 'Exploiting Green Strategies for Competitive Advantage', *Long Range Planning*, 27(6), pp. 69–81.

————Noci, G. (1997) 'At Last we are Creating Environmental Strategies which Work', *Long Range Planning*, 30, pp. 562–71.

——Noci, G. (1998) 'Seeing Ecology and "Green" Innovations as a Source of Change', *Journal of Organizational Change Management*, 11(2), pp. 94–111.

Bailey, K.D. (1994) 'Typologies and Taxonomies: An Introduction to Classification Techniques'. Sage University Paper Series on Quantitative Applications in the Social Sciences, Series Number 070102.

Baker, S. (1997) 'The Evolution of European Union Environmental Policy: From Growth to Sustainable Development?', in Baker, S., Kousis, M., Richardson, D. and Young, S. eds. *The Politics of Sustainable Development: Theory, Policy and Practice within the European Union*. London: Routledge, pp. 91–106.

——Kousis, M., Richardson, D. and Young, S. (1997) 'Introduction: The Theory and Practice of Sustainable Development in EU Perspective', in Baker, S., Kousis, M., Richardson, D. and Young, S. eds. *The Politics of Sustainable Development: Theory, Policy and Practice within the European Union*. London: Routledge, pp. 1–40.

————————eds. (1997) *The Politics of Sustainable Development: Theory, Policy and Practice within the European Union*. London: Routledge.

Banerjee, S.B. (2001) 'Corporate Environmental Strategies and Actions', *Management Decision*, 39(1), pp. 36–44.

——Iyer, E.S. and Kashyap, R.K. (2003) 'Corporate Environmentalism: Antecedents and the Influence of Industry Type', *Journal of Marketing*, 67, pp. 106–22.

Bansal, P. (2002) 'The Corporate Challenges of Sustainable Development', *Academy of Management Executive*, 16(2), pp. 122–31.

——(2005) 'Evolving Sustainably: A Longitudinal Study of Corporate Sustainable Development', *Strategic Management Journal*, 26, pp. 197–218.

——Bogner, W.C. (2002) 'Deciding on ISO14001: Economics, Institutions and Context', *Long Range Planning*, 35, pp. 269–90.

——Clelland, I. (2004) 'Talking Trash: Legitimacy, Impression Management, and Unsystematic Risk in the Context of the Natural Environment', *Academy of Management Journal*, 47(1), pp. 93–103.

——Howard, E. eds. (1997) *Business and the Natural Environment*. Oxford: Butterworth Heinemann.

——Hunter, T. (2003) 'Strategic Explanations for the Early Adoption of ISO14001', *Journal of Business Ethics*, 46, pp. 289–99.

——Roth, K. (2000) 'Why Companies Go Green: A Model of Ecological Responsiveness', *Academy of Management Journal*, 43(4), pp. 717–36.

Barbier, E.B. (1997) 'Introduction', *Environment and Development Economics: Special Edition on Environmental Kuznets Curves*, 2(4), pp. 369–81.

Barney, J. (1991) 'Firm Resources and Sustained Competitive Advantage', *Journal of Management*, 17(1), pp. 99–120.

Barney, J.B. and Hesterley, W.S. (2009) *Strategic Management and Competitive Advantage*, 3rd Edition. Harlow: Prentice Hall.

Baron, R.M. and Kenny, D.A. (1986) 'The Moderator-Mediator Variable Distinction in Social Psychology Research: Conceptual, Strategic, and Statistical Considerations', *Journal of Personality and Social Psychology*, 51(6), pp. 1173–82.

Barrow, C.J. (1999) *Environmental Management: Principles and Practice*. London: Routledge.

Bartolomeo, M., Bennett, M., Bouma, J.J., Heydkamp, P., James, P. and Wolters, T. (2000) 'Environmental Management Accounting in Europe: Current Practice and Future Potential', *The European Accounting Review*, 9(1), pp. 31–52.

Baylis, R., Connell, L. and Flynn, A. (1998a) 'Company Size, Environmental Regulation and Ecological Modernization: Further Analysis at the Level of the Firm', *Business Strategy and the Environment*, 7, pp. 285–96.

————————(1998b) 'Sector Variation and Ecological Modernization: Towards an Analysis at the Level of the Firm', *Business Strategy and the Environment*, 7, pp. 150–61.

Begg, K., Van Der Woerd, F. and Levy, D. eds. (2005) *The Business of Climate Change: Corporate Responses to Kyoto*. Sheffield: Greenleaf.

Bemelmans-Videc, M., Rist, R. and Vedung, E. (1998) *Carrots, Sticks and Sermons: Policy Instruments and Their Evaluation*. New York: Transaction Publishers.

Bendell, J. and Sullivan, F. (1996) 'Sleeping with the Enemy? Business-Environmentalist Partnerships for Sustainable Development: The Case of the WWF 1995 Group', in Aspinwall, R. and Smith, J. eds. *Environmentalist and Business Partnerships: A Sustainable Model?* Cambridge: The White Horse Press, pp. 3–33.

Bennett, S.J. (1991) *Ecopreneuring: The Complete Guide to Small Business Opportunities from the Environmental Revolution*. New York: Wiley.

Bennett, M. and James, P. (2000) 'The Green Bottom Line', in Bennett, M. and James, P. eds. *The Green Bottom Line: Environmental Accounting for Management: Current Practice and Future Trends*. Sheffield: Greenleaf, pp. 30–60.

Bennett, M. and James, P. eds. (2000) *The Green Bottom Line: Environmental Accounting for Management: Current Practice and Future Trends*. Sheffield: Greenleaf.

Berry, M.A. and Rondinelli, D.A. (1998) 'Proactive Corporate Environmental Management: A New Industrial Revolution', *Academy of Management Executive*, 12(2), pp. 1–13.

Bianchi, R. and Noci, G. (1998) '"Greening" SMEs' Competitiveness', *Small Business Economics*, 11, pp. 269–81.

Biddle, D. (2000) 'Recycling for Profit: The New Green Business Frontier', *Harvard Business Review on Business and the Environment*. Boston, MA: Harvard Business School Press, pp. 169–99.

Biondi, V., Iraldo, F. and Meredith, S. (2002) 'Achieving Sustainability through Environmental Innovation: The Role of SMEs', *International Journal of Technology Management*, 24(5/6), pp. 612–26.

Blair, A. and Hitchcock, D. (2001) *Environment and Business*. London: Routledge.

Bluffstone, R.A. (2003) 'Environmental Taxes in Developing and Transition Economies', *Public Finance and Management*, 3(1), pp. 143–75.

Boiral, O. (1998) 'ISO14001: Against the Tide of Modern Management', *Journal of General Management*, 24 (1), pp. 35–52.

Bonifant, B.C., Arnold, M.B. and Long, F.J. (1995) 'Gaining Competitive Advantage through Environmental Investments', *Business Horizons*, 38(4), pp. 37–47.

Boons, F. and Roome, N. (2005) 'Sustainable Enterprise in Clusters of Innovation: New Directions in Corporate Sustainability Research and Practice', in Sharma, S. and Aragón-Correa, J.A. eds. *Corporate Environmental Strategy and Competitive Advantage*. Cheltenham: Edward Elgar, pp. 259–85.

Börkey, P., Glachant, M. and Lévêque, F. (1998) *Voluntary Approaches for Environmental Policy in OEDC Countries: An Assessment*. Paris: CERNA.

Bowen, F.E. (2000a) 'Does Size Matter? Organizational Slack and Visibility as Alternative Explanations for Environmental Responsiveness', *Business and Society*, 41(1), pp. 118–24.

——(2000b) 'Environmental Visibility: A Trigger of Green Organizational Response?', *Business Strategy and the Environment*, 9, pp. 92–107.

——(2002) 'Organizational Slack and Corporate Greening: Broadening the Debate', *British Journal of Management*, 13, pp. 305–16.

——Cousins, P.D., Lamming, R.C. and Faruk, A.C. (2001) 'The Role of Supply Management Capabilities in Green Supply', *Production and Operations Management*, 10(2), pp. 174–89.

————————(2006) 'Horses for Courses: Explaining the Gap Between the Theory and Practice of Green Supply', in Sarkis, J. ed. *Greening the Supply Chain*. London: Springer, pp. 151–72.

Braadbaart, O. (1998) 'American Bias in Environmental Economics: Industrial Pollution Abatement and 'Incentives versus Regulations'', *Environmental Politics*, 7(2), pp. 134–52.

Bradford, J. and Fraser, E.D.G. (2008) 'Local Authorities, Climate Change and Small and Medium Enterprises: Identifying Effective Policy Instruments to Reduce Energy Use and Carbon Emissions', *Corporate Social Responsibility and Environmental Management*, 15, pp. 156–72.

Bragd, A., Bridge, G., den Hond, F. and Jose, P.D. (1998) 'Beyond Greening: New Dialogue and New Approaches for Developing Sustainability', *Business Strategy and the Environment*, 7, pp. 179–92.

Branzei, O. and Vertinsky, I. (2002) 'Eco-sustainability Orientation in China and Japan: Differences between Proactive and Reactive Firms', in Sharma, S. and Starik, M. eds. *Research in Corporate Sustainability: The Evolving Theory and Practice of Organizations in the Natural Environment*. Cheltenham: Edward Elgar, pp. 85–121.

Bridges, C.M. and Wilhelm, W.B. (2008) 'Going beyond Green: The "Why and How" of Integrating Sustainability Into the Marketing Curriculum', *Journal of Marketing Education*, 30(1), pp. 33–46.

Brockhoff, K., Chakrabarti, A.K. and Kirchgeorg, M. (1999) 'Corporate Strategies in Environmental Management', *Research Technology Management*, July/August, pp. 26–30.

Buchholz, R.A. (1998) *Principles of Environmental Management: The Greening of Business*, 2nd Edition. New Jersey: Prentice Hall.

Burke, L. and Logsdon, J.M. (1996) 'How Corporate Social Responsibility Pays Off', *Long Range Planning*, 29(4), pp. 495–502.

Burritt, R.L. (2004) 'Environmental Management Accounting: Roadblocks on the Way to The Green and Pleasant Land', *Business Strategy and the Environment*, 13, pp. 13–32.

Busse, M. (2004) 'Trade, Environmental Regulations and the World Trade Organization: New Empirical Evidence', *Journal of World Trade*, 38(2), pp. 285–306.

Bussye, K. and Verbeke, A. (2003) 'Proactive Environmental Strategies: A Stakeholder Management Perspective', *Strategic Management Journal*, 24, pp. 453–70.

Cairncross, F. (1991) *Costing the Earth*. London: Economist Publications.

——(1993) *Costing the Earth: The Challenge for Governments, the Opportunities for Business*. Boston, MA: Harvard Business School Press.

——(1995) *Green, Inc.: Guide to Business and the Environment*. London: Earthscan.

Callon, M. (1998) 'An Essay on Framing and Overflowing: Economic Externalities Revisited by Sociology', in Callon, M. ed. *The Laws of the Markets*. Oxford: Blackwell, pp. 244–69.

Carroll, A.B. and Buchholtz, A.K. (2009) *Business and Society: Ethics and Stakeholder Management*, 7th Edition. Mason, OH: South Western Cengage Learning.

Carson, R. (1962) *Silent Spring*. New York: Fawcett Crest.

Carter, C. and Ellram, L. (1998) 'Reverse Logistics: A Review of the Literature and Framework for Future Investigation', *Journal of Business Logistics*, 19(1), pp. 85–102.

————Ready, K.J. (1998) 'Environmental Purchasing: Benchmarking our German Counterparts', *International Journal of Purchasing and Materials Management*, 34(4), pp. 28–38.

——Kale, R. and Grimm, C.M. (2000) 'Environmental Purchasing and Firm Performance: An Empirical Investigation', *Transportation Research Part E*, 36(3), pp. 219–28.

Cashore, B. (2002) 'Legitimacy and the Privatization of Environmental Governance: How Non-State Market-Driven (NMSD) Governance Systems Gain Rule-Making Authority', *Governance: An International Journal of Policy, Administration, and Institutions*, 15(4), pp. 503–29.

Cassing, J. and Kuhn, T. (2003) 'Strategic Environmental Policies when Waste Products are Tradable', *Review of International Economics*, 11(3), pp. 495–511.

Chamorro, A. and Banegil, T.M. (2006) 'Green Marketing Philosophy: A Study of Spanish Firms with Ecolabels', *Corporate Social Responsibility and Environmental Management*, 13, pp. 11–24.

Chapple, W., Cooke, A., Galt, V. and Paton, D. (2001) 'The Characteristics and Attributes of UK Firms Obtaining Accreditation to ISO14001', *Business Strategy and the Environment*, 10, pp. 238–44.

Chen, Y.-S. (2008) 'The Positive Effect of Green Intellectual Capital on Competitive Advantages in Firms', *Journal of Business Ethics*, 77, pp. 271–86.

Christmann, P. (2000) 'Effects of "Best Practices" of Environmental Management on Cost Advantage: The Role of Complementary Assets', *Academy of Management Journal*, 45(4), pp. 663–80.

Christmann, P. (2004) 'Multinational Companies and the Natural Environment: Determinants of Global Environmental Policy Standardization', *Academy of Management Journal*, 47(5), pp. 747–60.

Chryssides, G.D. and Kaler, J.H. (1993) *An Introduction to Business Ethics*. London: International Thomson Business Press, Chapter 9.

Clarke, S. and Roome, N. (1999) 'Sustainable Business: Learning-Action Networks as Organizational Assets', *Business Strategy and the Environment*, 8(5), pp. 296–310.

Clarkson, P.M., Li, Y., Richardson, G.D. and Vasvari, F.P. (2010) 'Does it Really Pay to be Green? Determinants and Consequences of Proactive Environmental Strategies', *Journal of Accounting and Public Policy*, 30(2), pp. 122–44.

Claver, E., Lopéz, M.D., Molina, J.F. and Tarí, J.J. (2007) 'Environmental Management and Firm Performance: A Case Study', *Journal of Environmental Management*, 84, pp. 606–19.

Claver-Cortés, E., Molina-Azorín, J.F., Tarí-Guillo, J.J. and López-Gamero, M.D. (2005) 'Environmental Management, Quality Management and Firm Performance: A Review of Empirical Studies', in Sharma, S. and Aragón-Correa, J.A. eds. *Corporate Environmental Strategy and Competitive Advantage*. Cheltenham: Edward Elgar, pp. 157–82.

Clemens, B. (2001) 'Changing Environmental Strategies over Time: An Empirical Study of the Steel Industry in the United States', *Journal of Environmental Management*, 62, pp. 221–31.

——(2006) 'Economic Incentives and Small Firms: Does it Pay to be Green?', *Journal of Business Research*, 59, pp. 492–500.

——Douglas, T.J. (2006) 'Does Coercion Drive Firms to Adopt "Voluntary" Green Initiatives? Relationships among Coercion, Superior Firm Resources, and Voluntary Green Initiatives', *Journal of Business Research*, 59, pp. 483–91.

Clement, K. and Bachtler, J. (2000) 'European Union Perspectives on the Integration of Environmental Protection and Economic Development', in Gouldson, A. and Roberts, P. eds. *Integrating Environment and Economy: Strategies for Local and Regional Government*. London: Routledge, pp. 25–38.

——Hansen, M. (2003) 'Financial Incentives to Improve Environmental Performance: A Review of Nordic Public Sector Support for SMEs', *European Environment*, 13, pp. 34–47.

Cockburn, I.M., Henderson, R.M. and Stern, S. (2000) 'Untangling the Origins of Competitive Advantage', *Strategic Management Journal*, 21, pp. 1123–45.

Coglianese, C. and Nash, J. eds. (2001) *Regulating from the Inside: Can Environmental Management Systems Achieve Policy Goals*. Washington, DC: Resources for the Future.

Cole, M.A. and Elliott, R.J.R. (2003) 'Determining the Trade-Environment Composition Effect: The Role of Capital, Labor and Environmental Regulations', *Journal of Environmental Economics and Management*, 46(3), pp. 363–83.

Collins, E., Lawrence, S., Pavlovich, K. and Ryan, C. (2007) 'Business Networks and the Uptake of Sustainability Practices: The Case of New Zealand', *Journal of Cleaner Production*, 15, pp. 729–40.

Condon, L. (2004) 'Sustainability and Small and Medium Sized Enterprises—How to Engage Them', *Australian Journal of Environmental Education*, 20(1), pp. 57–67.

Copeland, B.R. and Scott Taylor, M. (2004) 'Trade, Growth and the Environment', *Journal of Economic Literature*, XLII, pp. 7–71.

Cordano, M. and Frieze, I.H. (2000) 'Pollution Reduction Preferences of U.S. Environmental Managers: Applying Ajzen's Theory of Planned Behavior', *Academy of Management Journal*, 43(4), pp. 627–41.

Cordeiro, J.J. and Sarkis, J. (1997) 'Environmental Proactivism and Firm Performance: Evidence from Security Analyst Earnings Forecasts', *Business Strategy and the Environment*, 6, pp. 104–14.

Coulson, A.B. and Monks, V. (1999) 'Corporate Environmental Considerations Within Bank Lending Decisions', *Eco-Management and Auditing*, 6, pp. 1–10.

Cramer, J. (1998) 'Environmental Management: From "Fit" to "Stretch"', *Business Strategy and the Environment*, 7, pp. 162–72.

Crane, A. (2000) 'Facing the Backlash: Green Marketing and Strategic Reorientation in the 1990s', *Journal of Strategic Marketing*, 8, pp. 277–96.

——(2001) 'Unpacking the Ethical Product', *Journal of Business Ethics*, 30, pp. 361–73.

Cronin, J.J., Smith, J.S., Gleim, M.R., Ramirez, E. and Martinez, J.D. (2011) 'Green Marketing Strategies: An Examination of Stakeholders and the Opportunities they Present', *Journal of the Academy of Marketing Science*, 39, pp. 158–74.

Curkovic, S., Sroufe, R. and Melnyk, S. (2005) 'Identifying the Factors which Affect the Decision to Attain ISO14000', *Energy*, 30, pp. 1387–407.

Curtin, T. and Jones, J. (2000) *Managing Green Issues*. Basingstoke: Macmillan.

Daly, H.E. (1996) *Beyond Growth: The Economics of Sustainable Development*. Boston, MA: Beacon Press.

Darnall, N. (2002) 'Motivations for Participating in a US Voluntary Environmental Initiative: The Multi-State Working Group and EPA's EMS Pilot Program', in Sharma, S. and Starik, M. eds. *Research in Corporate Sustainability: The Evolving Theory and Practice of Organizations in the Natural Environment*. Cheltenham: Edward Elgar, pp. 123–53.

——Ytterhus, B. (2005) 'Environmental and Financial Performance: Do Industrial Sectors Differ in their Ability to Derive Financial Benefits from Environmental Actions?', in Proceedings of Business Strategy and the Environment Conference, University of Leeds, UK, 5–6 September.

Davis, J. (1991) *Greening Business: Managing for Sustainable Development*. Oxford: Blackwell.

De Simone, L.D. and Popoff, F. (1997) *Eco-efficiency: The Business Link to Sustainable Development*. Cambridge, MA: MIT Press.

Dean, T.J. and Brown, R.L. (1995) 'Pollution Regulation as a Barrier to New Firm Entry: Initial Evidence and Implications for Future Research', *Academy of Management Journal*, 38(1), pp. 288–303.

————Stango, V. (2000) 'Environmental Regulation as a Barrier to the Formation of Small Manufacturing Establishments: A Longitudinal Examination', *Journal of Environmental Economics and Management*, 40, pp. 56–75.

Dechant, K. and Altman, B. (1994) 'Environmental Leadership: From Compliance to Competitive Advantage', *Academy of Executive Management*, 8(3), pp. 7–20.

del Brío, J. and Junquera, B. (2003) 'A Review of the Literature on Environmental Innovation Management in SMEs: Implications for Public Policies', *Technovation*, 23, pp. 939–49.

Dennis, B., Neck, C.P. and Goldsby, M. (1998) 'Body Shop International: An Exploration of Corporate Social Responsibility', *Management Decision*, 36(10), pp. 649–53.

Denton, K. (1994) *Enviro-Management: How Smart Companies Turn Environmental Costs Into Profits*. Englewood Cliffs, NJ: Prentice Hall.

Dieleman, H. and de Hoo, S. (1993) 'Towards a Tailor-made Process of Pollution Prevention and Cleaner Production: Results and Implications of the PRISMA Project', in Fischer, K. and Schot, J. eds. *Environmental Strategies for Industry: International Perspectives on Research Needs and Policy Implications*. Washington, DC: Island Press, pp. 245–75.

Diesendorf, M. (2000) 'Sustainability and Sustainable Development', in Dunphy, D., Benveniste, J., Griffiths, A. and Sutton, P. eds. *Sustainability: The Corporate Challenge for the 21st Century*. Crows Nest, Australia: Allen and Unwin, pp. 19–37.

Dion, M. (1998) 'A Typology of Corporate Environmental Policies', *Environmental Ethics*, 20(2), pp. 151–62.

Dobers, P. and Wolff, R. (2000) 'Competing with 'Soft' Issues—From Managing the Environment to Sustainable Business Strategies', *Business Strategy and the Environment*, 9, pp. 143–50.

Dobilas, G. and MacPherson, A. (1997) 'Environmental Regulation and International Sourcing Policies of Multinational Firms', *Growth and Change*, 28, pp. 7–23.

Dobson, A. (1995) *Green Political Thought*, 2nd Edition. London: Unwin Hyman.

Doty, D.H. and Glick, W.H. (1994) 'Typologies as a Unique Form of Theory Building: Towards Improved Understanding and Modeling', *Academy of Management Review*, 19(2), pp. 230–51.

Dowell, G., Hart, S. and Yeung, B. (2000) 'Do Corporate Global Environmental Standards Create or Destroy Market Value?', *Management Science*, 46(8), pp. 1059–74.

Drake, F., Purvis, M. and Hunt, J. (2004) 'Meeting the Environmental Challenge: A Case of Win-Win or Lose-Win? A Study of the UK Baking and Refrigeration Industries', *Business Strategy and the Environment*, 13, pp. 172–86.

Driscoll, C. and Crombie, A. (2001) 'Stakeholder Legitimacy Management and the Qualified Good Neighbor: The Case of Nova Nada and JDI', *Business and Society*, 40(4), pp. 442–71.

Drobny, N. (1997) 'Environmental Management for the 21st Century', in Tibor, T. and Feldman, I. eds. *Implementing ISO 14000*. Chicago, IL: Irwin, pp. 1–14.

Drumwright, M.E. (1994) 'Socially Responsible Organizational Buying: Environmental Concern as a Non-economic Buying Criterion', *Journal of Marketing*, 58, pp. 1–19.

Dubey, P. (2008) 'Recycling Businesses: Cases of Strategic Choice for Green Marketing in Japan', *IIMB Management Review*, September, pp. 263–78.

Dunphy, D. and Benveniste, J. (2000) 'An Introduction to the Sustainable Corporation', in Dunphy, D., Benveniste, J., Griffiths, A. and Sutton, P. eds. *Sustainability: The Corporate Challenge for the 21st Century*. Crows Nest, NSW, Australia: Allen and Unwin, pp. 3–18.

————Griffiths, A. and Sutton, P. (2000) *Sustainability: The Corporate Challenge for the 21st Century*. Crows Nest, NSW, Australia: Allen and Unwin.

——Griffiths, A. and Benn, S. (2003) *Organizational Change for Corporate Sustainability*. London: Routledge.

Dyllick, T. and Hockerts, K. (2002) 'Beyond the Business Case for Corporate Sustainability', *Business Strategy and the Environment*, 11, pp. 130–41.

Eden, S. (1996) *Environmental Issues and Business: Implications of a Changing Agenda*. Chichester: John Wiley.

Ederington, J. and Minier, J. (2003) 'Is Environmental Policy a Secondary Trade Barrier? An Empirical Analysis', *Canadian Journal of Economics*, 36(1), pp. 137–54.

EEA (1996) *Environmental Taxes: Implementation and Environmental Effectiveness*. Copenhagen: European Environment Agency.

Egri, C.P. and Herman, S. (2000) 'Leadership in the North American Environment Sector: Values, Leadership Styles, and Contexts of Environmental Leaders and Their Organizations', *Academy of Management Journal*, 43(4), pp. 571–604.

Ehrlich, P.R. (1968) *The Population Bomb*. New York: Ballantine.

Ekins, P. (1997) 'The Kuznets Curve for the Environment and Economic Growth: Examining the Evidence', *Environment and Planning A*, 29(5), pp. 805–30.

——(1999) 'European Environmental Taxes and Charges: Recent Experience, Issues and Trends', *Ecological Economics*, 31, pp. 39–62.

El Dief, M. and Font, X. (2010) 'The Determinants of Hotels' Marketing Managers' Green Marketing Behaviour', *Journal of Sustainable Tourism*, 18(2), pp. 157–74.

Elkington, J. (1994) 'Towards the Sustainable Corporation: Win-Win-Win Business Strategies for Sustainable Development', *California Management Review*, 36(2), pp. 90–100.

——(1999) *Cannibals With Forks: The Triple Bottom Line of 21st Century Business*. Oxford: Capstone Publishing.

——Trisoglio, A. (1996) 'Developing Realistic Scenarios for the Environment: Lessons from 'Brent Spar'', *Long Range Planning*, 29(6), pp. 762–9.

Elliott, J.A. (1999) *An Introduction to Sustainable Development*, 2nd Edition. London: Routledge.

Engels, A. (2009) 'The European Emissions Trading Scheme: An Exploratory Study of How Companies Learn to Account for Carbon', *Accounting, Organizations and Society*, 34, pp. 488–98.

——Knoll, L. and Huth, M. (2008) 'Preparing for the 'Real' Market: National Patterns of Institutional Learning and Company Behaviour in the European Emissions Trading Scheme (EU ETS)', *European Environment*, 18, pp. 276–97.

Enmarch-Williams, H., ed. (1996) *Environmental Risks and Rewards in Business*. Chichester: John Wiley.

Environment Agency (2003) *NetRegs Benchmarking Survey: How Green are Small Businesses?* Available at www.environment-agency.gov.uk/

——(2009) *NetRegs SME-nvironment Survey*. Available at www.environment-agency.gov.uk/

Epstein, M.J. (1996) 'You've Got a Great Environmental Strategy—Now What?', *Business Horizons*, September/October, pp. 53–9.

——Roy, M.-J. (2000) 'Strategic Evaluation of Environmental Projects in SMEs', *Environmental Quality Management*, Spring, pp. 37–47.

————(2001) 'Sustainability in Action: Identifying and Measuring the Key Performance Drivers', *Long Range Planning*, 34, pp. 585–604.

Esty, D.C. and Porter, M.E. (1998) 'Industrial Ecology and Competitiveness: Strategic Implications for the Firm', *Journal of Industrial Ecology*, 2(1), pp. 35–43.

——Winston, A.S. (2006) *Green to Gold: How Smart Companies Use Environmental Strategy to Innovate, Create Value and Build Competitive Advantage*. New Haven and London: Yale University Press.

Etzion, D. (2007) 'Research on Organizations and the Natural Environment, 1992–Present: A Review', *Journal of Management*, 33(4), pp. 637–64.

Faulkner, D., Carlisle, Y.M. and Viney, H.P. (2005) 'Changing Corporate Attitudes towards Environmental Policy', *Management of Environmental Quality: An International Journal*, 16(5), pp. 476–89.

Field, B.C. (1994) *Environmental Economics: An Introduction*. Singapore: McGraw-Hill.

Fineman, S. (1997) 'Constructing the Green Manager', *British Journal of Management*, 8, pp. 31–8.

——ed. (2000) *The Business of Greening*. London: Routledge.

Fischer, K. and Schot, J. eds. (1993) *Environmental Strategies for Industry: International Perspectives on Research Needs and Policy Implications*. Washington, DC: Island Press.

Fisk, G. (1973) 'Criteria for a Theory of Responsible Consumption', *Journal of Marketing*, 37(2), pp. 24–31.

Flannery, B.L. and May, D.R. (2000) 'Environmental Ethical Decision Making in the U.S. Metal-Finishing Industry', *Academy of Management Journal*, 43(4), pp. 642–62.

Florida, R. and Davison, D. (2001) 'Gaining from Green Management: Environmental Management Systems Inside and Outside the Factory', *California Management Review*, 43(3), pp. 64–84.

Follows, S.B. and Jobber, D. (2000) 'Environmentally Responsible Purchasing Behaviour: A Test of the Consumer Model', *European Journal of Marketing*, 34(5/6), pp. 723–46.

Frankel, C. (1998) *In Earth's company: Business, Environment and the Challenge of Sustainability*. Gabriola Island, BC: New Society Publishers.

Freeman, R.E. (1984) *Strategic Management: A Stakeholder Perspective*. Englewood Cliffs, NJ: Prentice Hall.

Friedman, M. (1970) 'The Social Responsibility of Business is to Increase its Profits', *The New York Times Magazine*, 13 September (reprinted in Chryssides and Kaler, *op. cit.*).

Friedman, A.L. and Miles, S. (2002) 'SMEs and the Environment: Evaluating Dissemination Routes and Handholding Levels', *Business Strategy and the Environment*, 11, pp. 324–41.

————Adams, C. (2000) 'Small and Medium-sized Enterprises and the Environment: Evaluation of a Specific Initiative Aimed at All Small and Medium-sized Enterprises', *Journal of Small Business and Enterprise Development*, 7(4), pp. 325–42.

Fryxell, G.E. and Szeto, A. (2002) 'The Influence of Motivations for Seeking ISO14001 Certification: An Empirical Study of ISO14001 Certified Facilities in Hong Kong', *Journal of Environmental Management*, 65, pp. 223–38.

Fuchs, D.A. and Mazmanian, D.A. (1998) 'The Greening of Industry: Needs of the Field', *Business Strategy and the Environment*, 7, pp. 193–203.

Gadenne, D.L., Kennedy, J. and McKeiver, C. (2009) 'An Empirical Study of Environmental Awareness and Practices in SMEs', *Journal of Business Ethics*, 84, pp. 45–63.

Gallarotti, G. (1995) 'It Pays to be Green: The Managerial Incentive Structure and Environmentally Bound Strategies', *Columbia Journal of World Business*, 30(4), pp. 38–57.

Garner, R. (2000) *Environmental Politics: Britain, Europe and the Global Environment*, 2nd Edition. Basingstoke: Macmillan.

Garrod, B. and Chadwick, P. (1996) 'Environmental Management and Business Strategy: Towards a New Strategic Paradigm', *Futures*, 28(1), pp. 37–50.

Georg, S. and Fussel, L. (2000) 'Making Sense of Greening and Organizational Change', *Business Strategy and the Environment*, 9, pp. 175–85.

Gerrans, P. and Hutchinson, B. (2000) 'Sustainable Development and Small to Medium-sized Enterprises: A Long Way to Go', in Hillary, R. ed. *Small and Medium-Sized Enterprises and the Environment: Business Imperatives*. Sheffield: Greenleaf, pp. 75–81.

Gerstenfeld, A. and Roberts, H. (2000) 'Size Matters: Barriers and Prospects for Environmental Management in Small and Medium-sized Enterprises', in Hillary, R. ed. *Small and Medium-Sized Enterprises and the Environment: Business Imperatives*. Sheffield: Greenleaf, pp. 106–18.

Ghobadian, A., Viney, H., James, P. and Lui, J. (1995) 'The Influence of Environmental Issues in Strategic Analysis and Choice: A Review of Environmental Strategy among Top UK Corporations', *Management Decision*, 33(10), pp. 46–58.

————Liu, J. and James, P. (1998) 'Extending Linear Approaches to Mapping Corporate Environmental Behaviour', *Business Strategy and the Environment*, 7, pp. 13–23.

Gilley, K.M., Worrell, D.L. and El-Jelly, A. (2000) 'Corporate Environmental Initiatives and Anticipated Firm Performance: The Differential Effects of Process-Driven Versus Product-Driven Greening Initiatives', *Journal of Management*, 26(6), pp. 1199–216.

Ginsberg, J.M. and Bloom, P.N. (2004) 'Choosing the Right Green Marketing Strategy', *MIT Sloan Management Review*, Fall, 79–84.

Gladwin, T.N. (1993) 'The Meaning of Greening: A Plea for Organizational Theory', in Fischer, K. and Schot, J. eds. *Environmental Strategies for Industry: International Perspectives on Research Needs and Policy Implications.* Washington, DC: Island Press, pp. 37–61.

——Kennelly, J.J. (1997) 'Sustainable Development: A New Paradigm for Management Theory and Practice', in Bansal, P. and Howard, E. eds. *Business and the Natural Environment.* Oxford: Butterworth-Heinemann, pp. 13–39.

——Walter, I. (1980) 'How Multinationals Can Manage Social and Political Forces', *Journal of Business Strategy*, 1(1), 54–68.

Golub, J. (1998) 'New Instruments for Environmental Policy in the EU: Introduction and Overview', in Golub, J. ed. *New Instruments for Environmental Policy in the EU.* London: Routledge, pp. 1–29.

González-Benito, J. and González-Benito, O. (2005) 'An Analysis of the Relationship between Environmental Motivations and ISO14001 Certification', *British Journal of Management*, 16(2), pp. 133–48.

Gouldson, A. (2004) 'Cooperation and the Capacity for Control: Regulatory Styles and the Evolving Influence of Environmental Regulations in the UK', *Environment and Planning C: Government and Policy*, 22, pp. 583–603.

——Murphy, J. (1996) 'Ecological Modernisation and the European Union', *Geoforum*, 27(1), pp. 11–21.

————(1997) 'Ecological Modernisation: Economic Restructuring and the Environment', *Political Quarterly*, 68(5), pp. 74–86.

————(1998) *Regulatory Realities: The Implementation and Impact of Industrial Environmental Regulation.* London: Earthscan.

——Roberts, P. (2000) 'Integrating Environment and Economy: The Evolution of Theory, Policy and Practice', in Gouldson, A. and Roberts, P. eds. *Integrating Environment and Economy: Strategies for Local and Regional Government.* London: Routledge, pp. 3–21.

Graedal, T. (1994) 'Industrial Ecology: Definition and Implementation', in Socolow, R., Andrews, C., Berkhout, F. and Thomas, V. eds. *Industrial Ecology and Global Change.* Cambridge: Cambridge University Press, pp. 23–41.

Graff, R.G., Reiskin, E.D., White, A.L. and Bidwell, K. (1998) *Snapshots of Environmental Cost Accounting. A Report to USEPA Environmental Accounting Project.* Boston, MA: Tellus Institute.

Grant, J. (2007) *The Green Marketing Manifesto.* Chichester: John Wiley & Sons.

Gray, R. and Bebbington, J. (2000) 'Environmental Accounting, Managerialism and Sustainability: Is the Planet Safe in the Hands of Business and Accounting?', *Advances in Environmental Accounting and Management*, 1, pp. 1–44.

————(2001) *Accounting for the Environment*, 2nd Edition. London: Sage.

——Walters, D., Bebbington, J. and Thompson, I. (1995) 'The Greening of Enterprise: An Exploration of the (Non)Role of Environmental Accounting and Environmental Accountants in Organizational Change', *Critical Perspectives on Accounting*, 6, pp. 211–39.

Green, K., Morton, B. and New, S. (1996) 'Purchasing and Environmental Management: Interactions, Policies and Opportunities', *Business Strategy and the Environment*, 5, pp. 188–97.

Green, K., Morton, B. and New, S. (1998) 'Green Purchasing and Supply Policies: Do they Improve Companies' Environmental Performance?', *Supply Chain Management*, 3(2), pp. 89–95.

————(2000) 'Greening Organizations: Purchasing, Consumption and Innovation', *Organization and Environment*, 13(2), pp. 206–25.

Greenan, K., Humphreys, P. and McIvor, R. (1997) 'The Green Initiative: Improving Quality and Competitiveness for European SMEs, *European Business Review*, 97(5), pp. 208–14.

Greenham, T. (2010) 'Green Accounting: A Conceptual Framework', *International Journal of Green Economics*, 4(4), pp. 333–45.

Griffiths, A. (2000) 'New Organisational Architectures: Creating and Retrofitting for Sustainability', in Dunphy, D., Benveniste, J., Griffiths, A. and Sutton, P. eds. *Sustainability: The Corporate Challenge for the 21st Century*. Crows Nest, Australia: Allen and Unwin, pp. 219–35.

Grossman, G.M. and Krueger, A.B. (1995) 'Economic Growth and the Environment', *Quarterly Journal of Economics*, 112, pp. 353–78.

Groundwork (1998) *Small Firms and the Environment: A Groundwork Report*. Birmingham: Groundwork Foundation.

Guimaraes, T. and Liska, K. (1995) 'Exploring the Business Benefits of Environmental Stewardship', *Business Strategy and the Environment*, 4, pp. 9–22.

Gunningham, N. and Grabosky, P. (1998) *Smart Regulation: Designing Environmental Policy*. Oxford: Clarendon Press.

——Sinclair, D. (2002) *Leaders and Laggards: Next-Generation Environmental Regulation*. Sheffield: Greenleaf Publishing.

Gurau, C. and Ranchhod, A. (2005) 'International Green Marketing: A Comparative Study of British and Romanian Firms', *International Marketing Review*, 22(5), pp. 547–61.

Gurtoo, A. and Anthony, S.J. (2007) 'Environmental Regulations: Indirect and Unintended Consequences on Economy and Business', *Management of Environmental Quality: An International Journal*, 18(6), pp. 626–42.

Hahn, T. and Scheermesser, M. (2006) 'Approaches to Corporate Sustainability among German Companies', *Corporate Social Responsibility and Environmental Management*, 13, pp. 150–65.

Haigh, M. and Jones, M.T. (2006) 'The Drivers of Corporate Social Responsibility: A Critical Review', *The Business Review, Cambridge*, 5(2), pp. 245–51.

Halila, F. (2007) 'Networks as a Means of Supporting the Adoption of Organizational Innovations in SMEs: The Case of Environmental Management Systems (EMSs) Based on ISO 14001', *Corporate Social Responsibility and Environmental Management*, 14, pp. 167–81.

Halme, M. and Niskanen, J. (2001) 'Does Corporate Environmental Protection Increase or Decrease Shareholder Value? The Case of Environmental Investments', *Business Strategy and the Environment*, 10, pp. 200–14.

Hamilton, J.T. (1995) 'Pollution as News: Media and Stock Market Reactions to the Toxics Release Inventory Data', *Journal of Environmental Economics and Management*, 28, pp. 98–113.

Hamner, B. (2006) 'Effects of Green Purchasing Strategies on Supplier Behaviour', in Sarkis, J. ed. *Greening the Supply Chain*. London: Springer, pp. 25–37.

Handfield, R.B. and Melnyk, S.A. (1996) 'GreenSpeak', *Purchasing Today*, July, pp. 32–36.

Handfield, R., Sroufe, R. and Walton, S. (2005) 'Integrating Environmental Management and Supply Chain Strategies', *Business Strategy and the Environment*, 14, pp. 1–19.

——Walton, S.V., Sroufe, R. and Melnyk, S.A. (2002) 'Applying Environmental Criteria to Supplier Assessment: A Study in the Application of the Analytical Hierarchy Process', *European Journal of Operational Research*, 141(1), pp. 70–87.

Harris, L.C. and Crane, A. (2002) 'The Greening of Organizational Culture: Management Views on the Depth, Degree and Diffusion of Change', *Journal of Organizational Change Management*, 15(3), pp. 214–34.

Hart, S.L. (1995) 'A Natural Resource-based View of the Firm', *Academy of Management Review*, 20, pp. 986–1014.

——(1997) 'Beyond Greening: Strategies for a Sustainable World', *Harvard Business Review*, January–February, pp. 66–76.

——(1999) 'Corporations as Agents of Global Sustainability', in Cooperrider, D.L. and Dutton, J.E. eds. *Organizational Dimensions of Global Change*. Thousand Oaks, CA: Sage, pp. 346–61.

——Ahuja, G. (1996) 'Does it Pay to be Green? An Empirical Examination of the Relationship between Emission Reduction and Firm Performance', *Business Strategy and the Environment*, 5, pp. 30–7.

——Milstein, M.B. (1999) 'Global Sustainability and the Creative Destruction of Industries', *Sloan Management Review*, 41(1), pp. 22–33.

————(2003) 'Creating Sustainable Value', *Academy of Management Executive*, 17(2), pp. 56–67.

Hartman, C.L., Hofman, P.S. and Stafford, E.R. (1999) 'Partnerships: A Path to Sustainability', *Business Strategy and the Environment*, 8(5), pp. 255–66.

Hass, J.L. (1996) 'Environmental ('Green') Management Typologies: An Evaluation, Operationalisation and Empirical Development', *Business Strategy and the Environment*, 5, pp. 59–68.

Hawken, P. (1996) 'A Teasing Irony', in Welford, R. and Starkey, R. eds. *Business and the Environment*. London: Earthscan, pp. 5–16.

Henriques, I. and Sadorsky, P. (1996) 'The Determinants of an Environmentally Responsive Firm: An Empirical Approach', *Journal of Environmental Economics and Management*, 30, pp. 381–95.

————(1999) 'The Relationship between Environmental Commitment and Managerial Perceptions of Stakeholder Importance', *Academy of Management Journal*, 42(1), pp. 87–99.

Hervani, A.A., Helms, M.M. and Sarkis, J. (2005) 'Performance Measurement for Green Supply Chain Management', *Benchmarking: An International Journal*, 12(4), pp. 330–53.

Hildebrand, P.M. (1992) 'The European Community's Environmental Policy, 1957 to '1992': From Incidental Measures to an International Regime?', *Environmental Politics*, 1(4), pp. 15–44.

Hillary, R. (1995) *Small Firms and the Environment: A Groundwork Status Report*. Birmingham: Groundwork Foundation.

——ed. (2000) *Small and Medium-Sized Enterprises and the Environment: Business Imperatives*. Sheffield: Greenleaf.

——(2004) 'Environmental Management Systems and the Smaller Enterprise', *Journal of Cleaner Production*, 12, pp. 561–9.

Hilliard, R. (2004) 'Conflicting Views: Neo-Classical, Porterian and Evolutionary Approaches to the Analysis of the Environmental Regulation of Industrial Activity', *Journal of Economic Issues*, xxxviii(2), pp. 509–17.

Hitchens, D.M.W.N., Birnie, J.E., McGowan, A., Triebswetter, U. and Cottica, A. (1998) 'Investigating the Relationship between Company Competitiveness and Environmental Regulation in European Food Processing: Results of a Matched Firm Comparison', *Environment and Planning A*, 30, pp. 1585–602.

Hitchens, D., Thankappan, S., Trainor, M., Clausen, J. and De Marchi, B. (2005) 'Environmental Performance, Competitiveness and Management of Small Businesses in Europe', *Tijdschrift voor Economische en Sociale Geografie*, 96(5), pp. 541–57.

Hoevenagel, R. and Wolters, T. (2000) 'Small and Medium-Sized Enterprises, Environmental Policies and the Supporting Role of Intermediate Organisations in the Netherlands', *Greener Management International*, 30, pp. 61–9.

Hoffman, A.J. (1993) 'The Importance of Fit between Individual Values and Organizational Culture in the Greening of Industry', *Business Strategy and the Environment*, 2, pp. 10–18.

——(1999) 'Institutional Evolution and Change: Environmentalism and the U.S. Chemical Industry', *Academy of Management Journal*, 42(4), pp. 351–71.

——(2000) *Competitive Environmental Strategy: A Guide to the Changing Business Landscape*. Washington, DC: Island Press.

——(2001a) *From Heresy to Dogma: An Institutional History of Corporate Environmentalism*. Stanford: Stanford University Press.

——(2001b) 'Linking Organizational and Field Level Analyses: The Diffusion of Corporate Environmental Practice', *Organization and Environment*, 14(2), pp. 133–56.

——Bazerman, M.H. (2005) 'Changing Practice on Sustainability: Understanding and Overcoming the Organizational and Psychological Barriers to Action', *Organizations and the Sustainability Mosaic: Crafting Long-Term Ecological and Societal Solutions*, Volume 3. Cheltenham: Edward Elgar.

——Riley, H.C., Troast Jr, J.G. and Bazerman, M. (2002) 'Cognitive and Institutional Barriers to New Forms of Cooperation on Environmental Protection: Insights from Project XL and Habitat Conservation Plans', *The American Behavioral Scientist*, 45(5), pp. 820–45.

——Ventresca, M.J. eds. (2002) *Organizations, Policy and the Natural Environment*. Stanford, CA: Stanford University Press.

Holland, L. and Gibbon, J. (1997) 'SMEs in the Metal Manufacturing, Construction and Contracting Service Sectors: Environmental Awareness and Actions', *Eco-Management and Auditing*, 4, pp. 7–14.

Holliday Jr, C.O., Schmidheiny, S. and Watts, P. (2002) *Walking the Talk: The Business Case for Sustainable Development*. Sheffield: Greenleaf.

Holt, D., Anthony, S. and Viney, H. (2000) 'Supporting Environmental Improvements in Small and Medium-Sized Enterprises in the UK', *Greener Management International*, 30, pp. 29–49.

Huang, C.-L. and Kung, F.-H. (2010) 'Drivers of Environmental Disclosure and Stakeholder Expectation: Evidence from Taiwan', *Journal of Business Ethics*, 96, pp. 435–51.

Hunt, C. and Auster, E. (1990) 'Proactive Environmental Management: Avoiding the Toxic Trap', *Sloan Management Review*, Winter, pp. 7–18.

Husted, B.W. and De Jesus Salazar, J. (2006) 'Taking Friedman Seriously: Maximizing Profits and Social Performance', *Journal of Management Studies*, 43(1), pp. 75–91.

Hutchinson, C. (1996) 'Integrating Environment Policy with Business Strategy', *Long Range Planning*, 29(1), pp. 11–23.

Hutchison, J. (1998) 'Integrating Environmental Criteria into Purchasing Decisions: Value Added?', in Russel, T. ed. *Greener Purchasing: Opportunities and Innovations*. Sheffield: Greenleaf Publishing, pp. 164–78.

International Chamber of Commerce (1992) *From Ideas to Action*. Paris: ICC.

Isaak, R. (2002) 'The Making of the Ecopreneur', *Greener Management International*, 38, pp. 81–91.

Jacobs, M. (1996) *The Politics of the Real World: Meeting the New Century*. London: Earthscan.

Jaffe, A.B., Peterson, S.R., Portney, P.R. and Stavins, R.N. (1995) 'Environmental Regulation and the Competitiveness of U.S. Manufacturing: What Does the Evidence Tell Us?', *Journal of Economic Literature*, XXXIII, pp. 132–63.

James, P., Ghobadian, A., Viney, H. and Liu, J. (1999) 'Addressing the Divergence between Environmental Strategy Formulation and Implementation', *Management Decision*, 37(4), pp. 338–47.

Jänicke, M. and Jörgens, H. (2000) 'Strategic Environmental Planning and Uncertainty: A Cross-National Comparison of Green Plans in Industrialized Countries', *Policy Studies Journal*, 28(3), pp. 612–32.

Jennings, P.D. and Zandbergen, P.A. (1995) 'Ecologically Sustainable Organizations: An Institutional Approach', *Academy of Management Review*, 20, pp. 1015–52.

Jeppesen, T., List, J.A. and Folmer, H. (2002) 'Environmental Regulations and New Plant Location Decisions: Evidence from a Meta-Analysis', *Journal of Regional Science*, 42(1), pp. 19–49.

Johansson, L. (2000) 'Small Business, Sustainability and Trade', in Hillary, R. ed. *Small and Medium-Sized Enterprises and the Environment: Business Imperatives*. Sheffield: Greenleaf, pp. 82–93.

Johnson, G., Scholes, K. And Whittington, R. (2005) *Exploring Corporate Strategy: Text and Cases*, 7th Edition. Harlow: FT/Prentice Hall.

Johri, L.M. and Sahasakmontri, K. (1998) 'Green Marketing of Cosmetics and Toiletries in Thailand', *Journal of Consumer Marketing*, 15(3), pp. 265–81.

Jones, M.T. (1999) 'The Institutional Determinants of Social Responsibility', *Journal of Business Ethics*, 20, pp. 163–79.

Jordan, A., Wurzel, R., Zito, A.R. and Brückner, L. (2003a) 'European Governance and the Transfer of 'New' Environmental Policy Instruments (NEPIs) in the European Union', *Public Administration*, 81(3), pp. 555–74.

——Wurzel, R.K.W. and Zito, A.R. (2003b) 'New Instruments of Environmental Governance: Patterns and Pathways of Change, *Environmental Politics*, 12(1), pp. 1–24.

Jørgensen, T.H. (2000) 'Environmental Management Systems and Organizational Change', *Eco-Management and Auditing*, 7, pp. 60–6.

Judge, W.Q. and Douglas, T.J. (1998) 'Performance Implications of Incorporating Natural Environmental Issues into the Strategic Planning Process: An Empirical Assessment', *Journal of Management Studies*, 35 (2), pp. 241–62.

Kalafatis, S.P., Pollard, M., East, R. and Tsogas, M.H. (1999) 'Green Marketing and Ajzen's Theory of Planned Behaviour: A Cross-market Examination', *Journal of Consumer Marketing*, 16(5), pp. 441–60.

Karagozoglu, N. and Lindell, M. (2000) 'Environmental Management: Testing the Win-Win Model', *Journal of Environmental Planning and Management*, 43(6), pp. 817–29.

Kasim, A. (2007) 'Corporate Environmentalism in the Hotel Sector: Evidence of Drivers and Barriers in Penang, Malaysia', *Journal of Sustainable Tourism*, 15(6), pp. 680–99.

Kassaye, W.W. (2001) 'Green Dilemma', *Marketing Intelligence and Planning*, 19, pp. 444–55.

Kassinis, G. and Vafeas, N. (2002) 'Corporate Boards and Outside Stakeholders as Determinants of Environmental Litigation', *Strategic Management Journal*, 23(5), pp. 399–415.

Kassinis, G.I. and Soteriou, A.C. (2005) 'Greening Service Organizations: Environmental Management Practices and Performance', in Sharma, S. and Aragón-Correa, J.A. eds. *Corporate Environmental Strategy and Competitive Advantage*. Cheltenham: Edward Elgar, pp. 115–37.

Kellow, A. and Zito, A.R. (2002) 'Steering through Complexity: EU Environmental Regulation in the International Context', *Political Studies*, 50, pp. 43–60.

Khanna, M. and Anton, W.R.Q. (2002a) 'Corporate Environmental Management: Regulatory and Market-Based Incentives', *Land Economics*, 78(4), pp. 539–58.

————(2002b) 'What is Driving Corporate Environmentalism: Opportunity or Threat?', *Corporate Environmental Strategy*, 9(4), pp. 409–17.

Kilbourne, W.E. (1998) 'Green Marketing: A Theoretical Perspective', *Journal of Marketing Management*, 14, pp. 641–55.

King, A. (2000) 'Organizational Response to Environmental Regulation: Punctuated Change or Auto-genesis', *Business Strategy and the Environment*, 9, pp. 224–38.

King, A.A. and Lenox, M.J. (2000) 'Industry Self-regulation without Sanctions: The Chemical Industry's Responsible Care Programme', *Academy of Management Journal*, 43(4), pp. 698–716.

————(2001) 'Does It *Really* Pay to Be Green?', *Journal of Industrial Ecology*, 5(1), pp. 105–16.

Kinnear, T.C., Taylor, J.E. and Ahmed, S.A. (1974) 'Ecologically Concerned Consumers: Who Are They?', *Journal of Marketing*, 38(2), pp. 20–4.

Kirchgeorg, M. (1993) 'Oekologieorientiertes Unternehmensverhalten, Gabler Verlag, Wiesbaden 1990', Nitsche, C. trans. *Banks and the Environment—A European Comparison, First Year Report*. Cambridge: The Judge Institute of Management Studies, University of Cambridge, pp. 16–20.

Klassen, R.D. (2000) 'Exploring the Linkage between Investment in Manufacturing and Environmental Technologies', *International Journal of Operations and Production Management*, 20(2), pp. 127–47.

——McLaughlin, C.P. (1996) 'The Impact of Environmental Management on Firm Performance', *Management Science*, 42(8), pp. 1199–214.

——Whybark, D.C. (1999) 'The Impact of Environmental Technologies on Manufacturing Performance', *Academy of Management Journal*, 42(6), pp. 599–615.

Kolk, A. (2000) *Economics of Environmental Management*. Harlow: Financial Times/Prentice Hall.

——Mauser, A. (2002) 'The Evolution of Environmental Management. From Stage Models to Performance Evaluation', *Business Strategy and the Environment*, 11, pp. 14–31.

——Pinkse, J. (2005) 'Business Response to Climate Change: Identifying Emergent Strategies', *California Management Review*, 47(3), pp. 6–20.

Kollman, K. and Prakash, A. (2001) 'Green by Choice? Cross-National Variations in Firms' Responses to EMS-Based Environmental Regimes', *World Politics*, 53, pp. 399–430.

KPMG (1997) *The Environmental Challenge and Small and Medium Sized Enterprises in Europe*. The Hague: KPMG Consulting.

Kruger, J.K. and Pizer, W.A. (2004) 'Greenhouse Gas Trading in Europe: The Grand New Policy Experiment', *Environment*, 46, pp. 8–23.

Krut, R. and Gleckman, H. (1998) *ISO14001: A Missed Opportunity for Sustainable Global Industrial Development*. London: Earthscan.

Kuhn, M. (2005) *The Greening of Markets: Product Competition, Pollution and Policy Making in a Duopoly*. Cheltenham: Edward Elgar.

LaFrance, J. and Lehmann, M. (2005) 'Corporate Awakening-Why (Some) Corporations Embrace Public-Private Partnerships', *Business Strategy and the Environment*, 14, pp. 216–29.

Lamming, R., Faruk, A. and Cousins, P. (1999) 'Environmental Soundness: A Pragmatic Alternative to Expectations of Sustainable Development in Business Strategy', *Business Strategy and the Environment*, 8, pp. 177–88.

——Hampson, J. (1996) 'The Environment as a Supply Chain Management Issue', *British Journal of Management*, 7(Special Issue), S45–S62.

Lampe, M. and Gazda, G.M. (1995) 'Green Marketing in Europe and the United States: An Evolving Business and Society Interface', *International Business Review*, 4(3), pp. 295–312.

Landis-Gabel, H. and Sinclair-Désgagné, B. (1994) 'From Market Failure to Organisational Failure', *Business Strategy and the Environment*, 3(2), pp. 50–8.

Langerak, F., Peelen, E. and van der Veen, M. (1998) 'Exploratory Results on the Antecedents and Consequences of Green Marketing', *Journal of the Market Research Society*, 40(4), pp. 323–35.

Lankoski, L. (2006) 'Environmental and Economic Performance: The Basic Links', in Schaltegger, S. and Wagner, M. eds. *Managing the Business Case for Sustainability*. Sheffield: Greenleaf Publishing, pp. 32–46.

Lanoie, P. and Tanguay, G.A. (2000) 'Factors Leading to Green Profitability', *Greener Management International*, 31, pp. 39–51.

Larringa-Gonzalez, C. and Bebbington, J. (2001) 'Accounting Change or Institutional Appropriation?—A Case Study of the Implementation of Environmental Accounting', *Critical Perspectives on Accounting*, 12, pp. 269–92.

Lash, J. and Wellington, F. (2007) 'Competitive Advantage on a Warming Planet', *Harvard Business Review*, 85(3), pp. 94–102.

Laszlo, C. (2008) *Sustainable Value: How the World's Leading Companies are Doing Well by Doing Good*. Sheffield: Greenleaf.

——Zhexembayeva, N. (2011) *Embedded Sustainability: The Next Big Competitive Advantage*. Sheffield: Greenleaf Publishing.

Lawrence, A.T. and Morell, D. (1995) 'Leading-edge Environmental Management: Motivation, Opportunity, Resources and Processes', in Collins, D. and Starik, M. eds. *Research in Corporate Social Performance and Policy*. Greenwich, CT: JAI Press, pp. 99–126.

Lawrence, S.R., Collins, E., Pavlovich, K. and Arunachalam, M. (2006) 'Sustainability Practices of SMEs the Case of NZ', *Business Strategy and the Environment*, 15, pp. 242–57.

Ledgerwood, G. and Broadhurst, A.I. (2000) *Environment, Ethics and the Corporation*. Basingstoke: Macmillan.

Lee, K. (2008) 'Opportunities for Green Marketing: Young Consumers', *Marketing Intelligence and Planning*, 26(6), pp. 573–86.

Lee, S.-Y. (2008) 'Drivers for the Participation of Small and Medium-sized Suppliers in Green Supply Initiatives', *Supply Chain Management: An International Journal*, 13(3), pp. 185–98.

——Rhee, S-K. (2007) 'The Change in Corporate Environmental Strategies: A Longitudinal Empirical Study', *Management Decision*, 45(2), pp. 196–216.

Lefebvre, E., Lefebvre, L.A. and Talbot, S. (2003) 'Determinants and Impacts of Environmental Performance in SMEs', *R&D Management*, 33(3), pp. 263–83.

Lepoutre, J. and Heene, A. (2006) 'Investigating the Impact of Firm Size on Small Business Social Responsibility: A Critical Review', *Journal of Business Ethics*, 67, pp. 257–73.

Levinson, A. (1996) 'Environmental Regulations and Manufacturers' Location Choices: Evidence from the Census of Manufactures', *Journal of Public Economics*, 62(1/2), pp. 5–29.

Levy, D.L. (1995) 'The Environmental Practices and Performances of Transnational Corporations', *Transnational Corporations*, 4(1), pp. 44–67.

Levy, D.L. and Kolk, A. (2002) 'Strategic Responses to Global Climate Change: Conflicting Pressures on Multinationals in the Oil Industry', *Business and Politics*, 4(3), pp. 275–300.

Liedtka, J. (1991) 'Organizational Value Contention and Managerial Mindsets', *Journal of Business Ethics*, 10, pp. 543–57.

Lindell, M. and Karagozoglu, N. (2001) 'Corporate Environmental Behaviour—A Comparison Between Nordic and US Firms', *Business Strategy and the Environment*, 10, pp. 38–52.

Litvine, D. and Wüstenhagen, R. (2011) 'Helping "Light Green" Consumers Walk the Talk: Results of a Behavioural Intervention Survey in the Swiss Electricity Market', *Ecological Economics*, 70, pp. 462–74.

Lloyds TSB/Small Business Research Trust (1999) 'Small Firms & the Environment', *Quarterly Small Business Management Report*, 6(4). Milton Keynes: Lloyds/SBRT.

Lober, D.J. (1998) 'Pollution Prevention as Corporate Entrepreneurship', *Journal of Organizational Change Management*, 11(1), pp. 26–37.

Löfstedt, R.E. and Vogel, D. (2001) 'The Changing Character of Regulation: A Comparison of Europe and the United States', *Risk Analysis*, 21(3), pp. 399–416.

Lovelock, J. (1979) *Gaia*. Oxford: Oxford University Press.

Lowe, E. (1990) 'Industrial Ecology—An Organizing Framework for Environmental Management', *Environmental Quality Management*, 3(I), pp. 73–85.

Lowe, P. and Ward, S. eds. (1998) *British Environmental Policy and Europe: Politics and Policy in Transition*. London: Routledge.

Lynch, R. (2006) *Corporate Strategy*, 4th Edition. Harlow: FT/Prentice Hall.

Lynes, J.K. and Andrachuk, M. (2008) 'Motivations for Corporate Social and Environmental Responsibility: A Case Study of Scandinavian Airlines', *Journal of International Management*, 14, pp. 377–90.

——Dredge, D. (2006) 'Going Green: Motivations for Environmental Commitment in the Airline Industry. A Case Study of Scandinavian Airlines', *Journal of Sustainable Tourism*, 14(2), pp. 116–38.

Lyon, T.P. and Maxwell, J.W. (1999) 'Corporate Environmental Strategies as Tools to Influence Regulation', *Business Strategy and the Environment*, 8, pp. 189–96.

————(2003) 'Mandatory and Voluntary Approaches to Mitigating Climate Change', Available online at http://webuser.bus.umich.edu

————(2007) 'Environmental Public Voluntary Programs Reconsidered', *The Policy Studies Journal*, 35 (4), pp. 723–50.

Madsen, P.M. (2009) 'Does Corporate Investment Drive a "Race to the Bottom" in Environmental Protection? A Re-examination of the Effect of Environmental Regulation on Investment', *Academy of Management Journal*, 52(6), pp. 1297–318.

Maignan, I., Ferrell, O.C. and Ferrell, L. (2005) 'A Stakeholder Model for Implementing Social Responsibility in Marketing', *European Journal of Marketing*, 39(9/10), pp. 956–77.

Majumdar, S.K. (1997) 'Incentive Regulation and Productive Efficiency in the U.S. Telecommunications Industry', *The Journal of Business*, 70(4), pp. 547–76.

——Marcus, A.A. (2001) 'Rules versus Discretion: The Productivity Consequences of Flexible Regulation', *Academy of Management Journal*, 44(1), pp. 170–9.

Makower, J. (1993) *The E-Factor: The Bottom-Line Approach to Environmentally Responsible Business*. New York: Times Books.

Marcus, A. and Geffen, D. (1998) 'The Dialectics of Competency Acquisition: Pollution Prevention in Electric Generation', *Strategic Management Journal*, 19(8), pp. 1145–68.

Marcus, A.A. (2005) 'Research in Strategic Environmental Management', in Sharma, S. and Aragón-Correa, J.A. eds. *Corporate Environmental Strategy and Competitive Advantage*. Cheltenham: Edward Elgar, pp. 27–48.

Marshall Report (1998) *Economic Instruments and the Business Use of Energy*. London: Stationery Office.

Marshall, R.S. and Brown, D. (2003) 'Corporate Environmental Reporting: What's in a Metric?', *Business Strategy and the Environment*, 12, pp. 87–106.

——Cordano, M. and Silverman, M. (2005) 'Exploring Individual and Institutional Drivers of Proactive Environmentalism in the US Wine Industry', *Business Strategy and the Environment*, 14, pp. 92–109.

Martín-Tapia, I., Aragón-Correa, J.A. and Rueda-Manzanares, A. (2010) 'Environmental Strategy and Exports in Medium, Small and Micro-enterprises', *Journal of World Business*, 45(3), pp. 266–75.

Masurel, E. (2007) 'Why SMEs Invest in Environmental Measures: Sustainability Evidence from Small and Medium-Sized Printing Firms', *Business Strategy and the Environment*, 16, pp. 190–201.

Matthews, D.H. (2003) 'Environmental Management Systems for Internal Corporate Environmental Benchmarking', *Benchmarking: An International Journal*, 10(2), pp. 95–106.

Maxwell, J., Rothenburg, S., Briscoe, F. and Marcus, A. (1997) 'Green Schemes: Corporate Environmental Strategies and their Implementation', *California Management Review*, 39(3), pp. 118–34.

Maxwell, J.W. (1996) 'What To Do When Win-Win Won't Work: Environmental Strategies for Costly Regulation', *Business Horizons*, 39(5), September/October, pp. 60–3.

McCormick, J. (1995) *The Global Environmental Movement*, 2nd Edition. Chichester: John Wiley.

McCoy, M. and McCully, P. (1993) *The Road from Rio: An NGO Action Guide to Environment and Development*. Amsterdam: International Books/WISE.

McDaniel, S.W. and Rylander, D.H. (1993) 'Strategic Green Marketing', *Journal of Consumer Marketing*, 10(3), pp. 4–10.

McDonagh, P. and Prothero, A. eds. (1997) *Greener Management: A Reader*. London: Dryden Press.

McKeiver, C. and Gadenne, D. (2005) 'Environmental Management Systems in Small and Medium Businesses', *International Small Business Journal*, 23(5), pp. 513–37.

McWilliams, A. and Siegel, D. (2001) 'Corporate Social Responsibility: A Theory of the Firm Perspective', *Academy of Management Review*, 26, pp. 117–27.

————Wright, P.M. (2006) 'Corporate Social Responsibility: Strategic Implications', *Journal of Management Studies*, 43(1), pp. 1–17.

Meadows, D.H., Meadows, D.L., Randers, J. and Behrens III, W. (1972) *The Limits to Growth: A Report for the Club of Rome's Project on the Predicament of Mankind*. New York: Universe.

Melnyk, S.A., Sroufe, R.P. and Calantone, R. (2003) 'Assessing the Impact of Environmental Management Systems on Corporate and Environmental Performance', *Journal of Operations Management*, 21, pp. 329–51.

Mendleson, N. and Polonsky, M.J. (1995) 'Using Strategic Alliances to Develop Credible Green Marketing', *Journal of Consumer Marketing*, 12(2), pp. 4–18.

Menon, A. and Menon, A. (1997) 'Enviropreneurial Market-Strategy: Emergence of Corporate Environmentalism as a Market Strategy', *Journal of Marketing*, 61, pp. 51–67.

Meyer, A. (2001) 'What's in it for the Customers? Successfully Marketing Green Clothes', *Business Strategy and the Environment*, 10, pp. 317–30.

Miles, M.P. and Covin, J.G. (2000) 'Environmental Marketing: A Source of Reputational, Competitive and Financial Advantage', *Journal of Business Ethics*, 23, pp. 299–311.

Miles, M.P., Munilla, L.S. and McClurg, T. (1999) 'The Impact of ISO14000 Environmental Management Standards on Small and Medium Sized Enterprises', *Journal of Quality Management*, 4(1), pp. 111–22.

Miles, R.E. and Snow, E.E. (1978) *Organizational Strategy, Structure, and Process*. New York: McGraw Hill.

Min, H. and Galle, W.P. (1997) 'Green Purchasing Strategies: Trends and Implications', *International Journal of Purchasing and Materials Management*, 33(3), pp. 10–17.

————(2001) 'Green Purchasing Practices of US Firms', *International Journal of Operations and Production Management*, 21(9), pp. 1222–38.

Mintzberg, H., Ahlstrand, B. and Lampel, J. (1998) *Strategy Safari: A Guided Tour through the Wilds of Strategic Management*. New York: The Free Press.

Mir, D.F. (2008) 'Environmental Behaviour in Chicago Automotive Repair Micro-Enterprises (MEPs)', *Business Strategy and the Environment*, 17, pp. 194–207.

——Feitelson, E. (2007) 'Factors Affecting Environmental Behaviour in Micro-enterprises: Laundry and Motor Vehicle Repair Firms in Jerusalem', *International Small Business Journal*, 25(4), pp. 383–415.

——Sanchez, A.E. (2009) 'Impact of Gentrification on Environmental Pressure in Service Micro-enterprises', *Business Strategy and the Environment*, 18(7), pp. 417–31.

Mol, A. and Sonnenfeld, D. (2000) *Ecological Modernisation Around the World: Perspectives and Critical Debates*. London: Cass.

Mol, A.P.J. (2003) 'Joint Environmental Policymaking in Europe: Between Deregulation and Political Modernization', *Society and Natural Resources*, 16, pp. 335–48.

Monaghan, M. (1997) 'Management Systems: Environment and Economic Management', in Bansal, P. and Howard, E. eds. *Business and the Natural Environment*. Oxford: Butterworth Heinemann, pp. 239–65.

Montabon, F., Melnyk, S.A., Sroufe, R.P. and Calantone, R.J. (2000) 'ISO 14000: Assessing Its Perceived Impact on Corporate Performance', *The Journal of Supply Chain Management*, 36(2), pp. 4–16.

Morrow, D. and Rondinelli, D. (2002) 'Adopting Corporate Environmental Management Systems: Motivations and Results of ISO14001 and EMAS Certification', *European Management Journal*, 20(2), pp. 159–71.

Murphy, D.F. and Bendell, J. (1997) *In the Company of Partners: Business, Environmental Groups and Sustainable Development Post-Rio*. Bristol: Policy Press.

Naess, A. (1973) 'The Shallow and the Deep, Long Range Ecology Movement: A Summary', *Inquiry*, 16, pp. 95–100.

Naffziger, D.W., Ahmed, N.U. and Montagno, R.V. (2003) 'Perceptions of Environmental Consciousness in U.S. Small Businesses: An Empirical Study', *S.A.M. Advanced Management Journal*, 68(2), pp. 23–31.

Nair, S.R. and Menon, C.G. (2008) 'An Environmental Marketing System—A Proposed Model Based on Indian Experience', *Business Strategy and the Environment*, 17, pp. 467–79.

Narasimhan, R. and Carter, J.R. (1998) *Environmental Supply Chain Management*. Tempe, AZ: The Center for Advanced Purchasing Studies, Arizona State University.

Nehrt, C. (1996) 'Timing and Intensity Effects of Environmental Investments', *Strategic Management Journal*, 17, pp. 535–47.

——(1998) 'Maintainability of First Mover Advantages When Environmental Regulations Differ between Countries', *Academy of Management Review*, 23(1), pp. 77–97.

New, S., Green, K. and Morton, B. (2000) 'Buying the Environment: The Multiple Meanings of Green Supply', in Fineman, S. ed. *The Business of Greening*. London: Routledge, pp. 35–53.

Newton, T. and Harte, G. (1997) 'Green Business: Technicist Kitsch?', *Journal of Management Studies*, 34(1), January, pp. 75–98.

Newton, T.J. (2002) 'Creating the New Ecological Order? Elias and Actor-Network Theory', *Academy of Management Review*, 27(4), pp. 523–40.

Ng, C.B. (2005) 'Deriving Competitive Advantage from Environmental Regulations', in Proceedings of Business Strategy and the Environment Conference, University of Leeds, UK, 5–6 September.

Noci, G. and Verganti, R. (1999) 'Managing 'Green' Product Innovation in Small Firms', *R & D Management*, 29, pp. 3–15.

OECD (1994) *Managing the Environment: The Role of Economic Instruments*. Paris: Organisation for Economic Co-operation and Development.

——(2001) *Environmental Taxes and Competitiveness: An Overview of Issues, Policy Options and Research Needs*. Paris: Organisation for Economic Co-operation and Development.

Okereke, C. (2007) 'An Exploration of Motivations, Drivers and Barriers to Carbon Management: The UK FTSE 100', *European Management Journal*, 25(6), pp. 475–86.

O'Laoire, D. and Welford, R. (1996) 'The EMS in the SME', in Welford, R. ed. *Corporate Environmental Management: Systems and Strategies*. London: Earthscan, pp. 201–11.

Oliver, C. (1991) 'Strategic Responses to Institutional Processes', *Academy of Management Review*, 16(1), pp. 145–79.

——(1997) 'Sustainable Competitive Advantage: Combining Institutional and Resource-Based Views', *Strategic Management Journal*, 18(9), pp. 697–713.

O'Riordan, T. (1981) *Environmentalism*, 2nd Edition. London: Pion Press.

——(1985) 'What does Sustainability Really Mean? Theory and Development of Concepts of Sustainability', in Proceedings of the Sustainable Development in an Industrial Economy Conference, Queen's College, Cambridge, 23–5 June.

Orsato, R.J. (2006) 'Competitive Environmental Strategies: When Does It Pay To Be Green?', *California Management Review*, 48(2), pp. 127–43.

——Clegg, S.R. (1999) 'The Political Ecology of Organizations: Toward a Framework for Analyzing Business-Environment Relationships', *Organization & Environment*, 12(3), pp. 263–79.

————(2005) 'Radical Reformism: Towards *Critical* Ecological Modernization', *Sustainable Development*, 13, pp. 253–67.

Ottman, J.A. (2010) *The New Rules of Green Marketing: Strategies, Tools, and Inspiration for Sustainable Branding*. Sheffield: Greenleaf Publishing.

——Stafford, E.R. and Hartman, C.L. (2006) 'Avoiding Green Marketing Myopia: Ways to Improve Consumer Appeal for Environmentally Preferable Products', *Environment*, 48(5), pp. 22–36.

Oxley-Green, A. and Hunton-Clarke, L. (2003) 'A Typology of Stakeholder Participation for Company Environmental Decision-Making', *Business Strategy and the Environment*, 12, pp. 292–9.

Pagell, M., Yang, C.-L., Krumwiede, D.W. and Sheu, C. (2004) 'Does the Competitive Environment Influence the Efficacy of Investments in Environmental Management?', *Journal of Supply Chain Management*, 40(3), pp. 30–9.

Palmer, K.P., Oates, W.E. and Portney, P.R. (1995) 'Tightening Environmental Standards: The Benefit-Cost or the No-Cost Paradigm?', *Journal of Economic Perspectives*, 9(4), pp. 119–32.

Panayotou, T. (1994) 'Economic Instruments for Environmental Management and Sustainable Development', A report to the UNEP Expert Group Meeting on Use and Development of Economic Policy Instruments for Environmental Management, Nairobi, August.

Parker, C.M., Redmond, J. and Simpson, M. (2009) 'A Review of Interventions to Encourage SMEs to Make Environmental Improvements', *Environment and Planning C: Government and Policy*, 27, pp. 279–301.

Paton, B. (2000) 'Voluntary Environmental Initiatives and Sustainable Industry', *Business Strategy and the Environment*, 9, pp. 328–38.

Patton, D. and Worthington, I. (2003) 'SMEs and Environmental Regulations: A Study of the UK Screen-Printing Sector, *Environment and Planning C: Government and Policy*, 21, pp. 549–66.

Pearce, D. and Barbier, E.B. (2000) *Blueprint for a Sustainable Economy*. London: Earthscan.

——Markandya, A. and Barbier, E.B. (1994) *Blueprint for a Green Economy*. London: Earthscan.

Pearce, D.W. and Kerry Turner, R. (1990) *Economics of Natural Resources and the Environment*. Hemel Hempstead: Harvester Wheatsheaf.

——Markendya, A. and Barbier, E.B. (1989) *Blueprint for a Green Economy*. London: Earthscan.

Peart, R. (2001) 'External Factors Influencing the Environmental Performance of South African Firms', *South African Journal of Science*, 97, pp. 2–8.

Peattie, K. (1995) *Environmental Marketing Management: Meeting the Green Challenge*. London: Pitman.

——(1997) 'Environmental Marketing', in Bansal, P. and Howard, E. eds. *Business and the Natural Environment*. Oxford: Butterworth Heinemann, pp. 195–220.

——(2001a) 'Golden Goose or Wild Goose? The Hunt for the Green Consumer', *Business Strategy and the Environment*, 10, pp. 187–99.

——(2001b) 'Towards Sustainability: The Third Age of Green Marketing', *The Marketing Review*, 2, pp. 129–46.

——Charter, M. (1997) 'Green Marketing', in McDonagh, P. and Prothero, A. eds. *Greener Management: A Reader*. London: Dryden Press, pp. 388–412.

——and Crane, A. (2005) 'Green Marketing: Legend, Myth, Farce or Prophesy?', *Qualitative Market Research: An International Journal*, 8(4), pp. 357–70.

Pedersen, C. (2000) 'Local Authorities in Dialogue with Small And Medium-sized Enterprises', in Hillary, R. ed. *Small and Medium-Sized Enterprises and the Environment: Business Imperatives*. Sheffield: Greenleaf, pp. 203–18.

Perez-Sanchez, D., Barton, J.R. and Bower, D. (2003) 'Implementing Environmental Management in SMEs', *Corporate Social Responsibility and Environmental Management*, 10, pp. 67–77.

Petts, J. (2000) 'The Regulator-Regulated Relationship and Environmental Protection: Perceptions in Small And Medium-sized Enterprises', *Environment and Planning C: Government and Policy*, 18, pp. 191–206.

——Herd, A., Gerrard, S. and Horne, C. (1999) 'The Climate and Culture of Environmental Compliance within SMEs', *Business Strategy and the Environment*, 8, pp. 14–30.

———O'heocha, M. (1998) 'Environmental Responsiveness, Individuals and Organizational Learning: SME Experience', *Journal of Environmental Planning and Management*, 41(6), pp. 711–30.

Petulla, J.M. (1987) *Environmental Protection in the United States: Industry, Agencies, Environmentalists*. San Francisco, CA: San Francisco Study Center.

Pezzoli, K. (1997) 'Sustainable Development: A Transdisciplinary Overview of the Literature', *Journal of Environmental Planning and Management*, 40(5), pp. 549–74.

Pimenova, P. and van der Vorst, R. (2004) 'The Role of Support Programmes and Policies in Improving SMEs Environmental Performance in Developed and Transition Economies', *Journal of Cleaner Production*, 12, pp. 549–59.

Polonsky, M.J. (1994) 'An Introduction to Green Marketing', *Electronic Green Journal*, 1(2), pp. 1–10.

——(1995) 'A Stakeholder Theory Approach to Designing Environmental Marketing Strategy', *Journal of Business & Industrial Marketing*, 10(3), pp. 29–46.

——(2011) 'Transformative Green Marketing: Impediments and Opportunities', *Journal of Business Research*, 64(12), pp. 1311–19.

——Rosenberger III, P.J. (2001) 'Re-evaluating Green Marketing: A Strategic Approach, *Business Horizons*, 44(5), pp. 21–30.

Porritt, J. (1984) *Seeing Green*. Oxford: Blackwell.

Porter, M.E. (1980) *Competitive Strategy: Techniques for Analysing Industries and Competitors*. New York: Free Press.

——(1985) *Competitive Advantage: Creating and Sustaining Superior Performance*. New York: Free Press.

——(1991) 'America's Green Strategy', *Scientific American*, 264(4), p. 168.

——Kramer, M.R. (2002) 'The Competitive Advantage of Corporate Philanthropy', *Harvard Business Review*, December, pp. 5–16.

————(2011) 'Creating Shared Value: How to Reinvent Capitalism—And Unleash a Wave of Innovation and Growth', *Harvard Business Review*, January/February, pp. 63–77.

——Reinhardt, F.L. (2007) 'A Strategic Approach to Climate Change', *Harvard Business Review*, 85(10), pp. 22–6.

——van der Linde, C. (1995a) 'Green Competitive: Ending the Stalemate', *Harvard Business Review*, September–October, pp. 120–34.

————(1995b) 'Towards a New Conception of the Environment-Competitiveness Relationship', *Journal of Economic Perspectives*, 9(4), pp. 97–118.

Post, J.E. (1994) 'Environmental Approaches and Strategies: Regulation, Markets and Management Education', in Kolluru, R.B. ed. *Environmental Strategies Handbook*. New York: McGraw Hill, pp. 11–30.

——Altman, B.W. (1994) 'Managing the Environmental Change Process: Barriers and Opportunities', *Journal of Organizational Change Management*, 7(4), pp. 64–81.

——Frederick, W.C., Lawrence, A.T. and Weber, J. (1996) *Business and Society: Corporate Strategy, Public Policy and Ethics*, 8th Edition. New York: McGraw-Hill.

Potoski, M. and Prakash, A. (2004) 'The Regulation Dilemma: Cooperation and Conflict in Environmental Governance', *Public Administration Review*, 64(2), pp. 152–63.

Prahalad, C.K. and Hamel, G. (1990) 'The Core Competence of the Organization', *Harvard Business Review*, 90, pp. 79–93.

Prakash, A. (1999) 'A New-Institutionalist Perspective on ISO 14000 and Responsible Care', *Business Strategy and the Environment*, 8, pp. 322–35.

——(2000a) *Greening the Firm: The Politics of Corporate Environmentalism*. Cambridge: Cambridge University Press.

——(2000b) 'Responsible Care: An Assessment', *Business and Society*, 39(2), pp. 183–209.

——(2001) 'Why Do Firms Adopt Beyond-Compliance Environmental Policies?', *Business Strategy and the Environment*, 10, pp. 286–99.

——(2002) 'Green Marketing, Public Policy and Managerial Strategies', *Business Strategy and the Environment*, 11, pp. 285–97.

Prakash, A. and Kollman, K. (2004) 'Policy Modes, Firms and the Natural Environment', *Business Strategy and the Environment*, 13, pp. 107–28.

Preuss, L. (2001) 'In Dirty Chains? Purchasing and Greener Manufacturing', *Journal of Business Ethics*, 34, pp. 345–59.

——(2005a) 'Rhetoric and Reality of Corporate Greening: A View from the Supply Chain Management Function', *Business Strategy and the Environment*, 14, pp. 123–39.

——(2005b) *The Green Multiplier: A Study of Environmental Protection and the Supply Chain*. Basingstoke: Palgrave Macmillan.

Priebe, M.B. (2010) 'What is Green Marketing', Available at http://www.greenmarketing.tv/2010/06/27/what-is-greenmarketing

Purser, R.E., Park, C. and Montuori, A. (1995) 'Limits to Anthropocentrism: Towards an Ecocentric Organization Paradigm?', *Academy of Management Review*, 20(4), pp. 1053–89.

Quentin Merritt, J. (1998) 'EM into SME won't Go? Attitudes, Awareness and Practices in the London Borough of Croydon', *Business Strategy and the Environment*, 7, pp. 90–100.

Ramus, C.A. and Montiel, I. (2005) 'When are Corporate Environmental Policies a Form of Greenwashing?', *Business and Society*, 44(4), pp. 377–414.

——Steger, U. (2000) 'The Role of Supervisory Support Behaviors and Environmental Policy in Employee "Ecoinitiatives" at Leading-Edge European Companies', *Academy of Management Journal*, 43(4), pp. 605–26.

Randjelovic, J., O'Rourke, A.R. and Orsato, R.J. (2003) 'The Emergence of *Green* Venture Capital', *Business Strategy and the Environment*, 12, pp. 240–53.

Ransom, P. and Lober, D.J. (1999) 'Why do Firms Set Environmental Performance Goals? Some Evidence from Organizational Theory', *Business Strategy and the Environment*, 8, pp. 1–13.

Rao, P. (2002) 'Greening the Supply Chain: A New Initiative in South East Asia', *International Journal of Operations and Production Management*, 22(6), pp. 632–55.

——Holt, D. (2005) 'Do Green Supply Chains Lead to Competitiveness and Green Performance?', *International Journal of Operations and Production Management*, 25(9), pp. 898–916.

Räsänen, K., Meriläinen, S. and Lovio, R. (1995) 'Pioneering Descriptions of Corporate Greening: Notes and Doubts on the Emerging Discussion', *Business Strategy and the Environment*, 3(4), pp. 9–16.

Redmond, J., Walker, E. and Wang, C. (2008) 'Issues for Small Businesses with Waste Management', *Journal of Environmental Management*, 88, pp. 275–85.

Reinhardt, F.L. (1998) 'Environmental Product Differentiation: Implications for Corporate Strategy', *California Management Review*, 40(4), pp. 43–73.

——(1999a) 'Bringing the Environment Down to Earth', *Harvard Business Review*, July–August, pp. 149–57.

——(1999b) 'Market Failure and the Environmental Policies of Firms: Economic Rationales for "Beyond Compliance" Behavior', *Journal of Industrial Ecology*, 3(1), pp. 9–21.

Remmen, A. (2001) 'Greening of Danish Industry—Changes in Concepts and Policies', *Technology Analysis and Strategic Management*, 13(1), pp. 53–69.

Revell, A. (2003) 'Environmental Policy and the Small Firm in Japan', *Journal of Environmental Policy and Planning*, 5(4), pp. 397–413.

——(2007) 'The Ecological Modernisation of SMEs in the UK's Construction Industry', *Geoforum*, 38, pp. 114–26.

——Blackburn, R. (2007) 'The Business Case for Sustainability? An Examination of Small Firms in the UK's Construction and Restaurant Sectors', *Business Strategy and the Environment*, 16, pp. 404–20.

——Rutherfoord, R. (2003) 'UK Environmental Policy and the Small Firm: Broadening the Focus', *Business Strategy and the Environment*, 12, pp. 26–35.

Rex, E. and Baumann, H. (2007) 'Beyond Ecolabels: What Green Marketing can Learn from Conventional Marketing', *Journal of Cleaner Production*, 15, pp. 567–76.

Rhee, S.-K. and Lee, S.-Y. (2003) 'Dynamic Change of Corporate Environmental Strategy: Rhetoric and Reality', *Business Strategy and the Environment*, 12, pp. 175–90.

Rivera-Camino, J. (2007) 'Re-evaluating Green Marketing Strategy: A Stakeholder Perspective', *European Journal of Marketing*, 41(11/12), pp. 1328–58.

Robbins, P.T. (2001) *Greening the Corporation: Management Strategy and the Environmental Challenge*. London: Earthscan Publications.

Roberts, P. (1995) *Environmentally Sustainable Business: A Local and Regional Perspective*. London: Paul Chapman Publishing.

——Gouldson, A. (2000) 'Retrospect and Prospect: Designing Strategies for Integrated Economic Development and Environmental Management', in Gouldson, A. and Roberts, P. eds. *Integrating Environment and Economy: Strategies for Local and Regional Government*. London: Routledge, pp. 257–69.

Roberts, S. (2003) 'Supply Chain Specific: Understanding the Patchy Success of Ethical Sourcing Initiatives', *Journal of Business Ethics*, 44, pp. 159–70.

——Lawson, R. and Nicholls, J. (2006) 'Generating Regional-Scale Improvements in SME Corporate Responsibility Performance: Lessons from Responsibility Northwest', *Journal of Business Ethics*, 67, pp. 275–86.

Rondinelli, D. and London, T. (2003) 'How Corporations and Environmental Groups Cooperate: Assessing Cross-sector Alliances and Collaborations', *Academy of Management Executive*, 17(1), pp. 61–75.

——Vastag, G. (1996) 'International Environmental Standards and Corporate Policies: An Integrative Framework', *California Management Review*, 39(1), pp. 106–22.

————(2000) 'Panacea, Common Sense or Just a Label? The Value of ISO14001 Environmental Management Systems', *European Journal of Management*, 18(5), pp. 499–510.

Roome, N. (1992) 'Developing Environmental Management Strategies', *Business Strategy and the Environment*, 1, pp. 11–24.

——(1994) 'Business Strategy, R & D Management and Environmental Imperatives', *R & D Management*, 24(1), pp. 65–82.

——(1997) 'Corporate Environmental Responsibility', in Bansal, P. and Howard, E. eds. *Business and the Natural Environment*. Oxford: Butterworth-Heinemann, pp. 40–62.

——ed. (1998) *Sustainability Strategies for Industry: The Future of Corporate Practice*. Washington, DC: Island Press.

Ross, A. and Rowan-Robinson, J. (1997) 'It's Good to Talk! Environmental Information and the Greening of Industry', *Journal of Environmental Planning and Management*, 40(1), pp. 111–24.

Rowe, J. and Hollingsworth, D. (1996) 'Improving Environmental Performance of SMEs', *Eco-management and Auditing*, 3, pp. 97–107.

Roy, M.-J. and Therin, F. (2008) 'Knowledge Acquisition and Environmental Commitment in SMEs', *Corporate Social Responsibility and Environmental Management*, 15, pp. 249–59.

Rugman, A.M. and Verbeke, A. (1998a) 'Corporate Strategies and Environmental Regulations: An Organizing Framework', *Strategic Management Journal*, 19, pp. 363–75.

————(1998b) 'Corporate Strategy and International Environmental Policy', *Journal of International Business Studies*, 29(4), pp. 819–33.

————(2000) 'Six Cases of Corporate Responses to Environmental Regulation', *European Management Journal*, 18(4), pp. 377–85.

Russel, T. ed. (1998) *Greener Purchasing: Opportunities and Innovations*. Sheffield: Greenleaf Publishing.

Russell, C. and Powell, P. (1996) *Choosing Environmental Policy Tools*. Washington, DC: Inter-American Bank, Environment Division.

Russo, M.V. ed. (1999) *Environmental Management Readings and Cases*. Boston: Houghton Mifflin.

——Fouts, P.A. (1997) 'A Resource-Based Perspective on Corporate Environmental Performance and Profitability', *Academy of Management Journal*, 40(3), pp. 534–59.

Rutherfoord, R., Blackburn, R.A. and Spence, L.J. (2000) 'Environmental Management and the Small Firm: An International Comparison', *International Journal of Entrepreneurial Behaviour and Research*, 6(6), pp. 310–25.

——Spence, L.J. (1998) 'Small Business and the Perceived Limits of Responsibility: Environmental Issues', in Proceedings of 21st ISBA National Small Firms Conference.

Salzmann, O., Ionescu-Somers, A. and Steger, U. (2005) 'The Business Case for Corporate Sustainability: Literature Review and Research Options', *European Management Journal*, 23(1), pp. 27–36.

Sarkis, J. (2001) 'Manufacturing's Role in Corporate Environmental Sustainability: Concerns for the New Millennium', *International Journal of Operations and Production Management*, 21(5/6), pp. 666–86.

——(2003) 'A Strategic Decision Framework for Green Supply Chain Management', *Journal of Cleaner Production*, 11(4), pp. 397–409.

——Cordeiro, J.J. (2001) 'An Empirical Evaluation of Environmental Efficiencies and Performance: Pollution Prevention versus End-of-Pipe Practice', *European Journal of Operational Research*, 135, pp. 102–13.

——Rasheed, A. (1995) 'Greening the Manufacturing Function', *Business Horizons*, September–October, pp. 17–27.

Schaefer, A. and Harvey, B. (1998) 'Stage Models of Corporate 'Greening': A Critical Evaluation', *Business Strategy and the Environment*, 7, pp. 109–23.

Schaltegger, S. and Burritt, R. (2000) *Contemporary Environmental Accounting: Issues, Concepts and Practice*. Sheffield: Greenleaf Publishing.

————Petersen, H. (2003) *An Introduction to Corporate Environmental Management: Striving for Sustainability*. Sheffield: Greenleaf Publishing.

——Synnestvedt, T. (2002) 'The Link between 'Green' and Economic Success: Environmental Management as the Crucial Trigger between Environmental and Economic Performance', *Journal of Environmental Management*, 65, pp. 339–46.

Schaper, M. (2002) 'The Essence of Ecopreneurship', *Greener Management International*, 38, pp. 26–30.

Schmidheiny, S. (1992) *Changing Course: A Global Business Perspective on Development and the Environment*. Cambridge, MA: The MIT Press.

Schnaiberg, A. (1997) 'Sustainable Development and the Treadmill of Production', in Baker, S., Kousis, M., Richardson, D. and Young, S. eds. *The Politics of Sustainable Development: Theory, Policy and Practice within the European Union*. London: Routledge, pp. 72–88.

Schot, J. and Fischer, K. (1993) 'The Greening of the Industrial Firm', in Fischer, K. and Schot, J. eds. *Environmental Strategies for Industry: International Perspectives on Research Needs and Policy Implications*. Washington, DC: Island Press, pp. 3–33.

Seik, F.T. (1996) 'Urban Environmental Policy—The Use of Regulatory and Economic Instruments in Singapore', *Habitat International*, 20(1), pp. 5–22.

Seuring, S., Sarkis, J., Muller, M. and Rao, P. (2008) 'Sustainability and Supply Chain Management—An Introduction to the Special Issue', *Journal of Cleaner Production*, 16(15), pp. 1545–51.

Sharfman, M., Ellington, R.T. and Meo, M. (1997) 'The Next Step in Becoming "Green": Life-Cycle Orientated Environmental Management', *Business Horizons*, 40(3), pp. 13–22.

Sharma, A., Iyer, G.R., Mehotra, A. and Krishnan, R. (2010) 'Sustainability and Business-to-Business Marketing: A Framework and Implications', *Industrial Marketing Management*, 39, pp. 330–41.

Sharma, S. (2000) 'Managerial Interpretations and Organizational Context as Predictors of Corporate Choice of Environmental Strategy', *Academy of Management Journal*, 43(4), pp. 681–97.

——(2002) 'Research in Corporate Sustainability: What Really Matters?', in Sharma, S. and Starik, M. eds. *Research in Corporate Sustainability: The Evolving Theory and Practice of Organizations in the Natural Environment*. Cheltenham: Edward Elgar, pp. 1–29.

——Aragón-Correa, J.A. (2005) 'Corporate Environmental Strategy and Competitive Advantage: A Review from the Past to the Future', in Sharma, S. and Aragón-Correa, J.A. eds. *Corporate Environmental Strategy and Competitive Advantage*. Cheltenham: Edward Elgar, pp. 1–26.

——Henriques, I. (2005) 'Stakeholder Influences on Sustainability Practices in the Canadian Forest Products Industry', *Strategic Management Journal*, 26, pp. 158–80.

——Pablo, A.L. and Vredenburg, H. (1999) 'Corporate Environmental Responsiveness Strategies: The Importance of Issue Interpretation and Organizational Context', *Journal of Applied Behavioural Science*, 35(1), pp. 87–108.

——Vredenburg, H. (1998) 'Proactive Corporate Environmental Strategy and the Development of Competitively Valuable Organizational Capabilities', *Strategic Management Journal*, 19(8), pp. 729–53.

Sherman, W.R., Steingard, D.S. and Fitzgibbons, D.E. (2002) 'Sustainable Stakeholder Accounting beyond Complementarity and towards Integration in Environmental Accounting', in Sharma, S. and Starik, M. eds. *Research in Corporate Sustainability: The Evolving Theory and Practice of Organizations in the Natural Environment*. Cheltenham: Edward Elgar, pp. 257–94.

Shrivastava, P. (1992) 'Corporate Self-greenewal: Strategic Responses to Environmentalism', *Business Strategy and the Environment*, 1(3), pp. 9–21.

——(1995a) 'Ecocentric Management for a Risk Society', *Academy of Management Review*, 20, pp. 118–37.

——(1995b) 'Environmental Technologies and Competitive Advantage', *Strategic Management Journal*, 16, pp. 183–200.

——(1995c) 'The Role of Corporations in Achieving Ecological Sustainability', *Academy of Management Review*, 20(4), pp. 936–60.

——(1996) *Greening Business: Profiting the Corporation and the Environment*. Cincinnati: Thomson Executive Press.

——Hart, S. (1994) 'Greening Organizations-2000', *International Journal of Public Administration*, 17(3/4), pp. 607–35.

———(1995) 'Creating Sustainable Corporations', *Business Strategy and the Environment*, 4, pp. 154–65.

Simpson, D.F. and Power, D.J. (2005) 'Use the Supply Relationship to Develop Lean and Green Suppliers', *Supply Chain Management: An International Journal*, 10(1), pp. 60–8.

Simpson, M., Taylor, N. and Barker, K. (2004) 'Environmental Responsibility in SMEs: Does it Deliver Competitive Advantage?', *Business Strategy and the Environment*, 13, pp. 156–71.

Simula, H., Lehtimaki, T. and Salo, J. (2009) 'Managing Greenness in Technology Marketing', *Journal of Systems and Information Technology*, 11(4), pp. 331–46.

Sinding, K. (2000) 'Environmental Management Beyond the Boundaries of the Firm: Definitions and Constraints', *Business Strategy and the Environment*, 9, pp. 79–91.

Singh, R.K., Garg, S.K. and Deshmukh, S.G. (2008) 'Strategy Development by SMEs for Competitiveness: A Review', *Benchmarking: An International Journal*, 15(5), pp. 525–47.

Skidmore, D. (1995) 'Managing Responsiveness to Pressures for Change in Environmental Performance', *Business Strategy and the Environment*, 4, pp. 95–8.

Slater, J. and Angel, I.T. (2000) 'The Impact and Implications of Environmentally Linked Strategies on Competitive Advantage: A Study of Malaysian Companies', *Journal of Business Research*, 47, pp. 75–89.

Smallbone, T. (2004) 'Can "Market Transformation" Lead to "Sustainable Business"? A Critical Appraisal of the UK's Strategy for Sustainable Business', *Business Strategy and the Environment*, 13, pp. 96–106.

Smith, A., Kemp, R. and Duff, C. (2000) 'Small Firms and the Environment: Factors that Influence Small and Medium-sized Enterprises' Environmental Behaviour', in Hillary, R. ed. *Small and Medium-Sized Enterprises and the Environment: Business Imperatives*. Sheffield: Greenleaf, pp. 24–34.

Smith, D., ed. (1993) *Business and the Environment: Implications of the New Environmentalism*. London: Paul Chapman Publishing.

Socolow, R., Andrews, C., Berkhout, F. and Thomas, V. (1994) *Industrial Ecology and Global Change*. Cambridge: Cambridge University Press.

Sonneborn, C.L. (2004) 'Renewable Energy and Market-based Approaches to Greenhouse Gas Reduction—Opportunity or Obstacle?', *Energy Policy*, 32, pp. 1799–805.

Spence, L. (1999) 'Does Size Matter? The State of the Art in Small Business Research', *Business Ethics: A European Review*, 8(3), pp. 163–74.

Sprenger, R.-U. (2000) 'Market-based Instruments in Environmental Policies: The Lessons of Experience', in Andersen, M.S. and Sprenger, R.-U. eds. *Market-based Instruments for Environmental Management: Policies and Institutions*. Cheltenham: Edward Elgar, pp. 3–24.

Srivastava, S.K. (2007) 'Green Supply-Chain Management: A State-of-the-Art Literature Review', *International Journal of Management Reviews*, 9(1), pp. 53–80.

Sroufe, R. (2006) 'A Framework for Strategic Environmental Sourcing', in Sarkis, J. ed. *Greening the Supply Chain*. London: Springer, pp. 3–23.

——Curkovic, S., Montabon, F. and Melnyk, S.A. (2000) 'The New Product Design Process and Design for the Environment "Crossing the Chasm"', *International Journal of Operations & Production Management*, 20(2), pp. 267–83.

Sroufe, R.P., Melynk, S.A. and Vastag, G. (1998) 'Environmental Management Systems as a Source of Competitive Advantage', A paper submitted by the Department of Marketing and Supply Chain Management, Michigan State University, available via Google Scholar (accessed 27/11/2009).

Stafford, E.R. and Hartman, C.L. (1996) 'Green Alliances: Strategic Relations Between Businesses and Environmental Groups', *Business Horizons*, March/April, pp. 50–9.

——Polonsky, M.J. and Hartman, C.L. (2000) 'Environmental NGO–Business Collaboration and Strategic Bridging: A Case Analysis of the Greenpeace-Foron Alliance', *Business Strategy and the Environment*, 9, pp. 122–35.

Stainer, A. and Stainer, L. (1997) 'Ethical Dimensions of Environmental Management', *European Business Review*, 97(5), pp. 224–30.

Stanwick, P.A. and Stanwick, S.D. (2001) 'CEO Compensation: Does it Pay to Be Green?', *Business Strategy and the Environment*, 10, pp. 176–82.

Starik, M. and Marcus, A.A. (2000) 'Introduction to the Special Research Forum on the Management of Organizations in the Natural Environment: A Field Emerging from Multiple Paths, with Many Challenges Ahead', *The Academy of Management Journal*, 43(4), pp. 539–46.

——Rands, G. (1995) 'Weaving an Integrated Web: Multilevel and Multisystem Perspectives of Ecologically Sustainable Organizations', *Academy of Management Review*, 20(4), pp. 908–35.

——Throop, G., Doody, J.R. and Joyce, M.E. (1996) 'Growing an Environmental Strategy', *Business Strategy and the Environment*, 5, pp. 12–21.

Starkey, R. and Welford, R. eds. (2001) *The Earthscan Reader in Business and Sustainable Development*. London: Earthscan.

Steelman, T.A. and Rivera, J. (2006) 'Voluntary Environmental Programs In the United States: Whose Interests Are Served?', *Organization and Environment*, 19(4), pp. 505–25.

Steger, U. (1993) 'The Greening of the Board Room: How German Companies Are Dealing with Environmental Issues', in Fischer, K. and Schot, J. eds. *Environmental Strategies for Industry: International Perspectives on Research Needs and Policy Implications*. Washington, DC: Island Press, pp. 147–66.

——(2000) 'Environmental Management Systems: Empirical Evidence and Further Perspectives', *European Management Journal*, 18(1), pp. 23–37.

——Ionescu-Somers, A. and Salzmann, O. (2007) 'The Economic Foundations of Corporate Sustainability', *Corporate Governance*, 7(2), pp. 162–77.

——Meima, R. (1998) *The Strategic Dimensions of Environmental Management: Sustaining the Corporation During the Age of Ecological Discovery*. Basingstoke: Macmillan.

——Zhaoben, F. and Wei, L. (2003) *Greening Chinese Business: Barriers, Trends and Opportunities for Environmental Management*. Sheffield: Greenleaf Publishing.

Stern, D.I., Common, M.S. and Barbier, E.B. (1996) 'Economic Growth and Environmental Degradation: The Environmental Kuznets Curve and Sustainable Development', *World Development*, 24(7), pp. 1151–60.

Stern Review on the Economics of Climate Change (2006) Cambridge: Published on behalf of HM Treasury by Cambridge University Press.

Stoeckl, N. (2004) 'The Private Costs and Benefits of Environmental Self-Regulation', *Business Strategy and the Environment*, 13, pp. 135–55.

Stoker, G. (1998) 'Governance as Theory', *International Social Science Journal*, 155, pp. 17–28.

Studer, S., Tsang, S., Welford, R. and Hills, P. (2008) 'SMEs and Voluntary Environmental Initiatives: A Study of Stakeholders' Perspectives in Hong Kong', *Journal of Environmental Planning and Management*, 51(2), pp. 285–301.

——Welford, R. and Hills, P. (2006) 'Engaging Hong Kong Businesses in Environmental Change: Drivers and Barriers', *Business Strategy and the Environment*, 15, pp. 416–31.

Svoboda, S. (1999) 'Note on Life Cycle Analysis', in Russo, M.V. ed. *Environmental Management Readings and Cases*. Boston: Houghton Mifflin, pp. 217–27.

Takahashi, T. and Nakamura, M. (2005) 'Bureaucratization of Environmental Management and Corporate Greening: An Empirical Analysis of Large Manufacturing Firms in Japan', *Corporate Social Responsibility and Environmental Management*, 12, pp. 210–19.

Takala, T. and Pallab, P. (2000) 'Individual, Collective and Social Responsibility of the Firm', *Business Ethics: A European Review*, 9(2), pp. 109–18.

Taylor, N., Barker, K. and Simpson, M. (2003) 'Achieving 'Sustainable Business': A Study of the Perceptions of Environmental Best Practice by SMEs in South Yorkshire', *Environment and Planning C: Government and Policy*, 21, pp. 89–105.

Terence Tsai, S.-H. and Child, J. (1997) 'Strategic Responses of Multinational Corporations to Environmental Demands', *Journal of General Management*, 23(1), pp. 1–22.

Tews, K., Busch, P.-O., Jorgens, H. (2003) 'The Diffusion of New Environmental Policy Instruments', *European Journal of Political Research*, 42, pp. 569–600.

Thompson, J.L. (2001) *Strategic Management*, 4th Edition. London: Thomson Learning.

Tibor, T. and Feldman, I. (1999) 'Introduction to ISO14000', in Russo, M.V. ed. *Environmental Management Readings and Cases*. Boston: Houghton Mifflin, pp. 256–66.

Tilley, F. (1999) 'The Gap Between the Environmental Attitudes and Environmental Behaviour of Small Firms', *Business Strategy and the Environment*, 8, pp. 238–48.

——(2000) 'Small Firms' Ethics: How Deep do they Go?', in Hillary, R. ed. *Small and Medium-Sized Enterprises and the Environment: Business Imperatives*. Sheffield: Greenleaf, pp. 35–48.

Turunen-Red, A.H. and Woodland, A.D. (2004) 'Multilateral Reforms of Trade and Environmental Policy', *Review of International Economics*, 12(3), pp. 321–36.

United Nations (2007) *UN Millennium Ecosystem Assessment Report*. New York: UN.

United Nations Global Compact CEO Survey (2010) Produced for UNGC by Accenture.

United States Environmental Protection Agency (1995) *An Introduction to Environmenal Accounting as a Business Management Tool: Key Concepts and Terms*. Washington, DC: USEPA, available at www.epa.gov A shorter version can be found in Bennett and James (2000) *op. cit.* chapter 2.

Unruh, G. and Ettenson, R. (2010) 'Growing Green: Three Smart Paths to Developing Sustainable Products', *Harvard Business Review*, June, pp. 94–100.

Vaccaro, V.L. (2009) 'B2B Green Marketing and Innovation Theory for Competitive Advantage', *Journal of Systems and Information Technology*, 11(4), pp. 315–30.

Vachon, S. and Klassen, R.D. (2006) 'Extending Green Practices across the Supply Chain: The Impact of Upstream and Downstream Integration', *International Journal of Operations and Production Management*, 26(7), pp. 795–821.

Van de Ven, A.H. and Poole, M.S. (1995) 'Explaining Development and Change in Organizations', *Academy of Management Review*, 20(3), pp. 510–40.

Van Marrewijk, M. (2003) 'Concepts and Definitions of CSR and Corporate Sustainability: Between Agency and Communion', *Journal of Business Ethics*, 44, pp. 95–105.

van Someren, T.C.R. (1995) 'Sustainable Development and the Firm: Organizational Innovations and Environmental Strategy', *Business Strategy and the Environment*, 4, pp. 23–33.

Vastag, G. (2004) 'Revisiting ISO14000 Diffusion: A New "Look" at the Drivers of Certification', *Production and Operations Management*, 13(3), pp. 260–7.

——Kerekes, S. and Rondinelli, D. (1996) 'Evaluation of Corporate Environmental Management Approaches: A Framework and Application', *International Journal of Production Economics*, 43, pp. 193–211.

Verheul, H. (1999) 'How Social Networks Influence the Dissemination of Cleaner Technologies in SMEs', *Journal of Cleaner Production*, 7(3), pp. 213–19.

Visser, W. (2009) *Landmarks for Sustainability: Events and Initiatives that have Changed Our World*. Sheffield: Greenleaf Publishing.

Vlachou, A. (2004) 'Capitalism and Ecological Sustainability: The Shaping of Environmental Policies', *Review of International Political Economy*, 11(5), pp. 926–52.

Vogel, D. (2006) *The Market for Virtue: The Potential and Limits of Corporate Social Responsibility*. Washington, DC: Brookings Institution.

Waddock, S.A., Bodwell, C. and Graves, S.B. (2002) 'Responsibility: The New Business Imperative', *Academy of Management Executive*, 16(2), pp. 132–48.

Wagner, M. (2005) 'How to Reconcile Environmental and Economic Performance to Improve Corporate Sustainability: Corporate Environmental Strategies in the European Paper Industry', *Journal of Environmental Management*, 76, pp. 105–18.

——(2007) 'Integration of Environmental Management with Other Managerial Functions of the Firm: Empirical Effects on Drivers of Economic Performance', *Long Range Planning*, 40, pp. 611–28.

——Schaltegger, S. (2003) 'How Does Sustainability Performance Relate to Business Competitiveness?', *Greener Management International*, 44, pp. 5–16.

————(2004) 'The Effect of Corporate Environmental Strategy Choice and Environmental Performance on Competitiveness and Economic Performance: An Empirical Study of EU Manufacturing', *European Management Journal*, 22(5), pp. 557–72.

——Wehrmeyer, W. (2002) 'The Relationship of Environmental and Economic Performance at Firm Level: A Review of Empirical Studies in Europe and Methodological Comments', *European Environment*, 12, pp. 149–59.

Walker, H., Di Sistio, L. and McBain, D. (2008) 'Drivers and Barriers to Environmental Supply Chain Management Practices: Lessons from the Public and Private Sectors', *Journal of Purchasing & Supply Management*, 14, pp. 69–85.

Walley, E.E. and Taylor, D.W. (2002) 'Opportunists, Champions, Mavericks...? A Typology of Green Entrepreneurs', *Greener Management International*, 38, pp. 31–43.

Walley, N. and Whitehead, B. (1994) 'It's not Easy being Green', *Harvard Business Review*, 72(3), pp. 46–52.

Walton, S.V. and Galea, C. (2006) 'E-commerce Solutions to Environmental Purchasing', in Sarkis, J. ed. *Greening the Supply Chain*. London: Springer, pp. 379–91.

——Handfield, R.B. and Melnyk, S.A. (1998) 'The Green Supply Chain: Integrating Suppliers into Environmental Management Processes', *Journal of Supply Chain Management*, 34(2), pp. 2–11.

Ward, S. (2011) 'Green Marketing', Available at http://sbinfocanada.about.com/od/marketing/g/greenmarketing.htm

WCED (World Commission on the Environment and Development) (1987) *Our Common Future*. Oxford: Oxford University Press.

Welford, R. (1995) *Environmental Strategy and Sustainable Development: The Corporate Challenge for the 21st Century*. London: Routledge.

——ed. (1996) *Corporate Environmental Management: Systems and Strategies*. London: Earthscan.

——(1997a) *Corporate Environmental Management 2: Culture and Organisations*. London: Earthscan.

——(1997b) *Hijacking Environmentalism: Corporate Responses to Sustainable Development*. London: Earthscan.

——(2000) *Corporate Environmental Management 3: Towards Sustainable Development*. London: Earthscan.

——(2003) 'Beyond Systems: A Vision for Corporate Environmental Management for the Future', *International Journal of Environment and Sustainable Development*, 2(2), pp. 162–73.

——Gouldson, A. (1993) *Environmental Management and Business Strategy*. London: FT Management.

——Jones, D. (1996) 'Beyond Environmentalism and Towards the Sustainable Organization', in Welford, R. ed. *Corporate Environmental Management: Systems and Strategies*. London: Earthscan, pp. 239–55.

——Starkey, R. eds. (1996) *Business and the Environment*. London: Earthscan.

Wheeler, D. and Sillanpää, M. (1997) *The Stakeholder Corporation: The Body Shop: Blueprint for Maximizing Stakeholder Value*. London: Pitman.

Willard, B. (2002) *The Sustainability Advantage: Seven Business Case Benefits for a Triple Bottom Line*. Gabriola Island, BC: New Society Publishers.

Williamson, D. and Lynch-Wood, G. (2001) 'A New Paradigm for SME Environmental Practice', *The TQM Magazine*, 13(6), pp. 424–32.

————Ramsay, J. (2006) 'Drivers of Environmental Behaviour in Manufacturing SMEs and the Implications for CSR', *Journal of Business Ethics*, 67, pp. 317–30.

Williams, H., van Hooydonk, A., Dingle, P. and Annandale, D. (2000) 'Developing Tailored Environmental Management Systems for Small Business', *Eco-Management and Auditing*, 7(3), pp. 106–13.

Williams, H.E., Medhurst, J. and Drew, K. (1993) 'Corporate Strategies for a Sustainable Future', in Fischer, K. and Schot, J. eds. *Environmental Strategies for Industry: International Perspectives on Research Needs and Policy Implications*. Washington, DC: Island Press, pp. 117–46.

Winn, M.I. and Angell, L.C. (2000) 'Towards a Process Model of Corporate Greening', *Organization Studies*, 21(6), pp. 1119–47.

——Kirchgeorg, M. (2005) 'The Siesta is Over: A Rude Awakening from Sustainability Myopia', in Sharma, S. and Aragón-Correa, J.A. eds. '*Corporate Environmental Strategy and Competitive Advantage*. Cheltenham: Edward Elgar, pp. 232–58.

Winsemius, P. and Guntram, U. (1992) 'Responding to the Environmental Challenge', *Business Horizons*, March–April, pp. 12–20.

Wook Lee, B. and Green, K. (1994) 'Towards Commercial and Environmental Excellence: A Green Portfolio Matrix', *Business Strategy and the Environment*, 3(3), Autumn, pp. 1–9.

World Business Council for Sustainable Development (1996) *Sustainable Production and Consumption: A Business Perspective*. Geneva: WBCSD.

——(1997) *Environmental Performance and Shareholder Value*. Geneva: WBCSD.

——(2000) *Eco-efficiency: Creating More Value with Less Impact*. Geneva: WBCSD.

Worthington, I. (2005) 'Business, Government and the Natural Environment', in Worthington, I., Britton, C.B. and Rees, A. eds. *Economics for Business: Blending Theory and Practice*, 2nd Edition. Harlow: FT/Prentice-Hall, pp. 445–70.

——(2009) 'Corporate Perceptions of the Business Case for Supplier Diversity: How Socially Responsible Purchasing Can Pay', *Journal of Business Ethics*, 90, pp. 47–60.

——Britton, C.B. (2009) *The Business Environment*, 6th Edition. Harlow: FT/Prentice-Hall.

————Rees, A. (2005) *Economics for Business: Blending Theory and Practice*, 2nd Edition. Harlow: FT/Prentice-Hall.

——Patton, D. (2005) 'Strategic Intent in the Management of the Green Environment within SMEs: An Analysis of the UK Screen-Printing Sector', *Long Range Planning*, 38, pp. 197–212.

————Lindley, I. (2003) 'Local Authorities, Business and LA21: A Study of East Midlands Sustainable Development Partnerships', *Local Government Studies*, 29(1), pp. 91–110.

——Ram, M., Boyal, H. and Shah, M. (2008) 'Researching the Drivers of Socially Responsible Purchasing: A Cross-National Study of Supplier Diversity Initiatives', *Journal of Business Ethics*, 79, pp. 319–31.

Wright, C. and Rwabizambuga, A. (2006) 'Institutional Pressures, Corporate Reputation, and Voluntary Codes of Conduct: An Examination of the Equator Principles', *Business and Society Review*, 111(1), pp. 89–117.

Wubben, E. (1999) 'What's in it for Us? Or: The Impact of Environmental Legislation on Competitiveness', *Business Strategy and the Environment*, 8, pp. 95–107.

Wulfson, M. (2001) 'The Ethics of Corporate Responsibility and Philanthropic Ventures', *Journal of Business Ethics*, 29(1/2), pp. 135–45.

Yakhou, M. and Dorweiler, V.P. (2004) 'Environmental Accounting: An Essential Component of Business Strategy', *Business Strategy and the Environment*, 13, pp. 65–77.

Yaziji, M. (2004) 'Turning Gadflies into Allies', *Harvard Business Review*, February, pp. 1–8.

Yin, R.K. (1994) *Case Study Research: Design and Methods*, 2nd Edition. Thousand Oaks, CA: Sage Publications.

York, J.G. and Venkataraman, S. (2010) 'The Entrepreneur-Environment Nexus: Uncertainty, Innovation and Allocation', *Journal of Business Venturing*, 25, pp. 449–63.

Ytterhus, B.E. and Synnestvedt, T. (1996) 'The Process of Greening: Results from the Nordic Business Barometer', *Eco-Management and Auditing*, 3(1), pp. 30–6.

Zeffane, R.M., Polonsky, M.J. and Medley, P. (1995) 'Corporate Environmental Commitment: Developing the Operational Concept', *Business Strategy and the Environment*, 3(4), pp. 17–28.

Zhang, B., Bi, J. and Liu, B. (2009) 'Drivers and Barriers to Engage Enterprises in Environmental Initiatives in Suzhou Industrial Park, China', *Frontiers in Environmental Science & Engineering in China*, 3(2), pp. 210–20.

Zhu, Q. and Cote, R.P. (2004) 'Integrating Green Supply Chain Management into an Embryonic Eco-industrial Development: A Case Study of the Guitang Group', *Journal of Cleaner Production*, 12(8–10), pp. 1025–35.

——Sarkis, J. (2006) 'An Inter-sectoral Comparison of Green Supply Chain Management in China: Drivers and Practices', *Journal of Cleaner Production*, 14(5), pp. 472–86.

————Cordeiro, J.J. and Lai, K. (2008b) 'Firm-level Correlates of Emergent Green Supply Chain Management Practices in the Chinese Context', *Omega*, 36(4), pp. 577–91.

————Geng, Y. (2005) 'Green Supply Chain Management in China: Pressures, Practices and Performance', *International Journal of Operations and Production Management*, 25(5), pp. 449–68.

————Lai, K. (2007a) 'Green Supply Chain Management: Pressures, Practices and Performance within the Chinese Automobile Industry', *Journal of Cleaner Production*, 15(11/12), pp. 1041–52.

Zhu, Q. and Cote, R.P. and Lai, K. (2007b) 'Initiatives and Outcomes of Green Supply Chain Management Implementation by Chinese Manufacturers', *Journal of Environmental Management*, 85(1), pp. 179–89.

——————(2008a) 'Confirmation of a Measurement Model for Green Supply Chain Management Practices Implementation', *International Journal of Production Economics*, 111(2), pp. 261–73.

Zhuang, L. and Synodinos, D. (1997) 'Legislation for the Environment: Does it Work?—An Empirical Study into Selected UK-based Chemical Manufacturing Firms', *Management Decision*, 35(7), pp. 508–18.

Zsidisin, G.A. and Siferd, S.P. (2001) 'Environmental Purchasing: A Framework for Theory Development', *European Journal of Purchasing and Supply Management*, 7, pp. 61–73.

INDEX